Fine An... ...d Irish, and small collectors' items

A magnificent Charles II two-handled lidded Porringer made in London 1669-70 by Francis Leake.

Great Grooms Antiques Centre
Parbrook, Billingshurst, West Sussex RH14 9EU
Tel/Fax: 01403 786656 Mobile: 07885 643000
Email: silver@nicholas-shaw.com

Website:
www.nicholas-shaw.com

LAPADA
MEMBER

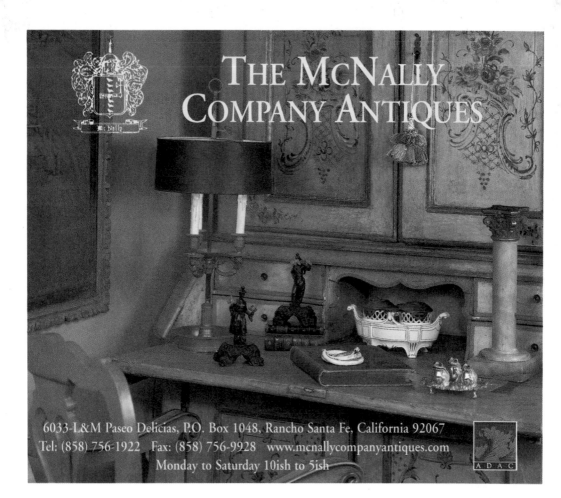

MILLER'S

silver & plate

MILLER'S SILVER & PLATE BUYER'S GUIDE

Created and designed by
Miller's Publications
The Cellars, High Street
Tenterden, Kent TN30 6BN
Telephone: 01580 766411
Fax: 01580 766100

Consultant: Daniel Bexfield
Managing Editor: Valerie Lewis
Project Co-ordinator: Deborah Wanstall
Production Co-ordinator: Kari Reeves
Editorial Assistants: Kim Cook, Rosemary Cooke, Maureen Horner
Designer: Philip Hannath
Advertisement Designer: Simon Cook
Jacket Design: Colin Goody
Advertising Executive: Jo Hill
Advertising Assistant: Melinda Williams
Production Assistants: Caroline Bugeja, Gillian Charles, Léonie Sidgwick, Ethne Tragett
Additional Photography: Robin Saker
Indexer: Hilary Bird

First published in Great Britain in 2002
by Miller's, a division of Mitchell Beazley,
imprints of Octopus Publishing Group Ltd,
2–4 Heron Quays, London E14 4JP

© 2002 Octopus Publishing Group Ltd

A CIP catalogue record for this book is
available from the British Library

ISBN 1 84000 555 6

Some images have appeared in previous editions of
Miller's Antiques Price Guide and *Miller's Collectables Price Guide*

Illustrations and film output by CK Litho, Whitstable, Kent
Printed and bound by Toppan Printing Co (HK) Ltd, China

Front cover illustration:
A Victorian silver rose bowl, by William Hutton & Sons,
London 1895, 9½in (24cm) diam, 22oz.
£350–450/$500–650 ⚒ CGC

MILLER'S

silver
& plate

DANIEL BEXFIELD CONSULTANT

Acknowledgments

Consultant

Daniel Bexfield has 21 years experience in the antiques business,19 of them in silver and is still one of the youngest dealers. He has a shop in Burlington Arcade, Mayfair, London, where he sells fine quality silver and jewellery from the 17th to the 20th centuries, and his website on silver is one of largest in the country. He prides himself on the care and attention he gives to his customers and willingly shares his extensive knowledge and enthusiasm for his subject.
Daniel Bexfield Antiques, 26 Burlington Arcade, Mayfair, London W1V 9AD www.bexfield.co.uk

Georg Jensen

Alastair Crawford is a director of The Silver Fund plc, who deal mainly in Georg Jensen silverware. Alastair started dealing in Antique silver in 1979 after leaving Edinburgh University and has traded internationally, especially in Australia, America and Europe. In 1996 he established, with Michael James, The Silver Fund, which is now recognized as the world's leading retailer of estate Georg Jensen silverware.
The Silver Fund plc, 40 Bury Street, London SW1Y 6AU www.thesilverfund.com

Old Sheffield Plate and Silver Plate

Hugh Gregory joined the saleroom of Knight, Frank & Rutley in 1962. He obtained a diploma in Gemology in 1966. From 1971–76 he worked for Phillips Auctioneers but since then has been self-employed. For the last ten years he has acted as a general valuer and specialist consultant in silver, clocks and watches and jewellery for Tennants Auctioneers.
Tennants, The Auction Centre, Harmby Road, Leyburn, Yorks, DL8 5SG

Decorative Arts

Fay Lucas established Fay Lucas Gallery and Fay Lucas Artmetal in 1980 and is a leading dealer in 20th-century applied and decorative arts, with emphasis on precious metals and signed exhibition furniture. Her gallery exhibition *Newave* which showed silver from each decade of the 20th century was a contributing factor in the classification and recognition of new innovative trends that had made the century such a challenging and fun period for old and new collectors. Fay has now retired from her gallery but is available for consultation, research and private commissions. She is a member of BADA, CIONA, the Silver Society and is a regular exhibitor at the fine arts and antique fairs at Olympia and BADA fairs. She can be contacted through the BADA association and by appointment only.

American Silver

Connie McNally opened her first antique shop in Palm Springs, California in 1976 and, with her husband, currently runs an antique shop in Rancho Santa Fe. They are members of the Antique Dealers' Association of California. The McNally Company Antiques offers one of the finest collections of antique silver in southern California, together with a good range of continental antiques. Her first love is silver, and in 1993 she purchased *Silver Magazine*, the only publication specializing in silver. Under her editorship the magazine has become a scholarly reference source read by collectors and researchers alike. Connie was a panel member at New York University's March 2000 conference, *Glistening Transmissions of style: American Silver and International Influence*, as well as their 2002 conference, *Sterling Modernities: International and American Silver from the Arts and Crafts Movement to the Present*. She is listed in the 2001 edition of *Who's Who in America*.
Silver Magazine, PO Box 9690, Rancho Santa Fe, CA 92067, USA www.silvermag.com

Russian Silver

Sheldon Shapiro has been established at Grays Antique Market for 21 years after being brought up in a family of jewellers and starting out in Portobello Road at the tender age of 17 years old. He specializes in the interesting and unusual including Imperial Russian works of art.
Sheldon Shapiro & Co Ltd, Stand 380, Grays Antique Market, Davies Street, London W1

Scottish Silver

Nicholas Shaw was recently voted Silver Dealer of the Year at the British Antiques and Collectables Awards (BACA) ceremony. He organized the hugely successful exhibition of York silver at the Merchant Adventurers' Hall in York, being the largest display of provincial silver ever mounted in the UK, some of which had never before been on public view. He specializes in Scottish and Irish pieces together with very fine quality early English and small collectors' items. He is a member of the Silver Society, BADA, LAPADA and CINOA.
Nicholas Shaw Antiques, Great Grooms Antiques Centre, Parbrook, Billingshurst, West Sussex RH14 9EU www.nicholas.shaw.com

Gorham Manufacturing Co

Loraine Turner started working in the antiques trade in 1977. She has worked with furniture and silver at retail and auction. She is currently working for Phillips Auctioneers in London.

Irish Silver

James Weldon has worked in the antiques trade since 1963, when he joined the family firm. The business was established in 1899 by his grandfather and has remained in the family ever since. J. W. Weldon are leading experts in Irish silver and have helped to build most of the existing collections of old Irish silver, but they also specialize in old jewellery, especially old diamond jewellery. They are constantly researching Irish marks, and have contributed considerably to the amount of information available on this subject.
J. W. Weldon, 55 Clarendon Street, Dublin 2

Contents

MILLER'S

How to use this book

I t is our aim to make this book easy to use. In order to find a particular item, consult the contents list on page 5 to find the main heading – for example, Spoons. Having located your area of interest, you will find that larger sections have been sub-divided. If you are looking for a particular factory, designer or craftsman, consult the index which starts on page 315.

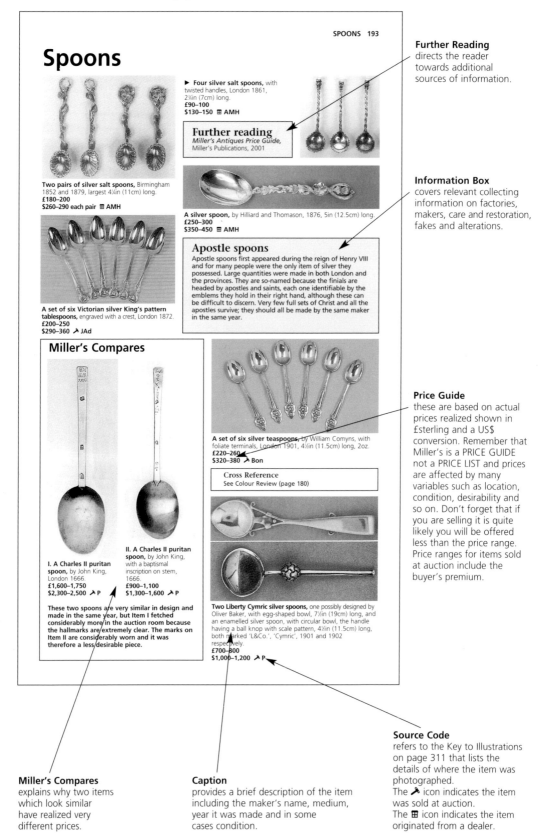

Spoons

Two pairs of silver salt spoons, Birmingham 1852 and 1879, largest 4¼in (11cm) long.
£180–200
$260–290 each pair ⊞ AMH

A set of six Victorian silver King's pattern tablespoons, engraved with a crest, London 1872.
£200–250
$290–360 ⚒ JAd

▶ Four silver salt spoons, with twisted handles, London 1861, 2¾in (7cm) long.
£90–100
$130–150 ⊞ AMH

Further reading
Miller's Antiques Price Guide,
Miller's Publications, 2001

A silver spoon, by Hilliard and Thomason, 1876, 5in (12.5cm) long.
£250–300
$350–450 ⊞ AMH

Apostle spoons
Apostle spoons first appeared during the reign of Henry VIII and for many people were the only item of silver they possessed. Large quantities were made in both London and the provinces. They are so-named because the finials are headed by apostles and saints, each one identifiable by the emblems they hold in their right hand, although these can be difficult to discern. Very few full sets of Christ and all the apostles survive; they should all be made by the same maker in the same year.

Miller's Compares

I. A Charles II puritan spoon, by John King, London 1666.
£1,600–1,750
$2,300–2,500 ⚒ P

II. A Charles II puritan spoon, by John King, with a baptismal inscription on stem, 1666.
£900–1,100
$1,300–1,600 ⚒ P

These two spoons are very similar in design and made in the same year, but Item I fetched considerably more in the auction room because the hallmarks are extremely clear. The marks on Item II are considerably worn and it was therefore a less desirable piece.

A set of six silver teaspoons, by William Comyns, with foliate terminals, London 1901, 4½in (11.5cm) long, 2oz.
£220–260
$320–380 ⚒ Bon

Cross Reference
See Colour Review (page 180)

Two Liberty Cymric silver spoons, one possibly designed by Oliver Baker, with egg-shaped bowl, 7½in (19cm) long, and an enamelled silver spoon, with circular bowl, the handle having a ball knop with scale pattern, 4½in (11.5cm) long, both marked 'L&Co.', 'Cymric', 1901 and 1902 respectively.
£700–800
$1,000–1,200 ⚒ P

Further Reading
directs the reader towards additional sources of information.

Information Box
covers relevant collecting information on factories, makers, care and restoration, fakes and alterations.

Price Guide
these are based on actual prices realized shown in £sterling and a US$ conversion. Remember that Miller's is a PRICE GUIDE not a PRICE LIST and prices are affected by many variables such as location, condition, desirability and so on. Don't forget that if you are selling it is quite likely you will be offered less than the price range. Price ranges for items sold at auction include the buyer's premium.

Source Code
refers to the Key to Illustrations on page 311 that lists the details of where the item was photographed.
The ⚒ icon indicates the item was sold at auction.
The ⊞ icon indicates the item originated from a dealer.

Miller's Compares
explains why two items which look similar have realized very different prices.

Caption
provides a brief description of the item including the maker's name, medium, year it was made and in some cases condition.

Introduction

For many centuries silver has been avidly sought after by collectors for its beauty, practicality and value. Traditionally, silver was paraded as a sign of the wealth and importance of families and religious establishments, with the added advantage that it could be melted down easily and sold as bullion or transported in times of trouble. When mined, silver is usually found as nuggets or grains and the most prolific areas for excavating silver ore are in Mexico, Australia, USA and Russia. Silver is often found near copper mines. I am sure it is the unique metallic lustre of silver, together with the craftsmanship of the silversmith, which lures one into craving ownership of this metal.

When you purchase a modern object today you are paying for the design and workmanship that goes into the item, whereas in times past, with the abundance of cheap labour, the majority of the cost was determined purely by its weight. It was also acceptable then to send an item to the silversmith to be reworked when fashions changed. Many examples of this are seen today which illustrate the changing tastes between the Georgian and Victorian era. Many Georgian pieces were plain and simple with maybe a bright-cut design, whereas heavy embossing and chasing were popular on Victorian wares. It was much cheaper to send your tea service off to be decorated than buy a new one. Today this is often thought of as vandalism and given a wide berth by collectors, as the pieces are no longer original. A tankard with later chasing, for instance, will sell for at least half the price of an unaltered one. Although this may sound like a good buy, as far as future investment is concerned it will always be a later chased item with a consequent low value.

Whether you are new to the world of collecting or have years of experience it is worth remembering to always handle, as well as look at, items you are considering purchasing. This may sound obvious but I have seen many a customer worried about leaving fingerprints on a shiny surface. A reputable dealer or auction house will never mind a customer handling an item. Handling a piece provides the opportunity to feel the weight and gauge of the silver, and also to feel for damage, repair or removal of an inscription. Run a finger and thumb together on the inside and outside of a christening mug, for instance, and you will be able to determine a change in thickness if any initials have been removed.

When I am looking at a piece to buy what I am really trying to do is find a reason not to purchase. This may sound strange but there is a lot of silver in the world and it is easy to spend money. The trick is finding those perfect items that will enhance, rather than lessen your collection. Never be afraid to ask questions about what you are looking at and listen carefully to the answers. If you have the slightest doubt about a dealer or auctioneer there is probably a reason why – trust should be earned. Try to keep away from worn, dented, repaired and altered silver, this will stand you in good stead in the future whether you decide to sell or pass on your collection. Only once you have satisfied yourself that all is well is it time to consider the price. There is a wonderful saying 'quality lives when price is forgotten'. This is very true.

There is enormous scope for the budding collector with prices ranging from a few pounds to tens of thousands. I am often asked 'what should I collect?'. I try to find out what interests the customer and whether they wish to use the pieces. Practical items such as cutlery make a good start as these can then be extended to include other tableware pieces, from small items such as salt cellars through to candlesticks and extravagant centrepieces. Other collectors specialize in defined areas with strict parameters such as only collecting a particular animal or bird, or one type of item, such as tea caddy spoons. It is simply a matter of choosing an area that arouses a passion, and whatever that may be, you are certain to discover it in silver in one form or another.

As far as prices are concerned, at the moment the market place can be defined in two areas, one excelling and the other declining. Poor quality, slightly damaged and uninteresting silver is now incredibly cheap, as collectors have learned that these pieces, although inexpensive, are not worth buying. However prices are very strong and still rising for the unusual, the best examples of their kind or pieces by famous silversmiths. George II silver with thick gauge and good hallmarks is certainly sought after. Provincial Scottish silver is also a keen market with pieces originating from Elgin, Perth, Tain and Wick finding many collectors with deep pockets. Small collectables such as wine labels, miniatures or nutmeg graters, basically anything which will fit comfortably in a little display cabinet, are rising to new heights. Tiny little pincushions with no weight to them are selling for £1,000 ($1,500), and I see no slow down at the moment. However, the biggest increase in interest and price is still with Irish silver. It is the early and provincial pieces that collectors hanker after, but in reality it seems anything with an Irish hallmark will do. Demand is exceeding supply and inevitably this will always have an effect on the price.

There have been hundreds of books written on the subject of silver and their makers and if the addiction of collecting has taken hold, a trip to a good book shop will feed your passion. Do remember that *Miller's Silver & Plate Buyer's Guide* is only a price guide, and that numerous factors will affect the price of an item so, with that in mind, I hope you enjoy this book and find it useful. Happy collecting! **Daniel Bexfield**

Silver Marks

The English hallmarking system began in 1300 to enforce the assay laws from the Goldsmiths' Hall (hence the term hallmark). Only silver containing at least 92.5 per cent of silver to 7.5 per cent copper could be termed sterling and receive the official mark. Marking also made it easier for customs officials to prevent the export of silver from England. Assay Offices were established across the country, although only five operate today: London, Birmingham, Dublin, Edinburgh and Sheffield. Each Office was autonomous, and therefore responsible for the design and cutting of its own punches. Thus the standard mark for sterling silver (Lion Passant) was of a different design at each Hall. The Hallmarking Act of 1973 tidied up many of the anomalies in the Law and simplified the marks so that they are easier to understand and recognize. Assaying has always applied to both the main body and any detachable parts.

Standard Marks

The Lion Passant was introduced in 1544 to designate silver of sterling standard (92.5 per cent). In 1696 the standard was raised to Britannia (95.8 per cent) by an Act of Parliament, the mark being the figure of Britannia and a Lion's head erased. Sterling was restored in 1720 and the Lion Passant reinstated. Its appearance has changed slightly over the years.

Sterling Silver

British sterling silver usually bears at least four marks: the maker's mark, standard mark, town mark and date letter; some items also bear a duty mark for the relevant period and a commemorative mark.

Date Letter

These appear as letters of the alphabet, though not all letters were used. Date letters before 1975 are best referred to by both the part years during which they were current. For example, in Edinburgh the letter was changed annually in September until 1832, and thereafter in October. In Birmingham and Sheffield it changed in July, in Dublin it changed in June until 1932 and thereafter in January. From 1975 all date letters change on 1 January, and so the assay year and calendar year now coincide. The various cycles of date letters are identifiable by the forms of the letters and the shapes of the shield which enclose them, and should be read in conjunction with the other marks on the piece.

Duty Marks

The sovereign's head was introduced as a Duty Mark in 1784. It was proof that duty had been paid to the government at the time of assay, and appears on all items made during that period, except those articles not liable to compulsory hallmarking. It was abolished in 1890. The sovereign's head was not introduced as Duty Mark at the Dublin Assay Office until 1807, and not until 1819 at Glasgow.

Commemorative Marks

The King's Jubilee Mark, which shows the heads of King George V and Queen Mary, accompanied by the date letters for the assay years 1934–35 and 1935–36, were used to commemorate the 25th anniversary of the King's accession. The Coronation Mark, showing the head of Queen Elizabeth II, and the date letters of either 1952 or 1953, were used to commemorate the coronation of Queen Elizabeth II. The Queen's Jubilee Mark, showing the head of Queen Elizabeth II, was used on silver assayed in 1977 to commemorate the 25th anniversary of the Queen's accession.

Marks of Origin

Each assay office had its own mark which makes it possible to identify the location of the assay.

London

From 1300 London-made sterling silver was marked with the Leopard's Head. From 1478 until 1820 it was surmounted with a crown, after which date the crown is deleted. Occasionally the mark was omitted, especially on smaller articles, between 1790 and 1820.

Outside London, a number of smaller towns marked their own silver. Compared with that of London, provincial marking was relatively haphazard and inconsistent, and pieces carrying rare or unusual provincial marks are highly prized among collectors.

Birmingham

An important centre for silver production during the late 18th century, especially for small items such as vinaigrettes and snuff boxes. An Assay Office was opened there in 1773 with the town mark designated by an anchor, and this is accompanied by a Lion Passant, a date letter, duty mark and maker's initials.

Chester

The town mark is a shield bearing the Arms of the city, three sheaves of wheat with a dagger. Marking there was not regulated until the end of the 17th century, the marks then used were similar to those found on London hallmarked silver of the same period. The Office was closed in 1962. Generally speaking smaller articles were assayed here, such as cream jugs, tumbler cups, tankards and beakers.

Dublin

The town mark is a Harp Crowned. It appears with a date letter and, after 1730, the figure of Hibernia. Irish silver does not always bear complete marks, but the workmanship was excellent and the designs decorative, encompassing the whole range of the silversmith's craft.

Edinburgh

Scottish silver marks were introduced in the mid-15th century. The town mark is a castle with three towers and the deacon's mark. In 1681 an assay master was appointed and a date letter system introduced. In 1759 the assay master's initials were replaced by a Scottish thistle, and in 1975 this was again replaced with a Lion Rampant.

Exeter

Silver was made here from the very earliest times, and the assay marks date from the mid-16th century. The mark of origin was in the form of the letter X, usually in a round shield surmounted by a crown. In 1701 this was replaced by a three-towered castle, and until 1720 the town and maker's marks were accompanied by the Britannia mark and Lion's head erased. These last two were replaced with the Leopard's Head (which was dropped in 1777) and Lion Passant in square shields after 1721. Some very good quality silver was produced in Exeter, notably ecclesiastical vessels, tankards, coffee pots and teapots. The Assay Office closed in 1882.

Glasgow

The first defining marks did not appear until the latter part of the 17th century. The town mark consisted of a Tree, Bird, Bell, Fish and Ring motif, with the maker's mark struck either side of the town mark. A date letter cycle mark was introduced in 1681 but abandoned after approximately 25 years. Locally struck marks ceased in 1784, after which nearly all work was sent to Edinburgh for assay until 1819, when Glasgow was given its own assay office. The new marks were the town mark (as before), a lion rampant, a date letter, the monarch's head and a duty mark where relevant. A thistle was added in 1914.

Norwich

Assay marks can be traced to the mid-16th century when the mark of origin was a Castle surmounting a Lion Passant, used with a date letter and maker's mark. During the early part of the 17th century a Seeded Rose was added to the town mark, which was altered to a Rose with a stem in the last half of the century. Silver marking was erratic at this office, and little, if any, was assayed after 1701. Production was chiefly confined to church and corporation plate, and spoons.

Newcastle

Silver was assayed here from the mid-17th century. The town mark was three Castles in a shield, but marking was erratic until 1702 when the Britannia standard was introduced. With the restoration of sterling in 1720, the Leopard's Head and Lion Passant were used with the town mark and date letter. The Lion faces to the right between 1721 and 1727.

Sheffield

This Office was established by an Act of Parliament opened in 1773. Until 1974 the mark of origin on silver was the Crown accompanied by the usual sequence of marks in use elsewhere. The date letters began with the letter E, and thereafter varied irregularly each year until 1824, after which they were arranged in alphabetical order. All forms of decorative and domestic silver in use during the 18th and 19th centuries were produced and marked in Sheffield, particularly candlesticks. Quantities of these were purchased by London and Edinburgh silversmiths who overstruck the marks of the original silversmiths.

York

Silver was assayed here from the mid-16th century. The mark of origin was a halved Leopard's Head and a halved fleur-de-lys conjoined in one shield, with date letters and maker's marks. In the late 1690s the Leopard's Head was replaced with a half Seeded Rose. In 1701 the town mark was altered to Five Lions Passant on a Cross. Early silverware produced in the city were of fine workmanship and design, consisting largely of ecclesiastical and domestic ware, including caudle cups and tankards. Between 1700 and 1780 very few articles were assayed, and from 1780 until the closure of the Office in 1856 the items produced were unremarkable and largely for domestic use.

Import Marks

The Customs Act of 1842 made it illegal to import gold or silver ware into Great Britain and Ireland unless they had been assayed at a British Office. From 1867 silver articles produced outside Britain were assigned a distinctive mark of foreign origin (the letter F within an oval escutcheon) in addition to the standard British hallmarks. After 1904 imported silver was stamped with a symbol designating the decimal value of the standard used, together with the annual date letter and a special assay office mark; the letter F was discontinued.

Continental European Silver Marks

Silver produced in continental Europe was not marked as systematically as English silver, although marks were used to signify quality or during periods when duty was payable. Several standards of silver were used but the only examples now seen are 800, 830, 900 and 950 parts per thousand, which do not correspond to contemporary English marks. Consequently items with Continental marks are often described as Continental Silver or silver-coloured metal. Town marks were frequently used however, and can provide useful clues for determining the date and place of manufacture of an item. Since the recognition of lower grade standards by the Assay Office, 800 standard silver is now officially accepted in Great Britain.

American Marks

There is no official marking system in the USA and the only assay office operated in Baltimore from 1814 until 1830. Most makers stamped their silver with abbreviated or full maker or company names. Sometimes the pattern number and standard of silver used would be added. Emblems were used by many makers, the shape of the enclosure around the mark can help establish where or when an item was made as shapes varied with place of production and period. Some firms also used their own date marks or stamped wares with the weight in ounces.

Old Sheffield Plate and Silver Plate

Early Sheffield plate was rarely marked, if at all. In 1784 legislation was introduced that allowed a maker's mark and device, a note of which was kept in a register at the Sheffield Assay Office. The practice of marking increased as the century progressed, but it was not until the late 18th century that a set of marks began to appear that were rather too similar to those being used on sterling silver. The Plate Assay (Sheffield and Birmingham) Act of 1772 ordered that these two assay offices ensured that no marks applied to plated goods resembled too closely those applied to silver. By the 1820s, makers marks often consisted of the name in full, split in two to fit a regular punch, although initials were still used. The Crown was frequently used from 1765–1880 by various makers as a guarantee of quality. During the second half of the 19th century the letters E.P.N.S. (Electroplated Nickel Silver) and E.P.B.M. (Electroplated Britannia Metal) appeared.

Shown here are the marks of some of the silversmiths we have featured in this book:

Hester Bateman
 Her initials 'HB' appeared in script.

William Bateman
 'WB'

Peter and Jonathan Bateman
 'PB.IB'. This is the rarest Bateman mark, entered on 7 December 1790. Jonathan died on 19 April 1791.

Peter and Anne Bateman
 'PB.AB'

Peter, Anne and William Bateman
 'PB.AB.WB'

Peter and William Bateman
 'PB.WB'

Gorham Manufacturing Co
 The earliest pieces of flatware show the 'Gorham' name written in full, with other items marked 'Gorham & Webster', 'Gorham Webster & Price'. From 1850 'Gorham & Sons' was used, and after 1855 'Gorham & Co'. Hollow ware marks are a lion rampant, similar to the English mark, but facing in the opposite direction, with an anchor, and a gothic G for Gorham. In 1868 they adopted the English sterling standard and this was usually incorporated alongside the other marks. At the same time Gorham introduced an alphabetical dating system which ran from 1868–84, with a different symbol being used after 1885. Electroplated items were stamped with the company's name.

Georg Jensen

Paul de Lamerie
 His early mark 'LA' with a star and crow above and fleur-de-lys below, was only used on items made from Britannia standard silver. In June 1739 he registered his initials 'PL' with a crown above and pellet below.

Sampson Mordan
 This mark was used on items made after 1890.

Omar Ramsden and Alwyn Carr
 The joint mark was registered in 1898. In 1918 Ramsden entered a gothic-style mark.

Paul Storr
His initials, 'PS' were entered in 1793.

Tiffany
From 1873–1965 the mark included the initial letter of the company presidents' surname.

This is only a brief introduction to hallmarks. For further information we suggest you refer to *Miller's Silver & Sheffield Plate Marks Pocket Fact File*, available from most book shops.

Baskets

A German parcel-gilt silver basket, by Samuel Schneeweiss, the basket-weave body applied with four enamel plaques, with foliate and fruit chased handles, Augsburg c1690, 27¼in (69cm) wide, 39oz.
£4,300–4,800
$6,500–7,000 ⚒ S(G)

A George III silver basket, maker's mark partially worn, London 1780, 14¾in (37.5cm) wide, 29oz.
£1,600–2,000
$2,300–3,000 ⚒ Bon

A George III silver basket, by Benjamin Smith, the central panel engraved with a crest and motto 'Coleum Non Solum', with a ribbon tied foliate border and stiff-leaf chased rim, with beaded double handle, tied by flowerheads and leaves, with circular box hinges and matching flowerhead and rope twist everted border, raised upon a stiff-leaf chased and bead cast rectangular foot, the base engraved 'Presented to Elizabeth Sophia Dawes by Her Uncle Joshua Horton on her Marriage', London 1814, 14in (36cm) wide, 36oz.
£3,000–4,000
$4,500–6,000 ⚒ HSS

A silver basket, with ruby glass liner, crested, pierced with leaves and scrolls, swing handle, marked 'II' over 'DM', London 1768, 4¾in (12cm) high, 2.5oz.
£550–650
$800–1,000 ⚒ S(Am)

A George III silver dessert basket and stand, with two medallions engraved with coats-of-arms, rams' heads and ring handles, on four bun feet, maker's mark of John Wakelin and William Taylor, London 1790, 15½in (39.5cm) wide.
£17,500–20,000
$25,500–29,000 ⚒ C(G)

A William IV silver swing-handled basket, by Howard and Hawksworth, heavily chased overall, the centre engraved with a full coat-of-arms, Sheffield 1835, 5in (12.5cm) diam, 34.75oz.
£1,200–1,500
$1,750–2,200 ⚒ L

◀ **A silver-gilt neo-classical-style dessert basket,** by Thomas William and Henry Holmes Dobson, the pierced sides with cast and applied ribbon-tied paterae swags, London 1881, 11½in (29cm) wide, 18oz.
£720–800
$1,000–1,200 ⚒ WW

A silver pierced basket, by Richard Mills, London 1772, 5in (12.5cm) wide.
£3,500–4,000
$5,000–5,800 ⊞ DIC

A George III silver basket, by Robert Sharp, with armorial engraving below a bright-cut band, London 1795, 14½in (37cm) wide, 34oz.
£3,500–4,000
$5,000–5,800 ⚒ S
The arms are those of Mark Sprot, one of the founders of the London Stock Exchange.

A pair of French silver baskets, foliate-pierced, on silver-plated stands, 19thC, 10in (25.5cm) wide.
£3,500–3,800
$5,000–5,500 ⚒ S

A pair of Howard & Co sterling silver baskets, after a design by Paul de Lamerie, of shell-form on dolphin feet, mid-19thC, 10½in (26.5cm) long, 68oz.
£4,000–4,500
$6,000–6,500 ⚒ SK

A Victorian silver swing-handled basket, by Thomas Bradbury & Sons, decorated with foliate and strap engraving within a floral border spaced with six oval embossed floral medallions, stylized rope handle, Sheffield 1882, 11in (28cm) diam, 15oz.
£400–500
$600–750 L

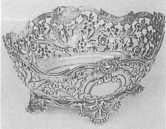

An Edwardian silver basket, by Sydney Bellamy Harman, the undulating border applied with flowers, the sides pierced with exotic birds and flowers and with a central cartouche, on four cast pierced shell and scroll feet, 1902, 9in (23cm) long, 18oz.
£600–700
$850–1,000 P(EA)

An Edward VII silver basket, chased and pierced with birds and animals among scrolls, flowers and foliage, with vine pattern edging, London 1909, 10in (25.5cm) diam, 10.5oz.
£350–400
$500–600 Bea

A pair of Edwardian silver baskets, Birmingham 1903, 4¾in (12cm) wide.
£220–240
$300–350 TGa

A pair of George V silver two-handled baskets, by D. and J. Wellby Ltd, the sides pierced and bright-cut, with foliate trellis-work and reeded handles, London 1910, 10in (25.5cm) long, 23.5oz.
£2,000–2,200
$2,900–3,500 Bea

◄ **A pair of George V silver baskets,** by William Comyns, with cast and pierced foliate decoration, London 1913, 6¼in (16cm) wide, 29oz.
£1,250–1,500
$1,800–2,200 Bea(E)
The baskets sold for well in excess of their estimate because they are of a good weight, and pairs are always desirable.

Bread Baskets

A George II silver bread basket, the detachable swing handle applied with a rococo cartouche engraved with a crest, the basket engraved with a coat-of-arms and later inscription beneath the base, marked on reverse, maker's mark of Samuel Herbert & Co, London 1754, 14½in (37cm) long, 44oz.
£7,000–8,000
$10,000–11,500 C
The inscription reads 'E. Dono B. Cust Baroneti Aug^st 31 1775'.

▶ **A George II silver bread basket,** on four shell and wheat ear feet, later engraved with a coat-of-arms, maker's mark of Frederick Kandler, marked under base, London 1750, 15in (38cm) long, 67oz.
£25,000–28,000
$36,000–40,500 C

◄ **A silver bread basket,** by R. Martin and E. Hall, Sheffield 1906, 12in (30.5cm) long.
£550–600
$800–880 THOM

Condition
The condition is absolutely vital when assessing the value of an antique. Damaged pieces on the whole appreciate much less than perfect examples. However a rare desirable piece may command a high price even when damaged.

Bonbon Baskets

A George III silver swing-handled bonbon basket, by William Plummer, with ropework borders, the wirework sides applied with fruiting vines, 1764, 6in (15cm) wide, 4.5oz.
£750–850
$1,000–1,200 ⚒ P

A silver pierced bonbon basket, London 1774, 6in (15cm) wide.
£700–800
$1,000–1,500 ⊞ DIC

A Victorian silver bonbon basket, by Yapp and Woodward, embossed at the centre with a view of York Minster, the sides embossed with fruit, flowers and foliage, Birmingham 1847, 6½in (16.5cm) diam, 4.5oz.
£450–550
$650–800 ⚒ Bea(E)

▶ **A graduated set of three silver pedestal boat-shaped bonbon baskets,** by Ball Brothers, chased and pierced with flowers, scrolls and foliage with tongue, bead and shell edging, Birmingham 1898, 6½ and 8½in (16 and 21cm) long, 14.5oz, in a fitted case.
£600–700
$900–1,000 ⚒ Bea

Cake Baskets

A George II silver cake basket, by John White, the centre engraved with a band of diaper work and scrolls, the swing handle engraved with the King crest, pierced and engraved on the outside with scrolling and foliage and centred on either side with roundels enclosing the King crest and baron's coronet, London 1734, 12¾in (32.5cm) wide, 80.75oz.
£66,000–72,000
$94,500–104,500 ⚒ S

A George II silver chinoiserie cake basket, by Samuel Herbert & Co, centrally engraved with a crest, the handle with old repairs, London 1754, 13½in (34.5cm) wide.
£2,500–3,000
$3,500–4,500 ⚒ DN
Samuel Herbert's first mark was entered in 1747, and he took an unnamed partner into the business at Foster Lane in 1750. He specialized in pierced work, in particular baskets.

A George II silver cake basket, with trellis pierced sides, rope edge, pierced plaited handle, maker's mark 'W.P.', London 1757, 12in (30.5cm) wide, 22oz.
£1,100–1,200
$1,600–1,800 ⚒ GAK

Miller's is a price GUIDE not a price LIST

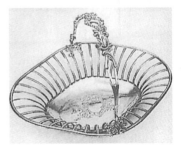

◀ **A George II silver cake basket,** by Edward Aldridge and John Stamper, with spiral beaded flutes and pierced panels, on mask and scroll feet, 1758, 15in (38cm) wide, 46oz.
£5,000–5,500
$7,250–8,000 ⚒ P(WM)

A George III silver openwork shaped oval cake basket, by John Henry Vere and William Lutwyche, the swing handle cast with a rococo cartouche and foliate scrolls, the base engraved with a rococo cartouche, London 1762, 14in (35.5cm) wide, 24oz.
£1,600–1,800
$2,300–2,600 ⚒ P(S)

An early George III silver cake basket, by William Penstone, with gadroon and shell cast rim, pierced sides, the centre engraved with the arms of Sir William Middleton 5th Baronet, London 1770, 15½in (39.5cm) long, 45oz.
£6,000–7,000
$8,700–10,500 ➤ AG

A George III silver cake basket, by Burrage Davenport, engraved with two later crests, London 1772, 13in (33cm) wide, 25oz.
£2,200–2,500
$3,200–3,600 ➤ S(NY)

A silver cake basket, by William Plummer, with pierced and chased beads, scrolls, paterae and foliage, with cast foliate border and pierced swing handle, 1772, 14¼in (36cm) wide, 30oz.
£3,200–3,500
$4,500–5,000 ➤ TEN

A George III silver panelled octagonal cake basket, with reeded edge and swing handle, the centre with a pierced band and border of bright-cut foliate swags, engraved with a crest of a horse's head, on a reeded pedestal foot, London 1788, 15¾in (40cm) wide, 26oz.
£1,100–1,300
$1,500–2,000 ➤ P(HSS)

A George III silver cake basket, by William Allen III, with pierced fret border, the swing handle with reeded moulding, damaged, London 1801, 15in (38cm) wide.
£700–800
$1,000–1,500 ➤ WW

A George III silver cake basket, by Thomas Wallis, the interior with floral and foliate-engraved border, London 1803, 13¾in (35cm) wide, 23.5oz.
£900–1,000
$1,300–1,500 ➤ Oli

A George III silver cartouche-shaped cake basket, the roll handles with rosettes, engraved with crests and initial 'M', inscribed, London 1807, 14¼in (36cm) wide.
£1,300–1,500
$2,000–2,200 ➤ DN

A George III silver cake basket, by Rebecca Emes and Edward Barnard, the reeded swing handle with raised hinges, cast shell and gadrooned border, London 1811, 14in (35.5cm) wide, 32oz.
£1,000–1,200
$1,500–2,000 ➤ GAK

A William IV silver cake basket, by H. Wilkinson & Co, with rococo scroll and floral embossed border, trailing ivy cast swing handle, the base inscribed and dated 'November 1st 1836', 10¼in (26cm) diam, 15oz.
£350–400
$500–600 ➤ HAM

◀ **An early Victorian silver cake basket,** with a shaped raised border and scrolling edge, the repoussé foliage with pierced hatched paterae panel to a matt ground, with pierced engraved swing handle, on pierced repoussé shell scroll panel feet, retailed by Hunt and Roskell, London 1847, 15in (38cm) high, 38oz.
£1,200–1,500
$1,750–2,200 ➤ WW

A Victorian silver cake basket, with openwork foot, maker's mark obscure, Birmingham 1897, 14in (35.5cm) long, 26.5oz.
£1,000–1,200
$1,500–2,000 ➤ SLN

A late Victorian silver cake basket, repoussé-decorated with flowers, leaves, scrolls and shell motifs, on oval foot, with scrolled and chased swing handle, Sheffield 1898, maker's mark 'F.Bs.Ltd.', 12in (30.5cm) long, 27oz.
£400–500
$600–750 ⚖ MCA

An Edward VII silver cake basket, by Lambert & Co, pierced and bright-cut with festoons and foliate motifs, with thread edging in 18thC style, London 1901, 10in (25cm) long, 11.5oz.
£400–450
$600–650 ⚖ Bea

An Edwardian silver cake basket, by Thomas Bradbury & Sons, the body with classical paterae and husk garlands on a pierced band, the leaf-capped swing handle with a band of husks within rope-twist border, 1903, 11½in (29cm) wide, 19oz.
£600–650
$900–950 ⚖ C(S)

A silver cake basket, by Charles Stuart Harris, with rope-twist borders, pierced sides, handle and foot, London 1914, 9½in (24cm) long, 17.5oz.
£900–1,100
$1,300–1,600 ⚖ DN

A silver cake basket, with Chippendale rim and swing handle, Sheffield 1918, 12in (30.5cm) long.
£700–800
$1,000–1,200 ⊞ CoHA

A silver cake basket, by Crichton Bros, the pierced and engraved edge with beaded border, London 1920, 13in (33cm) long, 25oz.
£800–900
$1,200–1,500 ⚖ SK

Fruit Baskets

A George III silver fruit basket, with reeded swing handle, the rim with pierced leaf pattern, London 1791, 7in (18cm) wide, 21oz.
£550–600
$800–900 ⚖ JAd

A George III boat-shaped silver fruit basket, by George Smith, with beaded rim, the sides with chased swags on a pierced-wave-patterned ground with loop handles, on pierced bracket feet with claw-and-ball supports, London 1817, 11in (28cm) wide, 14.5oz.
£900–1,100
$1,300–1,600 ⚖ AH

A Dutch 18thC-style silver fruit basket, pierced and engraved with foliage, flowers, beading and trelliswork, on lions' paw feet, import marks for Birmingham 1902, 11½in (29cm) wide, 16.25oz.
£900–1,100
$1,300–1,600 ⚖ CSK

An Edward VII silver fruit basket, by George Maudsley Jackson and David Landsborough Fullerton, London 1903, 14¾in (37.5cm) long, 33.5oz.
£520–575
$750–850 ⚖ Bea(E)

A silver fruit basket, by The Goldsmiths & Silversmiths Co, with chased flowers and scroll borders, pierced and engraved sides, London 1905, 9½in (24cm) wide, 19.25oz.
£900–1,100
$1,300–1,600 ⚖ DN

A George V silver-gilt fruit basket, by Mappin & Webb, with later presentation inscription, the pierced sides and base with chased vine pattern edging, Sheffield 1919, 4½in (11cm) long, 22.75oz.
£600–700
$900–1,000 ⚖ Bea

Sugar Baskets

A George III silver sugar basket, by William Plummer, the wirework sides with trailing vine leaves, London 1770, 3in (7.5cm) diam.
£400–450
$550–650 ✗ DN

A George III silver sugar basket, by William Vincent, the sides pierced with flowers, leaves and scrolls, with ropework rim and swing handles, on a trumpet foot, with blue glass liner, 1770, 3¼in (8cm) diam., 2.5oz.
£550–650
$800–950 ✗ P

A George III silver swing-handled sugar basket, by Richard Morton, the sides pierced with beads and slats above stamped and chased acanthus leaves, the foot crested, with blue glass liner, Sheffield 1778, 5in (12.5cm) diam, 4oz.
£700–800
$1,000–1,200 ✗ P

A George III silver swing-handled sugar basket, by William Plummer, with thread edging, pierced and bright-cut sides, on spreading pedestal base, with blue glass liner, London 1786, 7in (18cm) wide, 7.5oz.
£550–650
$800–950 ✗ Bea

A George III silver basket, by George Gray, with bright-cut engraving of foliage, glass liner missing, 1790, 4½in (11.5cm) wide, 5oz.
£300–350
$450–500 ✗ P

A George III silver sugar basket, with beaded borders and swing handle, embossed with fluting, swags of husks and paterae, with rams' head handles and oval base, foot repaired, the mark of George Gray overstriking that of Peter and Ann Bateman, London 1792, 5½in (14cm) wide, 5oz.
£350–400
$500–600 ✗ DN

A George III silver gilt-lined sugar basket, by Solomon Hougham, engraved with a band of bright-cut foliate decoration beneath the fluted rim, with two shield-shaped cartouches between reeds, on a raised foot, engraved with initials 'JEM', 1797, 6¾in (17cm) high, 8oz.
£420–480
$600–700 ✗ L

A silver swing-handled sugar basket, by Edward Barnard & Sons, with blue glass liner and a sugar sifter, monogrammed and dated, London 1858, 6¾in (17cm) high.
£280–320
$400–450 ✗ Bea(E)

A pierced silver sugar basket, by Henry Wilkinson & Co, with frosted glass liner, inscribed, Sheffield 1867, 5in (12.5cm) high.
£240–260
$350–400 ✗ Mit

A Victorian silver sugar basket, by R. Martin and E. Hall, with shaped border, panelled with embossed flowers, birds, snakes and fruits on a lobed oval foot, with swing handle, London 1868, 6½in (16.5cm) wide, 7oz.
£400–500
$600–750 ✗ DN

▶ **A Victorian silver sugar basket,** by George Unite of Birmingham, with deeply waved beaded rim, beaded foot and swing handle, the body pierced with scrolling foliates, stamped with petalled medallions joined by festoons of flowerheads, with fluted lower section, with blue glass liner, Chester 1900.
£400–500
$600–750 ✗ DA

A Victorian silver sugar basket, by J.and E. Bradbury, with swing handle, 1869, 6in (15cm) wide, 7.5oz.
£250–300
$350–450 ✗ L

A Victorian silver sugar basket, by Edward Barnard & Sons, pierced and engraved with foliate and arabesque designs, with blue glass liner, London 1870, 4in (10cm) high.
£275–325
$400–470 ✗ GAK

▶ **An Edwardian silver sugar basket,** by Richard Martin and Ebenezer Hall, with blue glass liner, Sheffield 1904, 5¼in (13.5cm) high.
£200–240
$300–350 ✗ P(O)

A Victorian silver swing-handled sugar basket, by Peter and Ann Bateman, with thread edging, pierced and bright-cut sides, on a pedestal base, with blue glass liner, London 1891, 5½in (14cm) wide, 4.75oz.
£650–750
$950–1,100 ✗ Bea

Sweetmeat Baskets

A George III silver sweetmeat basket, by Tudor and Leader, Sheffield 1776, 3in (7.5cm) high.
£500–600
$700–900 ⊞ TGa

▶ **An Edwardian silver sweetmeat basket,** by The Goldsmiths & Silversmiths Co, with reeded swing handle, on a pedestal foot, London 1907, 7in (18cm) wide.
£400–500
$600–750 ⊞ HofB

A George III silver swing-handled sweetmeat basket, by Thomas Wallis, with thread edging, bright-cut band and rim base, London 1801, 7½in (19cm) long, 9.5oz.
£700–800
$1,000–1,200 ✗ Bea

A silver sweemeat basket, by David Darling, chased with ribbon-tied flower festoons, reeded borders and swing handle, engraved with a monogram, Newcastle, c1803, 7½in (19cm) high, 6oz.
£380–420
$550–600 ✗ S(Am)
This basket has later Victorian decoration, would have been plain when new.

LOCATE THE SOURCE
The source of each illustration in Miller's can be found by checking the code letters below each caption with the Key to Illustrations, pages 311–314.

Beakers

A Dutch silver beaker, probably by Eelke Wyntiens, Leeuwarden, engraved with arabesques and strapwork enclosing leafy branches and flower-heads, gilt interior, the base set with a medal, c1651, 4¼in (11.5cm) high.
£1,100–1,200
$1,500–2,000 ⚒ S(Am)

A German parcel-gilt silver beaker, by Paulus Schütte, with embossed floral decoration, inscribed on base 'N4' and name, c1670, 5½in (14cm) high, 8oz.
£4,200–4,800
$6,000–7,000 ⚒ P

A Charles II silver beaker, by John Spackman, engraved with a coat-of-arms within plume mantling, on moulded skirt foot, London 1681, 4in (10.5cm) high, 7.75oz.
£3,200–3,600
$4,500–5,000 ⚒ S

A German parcel-gilt silver beaker, repoussé-decorated with a band of scroll and foliage on a matt ground chased with similar decoration under the reeded rim, early 18thC, 4¼in (11cm) high, 3.5oz.
£1,400–1,600
$2,000–2,500 ⚒ SLN

A Baltic parcel-gilt silver beaker, the tapering sides with a gilt and moulded rim, on a gadrooned foot with a zig-zag band, inscribed, marks probably for Riga, maker's mark 'ID' over 'R' beneath a crown, probably for I. D. Revald, c1730, 7in (18cm) high, with an associated cover, 15.5oz.
£1,750–2,000
$2,500–3,000 ⚒ DN
Parcel-gilt refers to an item that is partially gilded with silver.

A George III flared silver beaker, by Thomas Ray, lightly embossed and chased with a wooded scene, on a flared base, with gilt interior, 1763, 5in (12.5cm) high, 5oz.
£220–260
$300–400 ⚒ P(EA)

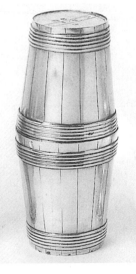

> **Cross Reference**
> See Colour Review (page 66)

◀ **A pair of George III silver provincial double beakers,** with reeded hoops and engraved staves, attributed to Joseph Walley of Liverpool, Chester 1779, 5½in (14cm) high, 7.75oz
£4,300–4,800
$6,250–7,000 ⚒ P

A French silver beaker, with reeded border, numbered 146, scratch initialled to base I. P., charge mark of Julien Alaterre, maker's mark of J. V. C., Paris 1768, 2½in (6.5cm) high, 3oz.
£300–360
$450–550 ⚒ Bon

A George III silver beaker, by John Lambe, with fluted decoration and a band of chased and embossed baskets of flowers, engraved coat-of-arms within a C-scroll cartouche, gilt interior, the foot with scalloped engraving, later inscription to base, 1786, 4in (10cm) high, 4.5oz.
£220–260
$300–380 ⚒ P

A George III silver beaker, by Henry Chawner, with engraved concentric bands, 1788, 4in (10cm) high, 6oz.
£480–520
$700–750 ⚒ P(WM)

A silver beaker, by John Hampston and John Prince, with contemporary crest, York 1788, 3in (7.5cm) high.
£850–950
$1,300–1,400 ⚒ DD

A Continental silver beaker, probably German, with reeded upper border, maker's mark of W. B., 4¼in (11cm) high, 5oz.
£250–300
$350–450 ⚒ Bon

A Guatemalan silver beaker, with flared moulded rim and gilt interior, marked on base with crowned tax stamp and Guatemala mark, c1800, 4in (10cm) high, 9.5oz.
£2,000–2,200
$2,900–3,200 ⚒ S(NY)

A silver beaker, by McHattie and Fenwick, engraved with crests and initials, Edinburgh 1802, 3in (7.5cm) high.
£450–500
$650–750 ⊞ HofB

A parcel-gilt silver beaker, nielloed with views of boats on the river Neva and scrolling foliage, maker's mark indistinct, Assay Master A. Kovalsky, Moscow 1844, 2in (5cm) high.
£1,600–1,800
$2,300–2,800 ⚒ S(G)

A parcel-gilt silver beaker, in the style of William Burges, raised on two falcon legs, chased with bands of medieval decoration with two knights jousting outside a castle, c1870, 3in (7.5cm) high, 2.5oz.
£450–550
$650–800 ⚒ S(S)

A George III crested silver beaker, by Rebecca Emes and Edward Barnard I, London 1813, 3½in (8cm) high, 4.5oz.
£400–450
$600–650 ⚒ DN

Insurance values

Always insure your valuable antiques for the cost of replacing them with similar items, regardless of the original price paid. Both dealers and auctioneers will provide a valuation service for a fee.

A silver beaker, in the 17thC German manner, the lobed heart decoration on a matt ground with traces of gilding, import marks for Chester 1898, importer's mark of B. Muller, 4in (10cm) high, 6oz.
£240–300
$350–440 ⚲ Bon

A Continental parcel-gilt 17thC-style beaker, embossed with mounted warriors being approached by a crowd of supplicant burghers, 19thC, 6in (15cm) high, 9oz.
£460–550
$650–800 ⚲ P(Ba)

A set of four graduated horn beakers, by Asprey, each mounted in silver, stacking together and contained in a leather case, London 1909, largest 5in (12.5cm) high, smallest 3¼in (8.5cm) high.
£350–400
$500–580 ⚲ CGC

◀ **A Dutch silver beaker,** by Gerritsen and van Kempen, with two wooden handles, Zeist 1933, 7½in (19cm) high.
£450–500
$650–720 ⚲ S(Am)

> **Miller's is a price GUIDE not a price LIST**

A Charles I silver wine cup, with bell-shaped bowl and baluster stem, maker's mark, London 1635, 6in (15cm) high, 6.5oz.
£4,000–4,500
$5,800–6,500 ⚲ S(NY)

A German silver-gilt wine goblet, the tapering bowl with panelled corners, on a fruit engraved panelled foot, 18thC, 6in (15cm) high.
£1,300–1,500
$2,000–2,200 ⚲ WW

A George I silver cup and cover, the bell-shaped body with a girdle moulding, on a moulded spreading foot, London 1714, 11in (28cm) high, 47oz.
£3,000–3,500
$4,400–5,000 ⚲ WW

A French parcel-gilt neo-Gothic chalice, by Placido Poussielgue-Rusand, enamelled and garnet set, Paris c1852, 10½in (26.5cm) high, 44oz.
£3,600–4,000
$5,000–5,800 ⚲ S
This chalice illustrates the resurgence of fine craftsmanship in French religious silver which occurred in the middle of the 19th century. Placide Poussielgue-Rusand is considered to be the principal goldsmith of this movement.

A set of four Victorian silver-gilt goblets, by Stephen Smith, the elongated vase-shaped bodies applied with a frieze of lions jumping through vine tendrils, the stems entwined with snakes, 1865, 8¼in (21cm) high.
£1,600–1,800
$2,300–2,600 ⚲ P

A silver thimble tot cup, by Hilliard and Thomason, inscribed 'Just a Thimble Full', Birmingham 1876, 2¼in (5.5cm) high, in original case.
£280–320
$410–465 ⊞ TC

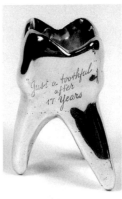

A silver tooth tot cup, by William Frederick Wright, inscribed 'Just a Toothful after 17 years', London 1906, 3¼in (8.5cm) high.
£550–650
$800–950 ⊞ TC

Bowls

The St John mazer, the silver-mounted maple bowl with a double moulded band, the rim mount with a central plaited wire, the upper strapwork bands with three rows of hyphens, later applied ox-eye handles, four hinged straps to the flared foot rim with egg-and-tongue border and lappets moulded to the wood, the rim and foot fully hallmarked, maker's mark a caltrap, London 1585, 7in (18cm) diam.
£55,000–60,000
$80,000–87,000 ⚒ WW
This silver-mounted mazer (hardwood drinking vessel) was found in a country house by Rev St John in Victorian times. Because it had been stored for such a long time it was in pristine condition, although the body was cracked due to shrinkage through lack of use. The non-original handles were added in 1630.

A Swiss silver-gilt bowl, by Hans Rudolph Mayer, decorated with an engraved armorial below a reeded rim, the domed foot embossed with foliage, c1680, 5in (12.5cm) diam, 5.5oz.
£2,250–2,750
$3,300–4,000 ⚒ S(G)

A French silver *coupe de mariage*, by Morlaix, the bowl with a griffin's head and scroll handles, engraved under the lip, on a waisted foot chased with foliage and ovolo and with spreading border, c1740, 5½in (14cm) wide, 4.25oz.
£3,200–3,500
$4,600–5,000 ⚒ C(G)

A Charles II silver bowl and cover, the bowl engraved with armorials between crossed plumes, maker's mark 'GC' in monogram reversed, 'WS' on bowl, London 1681, 5½in (14cm) diam, 19.25oz.
£22,000–25,000
$32,000–36,000 ⚒ S

A Continental silver *écuelle* and cover, the raised partly fluted cover chased with swirling flutes, applied rocaille and flower finial, inscribed, on three shell and hoof feet, maker's mark 'SH' and coronet, c1750, 9in (23cm) wide, 14oz.
£2,200–2,500
$3,000–3,600 ⚒ C(G)

A French silver-gilt *coupe de mariage*, with cover, stand and liner, the bowl on a spreading base with cornucopia handles each terminating in a ram's mask, applied twice with classical scenes, the cover with detachable finial formed as Hebe, the stand on four winged lion's mask and paw feet and with anthemion borders, the plain liner with two hinged handles, mark of Jean Baptiste Claude Odiot, Paris, c1820, 9½in (24cm) high, 69oz.
£12,000–14,000
$17,500–20,500 ⚒ C

▶ **A late Victorian silver-gilt bowl,** with an applied Islamic-style frieze of flowers and foliage, part fluted sides, two lion mask handles, on a round fluted foot, London 1898, 8¼in (21cm) diam.
£440–480
$650–700 ⚒ DN

A silver bowl and spoon, c1885, bowl 5in (12.5cm) diam, with case.
£300–350
$450–500 PC

A silver bowl, chased with foliate swags on a matted ground divided by winged putti masks and two double scroll handles, on a pedestal foot, import marks for London 1890, 4in (10cm) diam.
£250–300
$350–450 ⊞ HofB

Prices

The price ranges quoted in this book reflect the average price a purchaser might expect to pay for a similar item. The price will vary according to the condition, rarity, size, popularity, provenance, colour and restoration of the item, and this must be taken into account when assessing values. Don't forget that if you are selling it is quite likely that you will be offered less than the price range.

▶ **A silver bowl,** by H. C. Lambert, Coventry St, London 1905, stamped, 10in (25cm) long, 19oz.
£550–650
$800–950 ✠ DN

A Japanese silver bowl, decorated with irises, on a rim base, early 20thC, 10¼in (26cm) diam.
£1,650–1,800
$2,300–2,600 ✠ Bea(E)

◀ **A silver strawberry set,** Birmingham 1909, largest 6in (15cm) wide.
£220–260
$350–400 ⊞ CoHA

A silver-mounted palisander bowl, the silver rim chased with anthemion and the girdle decorated with silver acanthus leaves, marked 'Fabergé', Moscow c1910, 3¼in (8.5cm) diam.
£1,400–1,600
$2,000–2,300 ✠ CNY

An Edwardian silver presentation bowl, by The Goldsmiths & Silversmiths Co, partly fluted with embossed and chased panels and enamelled with arms of Hartlepool, inscribed, London 1911, 12¼in (31cm) diam, 105oz.
£3,200–3,500
$4,500–5,000 ✠ P(NE)

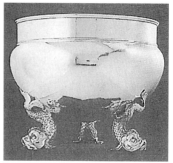

A Swedish silver bowl, with moulded rim, on three feet in the shape of dolphins with swept tails, maker's mark of C. G. Hallberg, Stockholm 1911, 12¼in (31cm) diam, 73.25oz.
£1,800–2,000
$2,500–2,900 ✠ C(G)

> **Miller's is a price GUIDE not a price LIST**

◀ **A pierced silver bowl,** with traces of gilding, inscribed, maker's mark worn, 1919, 11in (28cm) wide, 19.5oz.
£400–450
$580–650 ✠ P(B)

A silver dessert bowl, on three feet, London 1929, 12¼in (31cm) diam.
£200–225
$290–325 ⊞ SnA

▶ **A silver bowl,** by B. P. and S. Ltd, the scroll handles with lion mask finials, with egg-and-dart borders, on a spreading foot, together with a matching pair, c1935, 12¼in (31cm) diam, 44oz.
£700–800
$1,000–1,200 ✠ P(C)

Auction or dealer?

All the pictures in our price guides originate from auction houses and dealers. Look for the symbol at the end of each caption to identify the source.

When buying at auction, prices can be lower than those of a dealer, but a buyer's premium and VAT will be added to the hammer price. Equally, when selling at auction, commission, tax and photography charges must be taken into account. Dealers will often restore pieces before putting them back on the market.

Both dealers and auctioneers will provide professional advice, so it is worth researching both sources before buying or selling your antiques.

A silver tazza, by Charles Boyton, in lightly hammered silver, the bowl with a broad rim raised on six spheres above a spreading foot, the underside with designer's facsimile signature, maker's mark, London 1938, 5in (12.5cm) high.
£700–800
$1,000–1,200 ✠ S

Bleeding Bowls

A William III silver bleeding bowl, by Benjamin Braford, the flat pierced scroll handle with engraved shield, 4in (10cm) high, 4oz.
£3,400–3,800
$4,800–5,500 ⚘ C(G)
Many bowls of this type have had a lot of use. However, this example is engraved with contemporary arms, excellent marks and is in very good condition.

▶ **An American silver bleeding bowl,** by Paul Revere Jr, with a keyhole handle engraved with script 'L', marked '•REVERE', Boston, Massachusetts, c1790, 5½in (14cm) diam.
£12,000–13,000
$17,400–18,850 ⚘ S(NY)

▶ **A silver bleeding bowl,** by Paul Revere II, the pierced keyhole handle engraved, the reverse stamped 'Capt. Robert Wormsted, Æt 28, was lost at sea in Oct. 1782, R.W.A.', 8in (20.5cm) long, 9oz.
£13,000–15,000
$19,000–22,000 ⚘ Bon

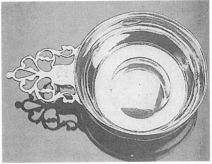

Did you know?

Bleeding bowls (known as porringers in the USA) were made in England for about 100 years following the accession of Charles I in 1625. Despite their name, they were probably used for food. The earliest examples have straight sides and are indistinguishable from skillet covers, the later ones have curved sides. Elaborately pierced handles were common throughout the 18th century. Bleeding bowls were not made in large quantities and can be expensive, those marked on both the handle and the rim fetching premium prices.

Brandy Bowls

A Dutch silver brandy bowl, by Hendrik van Manen, Sneek, engraved at the rim 'AE/1777', 1772, 10in (25.5cm) high, 6.5oz.
£850–950
$1,250–1,400 ⚘ S(Am)

A Dutch silver brandy bowl, the centre raised and chased with flowers, pierced handles, traces of gilding, maker's mark 'LA', Zwolle, 1670, 9in (23cm) wide, 5.5oz.
£1,400–1,600
$2,000–2,300 ⚘ S(Am)

A Dutch silver brandy bowl, the body chased with lobes and dots, the centre engraved with a scene of a meeting, the pierced handles cast with flowers, the reverse stamped with initials 'RY/GC', 8¾in (22.5cm) wide, 6.5oz.
£2,600–3,000
$3,800–4,500 ⚘ S(Am)

Fruit Bowls

▶ **A cut-glass fruit bowl,** with silver rim, c1886, 8¼in (21cm) diam.
£180–200
$260–290 ⊞ CB

An Edwardian silver fruit bowl, by Walker and Hall, formerly with inscription, Sheffield 1905, 15¾in (40cm) wide, 68oz.
£900–1,100
$1,300–1,600 ⚘ WW

▶ **A silver fruit bowl,** with radial-engraved dished centre, Birmingham 1933, 8in (20.5cm) diam, 15oz.
£200–250
$300–360 ⚘ GAK

A silver fruit bowl, by William Hutton & Sons, with blue glass liner, Sheffield 1912, 12¼in (31cm) wide, 26.5oz.
£950–1,150
$1,400–1,700 ⚘ WW

Monteiths

A William III silver monteith,
by Timothy Lea, the detachable rim
with wavy foliate scroll edge applied
with putto masks, the sides matted to
simulate shagreen and embossed with
gadrooned scrolls framing plain
panels, one engraved with armorial,
lion mask drop ring handles, 1696,
13¼in (33.5cm) diam, 89oz.
£20,000–22,000
$29,000–32,000 🔨 P

A late Victorian silver monteith,
by Martin and Hall, with scroll borders,
the sides with cartouche panels
within scale borders, cast lion mask
and ring handles, Sheffield 1890,
15in (38cm) diam, 98oz.
£3,400–3,800
$4,800–5,500 🔨 P(WM)

An Edwardian silver monteith, by
Charles Stuart Harris, with lions' heads
ring handles, London c1902,
11in (28cm) diam, 68oz.
£3,000–3,400
$4,400–4,900 🔨 SK(B)

> Items in the Bowls section have
> been arranged in date order
> within each sub-section.

Porringers

A Charles II silver porringer,
embossed with laurel wreaths above
acanthus leaves, maker's mark
'I.S.' intertwined, London 1680,
7in (18cm) wide, 5.75oz.
£2,000–2,200
$2,900–3,200 🔨 AH

A James II silver porringer cup,
chased with chinoiserie decoration
depicting two standing figures among
foliage and birds with scroll and head
handles, maker's mark 'PM', c1686,
4in (10cm) diam, 8oz.
£1,250–1,500
$1,800–2,200 🔨 L

A James II silver porringer, engraved
with initials 'M.C.' over 'A.W.', with a
band of stiff leaves, two scroll handles,
maker's mark 'E.G.' between mullets,
3¾in (9.5cm) diam, 5oz.
£1,300–1,500
$1,900–2,200 🔨 DN

◀ **A silver porringer,** with wrythen,
fluted and punched decoration,
London 1699, 3½in (9cm) high, 6oz.
£900–1,100
$1,300–1,600 🔨 GAK

A Queen Anne silver porringer,
by Nathaniel Lock, the front with a
vacant cartouche repoussé-decorated
and surmounted by a cherub's head,
London 1710, 2in (5cm) high, 11oz.
£1,150–1,400
$1,700–2,000 🔨 WW

**A George III silver porringer or
christening cup,** of Guernsey type,
the S-scroll handles with beaded
rat-tails, inscribed 'I.S.C, P.L.R.
1769', maker's mark 'IH' attributed
to John Hardie, Guernsey c1769,
2¾in (7cm) high, 4oz.
£880–1,000
$1,300–1,500 🔨 P

**A Channel Islands silver two-
handled cup,** by Pierre Maingy,
Guernsey, engraved on one side with
initials 'SRB' and on the other with
slightly later monogram 'EMR', maker's
mark, c1770, 2½in (6.5cm) high, 3oz.
£1,000–1,200
$1,500–1,800 🔨 S(NY)

A Queen Anne-style silver porringer,
with repoussé cable and scale pattern
and vacant cartouche, Sheffield 1891,
9½in (24cm) wide, 20oz.
£400–500
$600–750 🔨 L

Punchbowls

A George III silver punchbowl, by Charles Price, with an elaborate coat-of-arms and the motto 'Aquila Non Capit Muscas', the foot with similar gadrooning, the interior gilded, London 1813, 12in (30.5cm) diam, 63.25oz.
£7,000–7,500
$10,200–10,900 ⚶ HSS

A Victorian silver monteith-style punchbowl, by Robert Garrard, with notched rim and scroll edging with masks above reeded girdle, lion mask drop ring handles, London 1881, 12½in (32cm) diam, 66oz.
£2,400–2,600
$3,500–3,800 ⚶ Bea

A late Victorian silver punchbowl, by Walker and Hall, the border embossed with a frieze of chrysanthemums and leaves, Sheffield 1898, 9in (22.5cm) diam, 33oz.
£600–700
$870–1,000 ⚶ DN

A Victorian silver punchbowl, by Charles Stuart Harris, in the style of a late 17thC monteith, with ornate cartouche and cherubs' heads to the shaped rim, gilt lined, London 1881, 8½in (21.5cm) diam, 29oz.
£1,200–1,400
$1,700–2,000 ⚶ L

A Victorian silver monteith-style punchbowl, by Martin Hall & Co, with lobing to the lower body, the shaped scroll rim inscribed 'Won by Robert Usher's "Reiver" by Rostrevor', retailed by Brook & Son of Edinburgh, 1883, 12¾in (32.5cm) diam, 64oz.
£1,600–1,800
$2,300–2,600 ⚶ C(S)

A late Victorian silver punchbowl, with embossed gadrooned bead, scroll and floral decoration, by W. G., J. L., retailed by The Goldsmiths & Silversmiths Co, 9¾in (25cm) diam, 25oz.
£700–900
$1,000–1,300 ⚶ Gam

◄ **An Edwardian silver punchbowl,** with shaped mask, scroll and bead-decorated rim, the fluted body with embossed blind cartouche and scrolling foliate banding, on moulded circular foot, London 1902, 12¼in (32cm) wide, 44.5oz.
£1,600–1,800
$2,300–2,600 ⚶ AH

A Chinese silver punchbowl, the filigree sides decorated with entwined snakes, c1880, 15½in (39.5cm) diam.
£5,500–6,500
$8,000–9,500 ⊞ SFL

A Victorian Britannia standard silver-gilt punch bowl, by George Lambert, with nulled border, on a fluted foot, London 1882, 12½in (32cm) diam, 66oz.
£2,000–2,300
$2,900–3,350 ⚶ DN

A Victorian silver punchbowl, with moulded wave border, embossed flowers, foliate scrolls and leaf band, on a stem foot, London mark for 1889, 10½in (26.5cm) diam, 35oz.
£1,400–1,600
$2,000–2,300 ⚶ AG

A Victorian silver punchbowl, by C. S. Harris, with presentation inscription and armorials among a profusion of scrolls, flowers and foliage, on spreading base, London 1899, 11½in (29.5cm) wide, 39oz.
£1,000–1,200
$1,500–1,800 ⚶ Bea

Quaichs

A silver quaich, Sheffield 1928, 4in (10cm) diam.
£130–150
$190–220 ⊞ JAS

A silver quaich, c1900, 3½in (9cm) diam.
£150–200
$220–290 ⊞ BWA

Facts in brief

The quaich (or quaigh) is a drinking vessel resembling a shallow porringer with two (and occasionally three) flat handles. It originated in Scotland where it is still a popular Christening gift. The earliest examples were made of wood and featured vertical staves, silver rims and silver-mounted handles. The smaller quaichs were for individual use, the larger ones were passed around at ceremonial occasions. Examples made in the late 17th/early 18th century are keenly sought by collectors and command high prices.

A 16thC-style silver quaich, by J. Parkes & Co, the lobed bowl with a central rose head boss and flat scroll pierced handles, inscribed 'IF', London 1933, 7½in (19cm) wide.
£200–250
$290–360 ↗ DN

Rose Bowls

◀ **A silver rose bowl,** by Edward Hutton, with a reeded band and lion mask drop ring handles, vacant panels, reeded edging on spreading base, London 1887, 10¼in (26cm) diam, 36.25oz.
£700–850
$1,000–1,300 ↗ Bea(E)

A Victorian silver rose bowl, with gadrooned and shell rim, lion mask drop ring handles, leaf embossed body on flared base, with pierced and scrolled bracket feet, London 1890, 15in (38cm) wide, 53oz.
£2,000–2,250
$2,900–3,300 ↗ AH

◀ **An Edwardian silver rose bowl,** by The Goldsmiths & Silversmiths Co, chased and embossed with floral and foliate designs, with vacant cartouche, London 1901, 8in (20.5cm) diam, 32oz.
£550–650
$800–950 ↗ GAK

A half-fluted silver rose bowl, with a moulded rim over a band of embossed ribbon festoons, on black plinth with presentation plaque, London 1897, 9in (23cm) diam.
£350–400
$500–600 ↗ AH

▶ **A set of three silver rose bowls,** by Wakely and Wheeler, each with embossed bead and reeded borders, London, 1905 and 1907, largest 10½in (26.5cm) diam, 72oz gross.
£1,000–1,200
$1,500–1,800 ↗ P(Ed)

An Edwardian silver rose bowl, by Martin Hall & Co, part panelled, with a moulded rim, on a rising foot, Sheffield 1907, 8in (20.5cm) diam, 19.75oz.
£500–600
$700–870 ⚒ CSK

A silver rose bowl, by Charles Stuart Harris, with embossed husks, swags and ribbons, the base and foot with fluted decoration, 1907, 8in (20.5cm) diam, 12oz.
£250–300
$350–450 ⚒ P(EA)

A silver rose bowl, with wrythen and embossed decoration, on pedestal base, 10in (25.5cm) diam, 18.5oz.
£600–700
$870–1,000 ⚒ LF

Sugar Bowls

A George II silver sugar bowl, by John Gammon, with slightly domed cover and spreading foot, London 1735, 3½in (9cm) high, 7oz.
£2,600–2,800
$3,800–4,000 ⚒ C

A George IV silver lobed sugar bowl, with gadrooned border, acanthus and reeded handles, on four acanthus and shell cast paw feet, 1824, 4¼in (11cm) wide, 11oz.
£175–200
$255–290 ⚒ P(WM)

A William IV silver-gilt sugar bowl, by Charles Fox II, decorated with trailing roses, with acanthus leaf handles and shell foot, 1833, 5in (12.5cm) diam, 14oz.
£600–700
$870–1,000 ⚒ P

A George III silver two-handled sucrier, by Robert and Samuel Hennell, with part ribbed decoration, engraved with a crest, the cover with a reeded loop handle, the interior gilded, on a knopped stem and square foot, London 1805, 6½in (16.5cm) wide, 15.5oz.
£900–1,100
$1,300–1,600 ⚒ WW

A Victorian silver sugar bowl, by Robert Harper, with folded borders, repoussé-decorated with a deep band of foliate diaper pattern between beading, on a pedestal foot, 1871, 4¾in (12cm) diam, 6oz.
£140–180
$200–260 ⚒ P(EA)

▶ **A silver sugar basin,** London c1901, 4in (10cm) high.
£135–150
$200–220 ⊞ Rac

A pair of George III beaded sugar bowls, by James Young, on rising circular bases, each applied with two scrolling foliate handles and engraved with an armorial within an oval cartouche surrounded by paterae and bow and foliate swags, the waisted covers engraved with crests and balustroid finials, London 1777, 7in (18cm) high, 23.25oz.
£1,500–1,800
$2,200–2,600 ⚒ CSK

A Victorian silver-gilt quatrefoil sugar bowl, by William Smith, with pierced and cast swing handle and matching sifter spoon, flat chased foliate engraving, the handle chased with rosettes and a leaf, Chester 1876, 6in (15cm) wide, 5.5oz.
£380–420
$570–600 ⚒ DN

Boxes

A George I silver soap box,
on a spreading circular foot, the domed cover engraved with initials 'GW' beneath an earl's coronet, maker's mark of Isaac Liger, London 1717, Britannia standard, 3¾in (9.5cm) high, 11oz.
£15,000–18,000
$21,800–26,000 ⚒ C
The initials are those of George, 2nd Earl of Warrington.

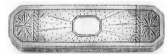

A George III silver toothpick box,
by Samuel Pemberton, engraved with ray decoration on a prick-dot ground, with vacant and foliate-filled cartouches, the red velvet lining and mirror both intact, Birmingham 1809, 3in (7.5cm) wide.
£500–550
$700–800 ⚒ P

A George IV silver-gilt seal box, the lidded box embossed with the Royal coat-of-arms, within a chased oak leaf border, the interior of the lid stamped '8', by John Bridge, London 1825, marks rubbed, 7in (18cm) diam, 17.5oz.
£1,700–2,000
$2,500–2,900 ⚒ L

A George II silver box and cover,
the body and detachable domed cover engraved with a coat-of-arms beneath an earl's coronet, on a moulded rim foot, maker's mark of James Shruder, London 1745, 5in (12.5cm) diam, 20oz.
£17,000–19,000
$24,650–27,500 ⚒ C
James Shruder was an exponent of some of the most individual English rococo designs. Little is known of Shruder's life and work but, because of his surname, he is thought to have been of German origin. He is recorded working in the parish of St Martin-in-the-Fields, London, and was declared bankrupt in 1749.

A miniature silver-mounted heart-shaped box, c1810, 2in (5cm) wide.
£120–150
$180–220 ⊞ MB

A Victorian silver heart-shaped box, with floral repoussé decoration, central medallion of Salisbury Cathedral, Birmingham 1887, 3¼in (8.5cm) high, 3oz.
£340–380
$500–570 ⚒ SLN

◀ **A silver box,** with small drawer, on cabriole legs, 1875, 5½in (14cm) wide.
£320–360
$450–550 ⊞ SSW

A German silver toilet box, the domed hinged cover with a shell and scroll cartouche and a shell thumbpiece, engraved with a coat-of-arms, on an oval lobed foot, with a key, maker's mark of Gottlieb Satzger, Augsburg, 1751–53, 8½in (21.5cm) long, 26oz.
£7,000–8,000
$10,500–11,500 ⚒ Bon

A George III silver and parcel-gilt box and cover, the hinged cover cast with an architectural ruin after Piranesi, initialled 'RB', London 1818, 3¾in (9.5cm) long, 6.25oz.
£750–850
$1,000–1,300 ⚒ EH
Piranesi was a Venetian architect who visited Rome in 1740 and made a large number of etchings of classical antiquities.

A Victorian silver trompe l'oeil box, by John Hunt of Hunt and Roskell, formed as a dinner plate with a folded damask napkin bearing the cypher 'CR VIII', London 1844, 11in (28cm) diam, 59oz.
£5,750–6,500
$8,500–9,500 ⚒ S
The cypher is that of Christian VIII of Denmark. Hunt and Roskell made a number of such boxes for European royal and noble families. This box is traditionally said to have been a gift from Queen Victoria who commissioned Hunt and Roskell to supply many of the gifts sent to European households.

Two silver sovereign cases:
l. Birmingham 1909,
r. W. M. Neale, Chester 1889,
1in (25mm) diam.
£220–260
$320–380 each ⊞ THOM

A silver double stamp box,
Birmingham 1897, 2¼in (5.5cm) wide.
£180–220
$250–320 ⊞ PSA

**A late Victorian silver playing
card box,** the hinged lid inscribed,
maker's mark of William Gibson
and John Langman, London 1899,
3½in (9cm) high.
£220–250
$320–360 ⚒ Bon

A silver box, by Thomas Hayes, the
sides embossed with classical figures,
the tortoiseshell cover inlaid in
Oriental style with finches amid
flowering branches, Birmingham
1899, 4¼in (11cm) wide.
£350–400
$500–580 ⚒ P

A silver box, set with emeralds,
rubies, sapphires and pearls, c1900,
3½in (9cm) wide.
£600–700
$870–1,000 ⊞ CoHA

A Chinese silver box, a presentation
piece for the Mosquito Yacht Club,
c1900, 4¼in (11cm) wide.
£350–400
$500–600 ⊞ ELI

A pierced silver jewellery box,
London 1900, 6in (15cm) wide.
£650–750
$1,000–1,200 ⊞ SHa

A silver sovereign case, with slide
top opening, by Levi and Salaman,
Birmingham 1902, 1in (2.5cm) diam.
£260–300
$380–450 ⊞ THOM

A silver biscuit box, by Roberts and
Belk, decorated with Gothic panels
around the sides, the lid with ring
handle, on three ball feet, Sheffield
1902, 6in (15cm) high.
£600–650
$870–1,000 ⊞ THOM

► **A silver hatpin
box,** Chester 1902,
9in (22.5cm) long.
£325–360
$470–550 ⊞ WN

◄ **A silver pierced box,** early 20thC,
6in (15cm) long.
£320–360
$470–550 ⊞ DaD

A silver box, embossed with
hunting scenes, London 1903,
3¼in (8.5cm) wide.
£1,100–1,250
$1,600–1,800 ⊞ SHa

► **A Continental silver
box,** modelled as a carp
with hinged head and
mouth and articulated
body, imported by
J. G. Piddington, 1904,
5in (12.5cm) long.
£750–900
$1,100–1,300 ⚒ TEN

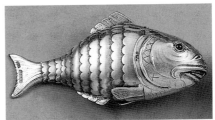

A German silver box, with hinged cover, embossed with a panel depicting a naval engagement with borders of military trophies and cornucopia, the sides with winged putti and birds, imported by Bertold Muller, Chester 1905, 7in (18cm) wide, 35oz.
£1,200–1,400
$1,800–2,000 ↗ DN

An Edwardian mid-18thC-style silver biscuit box, by Thomas Hayes, the sides embossed with flowers, leaves and scrolls around a large cartouche, with a gilt interior, Birmingham 1905, 8¾in (22cm) wide, 21oz.
£500–600
$700–870 ↗ P(S)

▶ **A Continental silver repoussé box,** the front with monogrammed cartouche, the lid with putti and a fairy, 7in (18cm) wide, 13oz.
£375–420
$550–650 ↗ SK

◀ **A silver jewellery casket,** by The Goldsmiths & Silver-smiths Co, with engine-turned decoration and foliate borders, on high scroll supports, London 1919, 5½in (14cm) wide.
£400–450
$580–650 ⊞ HofB

A silver dressing table ring box, by William Comyns, the top with mother-of-pearl, gold and silver-inlaid tortoiseshell panel, London 1907, 3½in (9cm) wide.
£280–320
$400–460 ↗ GAK

Compacts

An Italian engraved silver compact, with romantic scene enamelled on the lid, c1900, 3in (7.5cm) diam.
£180–200
$260–300 PC

A silver compact and perfume bottle on a chain, with heavy repoussé decoration, c1905, 2¼in (5.5cm) wide.
£140–160
$200–230 PC

A sterling silver compact, with enamelled seascape on the lid, and gilded interior, c1927, 2in (5cm) diam.
£90–120
$130–180 PC

▶ **An Asprey's sterling silver compact,** with gold inlay, ruby thumb catch and inner lid, Birmingham 1964, 2¾in (7cm) square.
£85–95
$125–140 PC

A Thai silver compact, with niello figure design on the lid, 1960s, 2in (5cm) diam.
£40–50
$60–75 PC

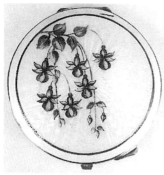

A sterling silver compact, the lid with fuchsias on white guilloché enamel, inner lid with Birmingham hallmark for 1961, 3in (7.5cm) diam.
£130–170
$200–250 PC

Beauty boxes

Modern compacts are the equivalent of the patch boxes used by Georgian women to hold their artificial beauty spots. During the 1920s many compacts sold in Britain were from French cosmetic houses, although English houses soon marketed similar products. Production virtually ceased during WWII but by 1950 makers were competing to satisfy the revived demand for luxury and glamour. Production gradually declined as cosmetics companies began to use plastic packaging and by 1997 the only surviving British manufacturer, Laughton & Sons, was taken over by Cork International.

Snuff Boxes

A silver and mother-of-pearl snuff box, 1680, 3in (7.5cm) diam.
£200–225
$300–325 ⊞ MB

A Continental parcel-gilt silver snuff box and watch, chased with trailing flowers, one side with hinged lid over snuff compartment, the other side with twin covers opening to reveal a verge watch with white enamel dial signed 'Pet Barth', marked on rim with 'H' crowned and a script 'T', possibly Belgian, c1760, 3in (7.5cm) wide.
£1,400–1,600
$2,000–2,500 ⚒ S(NY)

A George III silver snuff box, Birmingham 1795, 2½in (6.5cm) long.
£300–350
$440–500 ⊞ TGa

A George III silver snuff box, by John Death, the cover engraved with a hunting scene, London 1806, 3in (7cm) long, 2oz.
£400–500
$580–720 ⚒ DN

A Charles II silver and piqué snuff box, unmarked, c1680, 3½in (9cm) diam.
£1,800–2,000
$2,600–2,900 ⊞ BEX
Piqué is inlaid decoration of gold or silver, used on small objects such as boxes and fans.

A silver snuff box, engraved with floral sprays between arched borders, probably German, maker's mark 'DF', c1765, 3½in (9cm) wide, 3.75oz.
£575–625
$850–900 ⚒ S(S)

A George III silver and cowrie shell box, by James Kennedy, Dublin 1785, 3½in (9cm) long.
£700–800
$1,000–1,200 ⊞ WELD

A George III silver snuff box, by Thomas Phipps and Edward Robinson, with trellis and diaper engraving, London 1801, 3in (7.5cm) long.
£500–550
$700–800 ⚒ CGC

A Queen Anne silver tobacco box and cover, with rope-twist edging, the detachable cover embossed with beaded rope work, maker's mark 'B.E.', probably for Benjamin Bentley, London 1702, 4in (10cm) long, 4oz.
£1,200–1,400
$1,800–2,000 ⚒ Bea

A silver and mother-of-pearl mounted tortoiseshell snuff box, the shell with plain silver and mother-of-pearl hinged cover, c1780, 3in (7.5cm) long.
£450–550
$650–800 ⚒ Bea

A German silver-gilt snuff box, in the manner of Alexander Fromery, with rocaille decoration, inlaid with an enamel cartouche, marked 'AF', Berlin 18thC, 3in (7.5cm) wide.
£1,000–1,200
$1,500–1,800 ⚒ S(Z)

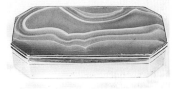

A George IV agate and silver snuff box, by Thomas Meriton, London 1822, 3in (7.5cm) long.
£500–550
$750–800 ⊞ CoHA

◄ **A George IV silver-gilt snuff box,** by Nathaniel Mills, the cover engine-turned within a broad floral and foliate border, Birmingham 1827, 3½in (8.5cm) long, 3.75oz.
£450–500
$650–750 ⚒ CGC

A George IV silver snuff box, by Edward Smith, Birmingham 1827, 3in (7.5cm) long.
£300–350
$450–500 ⊞ CoHA

A silver-gilt snuff box, engine-turned with raised floral borders, reeded sides, maker's mark probably of Ledsam and Vale, Birmingham 1831, 3in (7.5cm) long.
£320–350
$450–500 ⚒ Bon

A William IV silver-gilt snuff box, by Taylor and Perry, the cover with cast and chased hunting scene, Birmingham 1834, 3½in (9cm) wide, 5oz.
£2,300–2,500
$3,300–3,600 ⚒ S

A William IV silver regimental mess table snuff box, by Benjamin Smith, the cover with foliate scroll borders, 6in (15cm) long, 21oz.
£2,500–2,750
$3,600–3,900 ⚒ P

A Victorian silver table snuff box, by W. R. Smily, the cover with a hunting scene in relief, 1844, 3¼in (8.5cm) wide.
£1,000–1,200
$1,500–1,800 ⚒ P

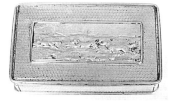

A William IV silver snuff box, by Nathaniel Mills, the cover engine-turned and applied with a scene of chasing hounds, Birmingham 1830, 3¼in (8.5cm) long, 3.25oz.
£240–280
$350–400 ⚒ CGC

A William IV silver snuff box, the cover chased with a hunting scene incorporating a later inset panel of a coach and horses, the gilt interior with inscription, maker's mark I. J., London 1831, 5oz.
£800–1,000
$1,200–1,500 ⚒ Bea(E)

A Victorian silver castle-top snuff box, by Nathaniel Mills, the hinged lid depicting a view of Kenilworth Castle, the sides with engraved chevron decoration, Birmingham 1837, 3½in (9cm) wide.
£1,200–1,400
$1,700–2,000 ⚒ Bon
Castle-top items, such as snuff boxes, card cases and vinaigrettes, have always been popular with collectors. With the advent of the railway during the early years of Queen Victoria's reign, the population became more mobile and people were keen to buy souvenirs of the places they visited. Nathaniel Mills of Birmingham was the first person to recognize the commercial aspect of this interest. His output of small silver objects was prolific, and is enthusiastically collected today.

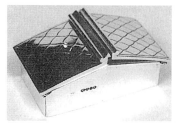

A silver snuff box, by Thomas Shaw, engraved with latticework around a monogrammed cartouche, the base with latticework and foliate scroll borders, Birmingham 1831, 2¼in (5.5cm) long.
£250–275
$360–400 ⚒ P

A George IV silver snuff box, by Charles Rawlings and William Summers, engine-turned, with leaf and flower chased thumbpiece, the cover inscribed 'J.A.' beneath a coronet, London 1833, 3in (7cm) long, 3oz.
£300–350
$440–500 ⚒ DN

Technical facts

Early snuff boxes were generally oval, square or rectangular and made in a range of styles and materials, from wood and horn to silver and enamel. Later ones were usually made of wood, but silver became more available to the mass market with the advent of mechanised techniques for die-stamping and rolling sheet silver. Novelty shapes such as shoes, hats and barrels joined the more traditional rectangle.

A silver snuff box, by Nathaniel Mills, engraved with scrolls, the base with a small scene, Birmingham 1839, 3½in (9cm) long.
£400–450
$580–650 ⊞ TEN

Cross Reference
See Miller's Compares (page 34)

◀ **A silver-gilt snuff box,** by John Keith, London 1852, 1½in (4cm) long.
£475–525
$690–760 ⊞ AMH

A silver snuff box, engraved with scrolls, makers F. H. and F., Birmingham 1857, 4in (10cm) long.
£320–385
$450–550 ↗ TEN

A granite curling trophy snuff mull, the silver cover set with a citrine, c1880, 11in (28cm) diam.
£2,500–3,000
$3,500–4,500 ⊞ BWA

A Victorian silver-mounted ram's horn snuff mull, c1860, 3½in (9cm) long.
£500–550
$700–800 ⊞ SHa

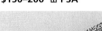

A silver snuff box, Birmingham 1894, 2½in (6.5cm) long.
£130–140
$150–200 ⊞ PSA

A Victorian fox's head silver snuff box, with risqué engraving inside, 3in (7cm) long.
£3,000–3,600
$4,400–5,200 ⊞ CRA

◀ **A silver snuff box,** with inscription, Birmingham 1907, 3in (7.5cm) long.
£120–150
$175–220 ⊞ PSA

A Victorian silver table snuff box, London 1899, 2¾in (7cm) diam.
£90–120
$130–180 ⊞ PSA
As these boxes are airtight they were also used for tobacco.

Vinaigrettes

A silver vinaigrette, Birmingham 1806, 1in (2.5cm) long.
£95–105
$140–150 ⊞ PSA

▶ **A George III silver vinaigrette,** by Samuel Pemberton, the cover engraved with floral basket, Birmingham 1809, 1¼in (3cm) diam.
£220–280
$320–400 ↗ CGC

A George III silver vinaigrette, by Cocks and Bettridge, in the shape of a scent bottle, the hinged cover and base engraved with a lozenge diaper panel border, engraved sides and screw stopper, Birmingham 1801, 2in (5cm) high.
£2,500–3,000
$3,500–4,500 ↗ DN

A silver vinaigrette, with embossed foliate decoration, the base with engine-turned decoration, the interior with a pierced silver-gilt foliate grille, maker's mark of John Shaw, Birmingham 1818, 2in (5cm) long.
£350–400
$500–600 ↗ Bon

A George III silver vinaigrette, by William Eley I, engraved with stylized branded and prick dot decoration, the interior fitted with a pierced grille with ferns and foliate decoration, London 1811, 1½in (4cm) long.
£280–320
$400–460 ↗ Bon

A William IV silver-gilt vinaigrette, the hinged lid, base and sides with raised stylized floral decoration, within foliate borders, maker's mark of Nathaniel Mills, Birmingham 1830, 1¾in (4.5cm) diam, 1.25oz.
£450–550
$650–800 ↗ Bon

Miller's is a price GUIDE not a price LIST

A George IV silver castle-top vinaigrette, by Nathaniel Mills, Birmingham 1827, 1¾in (4.5cm) wide.
£850–950
$1,300–1,400 ♦ CGC

A William IV silver vinaigrette, engine-turned, with pierced grille, maker's mark indistinct, possibly E. J, Birmingham 1834, 1½in (4cm) long.
£160–200
$230–290 ♦ P(Ed)

A silver-gilt vinaigrette, by George Tye, with embossed top, the grille pierced with musical instruments, Birmingham 1834, 2in (5cm) wide.
£400–450
$580–650 ⊞ DIC

Miller's Compares

I. A William IV silver vinaigrette, by Nathaniel Mills, depicting Abbotsford House, the grille with the remnants of a sterling lion punch, mostly lost in the piercing, Birmingham 1836, 1¾in (4.5cm) long.
£975–1,100
$1,400–1,600 ♦ P

II. A William IV silver vinaigrette, by Francis Clark, depicting Abbotsford House, the grille decorated with a basket of flowers and struck with a sterling lion only, Birmingham 1836, 1¾in (4.5cm) long.
£575–650
$850–950 ♦ P

These two vinaigrettes were made in the same year and depicted the same building, but the price realized for Item I was almost double that of Item II. This is mainly because Item I is more sharply executed, with a fuller, more attractive design that includes trees and a bridge. Item II is rather sparse in comparison. Furthermore, Item I is by the famous specialist maker of silver boxes, Nathaniel Mills, whose work is keenly collected, see page 32.

A Victorian silver castle-top vinaigrette, by Nathaniel Mills, the hinged cover with a view of Abbotsford House, foliate scroll borders, reeded sides, with a dependent loop, the interior fitted with a pierced foliate scroll grille, Birmingham 1839, 1½in (4cm) long.
£550–600
$800–870 ♦ Bon

A silver vinaigrette, by Edward Smith, the cover chased in low relief depicting Abbotsford House, the engine-turned base with vacant cartouches, Birmingham 1840, 2in (5cm) long.
£1,100–1,200
$1,600–1,750 ♦ P

A Victorian silver vinaigrette, by Nathaniel Mills, depicting York Minster, 1841, 1¾in (4.5cm) long.
£1,100–1,300
$1,600–1,900 ♦ G(L)

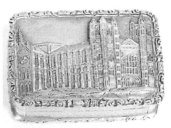

A Victorian silver castle-top vinaigrette, by Joseph Willmore, the cover depicting Beverley Minster, Birmingham 1843, 1¾in (4.5cm) long.
£1,000–1,200
$1,500–1,800 ♦ CGC

A silver vinaigrette, by E. H. Stockwell, modelled as a rose bud with petal hinged for access, 1881, 4½in (11.5cm) long, 3oz.
£1,200–1,400
$1,750–2,000 ♦ TEN

A Victorian silver vinaigrette, by Nathaniel Mills, engraved with scrolling foliage, the grille pierced with flowering foliage, Birmingham 1845, 1¾in (4.5cm) long.
£280–320
$400–460 ♦ P(Ed)

◄ **A silver vinaigrette,** engraved with Osborne House, with pierced scrolling foliate grille, maker's mark D. P., Birmingham 1853, 1¾in (4.5cm) wide.
£900–1,100
$1,300–1,600 ♦ P(Ed)

Buckles & Buttons

A triangular silver dress fastener, with linear decorated border, c9thC, 1¼in (3.8cm) long.
£30–35
$45–50 ⊞ ANG

◄ **A pair of George III silver and paste shoe buckles,** with facet-cut gold borders and steel prongs, c1790, 2¾in (7cm) wide, in original shagreen case.
£230–275
$330–400
⚒ P(EA)

A Victorian heart-shaped sterling silver button, depicting cherubs lighting a fire, c1890, 1½in (4cm) wide.
£40–45
$60–65 ⊞ TB

A Burmese low grade silver three-piece clasp, c1890, 6in (15cm) wide.
£75–85
$100–125 ⊞ JBB

A Dutch silver buckle, from the Province of Zeeland, 19thC, 7in (18cm) wide.
£75–85
$100–125 ⊞ JBB

A silver two-piece clasp, Birmingham 1898, 3½in (9cm) wide.
£120–140
$170–200 ⊞ JBB

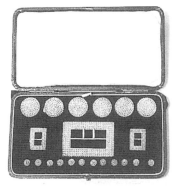

Three silver-handled button hooks, marked Birmingham 1899–1907, longest 4½in (11.5cm).
£30–40
$45–60 each ⚒ GAK
Button hooks were an essential Victorian accessory for doing up the tiny buttons on boots, gloves and tight-fitting clothing.

A set of six silver and paste coat buttons, c1900, 1¼in (3cm) diam.
£80–100
$115–145 ⊞ JBB

► **A set of six silver buttons,** with motif of a lady, Birmingham 1902, 1in (2.5cm) diam, in original box.
£250–270
$360–400 ⊞ AMH

A silver button and buckle set, by Charles Horner, Chester 1900, 9½in (24cm) wide, boxed.
£400–450
$550–650 ⊞ JBB

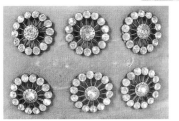

A set of six solid silver and paste buttons, c1900, 1¼in (3cm) diam.
£400–450
$550–650 ⊞ SLL

► **A silver and steel buttonhook,** by Crisford and Norris, depicting Mr Punch, Birmingham 1904, 4in (10cm) long.
£125–155
$180–250 ⊞ BEX

A set of six silver buttons, with motif of a cherub kissing a lady, Birmingham 1905, 1in (2.5cm) diam, in original box.
£250–275
$350–400 ⊞ AMH

Two Navajo stamped silver buttons, one with a scalloped border, the other set with matrix turquoise, c1910–30, largest 1½in (4cm) diam.
£40–45
$60–65 each ⊞ TB

Candle Snuffers & Trays

A George II cast-silver snuffer's stand, of shaped and waisted outline on four cast, husk and scroll feet with a reeded border interspersed by foliate motifs and a flying side handle, vacant oval cartouche, base engraved with motto 'Quod tibi, hoc alteri' and a coat-of-arms, London 1747, 8in (20.5cm) long, 11.5oz.
£900–1,000
$1,300–1,500 ⚒ WW
Coat-of-arms and motto are for Crawford or Hesketh.

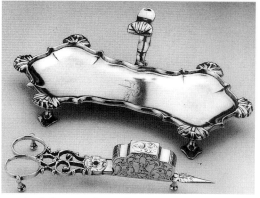

A pair of silver candle snuffers and tray, engraved with contemporary pelican crest, snuffers by John Booth, London 1769, 6½in (16.5cm), long, 3oz, tray by John Hyatt and Charles Semore, London 1760, 8½in (21.5cm) long, 10oz.
£1,800–2,000
$2,600–2,900 ⊞ PAY

A George III silver snuffer's tray, with beaded border, leaf capped beaded scroll handle, on four webbed feet, maker's mark of John Crouch I and Thomas Hannam, London 1773, 8in (20.5cm) long, 6oz.
£450–550
$650–800 ⚒ Bon

A pair of George III silver scissor snuffers, pierced and ring handles, engraved decoration, vacant cartouche, on three bun feet, maker's mark of I. B., London 1785, 6¼in (16cm) long, 2.5oz.
£300–340
$450–500 ⚒ Bon

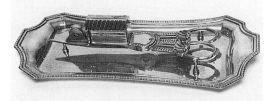

A pair of George III silver candle snuffers, by Joseph Cradock and William. Reid, with steel cutter and box, London and a George III tray by R. Gainsford, Sheffield 1813, tray 9½in (24cm) wide, 5.25oz.
£650–750
$950–1,200 ⚒ DD

A pair of George III silver candle snuffers, with engraved and beaded decoration, probably by John Baker, London 1787, 2.75oz.
£330–400
$480–580 ⚒ P(E)

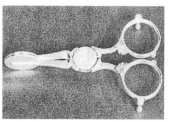

A silver candle snuffer, by Edward Hutton, London 1891, 3½in (9cm) long.
£360–390
$550–600 ⊞ BEX

Prices

The price ranges quoted in this book reflect the average price a purchaser might expect to pay for a similar item. The price will vary according to the condition, rarity, size, popularity, provenance, colour and restoration of the item, and this must be taken into account when assessing values. Don't forget that if you are selling it is quite likely that you will be offered less than the price range.

Two pairs of George IV silver candle snuffers, by Emes and Barnard, with a pair of snuffer trays, by Robert Garrard, 1826, snuffers 9¼in (23.5cm) long.
£2,800–3,200
$4,000–4,700 ⚒ P

Candlesticks & Chambersticks

A Queen Anne silver taperstick, by Thomas Merry I, the faceted baluster stem on moulded square base with canted corners, London 1706, 4½in (11.5cm) high, 4oz.
£2,600–2,800
$3,800–4,000 ⚒ WW

▶ **A pair of George II silver candlesticks,** by James Gould, with shaped circular bases, double knopped stems, detachable sconces with wavy edges, London 1734, 8in (20.5cm) high, 28oz.
£2,400–2,800
$3,500–4,000 ⚒ GAK

A pair of Queen Anne silver candlesticks, by Thomas Merry, with octagonal bases, initialled 'ET', London 1708, 6½in (16.5cm) high, 20.5oz.
£11,500–12,500
$16,700–18,200 ⚒ S

A pair of George II cast-silver table candlesticks, by Bennett Bradshaw and Robert Tyrill, with knopped fluted stems and square-shaped bases, London 1740, 6½in (16.5cm) high, 27.75oz.
£2,800–3,200
$4,000–4,650 ⚒ P(Sc)

Miller's is a price GUIDE not a price LIST

Two Dutch silver candlesticks, with shaped bases, octagonal baluster stems and slightly differing vase-shaped sockets, maker's mark of Hendrick van Beest, Rotterdam 1715 and 1723, 6¾in (17cm) high, 20.5oz.
£4,000–4,500
$5,800–6,500 ⚒ C(G)

▶ **A George II cast-silver taperstick,** by John Cafe, on a shaped square base with knopped stem, London 1743, 4in (10cm) high.
£600–700
$870–1,000 ⚒ GAK

Tapersticks

Tapersticks are small versions of candlesticks and were used primarily on a writing desk for holding a taper used to melt sealing wax. Unlike candlesticks they are usually found as single items.

A set of four George II silver candlesticks, by John Cafe, each with crested and numbered detachable nozzles, engraved with a coat-of-arms to the base, 1748 and 1756, 10in (25.5cm) high, 90oz.
£9,000–10,000
$13,000–14,500 ⚒ L

◀ **A pair of silver candlesticks,** by John Cafe, with loose sconces, knopped columns, saucer-shaped bases with cast shell feet, London 1748, 9in (23cm) high, 43oz.
£2,200–2,500
$3,200–3,600 ⚒ L&E

A pair of George III silver Corinthian column table candlesticks, by John Carter, on square bases chased with rams' masks and pendant husks, with detachable square nozzles, 1733, 13in (33cm) high.
£4,000–4,500
$5,800–6,500 ⚒ C

A George II silver taperstick, by William Cafe, on a shaped square base cast with shells at the angles, knopped baluster stem, detachable nozzle, 1747, 5½in (14cm) high, and matching extinguisher, maker's mark 'TW', 9oz.
£700–800
$1,000–1,200 ⚒ C(S)

▶ **A pair of George II cast-silver tapersticks,** by John Cafe, the baluster stems with fluted shoulders, spool-shaped holders on moulded square bases, London 1749, 4½in (11.5cm) high.
£2,200–2,600
$3,200–3,800 ⚒ WW

A George II silver taperstick, by James Gould, the hexagonal base shell-moulded at the angles, double knopped and faceted stem, spool-shaped sconce, London 1752, 5in (12.5cm) high.
£550–650
$800–1,000 ⚒ S

▶ **A pair of George III silver candlesticks,** by Ebenezer Coker, London 1761, 10½in (26.5cm) high, 48oz.
£3,500–3,800
$5,000–5,500 ⚒ Mit

LOCATE THE SOURCE
The source of each illustration in Miller's can be found by checking the code letters below each caption with the Key to Illustrations, pages 311–314.

A pair of silver candlesticks, by Ebenezer Coker, the knopped stems with cotton reel nozzles and spiral fluted drip pans, London 1762, 10¼in (26cm) high, 47oz.
£2,600–3,000
$3,800–4,500 ⚒ HAM

A George II silver chamberstick, by John Priest, engraved with a coat-of-arms, with detachable nozzle, London 1752, 6¼in (16cm) diam, 14oz.
£700–800
$1,000–1,200 ⚒ Bea(E)

A set of six Italian silver candlesticks, each on a circular base with moulded border, baluster stem, spool-shaped socket and circular drip pan, engraved with initial 'F' with crown above, maker's mark probably of Contardo Buccellatti, c1765, 5in (12.5cm) high, 42oz.
£20,000–23,000
$29,000–33,000 ⚒ C
The initial on these candlesticks is that of Franz I of Austria (1745–65).

A set of four George II cast-silver table candlesticks, by John Priest, the shaped square bases, knopped stems and detachable nozzles with shell corners, nozzles and bases numbered '1' to '4', London 1755, 9in (23cm) high, 74.5oz.
£7,000–8,000
$10,200–11,600 ⚒ Bea

A set of four German silver table candlesticks, two by Emanuel Abraham Drentwett, one by Caspar Kornmann, one by Johann Phillip Heckenauer, the shaped domed bases richly chased with rococo decoration, the twisted baluster stems cast to match, engraved with the cypher 'CG' on drapery mantle below a crown, the base rims engraved 'HF' and dated '1759', Augsburg c1758, 8in (20.5cm) high, 60.5oz.
£37,000–40,000
$54,000–58,000 ⚒ S(NY)
The cypher is that of Carl Georg, Duke of Anhalt-Köthen, 1730–89, who married, in 1763, Princess Louise of Schleswig-Holstein-Sonderburg (1749–1812).

Four Georgian silver Corinthian column table candlesticks, each with a papyrus sconce, fluted column and bead edging, on a stepped spreading square base, maker's mark 'IC' possibly for J. Collins, London 1759 and 1767, 13in (33cm) high.
£4,000–4,500
$5,800–6,500 ⚒ Bea

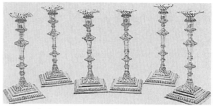

A set of six George III table candlesticks, by William Cafe, with detachable nozzles, two engraved with the crest of a falcon, four with a leopard holding a branch, London 1764, 10½in (27cm) high, 82oz.
£11,000–12,000
$16,000–17,500 ⚒ L

A set of four early George III-style candlesticks, by Ebenezer Coker, the acanthus leaf decorated candleholders with gadroon edge detachable nozzles, London 1766–67, 11½in (29cm) high.
£3,500–4,000
$5,000–5,800 ⚒ **WW**

A pair of early George III silver rococo candlesticks, with semi-fluted baluster sockets on waisted knopped stems and wrythen-fluted swept circular bases, cast with scrolls and acanthus leaves, repaired, maker's mark 'TE', London 1767, 11½in (29cm) high, 43oz, together with a pair of plated on copper detachable sconces.
£2,000–2,200
$2,900–3,200 ⚒ **HSS**

A pair of George III silver candlesticks, by Ebenezer Coker, London 1768, 10in (25.5cm) high.
£3,200–3,700
$4,700–5,000 ⊞ **TGa**

◄ **A set of four George III silver candlesticks,** by Ebenezer Coker, London 1770, 10in (25cm) high, 20oz each.
£8,000–9,000
$11,500–13,000 ⚒ **AAV**

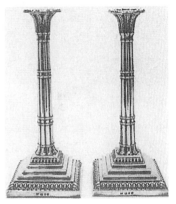

A pair of George III silver column candlesticks, by William Turton, with upper and lower beaded borders to the stepped square foot, classical column stems with palm capitals, London 1771, later removable sconces by Pairpoint, London 1925, 12½in (32cm) high, loaded, scratch weight for 24.5oz.
£1,800–2,000
$2,500–3,000 ⚒ **L**

Loaded candlesticks

The development of mechanization during the Industrial Revolution resulted in a proliferation of machine-made loaded candlesticks produced to meet the growing demands of the newly affluent merchant classes. Less metal was used to make a loaded candlestick than a cast one, as the stem was hollow and filled with pitch or sand for weight and stability, and therefore loaded candlesticks could be sold for a significantly lower price. Collectors should be careful when buying filled candlesticks as they often have holes worn through on edges and corners, due to the thinness of the silver.

A pair of loaded silver candlesticks, London 1771, 9in (23cm) high.
£1,800–2,000
$2,600–2,900 ⊞ **DIC**

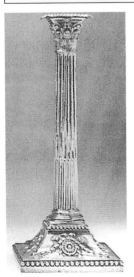

◄ **A pair of George III silver pillar candlesticks,** by John Carter, with fluted columns, Corinthian capitals and acanthus leaf designs, on square bases, London 1773, 12½in (32cm) high
£2,000–2,200
$2,900–3,200 ⚒ **RBB**

A George III silver chamberstick, by Robert Makepeace and Richard Carter, with gadrooned and harebell motif, London 1777, 4in (10cm) diam, 8oz, the snuffer also marked.
£620–680
$900-1,000 ⚒ **P(Ed)**

◄ **Four George III silver table candlesticks,** by Peter Desvignes, the bases cast and chased with flutes and paterae and engraved with armorials, detachable nozzles, engraved with a crest and the same armorials, London 1775, 11in (28cm) high, 90oz.
£14,000–16,000
$20,500–23,500 ⚒ **S**

A pair of George III silver candlesticks, by Robert Makepeace and Richard Carter, base monogrammed, London 1777, 9½in (24cm) high, 46oz.
£3,000–3,500
$4,500–5,000 ⚖ SK

A pair of George III silver fluted baluster candlesticks, by William Abdy, with roundel and reeded borders, on fluted bases, London 1785, 11½in (29cm) high.
£1,100–1,300
$1,600–1,900 ⚖ AG

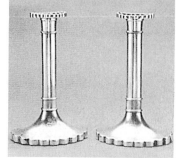

A pair of George III silver table candlesticks, engraved with a coat-of-arms, the plain oval bases and detachable nozzles with scalloped edges, maker's mark indistinct, London 1795, 9in (23cm) high.
£2,200–2,500
$3,200–3,600 ⚖ Bea

A set of four George III silver candlesticks, by John Green & Co, with plain columns, circular bases and detachable nozzles, Sheffield 1796, 6¼in (16cm) high.
£1,500–1,750
$2,200–2,500 ⚖ PFK

A George III silver chamberstick, by John Crouch I and Thomas Hannam, with reeded borders engraved with crests, with extinguisher and nozzle, London 1796, 5¾in (14.5cm) diam.
£700–800
$1,000–1,200 ⚖ DN

A pair of George III silver chambersticks, by John Edwards III, the circular pan with gadrooned border, snuffers and nozzles lacking, London 1800, 3¼in (8.5cm) high.
£650–700
$950–1,000 ⚖ RTo

A George III small silver chamberstick, by John Emes, with thread edging, initialled with detachable nozzle and extinguisher on chain, London 1807, 4in (10cm) diam, 3.5oz.
£720–800
$1,000–1,200 ⚖ Bea

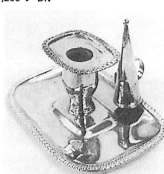

A George III silver chamberstick and snuffer, by T. Jones, with gadrooned edges and loop handle, London 1808, 4½in (11.5cm) wide.
£400–480
$580–700 ⚖ GAK

A George III silver chamberstick, by William Bateman, with gadrooned rim and detachable sconce, complete with snuffer, marked for London 1808, 5in (12.5cm) diam.
£700–800
$1,000–1,200 ⚖ GAK

▶ **A pair of Regency silver candlesticks,** with detachable sconces, the stems cast with shells, floral festoons, stiff acanthus and reeding, on hexagonal bases, the bases weighted with wood, Sheffield marks for John Roberts & Co, old repair to one stem, 1813, 10½in (26.5cm) high.
£1,000–1,500
$1,500–2,200 ⚖ MJB

A pair of rococo silver candlesticks, by Kirkby Waterhouse & Co, Sheffield 1816, 8in (20.5cm) high.
£1,800–2,000
$2,600–2,900 ⊞ DIC

A pair of George III silver chambersticks, by John and Thomas Settle, the detachable nozzles and bases with gadrooned edging and plain conical extinguishers, Sheffield 1818, 5½in (14cm) diam, 18.5oz.
£1,200–1,400
$1,800–2,000 ↗ Bea

A William IV silver chamberstick, 6in (15cm) diam, 3.25oz.
£380–450
$570–650 ⊞ DaD

A silver harlequin taper-stick, by Joseph Willmore, with a foliate chased base, Birmingham 1837, 5½in (14cm) high, 5oz.
£400–500
$580–720 ↗ DN

A pair of William IV silver candle-sticks, by Waterhouse, Hatfield & Co, each with leaf decoration, the bases with alternating C-scroll moulded decoration, Sheffield 1836, 11in (28cm) high.
£750–850
$1,100–1,300 ↗ TRM

A set of four Victorian silver table candlesticks, by William Smiley, the stems entwined with a serpent with gem set eyes, leaf-decorated sconces with plain detachable nozzles, each on three lion's leg supports conjoined by classical foliage and cartouches, engraved with crest, initials 'RJM' and inscription, London 1842, 11½in (29cm) high, 86oz.
£8,000–10,000
$11,500–14,500 ↗ S(NY)
Josiah Wedgwood II gave these candlesticks in the year of his death to his daughter-in-law's brother, Robert J. Mackintosh.

A pair of Victorian silver gilt four-light candelabra, by R. and S. Garrard & Co, in the manner of Paul de Lamerie, the central urn finials topped by a bud, guilloche borders, detachable nozzles, fully marked except one nozzle, London c1847, 27in (68.5cm) high, 417.5oz.
£35,000–38,000
$50,000–55,000 ↗ S(NY)

▶ **A Victorian silver chamberstick,** by William Comyns, on a heart-shaped tortoiseshell base, London 1890, 3½in (9cm) wide.
£400–450
$580–650 ↗ GTH

A pair of silver candle-sticks, the columns decorated with scrolls and simulated scales, the knops with leaf and scroll motifs, the base with shell, scroll and floral embossed bracket feet, Turkey 1876–1909, 12½in (32cm) high.
£2,200–2,500
$3,200–3,600 ↗ P

A Victorian silver taperstick, by Charles Stuart Harris, modelled as a drum, London 1887–88, 4in (10cm) high.
£1,500–1,650
$2,200–2,400 ⊞ BEX

A pair of late Victorian silver three-light candelabra, by Charles Boyton, the fluted stems decorated with creeping ivy motifs, the detachable nozzles and borders with beaded decoration, 1892, 20in (51cm) high.
£2,500–3,000
$3,600–4,000 ↗ P(B)

A pair of Victorian silver candlesticks, by John Dickson & Son, with Corinthian columns, Sheffield 1895, 8¾in (22cm) high.
£600–700
$870–1,000 ↗ TRM

A pair of late Victorian silver candlesticks, by J. N. Mappin, with Ionic capitals, spiral-fluted columns engraved with flowers, the bases embossed with swags of flowers, shell and leaf scroll corners, gadrooned borders, maker's marks for London 1896, 14½in (37cm) high.
£2,000–2,200
$2,900–3,200 ⚷ DN

A pair of silver candlesicks, by Hawkesworth and Eyre, Sheffield 1896, 9in (23cm) high.
£1,200–1,400
$1,750–2,000 ⊞ THOM

A pair of Victorian silver candlesticks, by Hawksworth, Eyre & Co, with octagonal bases, knopped baluster stems and detachable nozzles, Sheffield 1900, 6¾in (17cm) high.
£350–400
$500–580 ⚷ Bea(E)

Sets/pairs

Unless otherwise stated, any description which refers to 'a set' or 'a pair' includes a guide price for the entire set or the pair, even though the illustration may show only a single item.

A pair of silver candlesticks, London 1896, 4in (10cm) wide.
£750–850
$1,100–1,300 ⊞ PSA

A pair of Edwardian silver candlesticks, embossed with Adam-style urns, damaged, Sheffield 1898, 6½in (16.5cm) high.
£380–450
$570–650 ⚷ GAK

A pair of silver bedroom candlesticks, on shaped square bases, embossed with anthemions and fluted designs, with reeded columns and detachable sconces, Birmingham 1901, 5in (12.5cm) high.
£550–650
$800–950 ⚷ GAK

A pair of late Victorian silver candlesticks, by Hawksworth, Eyre & Co, with shell decoration, on stepped square, scroll bases, 11in (28cm) high.
£650–750
$900–1,100 ⚷ P(EA)

A pair of Adam-style silver candlesticks, Sheffield 1899, 10in (25.5cm) high.
£750–850
$1,100–1,300 ⚷ TMA

A pair of silver candlesticks, by The Goldsmiths & Silversmiths Co, the tapering Corinthian columns bound with spiral swags of acorns, on square spreading bases with urns, leaf scroll corners, gadrooned borders, London 1903, 10in (25.5cm) high.
£1,400–1,600
$2,000–2,300 ⚷ DN

◄ **A pair of Edwardian loaded silver three-light candelabra,** by William Hutton & Sons Ltd, the circular drip-pans and nozzles with gadrooned edging, with reeded scrolling branches and detachable flame finials, Sheffield 1903, 20½in (52cm) high.
£2,500–3,000
$3,500–4,500 ⚷ Bea(E)

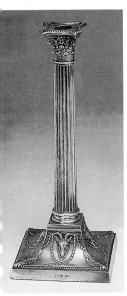

A pair of Edwardian silver loaded candlesticks, by Walker and Hall, with Corinthian columns, the bases embossed with wheat husk garlands draped with rams' heads, Sheffield 1903, 13½in (34.5cm) high.
£1,300–1,500
$1,900–2,200 ⚱ P(L)

A pair of Edwardian silver candlesticks, by Harrison Bros and Howson, with Corinthian columns, decorated with swags and beaded edging, Sheffield 1905, 8½in (21.5cm) high.
£700–800
$1,000–1,200 ⚱ MAT

A pair of 18thC-style silver candelabra, maker's mark, 'RC', London 1936, 13in (33cm) high, 27oz.
£1,150–1,300
$1,700–1,900 ⚱ S(S)

A pair of George II-style silver table candlesticks, with detachable nozzles, spool-shaped sconces, knopped baluster stems and shell-capped square bases, Sheffield 1904, 10in (25.5cm) high.
£750–850
$1,100–1,250 ⚱ N

An Edwardian silver chamberstick, by Thomas Bradbury & Sons, with detachable nozzle and oblong handle, all with gadrooned borders, 1904, 5in (12.5cm) wide, 10.5oz.
£450–550
$650–800 ⚱ C(S)

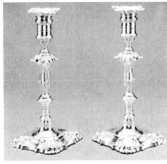

A pair of George V silver table candlesticks, by Hawksworth, Eyre & Co, the square bases, knopped stems and detachable nozzles with anthemion shell corners, Sheffield 1911, 9¾in (25cm) high.
£750–850
$1,100–1,300 ⚱ Bea

A pair of Edwardian silver chambersticks, by Charles Henry Townley and John William Thomas, the base with conical snuffer rest and gadrooned borders, engraved with crests, London 1904, 4in (10cm) high, 28oz.
£1,300–1,500
$1,900–2,200 ⚱ P(NE)

A pair of George V silver three-light candelabra, by Martin, Hall & Co, the fluted oval bases, tapering stems, drip pans and detachable nozzles with reeded edging, Sheffield 1913, 16¼in (41.5cm) high.
£1,800–2,000
$2,600–2,900 ⚱ Bea(E)

A set of four Edwardian Adam-style silver candlesticks, by Fordham and Faulkner, the faceted stems with urn-shaped candleholders and detachable nozzles, on loaded bases, Sheffield c1908, 12in (30.5cm) high.
£2,000–2,500
$2,900–3,600 ⚱ WW

A pair of silver candlesticks, by Leslie G. Durbin, stamped marks for 1966, 8¼in (21cm) high.
£1,700–2,000
$2,500–3,000 ⚱ P(Ba)
Durbin created the centrepiece for the 1951 Festival of Britain exhibition in London, and is considered to be one of the greatest silversmiths of the post-WWII era.

◀ **A silver chamberstick,** Sheffield 1923, 4in (10cm) wide.
£350–400
$500–580 ⊞ TGa

Canteens & Cutlery

A late 17thC silver trefid spoon, with plain rat-tail, the reverse of the handle prick dot initialled, 'E.y 168', the top side later monogrammed, date letter worn, maker's mark indistinct W., London c1680, 8in (20.5cm) long, 2oz.
£200–300
$300–450 ↗ Bon

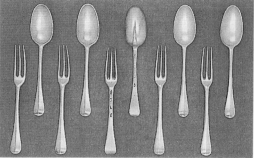

A set of 18 George I silver-gilt Hanoverian pattern dessert spoons and forks, the spoons with rat-tail bowls, the forks three-pronged, maker's mark of Philip Robinson, London 1714, some marks indistinct, spoons 6½in (16.5cm) long, 48oz.
£30,000–35,000
$43,500–50,500 ↗ C

◀ **A Georgian silver child's knife and fork,**
3½in (8.5cm) long.
£120–150
$180–220 ⊞ CRA

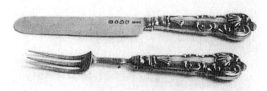

A set of 12 George I silver Hanoverian pattern table forks,
10 engraved with contemporary arms, by Lambe, 1723, two engraved with later crests and coronets, one engraved 'Nursery', by different makers, London 1719 and 1723, 26oz.
£2,200–2,500
$3,000–3,500 ↗ S(NY)

Two pairs of steel knives and forks, with stained ivory and silver collars, mark of the London Cutlery Co, c1730, largest 7in (18cm) long.
£120–150
$180–220 ⊞ ET

A canteen of George III and later silver cutlery, for 12 persons, Hanoverian and Old English patterns, engraved with initial 'M', London.
£1,200–1,700
$1,800–2,500 ↗ RBB

> **Cross Reference**
> See Colour Review (page 79)

◀ **A silver Fiddle and Thread pattern part-canteen of cutlery,** by Eley, Fearn and Chawner, comprising 103 pieces, 1809, including a pair of basting spoons and a soup ladle by Thomas Northcote, 1790, 107oz.
£1,400–1,700
$2,000–2,500 ↗ P(B)

▶ **A Georgian silver Old English and Hanoverian pattern table service,** comprising 12 place settings, later engraved 'C', various dates and makers, 1783–1832, 78oz.
£800–900
$1,200–1,500
↗ P(EA)

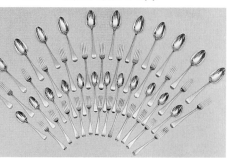

A George III Old English pattern silver-gilt dessert service, by George Smith and William Fearn, comprising 73 pieces, the terminals armorial engraved, the knife blades Edward Hunt II of London, c1790, the grape scissors Eley and Fearn, London 1814, 58oz, in contemporary brass-bound leather case.
£9,000–10,000
$13,000–14,500 ↗ S

A George III Old English pattern silver part table service, by Richard Crossley, for 12 place settings, comprising tablespoons, dessert spoons, table forks, dessert forks, engraved with griffin head crest, London 1793, 94.5oz.
£4,800–5,300
$7,000–7,800 ⚒ Bea(E)

A George III silver campaign set, comprising a beaker engraved with crest and monogram by Timothy Renou, a combined nutmeg grater and corkscrew, knife, fork and spoon, a marrow scoop, a pair of mounted glass condiments and a glass smelling bottle, c1800.
£7,500–8,250
$11,000–12,000 ⚒ P

A George III silver Old English pattern silver table service, by Eley, Fearn and Chawner, comprising 60 pieces, c1807, 73oz.
£3,500–4,000
$5,000–5,800 ⚒ C(S)

◀ **A set of 12 silver-gilt fish knives and forks,** with agate pistol grips and engraved crests, maker 'M.B.', knives London 1813, forks Sheffield 1907, in a mahogany case.
£1,400–1,800
$2,000–2,600 ⚒ RBB

▶ **A set of 12 George III silver Hour-Glass pattern teaspoons,** by Thomas Wallis and Jonathan Hayne, initialled 'R', London 1817, 12.5oz.
£160–190
$250–300 ⚒ Bea(E)

▶ **An oak canteen of matched silver Fiddle pattern cutlery and flatware,** London 1836–74, knives Sheffield 1966.
£1,400–1,600
$2,000–2,300 ⚒ WL

A George IV King's pattern silver table service, by John and Henry Lias, each piece additionally cast with foliage and a crest, comprising 282 spoons, 204 forks, 195 knives, two soup ladles, two pairs of asparagus tongs, four marrow scoops, four fish slices, two mustard spoons, four ice shovels, one pair of salad servers, six meat skewers and eight sauce ladles, all contained in three fitted wood boxes, 1821, 1406oz.
£45,000–55,000
$65,000–80,000 ⚒ C
The service was commissioned for the wedding in 1821 of William John Legh Esq, (d.1834) of Brymbo Hall, Co Denbigh and of Hordle, Co Hants and Mary Ann, (d.1838) eldest daughter and heir of John Wilkinson Esq, of Castlehead. Each piece is either cast or engraved with the crest-of-arms of Newton. Their fourth and eldest surviving son William John Legh (1828–98) succeeded to his father's estates in 1834 and to those of his uncle in 1857. He was later created 1st Baron Newton of Newton-in-Makerfield in 1892.

A George IV silver Fiddle pattern table service, engraved with monograms, various makers, c1820, 194.5oz.
£2,400–2,800
$3,500–4,000 ⚒ P(EA)

◀ **A Victorian silver canteen of 12 pairs of dessert cutlery,** Sheffield 1839, case 14in (35.5cm) wide.
£1,600–1,800
$2,300–2,600 ⊞ CoHA

An early Victorian silver canteen for 18, comprising 30 table forks, 30 table knives, 18 dessert forks, 12 dessert knives, 18 table spoons, 18 dessert spoons, six teaspoons, four sauce ladles, a soup ladle, a pair of basting spoons, a pair of graduated meat skewers, a marrow scoop, a condiment spoon, in a three drawer fitted wooden case, plus ten various items, maker's mark Mary Chawner, the knives by Thomas Chawner, London 1840, 265oz.
£6,500–7,500
$9,500–11,000 ⚲ **Bon**

A silver canteen of cutlery, by Chawner & Co, comprising 125 pieces, decorated with stylized scroll pattern, London 1850s, 202oz, in oak presentation case.
£4,500–5,000
$6,500–7,300 ⚲ **DD**

A Victorian silver christening set, by George Unite, Birmingham c1857, cutlery 6½in (16.5cm) long.
£120–150
$175–220 ⊞ **TVA**

A Victorian silver Fiddle, Thread, and Shell pattern table service, comprising 48 pieces, by George W. Adams, London c1842, 97oz.
£1,200–1,800
$1,800–2,600 ⚲ **HCH**

▶ **A Victorian silver Old English Thread pattern matched part-canteen,** by Mary Chawner, John and Henry Lias and Elizabeth Eaton, comprising 44 pieces, retailed by Carrington & Co, crested, c1850, 107oz, in fitted oak box.
£1,400–1,800
$2,000–2,600 ⚲ **P(B)**

A Victorian King's pattern silver table service for 12, by Henry John Lias & Son, with stag head crests, comprising 12 table forks, 12 table spoons, 12 dessert spoons, 12 dessert forks, 12 teaspoons, a pair of fish servers 1852 and 1860, a serving spoon, a soup ladle, a pair of sauce ladles and a pair of sugar tongs, London 1862, 168oz.
£2,700–3,000
$4,000–4,500 ⚲ **DN**

◀ **A silver Beaded-pattern service,** engraved with a crest, comprising 116 pieces, maker's mark of George Adams, London 1867, 236oz.
£7,000–8,000
$10,000–11,500 ⚲ **Bon**

A Victorian silver Prince's pattern table service, comprising 128 pieces, engraved with monogram, the majority by George Adams, 1849, 296oz.
£4,500–5,500
$6,600–8,000 ⚲ **Gam**

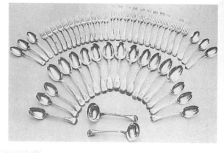

◀ **A Victorian silver Fiddle and Thread pattern part table service,** comprising 54 pieces, London mid-19thC, 112oz.
£1,800–2,000
$2,600–2,900 ⚲ **Bea**

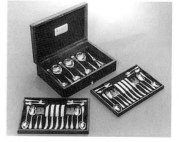

A Victorian silver-gilt Elizabethan pattern dessert service, by George Adams, comprising 39 pieces, London 1858–75, 63oz, in fitted oak box.
£1,000–1,200
$1,500–1,800 ⚲ **WW**

A set of 18 pairs of Victorian silver dessert knives and forks, by Martin Hall & Co, with matching servers, with strapwork engraved blades and tines, acanthus leaf stamped ferrules and leaf-capped carved mother-of-pearl handles, Sheffield 1865, in a walnut case with blue baize fitted interior and two lift-out compartments.
£1,800–2,000
$2,600–2,900 ⚲ **HSS**

A set of seven silver-bladed folding fruit knives, with mother-of-pearl handles, 1870–1900.
£40–70
$60–100 each ⊞ MB

◄ **A Victorian silver Bead edge canteen,** by George Adams, comprising 12 table spoons, 12 dessert spoons, 12 table forks, 12 dessert forks, 12 tea-spoons, London 1874–75, 12 table knives, 12 dessert knives by C. J. Vander Ltd, Sheffield 1985, 125.5oz.
£7,000–8,000
$10,000–11,500 ⊞ NS

Miller's is a price GUIDE not a price LIST

A French silver parcel-gilt Fiddle pattern table service, comprising 126 pieces, the stems chased with vine foliage, pearls and ribbons enclosing a cartouche engraved with armorials, the reverse chased with a hunting trophy, the knives with silver-gilt mounts, mother-of-pearl handles and steel blades, maker's mark 'PQ and Odiot', Paris c1880, 277oz.
£11,000–13,000
$16,000–19,000 ✗ C(G)

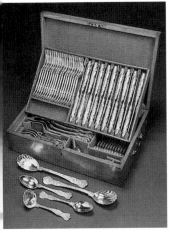

A silver-gilt Stag Hunt pattern dessert service, by George Adams, comprising 54 pieces, London 1874, 191oz, in a fitted oak case.
£8,500–10,000
$12,500–14,500 ✗ TEN

A set of six Victorian silver dessert knives and forks, with mother-of-pearl handles, by George Unite, Birmingham 1873, 12½in (32cm) wide, in carved walnut case.
£450–500
$650–720 ✗ TVA

A French silver dessert/table service, by G. Fouquet-Lapar, engraved with armorials, Paris c1880, 244.25oz, contained in three lined and fitted maroon leather travelling cases.
£6,800–7,500
$10,000–11,000 ✗ P

► **A silver folding blade and combination fruit knife and fork,** with mother-of-pearl handle, c1880, 3in (7.5cm) long.
£90–110
$130–160 ⊞ MB

A silver quill knife, decorated with flowers and leaves, c1880, 3in (7.5cm) long.
£70–80
$100–120 ⊞ MB

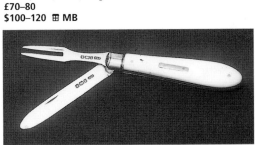

◄ **A sterling silver King's pattern flatware service,** by Dominick and Haff, comprising 144 pieces, monogrammed, 1880, 221oz.
£2,200–2,500
$3,200–3,600 ✗ SK(B)

► **A silver Fiddle and Thread pattern part table service,** by George Adams, comprising 28 crested pieces, London 1881, 57oz.
£1,200–1,400
$1,800–2,000 ✗ Bea(E)

A Victorian silver christening spoon and fork, engraved with floral pattern, London 1885, 6in (15cm) long.
£55–60
$80–90 ⊞ ASAA

▶ **A silver Queen's pattern canteen,** by Chawner & Co, and Elkington & Co, comprising 153 pieces, London 1888, 317.5oz, in brass-mounted oak case.
£7,000–8,000
$10,500–11,500
🔧 S

A set of four silver and parcel-gilt forks, by Martin and Hall, each finely engraved with fish and water weeds, the finials formed as scallop shells, Sheffield 1888, 6¼in (16cm) long.
£200–225
$300–350 ⊞ DAD

A set of 12 Victorian Vine pattern dessert knives and forks, by Aldwinckle and Slater, with engraved blades and tines, the loaded handles chased with fruiting vines, London 1889, in fitted rosewood case.
£700–900
$1,000–1,300 🔧 Bea

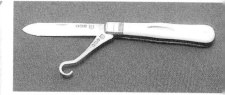

A silver combination fruit knife and button hook, with mother-of-pearl handle, c1890, 2¼in (5.5cm) long.
£60–65
$90–95 ⊞ MB

A silver sugar spoon, with foliate decoration, Birmingham 1894, 4¼in (11cm) long.
£110–130
$160–190 ⊞ AMH

▶ **A set of late Victorian silver Fiddle pattern cutlery,** by George Maudsley Jackson, comprising 62 pieces, London 1893, 109oz.
£1,800–2,200
$2,600–3,200 🔧 WW

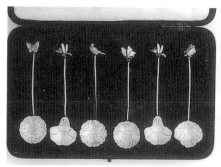

A set of six Arts and Crafts silver coffee spoons, London import mark for 1898, Liberty & Co sponsor's mark, 3½in (9cm) long, 1oz, in original fitted case,
£400–440
$580–640 ⊞ PAY
These spoons were originally made in Japan and imported by Liberty & Co to sell in their mail order catalogues.

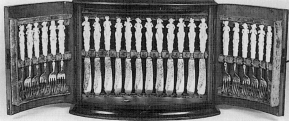

A set of 12 pairs of silver fish knives and forks, by J. H. Potter, each ivory handle carved as a boy or girl in a variety of costumes, with engraved blades and tines, Sheffield 1897, in a fitted wooden case.
£4,000–4,500
$5,800–6,500 🔧 P

▶ **A French silver-gilt christening set,** comprising 12 pieces, marked with retailer's name 'A. Aucoc, R. de la Paix', with a hand inscribed paper ticket 'Mgr. Le Duc d'Orléans à sa Filleule', 19thC, pan 9¼in (23.5cm) overall, in a plush and satin-lined tooled leather case.
£1,300–1,500
$2,000–2,200 🔧 CSK

◀ **A Victorian child's silver cutlery set,** London 1894–98, 8in (20.5cm) long, in a fitted box.
£110–130
$160–190 ⊞ TGa

◀ **A part canteen of silver Old English pattern cutlery,** by The Goldsmiths & Silversmiths Co, comprising five table forks, six dessert forks, six table spoons and four dessert spoons, London 1903, 42oz.
£550–650
$800–1,000 ⚒ Bon

An Edward VII silver Onslow pattern canteen of cutlery, by Mappin & Webb, comprising 133 pieces, Sheffield 1906, in a fitted oak table-top cabinet with three drawers.
£4,000–4,500
$5,800–6,500 ⚒ Bea(E)

A cased set of six silver napkin rings, plain cotton reel style, uninscribed, Sheffield 1906.
£280–300
$400–440 ⚒ GAK

A gold-washed sterling silver Francis I pattern flatware set, by Reed and Barton, comprising 39 pieces, 1907, 58oz.
£850–1,000
$1,250–1,500 ⚒ SK(B)

A set of six Liberty silver dessert knives, with steel blades, the square section handles cast in relief with stylized berries and leaf design, London 1908, in original fitted case.
£400–450
$580–650 ⚒ CSK

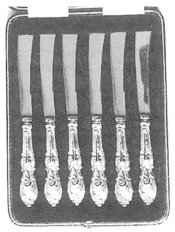

A set of six tea knives, with silver handles, Sheffield 1909, 7½in (19cm) wide, boxed.
£80–100
$120–150 ⊞ ABr

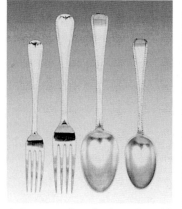

A George V silver feather-edge Old English pattern part service, by Mappin & Webb, comprising 39 pieces, London 1920, 83.5oz.
£800–900
$1,200–1,500 ⚒ Bea(E)

A Belgian set of table silver for 12 persons, by Wolfers Frères, some pieces with maker's marks Philippe Wolfers, Brussels, the majority c1929, 202oz excluding table and cheese knives with steel blades.
£4,800–5,500
$7,000–8,000 ⚒ S(G)

LOCATE THE SOURCE
The source of each illustration in Miller's can be found by checking the code letters below each caption with the Key to Illustrations, pages 311–314.

A part silver Old English pattern canteen, comprising six table forks, four dessert forks, six dessert spoons, six table spoons and four teaspoons, initialled, maker's mark Joseph Walton & Co, London 1933 and 1934, 50oz.
£450–550
$650–800 ⚒ Bon

◀ **A canteen of silver cutlery,** comprising 12 place settings, the knives with mother-of-pearl or ivory handles, Sheffield 1933, 200oz.
£4,000–4,600
$5,800–6,700 ⚒ JNic

◄ An Edwardian silver rococo Scroll pattern canteen, comprising 201 pieces, maker's mark of Elkington & Co, monogrammed, Birmingham 1903 and 1904, together with three pairs of electroplated nut crackers, 12 table knives, 12 dessert knives and a three-piece carving set with foliate pistol handles, London 1965 and 1972, 330oz, in a fitted six-drawer mahogany case.
£5,500–6,000
$8,000–8,700 ✦ Bon

◄ A George VI Hanoverian pattern table service, by The Goldsmiths & Silversmiths Co, Sheffield 1941, London 1935 and 1940, 56oz.
£900–1,200
$1,300–1,800
✦ Bea(E)

A silver Hanoverian pattern table service, each engraved with a crest, the majority Sheffield 1933, 180oz, in a fitted mahogany canteen.
£4,800–5,300
$7,000–7,700 ✦ Gam

Flatware

A set of six Queen Anne silver soup plates, with broad rims, each engraved with a coat-of-arms, maker's mark of Philip Rollos, London 1706, 10in (25.5cm) diam, 109oz.
£33,000–35,000
$48,000–51,000 ✦ C
These plates formed part of a large service made in 1706 and 1707 by Thomas Purr and Philip Rollos.

► A set of 14 silver soup plates, by Robert Makepeace and Richard Carter, engraved with armorials, applied buffed gadrooned borders, London 1778, 9¾in (25cm) diam, 255.75oz.
£3,500–4,200
$5,000–6,000 ✦ BB(S)

Two matching George III silver dinner plates, by James Young, London 1776 and by John Wakelin and John Garrard I, 1793, with shaped gadrooned borders and crests, 9½in (24cm) diam, 32oz.
£700–800
$1,000–1,200 ✦ DN

A George III plain silver serving dish, by W. Fountain, engraved with the arms and crest of Lawrence Monck of Caenby, Lincs, with reeded border, London mark 1798, 24in (61cm) wide.
£2,000–2,400
$2,900–3,500 ✦ AG

Sets/pairs

Unless otherwise stated, any description which refers to 'a set' or 'a pair' includes a guide price for the entire set or the pair, even though the illustration may show only a single item.

A set of 12 silver dinner plates, with gadrooned borders and engraved with a coat-of-arms, maker's mark of Paul Storr, London 1814, 10½in (26.5cm) diam, 262oz.
£8,000–9,000
$11,600–13,000 ✦ Bon

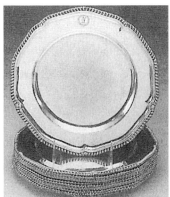

◄ A set of 12 Victorian silver dinner plates, by R. and S. Garrard, with shaped gadrooned rims, the borders engraved with contemporary crest within a motto, 9½in (24cm) diam, 183oz.
£5,500–6,500
$8,000–9,500 ✦ S(NY)
The crest and motto is that of Marton, Capernwray Hall, Lancaster.

Card Cases

The social grace of presenting a card printed with one's name was in full swing by the beginning of the 19th century. The presentation of a calling card was an important element of etiquette; even the design of the card, printed or hand-written gave away its owners's social standing. Other customs such as leaving a card with the lower right hand corner turned up indicated concern for an illness, another bent corner portayed an interest in marriage. Cards would be placed on a silver salver or waiter in the hallway if left, or carried through and presented by a maid or butler.

The majority of all silver cases produced came from the Birmingham quarter. The size of the cases is fairly standard, measuring 4 x 3in (10 x 7.5cm), with a hinged top. They were made in two halves and soldered together, so do check for splits and holes. The hallmarks are generally located on the inside lip of the main body with a part mark on the lid. These marks can be quite faint where the lid has rubbed over them with continuous opening and closing. Silver was certainly the main choice of material but cases were also made from mother-of-pearl, tortoise-shell, ivory and leather. With such variety, there is plenty of scope for a comprehensive collection and prices can range from £25 ($35) to several thousand pounds for an unusual silver one.

The most desirable of silver cases are those that are referred to as castle-tops. These were either hand-chased or die-stamped with views of famous landmarks, houses or castles. The most reproduced scenes are of Abbotsford, home of Sir Walter Scott and Newstead Abbey, home of Lord Byron. There are other castle-tops to choose from if you are able to find them, such as Windsor, Warwick and Kenilworth castles, St Paul's Cathedral and the Scott Memorial. It is possible to see exactly the same view by different silversmiths but on closer examination there will be variations.

Nathaniel Mills was the master at producing these cases but there are others who should be mentioned. Joseph Wilmore, Taylor & Perry and Francis Clark all turned out lovely cases from their workshops. As the Victorian industrial revolution took place and travelling by steam train made exploring Britain accessible to the public, even more scenes of monuments and places of interest were engraved on cases for travellers to take home as souvenirs. As fashions changed, so did the cases, as can be seen from Arts and Crafts, Art Nouveau and Art Deco designs, with the size also decreasing in keeping with the fashion for smaller waistcoat pockets.

Daniel Bexfield

A silver card case, by Nathaniel Mills, with pierced designs depicting Kenilworth and Warwick Castles, Birmingham 1825, 4in (10cm) high.
£1,000–1,100
$1,500–2,300 ⊞ DIC

A Victorian silver castle-top card case, by Nathaniel Mills, with a view of Windsor Castle in low relief on one side and Warwick Castle on the other, both scenes flanked by floral engraving, Birmingham 1840, 4in (10cm) high, 2oz.
£1,000–1,100
$1,500–1,600 ⚚ P

◀ **A Victorian silver card case,** by George Unite, embossed with a relief of the Scott memorial, the reverse with an initialled cartouche, Birmingham 1844, 4in (10cm) high, 2oz.
£800–900
$1,200–1,500 ⚚ S

▶ **A Victorian silver card case,** depicting St Paul's Cathedral, with chased scroll and foliate decoration, the reverse with initials engraved in a cartouche, Birmingham 1844, 4in (10cm) high.
£1,350–1,500
$2,000–2,200 ⚚ WW

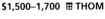

l. A silver card case, by Nathaniel Mills, depicting Kenilworth and Warwick Castles, Birmingham 1838, 4in (10cm) high.
£1,300–1,500
$2,000–2,200
r. A silver card case, by Taylor and Perry, depicting Windsor and Warwick Castles, Birmingham 1843, 4in (10cm) high.
£1,000–1,150
$1,500–1,700 ⊞ THOM

A Victorian silver embossed castle-top card case, by Taylor and Perry, with a view of Gloucester Abbey in relief on one side flanked by chased floral scrolls, the reverse with a lobed oval cartouche engraved with a vase of flowers, flanked by chased floral scrolls, Birmingham 1844, 4in (10cm) high, 2.5oz.
£2,100–2,500
$3,000–3,600 ⚒ P

An early Victorian silver castle-top card case, with a view of Westminster Abbey within foliate scroll decoration, the reverse with crested and mono-grammed scroll cartouche within foliate scrolls, maker's mark of Nathaniel Mills, Birmingham 1845, with French import marks, 4in (10cm) high.
£1,400–1,600
$2,000–2,300 ⚒ P

A Victorian silver castle-top card case, decorated with a view of the Royal Exchange within foliate scrolls, the reverse with foliate scrolls and cartouche, inscribed, slight damage, maker's mark of Nathaniel Mills, Birmingham 1845, 4in (10cm) high.
£900–1,100
$1,300–1,600 ⚒ Bon

A silver castle-top card case, by Nathaniel Mills, heavily embossed with a view of Windsor Castle, the reverse with foliate scrolls and vacant panel, Birmingham 1846, 4in (10cm) high.
£900–1,100
$1,300–1,600 ⚒ S(S)

An early Victorian silver castle-top card case, with a view of St Paul's Cathedral within foliate scroll decoration, the reverse with vacant scroll cartouche within foliate scrolls, maker's mark of Cronin and Wheeler, Birmingham 1847, 4in (10cm) high.
£1,200–1,400
$1,800–2,000 ⚒ Bon

A Victorian silver card case, with engraved decoration of a classical folly in landscape, flanked by a chequered border with vacant cartouche to the reverse, hallmarked, maker's mark Nathaniel Mills, Birimingham 1850, 4in (10cm) high.
£400–600
$580–870 ⚒ Mit

◀ **A mid-Victorian silver engraved castle-top card case,** with a view, possibly Burghley House, within scroll decoration, the reverse with monogrammed central cartouche, within scroll decoration, maker's mark of Foxall & Co, Birmingham 1850, 4in (10cm) high.
£900–1,100
$1,300–1,600 ⚒ Bon

A silver card case, embossed with a view of the Albert Memorial, London, within a scroll and leaf border, the hinged lid embossed with scroll decoration, Birmingham 1851, 4in (10cm) high.
£550–600
$800–880 ⚒ RTo

A Victorian silver engraved castle-top card case, by Foxall & Co, with a view of the Houses of Parliament and the river Thames, bordered by foliate scrolls, the reverse engraved with a vacant shield cartouche, Birmingham 1850, 4in (10cm) high, 2.5oz.
£1,500–1,800
$2,200–2,600 ⚒ P

Prices

The price ranges quoted in this book reflect the average price a purchaser might expect to pay for a similar item. The price will vary according to the condition, rarity, size, popularity, provenance, colour and restoration of the item, and this must be taken into account when assessing values. Don't forget that if you are selling it is quite likely that you will be offered less than the price range.

A silver castle-top card case, embossed and engraved with the 1851 Great Exhibition Hall in Hyde Park, within arabesque scrolls, maker's mark of D. P., Birmingham 1853, 4in (10cm) high, 2oz.
£1,800–2,000
$2,600–2,900 ⚹ **BR**

A silver castle-top card case, with a view of Bath Abbey within foliate scroll decoration, the reverse with a plain scroll cartouche, maker's mark of Alfred Taylor, Birmingham 1856, 4in (10cm) high.
£1,500–1,650
$2,200–2,400 ⚹ **Bon**

◀ **A Victorian silver castle-top card case,** with a view of St Anne's Chapel, Edinburgh Castle, within foliate scroll decoration, the reverse with vacant cartouche within foliate scrolls, maker's mark of Fredk Mason, Birmingham 1856, 4in (10cm) high.
£3,600–4,000
$5,300–5,800
⚹ **Bon**

▶ **A silver card case,** Birmingham 1871, 4in (10cm) high.
£120–160
$175–230 ⊞ **SnA**

A Victorian silver card case, by Cronin and Wheeler, decorated in high relief with St Paul's Cathedral, the reverse chased with foliate scrolls and flowers on a frosted ground around an initialled cartouche, Birmingham 1847.
£1,000–1,100
$1,500–1,600 ⚹ **P**

l. A silver card case, by David Pettifer, depicting St Paul's Cathedral, Birmingham 1848, 4in (10cm) high.
£1,400–1,500
$2,000–2,150
r. A silver card case, by Hilliard and Thomason, depicting Westminster Abbey, Birmingham 1868, 4in (10cm) high.
£2,000–2,200
$2,900–3,200 ⊞ **THOM**

A Victorian silver card case, engraved in the Japanesque style, mono-grammed, fitted leather case, Birmingham 1890, 4in (10cm) high.
£130–150
$190–220 ⚹ **P(S)**

A Victorian silver card case, embossed with a cartouche among flowers and scrolls, the interior fitted with a pen and an ivory sheet, Chester 1899, 4in (10cm) high, 3oz.
£100–120
$150–180 ⚹ **EH**

A Maltese silver card case and purse, with blue velvet lining, engraved with scroll-work around a monogram, marked for Francis Meli, late 19thC, 4½in (11.5cm) high.
£300–500
$450–750 ⚹ **P**

A silver card case, decorated in high relief with a stag, maker's mark 'C&N', Birmingham 1906, 4in (10cm) high.
£300–360
$450–550 ⊞ **DIC**

A silver card case, with scrolling foliate decoration, Chester 1911, 4in (10cm) high.
£160–200
$250–300 ⊞ **PSA**

Condition

The condition is absolutely vital when assessing the value of an antique. Damaged pieces on the whole appreciate much less than perfect examples. However a rare desirable piece may command a high price even when damaged.

Casters

A Queen Anne silver sugar caster, by Jonathan East, the lid pierced with flowerheads and leaves, the base and top of the lid with repoussé lobed horizontal bands, with a sleeve, London 1703, 5½in (14cm) high, 5.5oz.
£1,600–1,800
$2,300–2,600
🔨 RIT

A set of three Queen Anne silver-gilt casters, the finely pierced domed covers each with bayonet fittings and baluster finial, applied with bands of foliate and plain strapwork on a matt ground, with a band of shells, matt strapwork and foliate motifs, the bases with leaf-capped waved decoration, each engraved with crowned Royal cypher, attributed to Philip Rollos, c1705, largest 10½in (26.5cm) high, 56oz.
£150,000–165,000
$218,000–239,000 🔨 C
The cypher is that of Queen Anne.

▶ **A pair of George II silver casters,** by Samuel Wood, each on moulded foot, the covers pierced with stylized foliage, with baluster finial, 1731, 6in (15cm) high.
£2,200–2,500
$3,200–3,600 🔨 C

A set of three American silver sugar casters, by Samuel Edwards, mounted in an English silver frame by Samuel Wood, with two cut-glass bottles, the casters monogrammed 'TEA', marked 'SE' beneath a crown and within a shield, the frame with scrolled handle on four double scrolled legs and shell-form feet, London 1750, frame 8½in (21.5cm) high, 44oz.
£2,200–3,600
$3,200–5,500 🔨 S(Cg)
Samuel Edwards began woking as a silversmith in Boston in 1725. He probably made the three casters to replace or complete the English set.

A George III silver sugar caster, with reeded borders and pierced domed cover with bud finial, maker's mark of Samuel Wood, London 1752, 6½in (16.5cm) high, 5.5oz.
£340–400
$500–600 🔨 P(Ed)

A silver sugar caster, by Samuel Wood, London 1740, 7in (18cm) high.
£850–950
$1,300–1,400 ⊞ DIC

A George II silver inverted pear-shaped caster, on a rope-twist decorated rising foot, with a conforming body band, engraved with a crest, maker's mark indistinct, London 1745, 6in (15cm) high.
£450–550
$650–800 🔨 CSK

▶ **A Continental silver sugar caster,** the faceted body with gadrooned centre above repoussé caryatid decoration interspersed by foliate stems, with three hallmarks to the underside, probably Swiss, with French import marks for Annemasse, c1770, 9¾in (25cm) high.
£500–600
$700–900 🔨 Mit

A pair of George III silver casters, by Jabez Daniell and James Mince, with urn finials, beaded borders, engraved covers, crests and round bases, London 1770, 6¾in (17cm) high, 14oz.
£1,200–1,300
$1,750–1,900 🔨 DN

◀ **A George III silver sugar caster,** by Thomas and Jabez Daniell, monogrammed, 1772, 6¼in (16cm) high, 4oz.
£320–380
$450–600 🔨 P(O)

A George III silver muffineer, with reeded decoration, damaged, London 1795, 5½in (14cm) high.
£180–220
$260–320 ⚖ GAK
A muffineer is a small caster for sprinkling sugar, spice or salt on muffins. The holes are often finer than those on standard casters.

A George III silver sugar caster, with reeded bands, the cover with a ball finial, London 1800, 6½in (16.5cm) high, 3.75oz.
£275–325
$400–470 ⚖ CSK

A pair of George III Adam-style silver casters, on square bases with pierced campana-shaped lids, maker's mark rubbed, London 1805, 7in (18cm) high, 6.75oz.
£350–400
$500–580 ⚖ L

A pair of Austro-Hungarian silver cylindrical casters, the detachable tops with urn finials and decorative borders, Vienna 1806, 3½in (9cm) high, 5.75oz.
£280–350
$400–500 ⚖ DN

A George III silver sugar caster, by Thomas and George Hayter, with reeded band, on a square foot, 1816, 5½in (14cm) high.
£110–140
$150–200 ⚖ L

A George III silver caster, by Crispin Fuller, with shaped bun top and reeded borders, London 1808, 4in (10cm) high.
£190–220
$280–320 ⚖ DN

Three George III silver casters, with pull-off pierced covers, the raised circular bases on a square foot, initialled, various makers, London 1808, largest 4in (10cm) high, 7oz, in a later fitted case.
£420–500
$600–720 ⚖ Bon

A Victorian 18thC-style silver sugar caster, by George Fox, the pierced cover with bayonet fittings and baluster finial, London 1881, 8½in (21.5cm) high, 13.25oz.
£750–825
$1,000–1,200 ⚖ CSK

A pair of Dutch silver sugar casters, the covers pierced with scrolls and flowers, with wrythen knop finials, c1895, 12in (30.5cm) high, 44oz.
£1,200–1,400
$1,800–2,000 ⚖ P

A late Victorian silver sugar caster, with swirl fluted finial, the body embossed with floral and foliate strapwork, maker's mark of George Maudsley Jackson and David Landsborough Fullerton, London 1898, 9½in (24cm) high, 9oz.
£220–260
$320–380 ⚖ Bon

A pair of Victorian silver sugar casters, by Joseph Bradbury and John Henderson, decorated with spiral fluting and foliage and with C- and S-scroll, floral cartouches engraved with crests and mottos, each on a rocaille-decorated rising foot, London 1886, 8½in (21.5cm) high, 18.25oz, in a lined case.
£900–1,100
$1,500–1,500 ⚖ CSK

A late Victorian silver sugar caster, by Atkin Bros, the swirl-fluted pear-shaped body with foliate engraving, the cover with a swirling pear-shaped finial and a bayonet fitting, on a spreading foot, Sheffield 1890, 8in (20.5cm) high, 8oz.
£260–300
$380–440 ⚖ WW

A late Victorian silver sugar caster, with wrythen-fluted decoration and finial, Sheffield 1890, 8½in (21.5cm) high.
£220–260
$320–380 ↗ GAK

A late Victorian silver sugar caster, by Samuel Watton Smith, engraved with a crest, London 1896, 8in (20.5cm) high, 9.75oz.
£400–450
$580–650 ↗ CSK

A late Victorian silver baluster sugar caster, repoussé with ribbons and swags, bands of stiff leaf decoration, pierced cover with urn finial, Birmingham 1899, 8½in (21.5cm) high, 8oz.
£195–225
$280–350 ↗ P(EA)

A pair of George III-style silver sugar casters, by The Goldsmiths & Silversmiths Co, with rococo husk and foliage repoussé decoration, London 1898–1902, 9¼in (23.5cm) high, 31.5oz.
£1,400–1,700
$2,000–2,500 ↗ WW

An Edwardian silver openwork sugar caster, by Marston and Bayliss, with blue glass liner, 5¾in (14.5cm) high, 4.25oz.
£200–250
$300–360 ↗ CGC

An octagonal silver sugar caster, by J. R, Glasgow 1904, 8½in (21.5cm) high.
£175–200
$260–300 PC

A silver sugar caster, by Joel Phillips, engraved with rococo leaf and shell scrolls, enclosing diaper and fish scale panels, London 1905, 8in (20.5cm) high, 19oz.
£600–650
$900–950 ↗ P(NE)

A silver sugar caster, with turned finial on pedestal foot, London 1908, 8¾in (22cm) high 7.5oz.
£200–220
$300–350 ↗ Bea(E)

A pair of silver sugar casters, the pull-off pierced covers with swirl decoration, on a fluted foot, maker's mark of The Goldsmiths & Silversmiths Co, London 1913, largest 9in (23cm) high, 32oz.
£900–1,000
$1,300–1,500 ↗ Bon

◀ **A silver sugar caster,** on a stepped foot, Birmingham 1908, 9in (23cm) high, 11oz.
£270–300
$390–400 ↗ GAK

▶ **A silver sugar caster,** by William Comyns, with a detachable pierced fret cover, London 1915, 8½in (21.5cm) high, 8.5oz.
£260–320
$380–460 ↗ WW

A silver sugar caster, by The Goldsmiths & Silversmiths Co, London 1916, 7in (18cm) high, 5oz.
£250–300
$360–440 ⊞ TC

An early 18thC-style silver sugar caster, with quarter-fluted decoration, on a stepped circular foot, London 1924, 6½in (16.5cm) high, 8.5oz.
£250–300
$360–440 ⚒ GAK

A silver-gilt hammered baluster caster, by George Dimmer, with fluted finial, embossed with bands of lion masks, flowers, leaves and strapwork, London 1926, 6½in (16cm) high, 10oz.
£450–500
$650–750 ⚒ DN

A George I-style silver sugar caster, with central girdle, pull-off domed cover and knop finial, on a circular foot, maker's mark of Searle & Co, London 1932, 8oz.
£180–200
$260–300 ⚒ Bon

A silver sugar caster, Birmingham 1937, 6¼in (16cm) high, 7oz.
£140–170
$200–250 ⚒ P(B)

◀ **A silver sugar caster,** by Barker Bros, with moulded edge and girdle, the cover decoratively pierced below a bell finial, on a circular foot, Birmingham 1934, 7¾in (19.5cm) high, 5oz.
£100–130
$150–200 ⚒ CGC

▶ **A silver sugar caster,** by Mappin & Webb, with moulded edge and girdle below a pierced and engraved cover with wrythen finial, Birmingham 1966, 6½in (16.5cm) high, 5.5oz.
£75–95
$100–140 ⚒ CGC

Centrepieces

A silver-gilt tazza, probably German, the plaquette embossed and chased with 'The Binding of Isaac', on a later foot chased in conforming style, 17thC and later, 10in (25.5cm) diam, 38oz.
£5,000–6,000
$7,500–8,500 ⚒ S

A George II silver *épergne*, with four detachable scroll branches terminating in a detachable fluted dish, the handles formed as the head of Mercury, engraved with panels of scalework and a coat-of-arms, the dishes engraved with a crest, maker's mark of William Cripps, London 1754, 11in (28cm) high, 188oz.
£38,000–42,000
$55,000–61,000 ⚒ C

A George II silver *épergne*, with eight detachable leaf-capped branches, four terminating in a dish and four in a basket, each with a swing handle, engraved with crest and motto, maker's mark of Thomas Pitts, London 1759, with later French control marks, 23in (58.5cm) high, 194oz.
£55,000–60,000
$80,000–87,000 ⚒ C

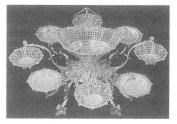

A George III silver basket *épergne*, by Thomas Pitts, engraved with contemporary arms and matching crest in rococo cartouches, fully marked on stand and central basket, maker's mark on all pieces and lion passant on four branches, London 1765, 26½in (67.5cm) wide, 166oz.
£30,000–34,000
$43,000–49,000 ⚒ S(NY)

A George III silver two-branch *épergne*, the baskets each with a cut-glass liner, maker's mark of William Holmes, London 1790, 16in (40.5cm) high, 147oz.
£8,000–9,000
$11,000–13,000 ⚒ L

A silver centrepiece, bowl damaged, maker's mark of John Mortimer and John Hunt, London 1843, 18¾in (47.5cm) high, 136oz.
£6,000–7,000
$8,500–10,000 ⚒ Bon

Insurance values

Always insure your valuable antiques for the cost of replacing them with similar items, regardless of the original price paid. Both dealers and auctioneers will provide a valuation service for a fee.

A George III silver canopied *épergne*, by Thomas Hemming, with nine baskets, engraved with contemporary arms and matching crests, fully marked, London 1765, 25in (63.5cm) high, 266.5oz.
£70,000–76,000
$101,000–110,000 ⚒ S(NY)
The arms are those of Montagu impaling Bulmer for Charles Greville, second son of Robert, third Duke of Manchester, born in 1741, and married on 20 September, 1765, Elizabeth, daughter of James Bulmer.

A George IV silver *épergne*, the central bowl supported by four scroll acanthus supports, baluster stem, with four foliate scroll branches, each supporting a glass bowl, on a shaped tapering square base, with shell and foliate decoration, on paw feet, crested, Birmingham 1823, 17½in (44.5cm) high, 92oz.
£8,000–9,000
$11,000–13,000 ⚒ Bon

A German silver centrepiece, the stem formed as a grapevine surrounded by three putti, the bowl with scrolled tendril handles, topped by seated putti, mid-19thC, 28in (71cm) high, 224oz.
£9,000–10,000
$13,000–14,500 ⚒ S(NY)

A George III silver-gilt basket *épergne*, by Thomas Pitts, the stand on four scroll supports linked by cast aprons of flowering foliage, detachable central basket and four circular baskets on detachable branches, later gilt, fully marked, London 1767, 15in (38cm) high, 91oz.
£9,000–11,000
$13,000–16,000 ⚒ S(NY)

An early Victorian silver comport, by Charles Reily & George Storer, decorated with latticework design and applied fruiting vine, on an oval stem foot, engraved inscription, London 1842, 11½in (29cm) high, 33oz.
£1,000–1,250
$1,500–1,800 ⚒ AG

A mid-Victorian silver *épergne* and mirror plateau, the central vertical vine column with hanging bunches of grapes supporting a wirework basket, on a raised circular rocky base mounted with playful putti putting garlands on a lion and embracing, the whole on a circular mirror plateau applied with an apron of trailing grape vine tendrils on three vine feet, with a cut glass bowl, maker's mark of William Gough and also marked with a Swedish import mark, Birmingham 1857, 18¼in (46.5cm) high, 121oz.
£4,700–5,200
$6,500–7,500 ⚒ Bon

A silver-gilt centrepiece, inscribed and marked with a registration mark, maker's mark of George Richard Elkington, London 1857, 19in (48.5cm) high.
£4,000–4,500
$5,800–6,500 ⚒ Bon

A Burmese silver and buffalo horn centrepiece, on an ebonized wooden stand, with three dog of Fo supports, presented in 1877 to Henry Montague Matthews CIE, Chief Engineer, South Burma Railway, 22½in (57cm) high.
£1,400–1,600
$2,000–2,300 ⚒ Bea

An Edwardian silver épergne, by Deakin and Deakin, with three small detachable vases and a larger central vase, Sheffield 1908, 14½in (37cm) high, 33oz.
£900–1,100
$1,300–1,600 ⚒ P(B)

A Victorian silver centrepiece, by Stephen Smith, 1866, 29in (73.5cm) high, 103oz.
£3,000–3,500
$4,500–5,000 ⚒ G(L)

A silver épergne, with reticulated and engraved floral and scroll design, with monogram and dated '1900', 14½in (37cm) high, 85oz.
£3,500–4,000
$5,000–5,800 ⚒ SK(B)

A silver épergne, by W. Hutton & Sons, London 1908, 12in (30.5cm) high.
£1,000–1,250
$1,500–1,800 ⊞ THOM

▶ **A silver and oxidised silver waterlily centrepiece,** by Stuart Devlin, the dish with removable oxidized silver-gilt cover comprising of a mesh of stylized lily pads of varying size in oxidized silver incorporating seven sockets for displaying flowers, stamped marks, 1976, 12in (30.5cm) diam.
£1,200–1,500
$1,800–2,200 ⚒ P(Ba)

A French silver centrepiece, with a figure of Plenty holding a cornucopia and laurel wreath, on a drum-shaped plinth applied with the Imperial eagle, the border of the bowl and the base of the plinth with inscriptions, maker's mark 'Christofle, Paris, 1866', 26in (66cm) high, 295oz.
£18,000–20,000
$26,000–29,000 ⚒ C

An Edward VII silver centrepiece, by J. W. D., Sheffield 1902 and London 1903, 15½in (39.5cm) high, 126oz.
£4,200–4,600
$6,000–6,700 ⚒ LT

A silver centrepiece, the bowls with shell and scroll borders, on four scroll legs with shell feet, maker's mark of James Dixon & Sons, Sheffield 1910, 13¾in (35cm) high, 106oz.
£3,000–3,400
$4,500–5,000 ⚒ Bon

A silver centrepiece, by Elkington & Co, applied with figures of a Chinaman and Sarawak tribesmen, Birmingham 1873, 19in (48.5cm) high, 115oz.
£6,500–7,000
$9,500–10,500 ⚒ S

An Edwardian centrepiece, by J. Davis & Son, composed of four intersecting open scroll branches supporting a central oval basket, with pierced foliate sides and floral scrolling rim, two smaller baskets similarly decorated and two trumpet-shaped vases, all with green glass liners, Sheffield 1907, 14½in (37cm) high, 91.5oz.
£6,000–6,750
$8,700–9,800 ⚒ P(WM)

A silver centrepiece, by J.& W. Dixon, Sheffield 1911, 15in (38cm) high, 34oz.
£900–1,100
$1,300–1,600 ⊞ PSA

Clocks & Watches

A Movado silver purse watch, with automatic wind, matt white dial with raised gilt numerals, gilt hands, inscribed 'Cartier', the movement signed 'Movado' with 15 jewels, screwed chatons and four adjustments, winding on ribbed and numbered '4256' opening case, with Cartier presentation box, 1¾ x ¾in (4.5 x 2cm).
£1,000–1,200
$1,500–1,800 ➤ C

A silver pair-cased verge stop watch, the *champlevé* dial signed 'Tho Rayment', London 18thC, 2in (5cm) diam.
£2,000–2,200
$2,900–3,200 ➤ P

◀ **A late Victorian silver and tortoiseshell watch stand,** fitted with a scroll wirework easel stand, the silver mounts embossed with floral and foliate scrolls and fitted with a hook from which to hang a pocket watch, maker's mark of William Comyns, London 1894, 6in (15cm) high.
£550–600
$800–870 ➤ Bon

A 17thC-style silver verge watch, by Jean Falise, the backplate with engraved decoration, the case pierced overall and engraved with hunting scenes, with detached wheels, 19thC, 4in (10cm) long.
£700–800
$1,000–1,200 ➤ S

◀ **An Omega silver and enamel lever dress watch,** the silvered dial with Arabic numerals, case, dial and movement signed, c1920.
£800–900
$1,200–1,500 ➤ S(Am)

A silver open-face keyless lever goliath watch, the enamel dial with Roman and Arabic numerals, subsidiary dials for day, date and seconds with moonphase, c1900, 3in (7.5cm) diam, with a leather-covered desk stand inscribed 'Giraudon, rue de la Paix, Paris'.
£850–950
$1,300–1,500 ➤ CSK

A Cyma Watch Co gold, silver, metal and enamel shutter clip watch, the nickel lever movement with 15 jewels, case signed Verger Frères, c1920, 1½in (4cm) long.
£1,200–1,400
$1,800–2,000 ➤ S(NY)

Auction or dealer?

All the pictures in our price guides originate from auction houses and dealers. Look for the symbol at the end of each caption to identify the source.

When buying at auction, prices can be lower than those of a dealer, but a buyer's premium and VAT will be added to the hammer price. Equally, when selling at auction, commission, tax and photography charges must be taken into account. Dealers will often restore pieces before putting them back on the market.

Both dealers and auctioneers will provide professional advice, so it is worth researching both sources before buying or selling your antiques.

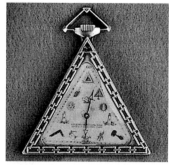

A Swiss silver masonic watch, with mother-of-pearl dial, 15 jewel movement adjusted to three positions, 1930s, 2in (5cm) wide, in fitted box.
£1,000–1,200
$1,500–1,800 ➤ Bon

◀ **A Dunhill silver watch, and cigarette lighter,** with nickel lever movement, signed, c1925, 2¼in (5cm) high.
£1,350–1,500
$2,000–2,200 ➤ S(NY)

Clocks

A silver-framed mantel clock, the dial cast with a hunting scene, the numbers in the form of bits and spurs, maker E. H. S., London 1890, 5in (12.5cm) diam.
£700–800
$1,000–1,200 ↗ RBB

A silver clock, depicting John Bull, inscribed 'Wake Up', marked, c1909, 6in (15cm) high.
£650–750
$900–1,100 ⊞ CHe

An Edwardian silver eight-day timepiece, by Grey & Co, fitted into a hinged and sprung silver frame upon a tortoiseshell base with gadrooned border, 1902, 5¼in (13.5cm) long.
£350–400
$500–580 ↗ P

A silver-cased clock, by Fattorini & Sons, Birmingham c1910, 9½in (24cm) high.
£500–600
$700–870 ↗ S(S)

> **Miller's is a price GUIDE not a price LIST**

▶ **A silver and guilloché enamel strut clock,** the blue guilloché enamel engraved with a floral spray and ribbon-tied foliate decoration over sun burst engine-turning, on three ball feet, maker's mark of R. C., London 1927, 4¼in (11cm) high.
£150–180
$220–260 ↗ Bon

A silver and enamel boudoir timepiece, the fan-shaped case enamelled in pink over feathered decoration, maker's mark possibly H. H., Birmingham 1928, 4in (10cm) high.
£450–500
$650–750 ↗ S(S)

Pocket Watches

◀ **A silver quarter-repeating verge pocket watch,** with concealed erotic scene, 2in (5cm) diam.
£1,800–2,000
$2,500–3,000 ↗ C

A gentleman's silver pair-cased open-face pocket watch, the silvered *champlevé* dial with Roman hour numerals, Arabic minute numerals, steel hand, the gilt fusee movement with a verge escapement, squared architectural pillars with scrolls at intervals, engraved and scroll pierced balance cock, the backplate signed 'HENY DEEME, HONITON, 2886', the inner case back initialled 'T.H.', plain outer case, minute hand missing, replacement base metal post and bow fittings, London 1759.
£500–600
$750–850 ↗ S(S)

Further reading

Miller's Clocks & Barometers Buyer's Guide (revised edition), Miller's Publications, 2002

A silver verge watch, the *champlevé* dial with date aperture, outer case missing, signed Rensman, London, 17thC, 2in (5cm) diam.
£450–550
$650–800 ↗ P

A George III silver pair-cased pocket watch, the case by William Howard, London 1763, 2in (5cm) diam.
£350–420
$500–600 ✗ DN

A silver pair-cased verge pocket watch, signed Thomas Haley, Oxford, c1785, 2in (5cm) diam.
£350–400
$500–580 ⊞ BSA

▶ **A silver rack lever pocket watch,** signed Litherland & Co, Liverpool 1799, 2¼in (5.5cm) diam.
£450–500
$650–750 ⊞ BSA

▶ **A silver pair-cased verge pocket watch,** by Edward Hemmen, with fusee movement, pierced and engraved balance clock, Tompion-type regulation and square pillars, marked H. M., London 1791, 2in (5cm) diam.
£300–350
$450–500 PC

A Dutch silver pair-cased verge watch, the pierced balance cock signed J. Strong, London, late 18thC, 2in (5cm) diam.
£300–330
$440–480 ✗ Bon(C)

A silver-gilt pedometer pocket watch, the movement signed Recordon, Spencer and Perkins, London, with white dial, the plain case marked 1807, 2in (5cm) diam.
£3,800–4,200
$5,500–6,000 ✗ GH

A Swiss silver quarter-repeating automaton verge open-face watch, with blue enamel dial, fusee movement, c1810, 2¼in (5.5cm) diam.
£2,700–3,000
$4,000–4,500 ⊞ PT

Items in the Clocks & Watches section have been arranged in date order within each sub-section.

A silver quarter-repeating automata open-face pocket watch, with blue enamel dial plate with central white dial and Arabic numerals, mounted with two gilt jacquemarts striking on bells, frosted gilt, fusee, verge with bridge cock repeating quarter hours on two gongs operated by the pendant, 2¼in (5.5cm) diam.
£1,300–1,500
$2,000–2,200 ✗ C

A silver pair-cased watch, with enamel dial decorated with a hunting scene, the black letters reading Richard Wakelin to record the hours, backplate signed 'Jn Roe', Coventry, Birmingham 1816, 1¾in (4.5cm) diam.
£420–470
$600–680 ✗ S(S)

▶ **A silver lever watch,** by Frodsham, with white enamel dial, the three train wheels under a single signed gilt cock, marked London 1825, 2¼in (5.5m) diam.
£480–535
$700–800 ⊞ PT

A French silver open-faced watch, by Robert and Courvoisier, with enamel dial, gilt fusee movement and verge escapement, c1840, 2¼in (5.5cm) diam.
£575–650
$850–1,000 ➶ S(S)

A Victorian silver lady's fob watch, 1¼in (32mm) diam.
£50–60
$75–90 ⊞ HEI

A silver full hunter verge watch, with fusee movement and enamel face, silver hands, key-wind and set, c1842, 2in (5cm) diam.
£400–450
$580–650 ⊞ DQ

▶ **A silver fusee lever pocket watch,** by Thomas Yates, Preston c1845, 2in (5cm) diam.
£150–180
$220–260 ⊞ BSA

A Swiss silver cased verge watch, with full plate gilt fusee movement, finely pierced and engraved bridge cock with steel coqueret, plain three arm gilt balance with blue steel spiral hairspring, silver regulator dial with blue steel indicator, round pillars, Roman numerals, blue steel hands, maker's mark 'ROJE' in an oval and London hallmark for 1850, 1in (2.5cm) diam.
£450–550
$650–800 ⊞ PT

A Swiss silver and enamel hunter watch, signed J. Ulman & Co, Hong Kong, with enamel dial, c1880, 2in (5cm) diam.
£250–300
$350–450 ➶ Bon(C)

◀ **A silver pocket watch,** by Kendal and Dent, with key wind fusee movement, restored, Birmingham 1891, 2in (5cm) diam.
£150–170
$220–250 ⊞ TIH

LOCATE THE SOURCE
The source of each illustration in Miller's can be found by checking the code letters below each caption with the Key to Illustrations, pages 311–314.

A Swiss silver fob watch, with key-wind and key set, late 19thC, 1½in (4cm) diam.
£125–150
$180–220 ⊞ DQ

A silver pocket watch, by J. W. Benson, signed 'The Ludgate watch by warrant to HM the Queen', 1893, 2in (5cm) diam.
£80–100
$115–145 ⊞ BSA

A silver cased open-face pocket watch, by J. W. Benson, London c1898, 2in (5cm) diam.
£125–150
$180–220 ⊞ PSA

A silver cased half hunter pocket watch, with Swiss 17 jewelled movement by Syren, separate jewel bearings, micrometer adjuster to regulator, Birmingham 1923, 2in (5cm) diam.
£250–300
$300–400 ⊞ PSA

Condition

The condition is absolutely vital when assessing the value of an antique. Damaged pieces on the whole appreciate much less than perfect examples. However a rare desirable piece may command a high price even when damaged.

A Swiss silver keyless lever watch, signed Rolex, with enamel dial, the movement jewelled to the centre with micrometer regulation, Birmingham 1940, 2in (5cm) diam.
£400–480
$580–700 ↗ P

A silver eight-day Goliath lever watch, by Octava Watch Co, with three-quarter plate keyless movement with going barrel, marked London 1920, 2½in (6.5cm) diam.
£375–425
$550–650 ⊞ PT

Wristwatches

A Rolex sterling silver watch, with hinged lugs, enamelled porcelain dial, the movement signed 'Rolex Breguet hairspring', case marked 'W. & D.' and 'Rolex 7 world records gold medal Geneva-Suisse', marked for 1924, 1in (2.5cm) wide.
£1,000–1,200
$1,500–1,750 ⊞ HARP

A silver cased wristwatch, by S.S. & Co, with gold button, red numeral '12', Swiss lever movement, original strap with hallmarked buckle, c1911, 1½in (4cm) diam.
£220–240
$300–350 ⊞ DQ

A Rolex silver half hunter watch, c1920, 1¼in (3cm) diam.
£1,600–1,800
$2,300–2,600 ⊞ TWD

A Rolex bracelet watch with silvered dial, diamond-set, signed for C. Bucherles, 1920, ½in (1.5cm) wide.
£600–700
$870–1,000 ↗ Bon

◀ **A French Favre-Leuba silver watch,** the leather strap with silver adornment, c1960, ¾in (2cm) wide.
£200–250
$290–360 ⊞ DID

▶ **A Samy Lay French silver wristwatch,** c1960, 1½in (1.5cm) diam.
£250–300
$350–450 ⊞ DID

A Harwood silver-cased automatic watch, with silvered dial, 1929, 1¼in (3cm) diam.
£300–350
$450–500 ↗ Bon

Colour Review

A George II silver basket, by Peter Archambo I, with pierced sides, the cartouches engraved with a coat-of-arms and motto, engraved crested handle, London 1734, 12in (30.5cm) wide, 69oz.
£40,000–45,000
$58,000–65,200 ➤ S

A George II silver basket, in the form of a scallop shell, on three cast dolphin feet, the handle later engraved with a crest and motto, maker's mark of Phillips Garden, London 1754, 13½in (34.5cm) wide, 58oz.
£36,000–38,000
$52,000–55,000 ➤ C

A George II silver basket, with swing handle, maker's mark of Samuel Herbert & Co, London 1754, 14½in (37cm) wide, 53oz.
£7,000–8,000
$10,500–11,500 ➤ Bon

A George III silver basket, by John Lawford and William Vincent, London 1762, 13¼in (33.5cm) wide, 24.5oz.
£2,800–3,200
$4,000–4,600 ➤ S

A George III silver cream pail, pierced with birds and scrolling foliage, London 1775, 2½in (6.5cm) high.
£450–550
$650–800 ➤ Bea(E)

A George III silver sugar basket, by John Emes, with later Victorian decoration, London 1805, 7in (18cm) wide.
£350–400
$500–600 ⊞ CoHA

◄ **A George III silver-gilt basket,** with mask and scroll handles, London 1791, 17¼in (44cm) wide.
£650–800
$950–1,200 ➤ WL

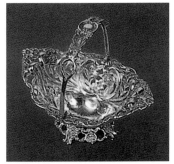

A set of four silver-gilt dessert baskets, with pierced fret sides, London 1899, 1905 and 1906, 12½in (32cm) wide, 180oz.
£11,000–13,000
$16,000–19,000 ➤ WW

A silver miniature basket, pierced and scrolled, Chester 1896, 4in (10cm) wide.
£160–180
$230–260 ⊞ AMH

◄ **A silver sweetmeat dish,** by Odiot of Paris, late 19thC, 5½in (14cm) high.
£1,750–2,000
$2,500–2,900 ⊞ SHa

An Edwardian silver sweetmeat dish, by Charles Stuart Harris, pierced sides, London 1903, 6in (15cm) wide.
£250–300
$350–450 ⊞ TGa

A silver bread basket, with maker's mark of Harrison Brothers & Howson, Sheffield 1910, 11in (28cm) wide.
£650–750
$950–1,100 ⊞ SHa

A silver-gilt basket, by Mappin & Webb, the scroll supports headed by busts of Ceres, London 1919, 15½in (39.5cm) wide, 98oz.
£5,500–6,000
$8,000–8,700 ⚒ S(S)

A silver bread basket, by Charles Boyton & Son, Sheffield 1929, 18in (45.5cm) long.
£900–1,100
$1,300–1,600 ⊞ JBU

A silver beaker, maker's mark 'WI', London 1599, 5½in (14cm) high, 7oz.
£11,500–13,000
$16,500–18,500 ⚒ S

A German silver and silver-gilt beaker, incised 'IVL 1653' above a blank baroque cartouche, Cologne, c1600, 3½in (9cm) high.
£7,000–7,500
$10,000–11,000 ⚒ ABB

A Swiss parcel-gilt silver beaker, by Heinrich Hoffmann II, Winterthur, c1660, 6¾in (17cm) high, 3¾oz.
£14,000–16,000
$20,300–23,200 ⚒ S(G)

A Victorian silver-mounted horn beaker, by Thomas Johnson, London 1880, 4½in (11.5cm) high.
£250–285
$360–400 ⊞ PAY

A German silver-gilt beaker cup, by Niclas Bille, Dresden c1680, 3¼in (8.5cm) high, 4oz.
£2,500–3,000
$3,500–4,500 ⚒ HAM

A Swedish silver tumbler, with parcel-gilt banding, late 18thC.
£170–200
$250–290 ⚒ G(B)

▶ **A French 950 standard silver-gilt beaker,** Paris c1880, 3½in (9cm) high.
£850–950
$1,200–1,400 ⊞ PAY

A silver-gilt shallow bowl, engraved, late 17thC, 5¼in (13.5cm) diam.
£4,500–5,000
$6,500–7,250 ⚒ S(G)

A silver rose bowl, by James Garrard, with detachable rim and gilt interior, 1887, 9½in (24cm) diam, 103oz.
£3,000–3,300
$4,400–4,800 ⚒ TEN

A Japanese compressed circular silver bowl, with everted rim, on a carved hardwood stand, the bowl signed, late 19thC, 10½in (26.5cm) diam.
£3,000–3,500
$4,400–5,000 ⚒ DN

▶ **A silver monteith,** by W. & J. Barnard, with detachable rim, London 1893, 9¾in (25cm) diam, 48oz.
£1,350–1,500
$2,000–2,200 ⚒ P(L)

◀ **A silver porringer,** c1925, 9in (23cm) diam.
£450–500
$650–700 ⊞ BWA

A Commonwealth silver porringer and cover, by John Thomason, York 1659, 5¼in (13.5cm) high, 17.5oz.
£25,000–30,000
$36,000–43,500 ⚒ S

◀ **A Victorian silver punch bowl,** by John Mortimer and John Samuel Hunt, embossed and chased with floral and fish motifs, on spreading foot, gilt interior, 1843, 15¼in (38.5cm) wide, 66oz.
£2,600–3,000
$3,800–4,400 ⚒ P(B)

A Victorian parcel-gilt silver punch bowl, maker's mark of Charles Frederick Hancock, London 1858, 21½in (54.5cm) diam, 329oz.
£32,000–35,000
$46,000–50,000 ⚒ C

A late Victorian silver rose bowl, by Martin, Hall & Co, with drop handles, London 1892, 16in (40.5cm) diam, 75oz.
£2,800–3,200
$4,000–4,500 ⚒ S(S)

A set of three Victorian silver rose bowls, by Horace Woodward & Co, chased with trailing foliage, the centre bowl crested with a demi-leopard gorged with a ducal coronet, London 1890, largest 12in (30.5cm) wide.
£3,700–4,000
$5,300–5,800 ⚒ S

A German parcel-gilt silver toilet box, by Albrecht Biller, with applied scrolling acanthus, nine embossed enamelled ovals, wood inserts and velvet lining, c1690, 14in (35.5cm) wide, 83oz.
£34,000–38,000
$49,000–55,000 ⚒ S

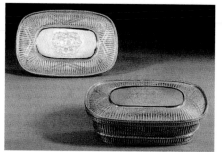

A pair of silver boxes and covers, in the form of baskets, maker's mark of Gabriel Sleath, London 1713, 7in (18cm) wide, 37oz.
£28,000–32,000
$40,500–46,500 ⚒ C

A Japanese silver and gilt *kogo*, signed 'Setsuho Hidetomo', Mejii period, 2¾in (7cm) diam.
£5,600–6,200
$8,000–9,000 ⚒ Bea(E)

◄ **A Victorian silver casket,** by Charles Reily and George Storer, chased with rococo ornament, dragons and demi-lions, hinged cover with lion's head finial, London 1844, 16½in (42cm) wide, 275oz.
£13,000–15,000
$19,000–22,000 ⚒ S(NY)

A silver-gilt case, for half and full sovereigns, 1880, 2in (5cm) wide.
£100–120
$145–175 ⊞ BHA

◄ **A French silver snuff box,** the engine-turned case with symmetrical scroll and floral decoration, 19thC, 3in (7.5cm) wide.
£225–250
$325–350 ⊞ WeH

A French silver and enamel singing bird box, maker's mark illegible, 19thC, 3½in (9cm) wide.
£3,200–3,600
$4,700–5,200 ⚒ C

► **A silver-topped box,** Birmingham 1906, 8½in (21.5cm) long.
£90–100
$130–145 ⊞ WN

A George V tortoiseshell and silver jewellery box, by Levi & Salaman, Birmingham 1917, 6in (15cm) wide.
£450–500
$650–700 ⊞ TGa

A silver and enamel compact, hand-painted with roses and gilt, Birmingham 1912, 2in (5cm) diam.
£165–185
$250–270 ⊞ JACK

A Continental silver singing bird box, in the form of a book, each corner set with a cabochon amethyst, opening to reveal a singing bird and winding screw, with sliding spine key compartment, importation mark for 1926, 4¼in (11cm) high.
£3,000–3,500
$4,500–5,000 ⚒ DD

◄ **An enamelled silver snuff bottle,** Kangxi/Yongzheng period, 2¾in (7cm) high.
£8,000–9,000
$11,500–13,000 ⊞ JWA

A silver-mounted mother-of-pearl snuff box, plain silver with reeding around base, engraved on the inside with the arms of the Courthope family in Sussex, the pull-off lid made of mother-of-pearl, carved with a naval scene, mounted with a reeded edge of silver, unmarked, 1698–1710, 3in (7.5cm) diam.
£1,800–2,200
$2,500–3,000 ⊞ SLI

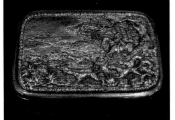

A George III silver snuff box, by Joseph Ash I, London 1809, 3¼in (8cm) wide.
£1,200–1,400
$1,800–2,000 ⊞ BEX

A Victorian silver snuff box, by Waterhouse & Ryland, engraved, Birmingham 1840, 3in (7.5cm) long.
£360–400
$500–600 ⊞ PAY

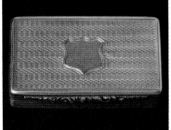

A silver snuff box, by Francis Clark, engine-turned with chased edge and engraving, Birmingham 1846, 2in (5cm) long.
£300–350
$450–500 ⊞ PAY

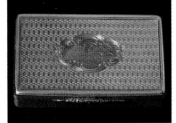

A silver snuff box, by Yapp & Woodward, engine-turned and engraved, with gilt interior, Birmingham 1848, 3in (7.5cm) long.
£300–350
$450–500 ⊞ PAY

A Victorian silver snuff box, by Edward Edwards, with chased edge and gilt interior, engraved, London 1844, 3in (7.5cm) wide.
£700–850
$1,000–1,250 ⊞ PAY

A silver-gilt vinaigrette, by N. Mills, in the shape of a pocket watch, Birmingham 1829, 1in (2.5cm) diam.
£670–720
$950–1,000 ⊞ THOM

A Regency silver-mounted vinaigrette, in the shape of a horn, chased with flowerheads, with a frosted and cut-glass body, c1830, 3in (7.5cm) long.
£350–400
$500–600 ⊞ HofB

An engraved silver snuff box, by George Unite, Birmingham 1880, 3in (7.5cm) long.
£320–360
$450–500 ⊞ PAY

▶ **A chased silver buckle with green stone,** by Heath & Middleton, Birmingham 1902, 4in (10cm) long.
£350–400
$500–600 ⊞ PAY

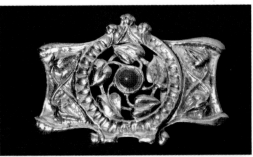

Six silver buttons, London 1770, 1¼in (3cm) diam.
£550–650
$800–1,000 ⊞ MCO

Two Victorian silver and steel shoe buckles, by Yapp & Woodward, Birmingham 1849, 3¾in (9.5cm) wide.
£150–165
$200–250 ⊞ BEX

A pair of William III silver candlesticks, maker's mark of John Laughton, repaired, London 1699, 6in (15cm) high.
£8,500–9,500
$12,500–13,500 ⚒ Bon

A pair of Dutch silver candlesticks, by Albert Gaillard, 1745, 13in (33cm) high.
£9,000–10,000
$13,000–14,500 ⚒ S(G)

A pair of George II silver candlesticks, by John Cafe, 1753, with later drip pans, 8½in (21.5cm) high.
£4,250–4,850
$6,200–7,000 ⊞ PAY

A pair of silver table candlesticks, by Ebenezer Coker, London 1764, 10in (25.5cm) high, 34oz.
£3,000–3,400
$4,500–5,000 ⚒ HCC

A pair of silver-gilt candlesticks, c1700, 25in (63.5cm) high.
£3,000–3,750
$4,500–5,500 ⊞ DBA

A pair of George III silver candlesticks, by William Cafe, London 1764–65, 10½in (27cm) high.
£6,200–6,800
$9,000–10,000 ⊞ PAY

▶ **A set of four German silver candelabra,** bases by Johann Philipp Heckenauer, c1767, 13¼in (33.5cm) high, 149oz.
£35,000–38,000
$50,000–55,000 ⚒ S(G)

A set of four silver candlesticks, by François de la Pierre, c1717, 8¾in (22cm) high, 89.25oz.
£55,000–60,000
$80,000–87,000 ⚒ S(G)

A silver chamberstick, by William Grundy, London 1758, 6in (15cm) diam.
£750–850
$1,000–1,250 ⊞ TGa

> **Miller's is a price GUIDE not a price LIST**

◀ **A George II cast-silver taperstick,** the knopped column on shaped and moulded base, engraved with crest and initials 'P*T', with snuffer, London 1739, 4in (10cm) high, 4.25oz.
£1,300–1,400
$1,900–2,000 ⚒ DN

A pair of George III silver tapersticks, by Emick Romer, London 1764, 7in (13cm) high.
£2,700–3000
$4,000–4,500 ⊞ PAY

► A pair of French silver three-light candelabra, by Jacques-Florent-Joseph Beydel, the armorial-engraved candle branches with flame finials, the bases on paw and leaf supports, Paris c1800, 18½in (47cm) high, 135oz.
£9,000–11,000
$13,000–16,000
🔨 S

A pair of George III silver candle-sticks, by John Carter, nozzles by W. Cafe, London 1768, 11in (28cm) high.
£5,400–6,000
$8,000–9,000 ⊞ PAY

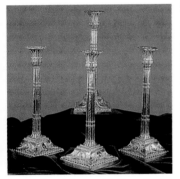

Two pairs of George III silver cluster column candlesticks, one pair by William Cripps, the other by Fenton Creswick & Co, London 1771, 12½in (32cm) high.
£8,000–9,000
$11,500–13,000 🔨 Bon

A pair of Georgian silver four-light candelabra, by William Pitts, London 1809, 8in (20.5cm) high, 415oz.
£22,000–25,000
$32,000–36,000 🔨 S(NY)

A pair of parcel-gilt silver table candlesticks, by L. R. Ruchmann, Paris c1825, 8¼in (21cm) high, 83oz.
£16,000–18,000
$23,000–26,000 🔨 S(NY)

A silver-gilt candlestick, London 1844, 8in (20.5cm) high.
£1,800–2,000
$2,500–3,000 ⊞ DIC

A pair of silver tapersticks, London 1890, 5in (12.5cm) high.
£550–650
$800–950 ⊞ PSA

A pair of Victorian five-light silver candelabra, engraved with two crests and mottos, maker's mark of Robert Garrard, London 1866, 32in (81.5cm) high, 600oz.
£50,000–55,000
$72,500–80,000 🔨 C

A pair of silver candlesticks, Sheffield 1894, 7in (18cm) high.
£1,100–1,300
$1,500–2,000 ⊞ THOM

◄ An Edwardian silver chamber-stick, by Atkin Brothers, Sheffield 1907, 7in (18cm) wide.
£575–650
$800–950 ⊞ ASAA

A set of four leaf-chased silver candlesticks, by Elkington & Co Ltd, Birmingham 1904, 12¾in (32.5cm) high.
£2,000–2,200
$3,000–3,200 🔨 DN

A William IV silver card case, by Taylor & Perry, one side depicts Abbotsford, the home of Sir Walter Scott, the other Newstead Abbey, the home of Lord Byron, Birmingham 1836, 3½in (9cm) high.
£1,700–1,800
$2,500–2,500 ⊞ BEX

An early Victorian silver card case, by Taylor & Perry, with a view of Windsor Castle on one side and Warwick Castle on the other, Birmingham 1838, 4in (10cm) high.
£1,000–1,100
$1,500–1,500 ⊞ PAY

A Victorian silver card case, by Taylor & Perry, engraved, Birmingham 1844, 4in (10cm) high.
£425–475
$600–700 ⊞ PAY

A castle-top silver card case, by Alfred Taylor, depicting King's College Chapel, Cambridge, Birmingham 1859, 4in (10cm) high.
£2,200–2,400
$3,200–3,500 ↗ Bon

An early Victorian silver card case, by Nathaniel Mills, with views of Windsor and Kenilworth Castles, Birmingham 1888, 4in (10cm) high, in original case.
£1,200–1,400
$1,500–2,000 ⊞ PAY

A Victorian silver card case, by George Unite, engraved in the aesthetic style, Birmingham 1879, 4in (10cm) high.
£525–585
$750–850 ⊞ PAY

A Victorian silver card case, by George Unite, highly embossed with flowers and seashells, Birmingham 1882, 4in (10cm) high.
£300–345
$450–500 ⊞ BEX

Items in the Colour Review have been arranged in date order within each sub-section.

A Victorian embossed silver card case, by Staiton Bros, Birmingham 1898, 3in (7.5cm) high.
£100–130
$150–200 ⊞ PAY

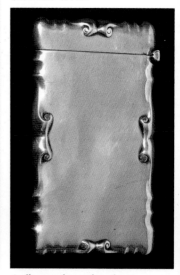

A silver embossed card case, by W. H. Haseler, Birmingham 1908, 3½in (9cm) high.
£150–175
$200–250 ⊞ PAY

A Queen Anne silver sugar caster, by Walter Scott, Assay Master Edward Penman, engraved, Edinburgh 1707–08, 8½in (21.5cm) high, 11.5oz.
£7,500–8,500
$11,000–12,500 ⊞ NS

▶ **A William III silver caster,** by Thomas Brydon, lighthouse-shaped, engraved with armorials above the applied girdle and lobed foot, bayonet lock cover pierced and engraved with vases of flowers below cut card work, baluster finial, London 1698, 8¼in (21cm) high.
£5,500–6,000
$8,000–8,500 ↗ S
The arms are those of Broadhurst.

A George II silver caster, by Samuel Wood, London 1728, 5in (12.5cm) high.
£1,000–1,150
$1,500–1,700 ⊞ JBU

An Edwardian silver cased sugar caster, with a blue glass liner, 7in (18cm) high.
£220–260
$300–380 ↗ SWO

◀ **A Victorian silver owl caster,** by George Unite, London 1867, 3½in (9cm) high.
£550–650
$800–1,000 ↗ P(Ed)

▶ **A silver sugar caster,** of panelled baluster form, beaded banding, Birmingham 1914, 4oz.
£140–180
$200–260 ↗ JAd

A silver-gilt historismus tazza, with vase-shaped stem, c1860, 7in (18cm) diam, 20oz.
£2,400–2,600
$3,500–3,800 ↗ S(G)

A George III silver épergne, by Thomas Pitts, London 1771, 16in (40.5cm) high, 131.5oz.
£20,000–22,000
$29,000–32,000 ↗ S

A George III silver épergne, by Thomas Pitts, the central basket engraved with a coat-of-arms, London 1773, 16in (40.5cm) high.
£35,000–40,000
$50,000–58,000 ↗ C

A George V pierced silver centre-piece, by William Hutton & Son, with applied border of scrolls, London 1910, 9¼in (23.5cm) high.
£3,500–4,000
$5,000–5,800 ↗ B&B

◀ **A Victorian silver centrepiece,** The Goodwood Cup, by R. & S. Garrard, London 1840, 21in (53.5cm) high.
$20,000–25,000
$29,000–36,000 ↗ S

A silver and glass centrepiece, by Bolin, Moscow c1896, 15¼in (38.5cm) high.
£38,000–42,000
$55,000–61,000 ↗ S(G)

An early silver waterproof free-sprung deckwatch, by Herbert Blockley & Co, with up-and-down indication, London No. 31629, in signed mahogany box.
£4,500–5,000
$6,500–7,000 ⚱ C

Two silver pocket watches, one movement signed 'William Eves', the other 'G. & R. Cathro London'.
£500–600
$700–850 ⚱ CSK

A silver pair-cased verge watch, the movement signed 'Forbes & Son', London c1796.
£450–550
$650–800 ⚱ CSK

A Swiss silver-gilt and enamel desk clock, by Henri Capt, c1910, 4in (10cm) high.
£1,600–1,800
$2,300–2,600 ⊞ SHa

▶ **A silver keyless Masonic fob watch,** by Golay, the mother-of-pearl dial painted with inscription, nickel-plated bar movement, bimetallic balance and cabochon winder, 1940s, 2in (5cm) long.
£1,600–1,800
$2,300–2,600 ⚱ C

◀ **A silver-gilt and enamel time-piece,** St. Petersburg, 1908–17, 4¼in (11cm) high, with later fitted case.
£10,000–11,000
$14,500–16,000 ⚱ S(G)

A George II silver cruet set, by George Methuen, the plain hexafoil stand with four leaf-capped scroll and shell supports, six large and six small bottle or box rings, two applied with shaped oval cartouches engraved with armorials, three crested baluster casters, three glass bottles with crested silver caps, six crested cylindrical spice boxes with detachable covers, London 1752, stand 10¾in (27.5cm) high, 110.5oz.
£35,000–40,000
$50,000–58,000 ⚱ S
The arms are those of Agar, Earls of Normanton. This set is the only example known to have six spice boxes.

A pair of George III silver-gilt spice boxes, covers and stands, engraved with crests and an earl's coronet, maker's mark of John Wakelin and Robert Garrard, London 1800, stands 8¾in (22cm) wide, 37oz.
£34,000–38,000
$49,000–55,000 ⚱ C

◀ **An Edward VII seven-piece silver condiment set,** made by C. B., comprising a mustard pot, four salts, two pepper casters and five Onslow pattern spoons, London 1902.
£320–400
$450–580 ⚱ PFK

A three-piece cased silver condiment set, comprising mustard pot and spoon, two peppers, pierced and engraved, Sheffield 1896–97, case 9in (23cm) wide.
£450–500
$650–700 ⊞ GLa

An Edwardian silver cruet set, by
Richard Richardson, Sheffield 1903,
5in (12.5cm) high.
£425–475
$600–700 ⊞ PAY

**An Edwardian oil and vinegar
stand,** by Thomas Bradbury, in the
Adam style, eliptical stand with
pierced fretwork borders, pierced
scroll points, fitted with two faceted
glass bottles, the mounts with hinged
lids and shell-shaped thumbpieces,
London 1902–03, 8¼in (21cm) high.
£360–400
$500–600 ⚹ P(L)

**A silver and glass four-piece cruet
set,** by Deykin & Harrison, Birmingham
1924, 4¾in (12cm) high.
£375–425
$550–600 ⊞ BEX

**A silver mounted novelty oil and
vinegar bottle,** by Hukin & Heath,
modelled as a duck in clear and green
glass, the hinged head set with glass
eyes and scrolled handles modelled
as wings, Birmingham 1931,
9½in (24cm) wide.
£800–1,000
$1,000–1,500 ⚹ Bon(M)

A silver condiment set, by The
Goldsmiths & Silversmiths Co,
London 1938, in a case, case
8 x 11in (20.5 x 28cm).
£550–600
$800–850 ⊞ JBU

A George III silver mustard pot,
by Charles Aldridge & Henry Green,
drum-shape, pierced, dome-shaped
lid, bifurcated thumbpiece, London
1771–72, 3in (7.5cm) high, 3oz.
£1,000–1,200
$1,500–1,750 ⊞ NS

◀ **A Victorian silver mustard pot,**
London 1855, spoon by John Figg,
London 1884, 2in (5cm) high.
£300–350
$450–500 ⊞ CoHA

A George III silver mustard pot, with
pierced decoration and beaded rim,
hinged and domed lid with turned
finial, blue glass liner, later spoon,
maker's mark of William Sutton,
London 1786, 3¾in (9.5cm) high.
£140–180
$200–250 ⚹ Bon(G)

A Victorian silver mustard pot, by
William Richardson, octagonal shape,
engraved and pierced, with an eagle
perched on the lid, London 1871–72,
3¼in (8.5cm) high, 3.75oz.
£600–700
$850–1,000 ⊞ NS

A silver mustard pot, with spoon,
Birmingham 1877, 2½in (6.5cm) high.
£500–550
$700–800 ⊞ AMH

**A novelty Victorian silver mustard
pot,** by Robert Hennell, cast in the
form of Mr Punch, London 1868,
4in (10cm) high, 7oz.
£10,000–11,000
$14,000–16,000 ⚹ S

A pair of Georgian-style silver mustard pots, with hinged lids above plain cylindrical bodies, reeded decoration and scroll handles, maker's mark 'HF', London 1921, one blue liner missing, 2¾in (7cm) high, 12oz.
£160–200
$250–300 ✗ Bon(G)

A pair of George III silver bun pepper pots, with knopped round pedestals, London 1813, 3½in (9cm) high.
£300–350
$450–500 ⊞ GLa

A Victorian sterling silver novelty pepper pot, by George Richards, in the shape of an owl, hallmarks, Birmingham 1854, 3½in (9cm) high.
£1,300–1,500
$2,000–2,200 ⊞ NS

A Victorian silver mustard pot, by George Richards, in the shape of an owl, London 1850–51, 4in (10cm) high.
£4,000–5,000
$5,800–7,000 ⊞ NS

A George II silver pepper pot, by Walter Brind, London 1754, 4¼in (11cm) high.
£360–400
$500–600 ⊞ GLa

A pair of silver pepper pots, Birmingham 1875, 3½in (9cm) high.
£175–200
$250–300 ⊞ CoHA

A Victorian sterling silver novelty pepper pot, by George Unite, in the shape of an owl, Birmingham 1867–68, 3¾in (9.5cm) high.
£850–950
$1,250–1,500 ⊞ SLI
Novelty pepper pots were extremely popular with the Victorians, particularly in the second half of the 19thC. Today these peppers are much sought after but hard to find in good condition.

A pair of George II silver salt cellars, by Edward Wood, embossed with garlands of flowers below shell-fluted rims, on three mask and shell supports, with blue glass liners, London 1748, 7oz.
£400–500
$600–700 ✗ P(L)

A pair of George III silver-gilt boat-shaped open salts, by William Abdy, later decoration, London 1792, 3in (7.5cm) high.
£250–300
$350–450 ⊞ CoHA

▶ **A set of four George III oval silver salts,** by R. H. & D. H., with pierced sides and blue glass liners, on claw and ball feet, London 1771, 3in (7.5cm) diam.
£700–800
$1,000–1,200 ✗ SWO

A silver novelty pepper pot, by Henry William Dee, modelled as Benjamin Disraeli, London 1878–79, 4in (10cm) high.
£5,500–6,500
$8,000–9,500 ⊞ NS

A pair of George III silver salts, London 1786, 2in (5cm) high.
£350–400
$500–600 ⊞ TGa

A set of four George III Egyptian Service silver salts, by Benjamin & James Smith, cauldron form with lion masks on graduated fluting above shield applied leaf-capped paw supports, circular bases hound crested below an earl's coronet with stylized palmette border and panel supports with anthemion ornament, London 1810, 4½in (11.5cm) diam.
£22,000–25,000
$32,000–36,000 ⚒ S
The crest is that of Talbot, Earls of Shrewsbury, for Charles, 15th Earl of Shrewsbury (1753–1827). The design for these salts, like so much early 19thC silver, was derived from Piranesi, in particular a marble antique tripod at Villa dell Emo.

► An early Victorian mustard and salt set, by Barnard & Co, London 1838, 2in (5cm) high.
£540–600
$800–850 ⊞ TGa

A pair of Georgian silver and cut glass salts, by T. Foster, London 1807, 4in (10cm) long.
£600–700
$850–1,000 ⊞ NOR

◄ A set of four silver salts, of circular form on three hoof feet, chased with flowerheads and foliage, engraved with initials, clear glass liner, two by George McHattie, Edinburgh 1814–26, two by J. E., Edinburgh 1819, 10oz.
£470–520
$650–750 ⚒ P(Ed)

A pair of George IV spool-shaped silver salts, by Jonathan Hayne, London 1828, 3½in (9cm) wide, 4oz.
£1,000–1,200
$1,500–1,750 ⚒ DN

A George III salt, by Edward Farrell, on lion mask capped paw feet, gilt interior, London 1814, 3¾in (9.5cm) diam, 7.25oz.
£600–700
$850–1,000 ⚒ P(Sy)

A pair of Victorian silver salts, by Henry Hyams, with matching spoons, London 1863, 1¾in (4.5cm) diam.
£250–300
$350–450 ⊞ CoHA

A set of six George IV silver salts, by Thomas Death, chased with flowers and scrolls, on rocaille and mask supports, London c1820, 4in (10cm) diam, 37oz.
£2,500–3,000
$3,500–4,500 ⚒ S

A pair of silver embossed salts, by William Eley, London 1829, 3½in (9cm) diam.
£700–800
$1,000–1,200 ⊞ DIC

A set of four Victorian cast silver salts, by J. C. Edington, each modelled as a mermaid supporting a large shell, on rock bases, gilt interiors, complete with four salt spoons with shell bowls and putto finials, 1849, 3¼in (8.5cm) high.
£3,800–4,200
$5,500–6,000 ⚒ P

A set of four lily pattern silver salts, by Martin Hall, London 1874, 4in (10cm) diam.
£1,000–1,250
$1,500–1,800 ⊞ AMH

A set of four silver hand-painted salts and spoons, raised on ball and claw feet, London 1901–02, salts 2in (5cm) high, box 8in (20.5cm) long.
£450–500
$650–700 ⊞ GLa

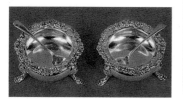

A pair of silver salts and spoons, by Jas Dixon & Sons, with foliate rims, on pad supports, Sheffield 1909–10, 2½in (6.5cm) diam.
£230–260
$300–400 ⊞ WeH

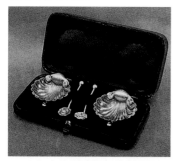

A set of four silver salts and spoons, by Hukin & Heath, London 1883, 3¼in (8.5cm) wide.
£1,000–1,100
$1,500–1,600 ⊞ AMH

A set of four silver salts and spoons, Birmingham 1908, box 17in (43cm) square.
£225–250
$325–360 ⊞ WAC

◄ **A pair of silver shell-shaped salts and spoons,** with gilt interiors, Birmingham 1916, boxed.
£80–100
$120–150 ⚒ PCh

► **Three engraved silver trefid spoons,** and similar forks, late 17thC, 4in (10cm) long.
£800–1,000
$1,200–1,500 ⚒ L

A pair of Victorian silver-gilt double salts and four spoons, by Hunt & Roskell, 1872, the twin shell containers with putti cartouches initialled 'HJ' and applied with winged cherubs, with twig-like stems and shell bowls, stamped 'Hunt & Roskell Late Storr & Mortimer 5940', the spoons by Francis Higgins, 1884, 5½in (14cm) long, 22oz.
£6,000–7,000
$8,500–10,000 ⚒ S

A silver-gilt salt cellar, by William Comyns & Sons, on a dolphin base, London 1960, 4½in (11.5cm) high.
£300–340
$450–500 ⊞ WeH

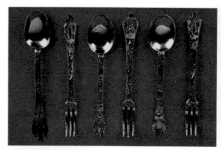

A William and Mary silver filigree *nécessaire,* maker's mark 'HS', London 1694, 4¾in (12cm) long.
£3,250–3,750
$4,500–5,500 ⚒ S(Am)

◄ **A German silver-gilt travelling** *nécessaire,* by Abraham Warnberger IV, egg cup by Johann Jakob Adam, comprising spoon, fork, knife with steel blades and fork with two-prong steel blade, egg cup, marrow scoop and double spice box, Augsburg 1761–63, Austro-Hungarian control marks for the town of Laibach 1806–24, spice box maker's mark indistinct, 10oz, later fitted leather case.
£4,600–5,000
$6,500–7,500 ⚒ S

A silver travelling knife and fork set, with mother-of-pearl handles, engraved 'James Norton', 1822–29, 6in (15cm) long, with original box.
£125–165
$200–250 ⊞ JBU

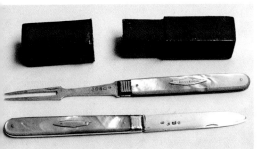

A set of six George IV silver Old English pattern dessert forks, by Barber, Cattle & North, York 1826–27, 6½in (16.5cm) long, 7.35oz.
£680–750
$950–1,000 ⊞ NS

A wooden canteen of silver-gilt dessert cutlery, by John Samuel Hunt, engraved with the crest of the Duke of St. Albans, with contents list on Hunt & Roskell notepaper, London 1862.
£12,000–14,000
$17,500–20,000 ⌲ C

A child's silver spoon and fork set, by Richard Marlin & Ebenezer Hall, registration mark London 1870, 6in (15cm) long, with original box.
£125–145
$200–250 ⊞ BEX

A French silver Fiddle pattern canteen of cutlery, by Jean Emile Puiforcat, comprising 163 pieces, slightly shaped monogrammed Fiddle pattern terminals, Paris early 20thC, 256oz.
£6,000–7,000
$8,500–10,000 ⌲ S

A French silver canteen of cutlery, by Bointaburet, with ribbon-tied reeded pattern, comprising 175 pieces including salad serving spoon and fork, cake lifter, pastry lifter, crumb pan, scoop, nut cracker and pair of sugar nips by other makers in a conforming pattern with different monogram, monogram 'OM', Paris c1900, 298oz, excluding knives with steel blades and nut cracker.
£9,500–11,000
$13,500–16,000 ⌲ S

A German four-piece silver cutlery set, by M. J. Rückert, the fork stamped 'Rückert' and maker's mark, dessert set engraved with monogram 'KW', Mainz 1901, knife 8in (20.5cm) long.
£4,000–4,500
$5,500–6,500 ⌲ S

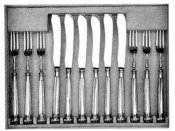

A canteen of Queen's pattern silver cutlery, by The Goldsmiths & Silversmiths Co, comprising 77 pieces including King's pattern butter spade, crested, London 1903, 191oz, in fitted oak case.
£4,500–5,500
$6,500–8,000 ⌲ S

A set of twelve silver dessert knives and fifteen forks, mother-of-pearl handles, shell motif terminals, Sheffield 1913, in a fitted wooden case.
£1,400–1,600
$2,000–2,500 ⌲ Bea(E)

A set of twelve fruit knives and forks, by The Goldsmiths & Silversmiths Co, with silver blades, Sheffield 1923, in wooden case.
£400–600
$600–900 ⌲ SWO

Two silver millennium spoons, designed by John Downes-Hall, limited edition of 50 made, Birmingham 1999, 7in (18cm) long.
£135–150
$200–250 ⊞ CoHA

◀ **A pair of silver second course dishes,** each with coat-of-arms and gadrooned border, maker's mark of George Methuen, London 1757, 16in (40.5cm) diam, 108oz.
£20,000–24,000
$29,000–35,000 ⚒ C

▶ **A George III silver warming pan entrée dish,** by William Pitts, London 1789, 9¾in (25cm) wide.
£3,100–3,450
$4,500–5,000
⊞ BEX

A pair of silver meat dishes and covers, the dishes with maker's mark of Thomas Heming, c1774, the covers William Brown and William Somersall, London 1838, 16in (40.5cm) wide, 171.75oz.
£6,000–6,500
$9,000–9,500 ⚒ S

Miller's is a price GUIDE not a price LIST

A Victorian silver bonbon dish, by William Comyns, London 1889, 4½in (11.5cm) diam.
£270–295
$400–450 ⊞ BEX

A set of 12 Victorian silver dinner plates, by John Hunt & Robert Roskell, London 1873, 9½in (24cm) diam, 222oz.
£7,500–8,500
$11,000–12,500 ⚒ C

A set of nine silver meat dishes, each engraved with the crest of Egerton and coronet, maker's mark of Robert Garrard, London 1857, one 1828, largest 23½in (59.5cm) long, 674oz.
£17,000–19,000
$24,500–27,500 ⚒ C

A Portuguese .833 silver dish, Oporto, c1890, 11¾in (30cm) diam.
£150–165
$200–250 ⊞ BEX

A sterling silver sweetmeat dish, with handle, Sheffield 1895, 7¼in (18.5cm) wide.
£180–200
$250–300 ⊞ WeH

A Victorian chased silver dish, by Elkington & Co, Birmingham 1891, 9in (23cm) long.
£270–300
$400–450 ⊞ PAY

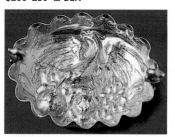

A silver dish, decorated with a bird and foliage, import marks for London 1896, 4in (10cm) wide.
£225–275
$325–400 ⊞ HofB

A Victorian silver bonbon dish, by Richard Martin & Ebenezer Hall, pierced and chased, Sheffield 1897, 9in (23cm) wide.
£350–390
$500–600 ⊞ PAY

An Empire-style silver-gilt breakfast service, by Puiforcat, the fan-shaped dishes and covers each with detachable seated dog finial, Paris, c1900, 16in (40.5cm) diam.
£14,000–16,000
$20,000–23,000 ⚒ C

Condiments

Condiment Sets

A French silver condiment set, comprising an oval sugar bowl and stand, a pair of oval salt cellars and a circular mustard pot, the stand engraved with monogram 'FD' beneath a count's coronet, maker's mark of Antoine Boullier, c1783, bowl 7¾in (19.5cm) wide, 43.75oz.
£3,400–3,600
$5,000–5,250 ⚡ C(G)

A Victorian silver condiment set, by Asprey, modelled as a street lamp and three bollards, the base engraved with initials, in original case, London 1877, 7¾in (19.5cm) high.
£1,750–2,000
$2,500–3,000 ⚡ AH

◄ **A silver seven piece condiment set,** by Walker and Hall, Sheffield 1910, 12in (30.5cm) wide, in a fitted case,
£625–700
$900–1,000 ⊞ CoHA

A pair of German silver novelty condiments each modelled as a donkey, with two panniers strapped to its side, one with English import marks for Chester 1906, one donkey lacking reins, 4¼in (11cm) high, 16.25oz.
£1,800–2,000
$2,600–3,000 ⚡ P

A silver three-piece condiment set, by Charles Boyton, with blue glass liner, London 1933, pepper 2¾in (7cm) high.
£400–450
$600–650 ⊞ BKK

Cruets

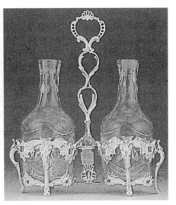

A Belgian silver cruet stand, moulded with matted rococo ornaments, pierced central handle, maker's mark of a crowned shell Stuyck 1612, Brussels 1773, 11in (28cm) wide, 16oz, excluding two associated glass bottles and stoppers.
£1,700–2,000
$2,500–3,000 ⚡ S(G)

Items in the Condiments section have been arranged in date order within each sub-section.

► **A George II silver cruet stand,** with a cartouche, with three casters and two mounted and crested cut-glass oil bottles, maker's mark of Samuel Wood, London 1749, 8¼in (21cm) high, 36oz.
£2,000–2,400
$2,900–3,500 ⚡ Bon

A Queen Anne silver cruet, by Charles Adam, the stepped frame with five pillar supports, scroll handle and simple ring holders, with three casters and glass oil and vinegar bottles with detachable caps, London 1708–09, 7¾in (19.5cm) high, 30.5oz.
£7,000–8,000
$10,500–11,500 ⚡ S

A George II silver cruet stand, by Samuel Wood, with foliate cartouche reserve, with two later cut-glass bottles and stoppers, 1751, 4in (10cm) high, 11oz.
£450–550
$650–800 ⚡ P(O)

A George III silver five-bottle cruet frame, cinquefoil form, central pierced carrying handle, pierced scroll gallery, gadrooned upper border, beaded lower border, with an applied oval cartouche, crested, on five pierced claw and ball feet, with two silver mounted oil jugs and three silver mounted cruet bottles, maker's mark unidentified, London 1770, 9in (23cm) high.
£1,200–1,400
$1,800–2,000 ⚒ Bon

A George III cruet stand, by Robert and David Hennell, containing eight silver topped cut-glass bottles, London c1800, 8in (20.5cm) wide, with a George III mustard spoon.
£1,200–1,400
$1,800–2,000 ⚒ P(S)

A George III cruet stand, the base with floral and leaf repoussé border, on four leaf-cast and shell feet, with five matched bottles, marks rubbed, London, 7½in (19cm) high.
£180–220
$250–350 ⚒ HYD

A George III silver cruet, by John Schofield, London 1792, bottles later, 14¼in (36cm) wide, 25oz.
£500–600
$700–870 ⚒ P(G)

A George III silver cruet, with carrying handle, on four ogee feet and wooden base, hallmarked London 1803, 8in (20.5cm) high, and seven flute-cut bottles with silver tops.
£800–900
$1,200–1,300 ⚒ GAK

A George III silver triangular cruet stand, by Robert Piercy, the stand with a pierced anthemion gallery, cartouche engraved with a stag, containing seven bottles, London 1774, 7in (18cm) wide, 21oz.
£4,500–5,000
$6,500–7,500 ⚒ S

A George III silver cruet stand, by Charles Chesterman, six stoppers with silver mounts, the stand with bands of bright-cut engraving and a monogrammed cartouche, with wooden base, maker's mark 'CC', London 1797, 10¼in (26cm) high.
£650–750
$950–1,100 ⚒ SK

A George III silver four-bottle cruet stand, with central fluted carrying handle, the four silver-mounted cut-glass cruet bottles with shell finials, maker's mark of Paul Storr, London 1806, 11in (28cm) high, 24oz.
£3,000–3,500
$4,500–5,000 ⚒ Bon

A Regency silver cruet stand, by Thomas Robinson, the base engraved with an initial, the frame with four reeded branches linked by rings for the cut-glass bottles and with rests for the stoppers, London 1815, 11¼in (28.5cm) wide.
£220–260
$320–380 ⚒ WW

A **Victorian silver five-cup egg cruet stand** the base shaped as a vine leaf with bifurcated fruiting vine handle, crested at front and raised on openwork vine supports, five egg cups chased with leaves, gilt interiors, five egg spoons with leaf terminals and tendril-wrapped bark stems, stand and cups by Robert Hennell, stand 1850, cups 1847, spoons by Francis Higgins 1850, except one, Birmingham 1883, made to match, 28.75oz.
£700–800
$1,000–1,200 ⚒ **P**

A **silver cruet stand,** with cut-glass bottles, by George Angell, London 1853, 10¾in (27cm) high.
£1,500–1,600
$2,200–2,300 ⊞ **WAC**

A **Victorian silver five-cup egg cruet stand,** by George Fox, circular stand with a pierced and lion mask border within a beaded rim, cups with wrythen piercing and lion mask handles, London 1860, 15.5oz.
£250–300
$350–450 ⚒ **P(E)**

A **Victorian silver seven-bottle cruet set,** on ornate scroll feet, three bottles with silver covers, maker's mark J. E., London 1861, 10¼in (26cm) high.
£650–750
$950–1,000 ⚒ **DDM**

A **Victorian silver cruet stand,** by Robert Harper, with pierced foliate sides and a central scroll-chased loop handle, supporting eight cut-glass bottles, by Robert Harper, with marks for London 1863, 11in (28cm) high, with Fiddle pattern mustard spoon, Exeter 1861.
£1,600–1,800
$2,300–2,600 ⚒ **DN**

◄ A **Victorian silver dinner cruet,** by Elkington & Co, the stand stamped with a frieze of stylized bulrushes, fitted with seven cut-glass bottles including three with silver mounts, Birmingham 1881, 10in (25.5cm) wide, 32oz.
£900–1,100
$1,300–1,600 ⚒ **P(L)**

A **pair of silver cruets,** c1888, 6in (15cm) high.
£450–500
$650–700 ⊞ **OBS**

A **Victorian George III-style silver four-piece cruet set,** by Thomas Hayes, pierced with birds amidst foliage below gadrooned rims, with blue glass liners, Birmingham 1898–1900, 3in (7.5cm) wide.
£550–650
$800–950 ⊞ **HofB**

A **Victorian silver cruet stand,** by Clift Alexander Clark, modelled as a sprig of thistle, the salt, pepper and mustard pots as flowers, with two spoons, London 1894, 4½in (11.5cm) wide, 7oz.
£800–900
$1,200–1,300 ⚒ **S**

► A **pair of novelty silver cruets,** the pepper pot modelled as a chauffeur, pull-off head, wearing goggles, a driving hat and coat, the salt modelled as a woman wearing Welsh national dress including a conical hat, both on filled circular bases, maker's mark of Cornelius Desormeaux Saunders and James Francis Hollings Shepherd, Chester 1906, chauffeur 3½in (9cm) high.
£1,800–2,000
$2,600–2,900 ⚒ **Bon**

A **silver thistle-shaped cruet set,** with original spoons, by Fenton Bros, Sheffield 1922, 6in (15cm) high.
£720–800
$1,000–1,200 ⊞ **THOM**

Mustard Pots

A George III silver mustard pot, by Jabez Daniell and James Mince, London 1768, 3¼in (8.5cm) high, 4oz.
£1,400–1,600
$2,000–2,300 ✦ S(S)

A George III oval silver mustard pot, reeded scroll handle, domed hinged cover with a ball finial, pierced and engraved decoration, beaded border, blue glass liner, maker's mark of Robert Hennell, London 1786, 3in (7.5cm), 3oz.
£380–420
$550–650 ✦ Bon

A late George III silver mustard pot, by Michael Starkey, with chased corder and crest, by Michael Starkey, London 1817, and a Fiddle and Thread pattern spoon by William Chawner II, 1826.
£420–480
$600–700 ✦ DN

▶ **A Victorian owl silver mustard pot,** by George Fox, chased with feathers and gilded around the red and black glass eyes, gilt interior and clear glass liner, complete with the original mustard spoon terminating in a mouse, the spoon sitting in the pot to give an impression of the mouse being held in the owl's beak, 1869, 7.25oz.
£3,500–3,800
$5,000–5,500 ✦ P

A pair of Dutch silver mustard pots, by Harmanus Heuvel, with blue liners and scroll handles applied with vines, hinged covers engraved with the monogram 'G' beneath a crown, one with rose finial, the other with aster finial, Amsterdam 1773, 4in (10cm) high.
£9,000–10,000
$13,000–14,500 ✦ S(Am)

A George III silver mustard pot, London 1789, 2¼in (5.5cm) high.
£450–500
$650–700 ⊞ TGa

A George IV silver mustard pot, by Joseph Angell, engraved with a crest, with blue glass liner, London 1825, 3in (7.5cm) high, 4oz.
£500–550
$700–800 ✦ S(S)

A German silver mustard pot, probably by Emden, lobed baluster form, scroll handle, domed hinged cover with a cone finial and pierced thumbpiece, the whole on a raised lead filled circular foot, with a blue glass liner, 18thC, 5¾in (14.5cm) high.
£1,300–1,500
$2,000–2,200 ✦ Bon

A George III oval silver mustard pot, by Peter, Ann and William Bateman, with thread edging, domed hinged cover with shell thumbpiece, blue glass liner and Old English pattern spoon, London 1804, 3½in (9cm) high.
£360–400
$520–550 ✦ Bea(E)

LOCATE THE SOURCE
The source of each illustration in Miller's can be found by checking the code letters below each caption with the Key to Illustrations, pages 311–314.

A Victorian circular silver mustard pot, by Charles Reily and George Storer, chased and engraved with flowers, leafy scrolls and a monogram, the flat cover with floral finial and foliate scroll handle, on anthemion feet, 1840, and a Fiddle pattern mustard spoon, engraved 'M', 1848, 4¾in (12cm) wide, 6oz, no liner.
£380–420
$570–600 ✦ P(EA)

◄ **A pair of silver mustard pots,** with blue glass liners and original spoons, hallmarked London 1896, 2in (5cm) high.
£450–500
$650–700 ⊞ WN

◄ **A Charles II-style silver mustard pot,** scroll handle, with a girdle of acanthus leaf decoration, hinged cover embossed with a mask, engraved with a coat-of-arms and inscribed 'Merchant Taylors Co. lst Charter 1327', 3¼in (8.5cm) high, 6oz.
£180–220
$260–320 ⚒ Bon

A Britannia standard silver mustard pot, with blue glass liner, London 1903, 5in (12.5cm) wide.
£275–325
$400–470 ⊞ CoHA

Pepper Pots

A George III silver pepper pot, by Thomas Shepherd, c1778, chased later, 5in (12.5cm) high.
£200–250
$300–360 ⊞ PSA

A mid-Victorian silver novelty pepper pot, modelled as a standing owl with red glass eyes, maker's mark of George Richards and Edward Brain, London 1864, 3in (7.5cm) high.
£450–550
$650–800 ⚒ Bon

A Victorian silver pepper caster, by E.H. Stockwell, cast in the shape of a cat, London 1874, 2½in (6cm) high, 2.5oz.
£1,000–1,250
$1,500–1,800 ⚒ CGC

A pair of Victorian cast silver peppers, by H. W. Curley, heavily chased with mythological figures, rams' mask mounts, London 1878, 3in (7.5cm) high.
£1,800–2,000
$2,600–2,900 ⚒ GAK

◄ **A Victorian novelty silver pepper,** modelled as a watering can, pull-off top, maker's mark J. T. in Gothic letters, Sheffield 1888, 3in (7.5cm) high.
£450–550
$650–800 ⚒ P

A silver egg-shaped pepper pot, marked London 1881, 1½in (4cm) high.
£55–65
$80–95 ⊞ VB

A silver pepper pot, by John Aldwinckle and Thomas Slater, in the shape of a fighting cock, London 1888, 3½in (9cm) high.
£420–480
$600–700 ⊞ TC

A pair of Dutch silver pepperettes, modelled as pigs, import mark for London 1895–1904, 4in (10cm) long, 6oz.
£1,200–1,300
$1,700–1,900 ⚒ S(S)

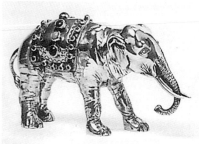

A German silver pepper pot, in the shape of an elephant, the pull-off head revealing a pepperette top, the elephant's back with a blanket set with various coloured pastes imitating gems, c1900, 3¾in (9.5cm) high, 9oz.
£360–400
$500–600 S

A novelty chick silver pepper pot, by William Hornsby, London 1902, 1½in (4cm) high.
£280–320
$400–460 ⊞ TC

A pair of Continental silver pepper casters, bearing Dutch tax marks only, of lobed baluster form chased with scrolls and figures, 19thC, 4¼in (11cm) high, 6.25oz.
£160–200
$230–290 CGC

▶ **A pair of Edwardian silver dog casters,** by William Edward Hurcomb, modelled as West Highland terriers, London 1906, 2¼in (5.5cm) high, 4.5oz.
£1,100–1,300
$1,600–1,900 P(Ed)

A pair of Edwardian novelty silver pepperettes, modelled as milk churns, Birmingham 1903, 1¾in (4.5cm) high.
£150–170
$220–250 ⊞ TVA

A novelty silver pepper, in the shape of a Toby jug with scrolled handle, Birmingham 1911, 3in (7.5cm) high.
£480–530
$700–750 GAK

A silver pepperette, modelled as a smiling cat, Birmingham 1911, 2½in (6.5cm) high.
£350–420
$500–600 RBB

◀ **A Continental silver parrot pepper shaker,** c1925, 3in (7.5cm) high.
£550–650
$800–950 ⊞ DIC

A pair of silver peppers, each modelled as Little Tommy Tucker, marked, Chester 1913, 2½in (6.5cm) high.
£575–650
$850–950 ⊞ SHa

▶ **A pair of novelty silver pepper pots,** in the shape of a pair of fighting cocks, the pull-off heads pierced, standing on textured circular bases, one base damaged, maker's mark of Frederick Charles Britten and Frederick William Britten, London 1919, 3¼in (8.5cm) high.
£220–280
$300–400 Bon

A pair of Norwegian silver peppers, modelled as a penguin and a polar bear, c1940, largest 2½in (6.5cm) high, 1.25oz.
£200–250
$300–360 S(S)

Salts

A set of four George II silver salts, by David Hennell, each engraved with two armorials within cartouches, later clear glass liners, London 1754, 2½in (6.5cm) high, 11oz.
£900–1,100
$1,300–1,600 ⚒ WW

▶ A Dutch silver salt cellar, chased with tulips, flowerheads and leaves, with gilt interior, c1660, 6¼in (16cm) high, 8.5oz.
£2,700–3,200
$3,900–4,700
⚒ S(Am)

A pair of George III two-handled boat-shaped silver salt cellars, by Wilkes Booth, crested, below undulating rims with thread edging, on pedestal supports, over handles, London 1787, 5¼in (13.5cm) high, 6.5oz.
£280–320
$400–470 ⚒ Bea(E)

A set of six George III silver salt cellars, oval form, reeded scroll handles, on raised oval pedestal bases, crested, maker's mark of Henry Chawner, London 1788, 5½in (14cm) long, 18oz.
£1,000–1,250
$1,500–1,800 ⚒ Bon

A pair of George III silver salt cellars, by William Fountain and Daniel Pontifex, of plain navette form below a reeded edge, raised on an oval pedestal foot, engraved with initials, London 1791, 2¼in (5.5cm) high, 3.25oz.
£120–160
$180–230 ⚒ CGC

A set of four George III silver salt cellars, of circular form, reeded borders, on a raised circular foot, gilded bowls, crested, with four silver salt spoons, maker's mark of John Emes, London 1798 and 1804, 3in (7.5cm) diam, 14oz.
£600–700
$870–1,000 ⚒ Bon
The crest is that of Verral.

Salt cellars

Salts are among the most varied and attractive small items of silver. From the late 17th century the most popular type was the trencher salt, of circular, octagonal or triangular form, with a central well. By the 1730s this style had been superseded by the circular cauldron salt cellar on three feet. Many cauldron salts, especially those made between the 1750s and 1780s, were inexpensively, and therefore lightly, constructed and are prone to damage. Condition is vital with salt cellars–the corrosive nature of salt, particularly when damp, means that many salts are corroded or stained with black spots, which reduces the value. Fine quality 20th century condiment sets signed by a renowned craftsman are very desirable, especially if sold in the original cases.

A matched set of four George III silver salt cellars, of shaped rectangular form, incurved corners, reeded borders, gilded bowls on a raised pedestal base, two initialled, one made by Solomon Hougham (the other maker's mark worn), London 1802 and 1803. 3¾in (9.5cm) long, 10oz.
£500–600
$700–850 ⚒ Bon

▶ A pair of George III silver salts, with trellis and foliate pierced sides, blue glass liners, London 1809, 3½in (9cm) long.
£175–200
$250–300 ⚒ GAK

A pair of George III Scottish silver salts, circular on three lion mask and paw feet, gadrooned border, engraved initial 'M', maker's mark of George Fenwick, Edinburgh 1812, 10oz.
£450–500
$650–700 ⚒ **P(Ed)**

A pair of George IV silver salts, by William Elliott, each with shell and leaf scroll rims, above foliate embossed bands, with gilt interiors, 1825, 3¼in (8.5cm) diam, 12oz.
£240–280
$350–400 ⚒ **P(S)**

A set of four late George III silver crested oval salts, by Philip Rundell, with flared rims, gadrooned and leaf scroll and acanthus chased borders, on scroll bracket and angled paw feet, London 1819, 4½in (11.5cm) diam, 28oz.
£1,800–2,000
$2,600–2,900 ⚒ **DN**

A set of four George IV silver table salts, with lobed lower bodies, gadrooned borders and a matching mustard pot, maker's mark 'CE', London 1824, 3½in (9cm) high.
£1,100–1,200
$1,600–1,750 ⚒ **HYD**

▶ **A pair of silver cauldron salts,** with gadrooned rims, embossed and chased rococo cartouches and flowers, rococo scroll feet, gilt interiors, marked 'Storr * Mortimer', London 1830, 3in (7.5cm) diam, 7.5oz.
£420–480
$600–700 ⚒ **P(S)**

A set of three Victorian silver salts, with pierced leaf rims, the sides pierced and chased with animals and fences, each with three shell feet headed by Chinamen, maker I. W., London 1841, 1842 and 1844, 2¼in (5.5cm) diam, 10oz, with liners.
£520–560
$750–800 ⚒ **DN**

▶ **A pair of Victorian silver salts,** with embossed scroll and foliate decoration, gadrooned edging, lion mask and claw-and-ball feet, London 1859, 3½in (9cm) diam.
£300–340
$450–500 ⚒ **Bea(E)**

◀ **A pair of silver salts,** by Robert Hennell, London 1859, 1½in (4cm) high.
£200–250
$300–350
⊞ **CoHA**

A set of four Victorian circular silver-gilt pedestal salts, with wrythen fluted and embossed decoration, maker R. S., London 1860, 2½in (6.5cm) diam.
£400–450
$600–650 ⚒ **GAK**

A pair of Victorian silver salts, by C. T. F. and G. F., shell-shaped, with a pair of shovel-shaped spoons, on three cast hoof feet, gilt lining, 1860, 4¼in (11cm) wide.
£750–900
$1,100–1,300 ⚒ **HYD**

A pair of silver salts, maker M. H. & Co, Sheffield 1862, 2½in (6.5cm) diam.
£180–200
$250–300 ⊞ WAC

A pair of silver and gilt salts, marked 'GM, JM', London 1872, 2¼in (5.5cm) diam.
£90–100
$130–150 ⊞ WAC

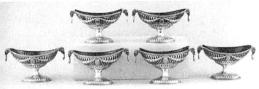

A set of six Victorian salt cellars, by Charles Stuart Harris, with beaded borders and rams' head handles, the pierced sides with swags and husks and paterae, on oval fluted bases, with blue glass liners, London 1880, 5in (12.5cm) wide.
£1,200–1,300
$1,800–2,000 🔨 DN

A composite set of six boat-shaped salts, the wirework sides with swags of drapery, reeded borders, and a matching mustard pot, Birmingham 1924, Chester 1905, London 1905, with blue glass liners, 16.5oz.
£600–700
$850–1,000 🔨 DN

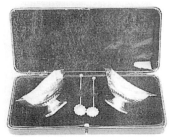

◄ **A set of silver salts and spoons,** Birmingham 1895, salts 3in (7.5cm) wide, in original box.
£120–140
$180–200 ⊞ WAC

► **A set of four silver salts and spoons,** Birmingham 1904–05, salts 2¼in (5.5cm) wide, in original box.
£250–300
$350–450 ⊞ RAC

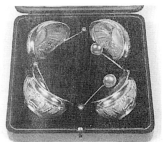

► **A pair of silver and gilt salts,** marked 'M.S.', Birmingham 1917, 5in (12.5cm) high.
£50–60
$75–90 ⊞ WAC

A pair of pierced silver salts, with original green glass liners, Chester 1909, 2in (5cm) high.
£200–230
$300–330 ⊞ CoHA

A pair of silver and gilt salts, Sheffield 1911, 2¼in (5.5cm) diam.
£100–120
$150–180 ⊞ WAC

Corkscrews

A silver and steel pocket corkscrew, c1780, 3in (7.5cm) long.
£575–650
$850–950 ⊞ BEX

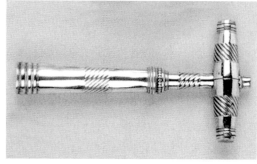

A silver pocket corkscrew, maker's mark of Samuel Pemberton, late 18th/early 19thC, 3¼in (8.5cm) long.
£600–700
$870–1,000 ⚒ Bon

A Dutch silver pocket corkscrew, the handle applied with swags, late 18thC, 3¼in (8.5cm) long.
£1,500–1,800
$2,200–2,600 ⚒ S(S)

l. A silver travelling corkscrew, by Thomas Willmore, with fluted pattern, silver handle and sheath, 1797, 3¼in (8.5cm) long.
£120–150
$175–220
r. A silver travelling corkscrew, by Samuel Pemberton, with fluted pattern mother-of-pearl barrel-shaped handle with silver bands and silver sheath, c1790, 3¼in (8.5cm) long.
£140–160
$200–230 ⊞ CS

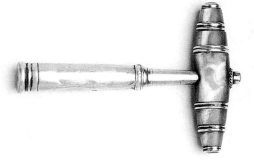

A pocket corkscrew, by Samuel Pemberton, with a barrel-shaped mother-of-pearl handle applied with reeded silver bands, maker's mark on base, Birmingham c1800, 2¾in (7cm) long.
£500–550
$720–800 ⚒ P

◀ **A Victorian silver folding corkscrew,** London 1876, 3in (7.5cm) long.
£360–440
$500–650
⊞ WELD

▶ **A silver fox corkscrew,** with red garnet eyes, hallmarked, 1920, 3½in (9cm) wide.
£220–250
$300–360 ⊞ RTh

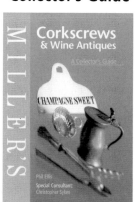

Dishes

A set of four William and Mary silver shell dishes, damaged, marks rubbed, London 1699, 5in (12.5cm) long, 7.5oz.
£2,500–3,000
$3,500–4,500 ⚖ S(NY)

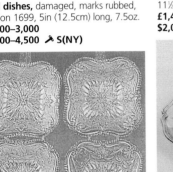

A set of four George IV silver dishes, with waisted sides, embossed beads, foliated scrolls and centre flowerheads, Edinburgh 1824, 6in (15cm) square, 20oz.
£420–480
$600–700 ⚖ AG

A set of four glass dishes on silver stands, with Greek key pattern border, the silver stands with central ball supported on three dolphins, each stand with registry mark for 1864, 17in (43cm) high.
£800–900
$1,000–1,300 ⚖ L

A set of four George II silver fruit dishes, by Edward Lothian, diamond-shaped, embossed with flowers, scale and foliated scrolls, with scroll and shell borders, Edinburgh 1738, 11½in (29cm) wide, 47oz.
£1,400–1,600
$2,000–2,300 ⚖ AG

A silver muffin dish, by Sebastian Crespel, London 1836, 7½in (19cm) diam.
£800–1,000
$1,200–1,500 ⊞ AMH

A pair of late Victorian silver dishes, embossed and chased with medallions of amorini beside trees, maker's mark 'T.S.', London 1882, 6½in (16.5cm) diam, 11oz.
£260–300
$400–450 ⚖ P(F)

Insurance values
Always insure your valuable antiques for the cost of replacing them with similar items, regardless of the original price paid. Both dealers and auctioneers will provide a valuation service for a fee.

◀ **A Victorian silver breakfast roll-top dish with liner,** by Walker and Hall, decorated with shells, applied crest with motto, Sheffield 1891, 15½in (39.5cm) wide, 73.25oz.
£1,250–1,500
$1,800–2,200 ⚖ Bea(E)

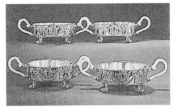

A set of four George IV silver-gilt dishes, the ivory scroll handles with cast foliage terminals, the sides applied in the neo-classical style with rosettes and husk swags and twice with a badge within the Garter motto and below duke's coronet, on four cast foliate scroll feet, maker's mark of Philip Rundell, marked on bases, London 1823, 8½in (21.5cm) diam, 207oz.
£14,000–16,000
$20,000–23,000 ⚖ C
The badge is that borne by the Dukes of Northumberland for Hugh, third Duke of Northumberland. These ivory handled chafing dishes display heraldic medallions with the Percy family badge of a saracenic crescent moon, wreathed by the garter ribbon and surmounted by the Duke's coronet, for Hugh.

An Austrian silver and gilt-embossed dish, decorated with a sacrificial scene within a border depicting the signs of the zodiac, Vienna 1857, 13in (33cm) wide.
£900–1,000
$1,300–1,500 ⚖ RTo

A Victorian silver-gilt dish, by Edward Brown, with a repoussé figure of a maiden amongst a border of flowers and bulrushes, on four scroll feet, London 1892, 8in (20.5cm) long, 6.5oz.
£460–500
$650–700 ⚖ WW

◀ **An oval silver dish,** by D. and A., pierced and decorated with scrolling foliage and gadrooned edge, Birmingham 1892, 8¼in (21cm) long, 11oz.
£200–220
$290–320 ⚒ **Bea**

A pair of Victorian parcel-gilt dishes, by W. Gibon & J. L. Langman, embossed with foliate scrolls, winged putti and flowers, London 1893, 6¾in (17cm) diam, 9oz.
£300–330
$450–500 ⚒ **DN**

▶ **A set of three late Victorian silver-gilt dessert dishes,** by W. J. Connell, the centres decorated with repoussé putti figures, scroll borders, on bun feet, London 1897, 8½in (21.5cm) diam, 28oz.
£2,000–2,400
$3,000–3,500
⚒ **WW**

◀ **An Edwardian silver muffin dish and cover,** with central scroll handle, scroll and shell border, maker's mark of James Dixon & Sons, Sheffield 1906, 8in (20.5cm) high, 14.5oz.
£240–280
$350–400 ⚒ **Bon(C)**

A silver soap dish and cover, with engraved band and trailing flowers, with liner, Ottoman Empire, late 19thC, 6¼in (16cm) long.
£1,100–1,200
$1,600–1,800 ⚒ **P**

▶ **A pair of silver bonbon dishes,** by Nathan & Hayes, Chester 1907, 6in (15cm) diam.
£380–420
$550–600 ⊞ **PSA**

Two silver dessert dishes, by Alfred, James, Francis and Arthur Walter Pairpoint, the open basketwork sides applied with grape vines and a gadrooned edge, on a panelled skirt foot, London 1912 and 1922, 10in (25.5cm) diam, 44.5oz.
£1,800–2,000
$2,600–3,000 ⚒ **WW**

A pair of silver bonbon dishes, by Mappin & Webb, London 1910, 3in (7.5cm) high.
£600–650
$850–1,000 ⊞ **AMH**

◀ **A silver dish,** with twin snake handles, c1911, 10in (25.5cm) wide, 65oz.
£1,200–1,500
$1,800–2,200 ⊞ **PSA**

Auction or dealer?

All the pictures in our price guides originate from auction houses and dealers. Look for the symbol at the end of each caption to identify the source.

When buying at auction, prices can be lower than those of a dealer, but a buyer's premium and VAT will be added to the hammer price. Equally, when selling at auction, commission, tax and photography charges must be taken into account. Dealers will often restore pieces before putting them back on the market.

Both dealers and auctioneers will provide professional advice, so it is worth researching both sources before buying or selling your antiques.

A set of three George V silver dishes, each with knotted dragon and boss band to the rim, Dublin 1920 and 1921, largest 13in (33cm) wide, 71oz.
£1,650–2,000
$2,500–3,000 ⚒ **DN(H)**

Butter Dishes

A set of three George III silver shell-form butter dishes, each engraved with a crest, maker's mark of Henry Green, London 1792, 5¾in (14.5cm) long, 9oz.
£700–850
$1,000–1,300 ⚒ Bon

▶ **A set of six silver and cut-glass butter dishes and knives,** by Mappin & Webb, Birmingham 1906, 14in (35.5cm) wide, in a fitted case.
£225–250
$300–350 ⊞ NAW

A late William IV butter dish, cover and liner, by Edward Barnard & Sons, the frosted glass bowl cut to simulate staved wood, the panelled lift-off cover with cow knop, on a panelled circular base, London 1836, 7in (18cm), 11.5oz.
£900–1,100
$1,300–1,600 ⚒ HSS

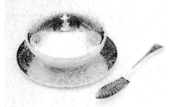

A Victorian silver butter dish, cover, stand and knife, by Edward Barnard & Sons, engraved with fern sprays, London 1875–76, stand 7½in (19cm) diam, together with a cut-glass dish, in a fitted leather case.
£400–440
$580–640 ⚒ Bea

A silver and glass butter dish and knife, by John Thomas Heath and John Hartshorne Middleton, London c1889, 4¾in (12cm) wide, in a lined case.
£400–450
$600–650 ⊞ AMH

Entrée Dishes

◀ **A French circular silver entrée dish and cover,** with foliate borders, the base with two scroll and shell handles, pull-off domed cover with pierced pine cone finial, 10¾in (27.5cm) wide, 28oz.
£250–350
$350–500 ⚒ Bon

Items in the Dishes section have been arranged in date order within each sub-section.

A pair of George III silver entrée dishes with covers and handles, by T. and J. Guest and Joseph Cradock, the covers engraved with armorials, the fluted and foliate-decorated handles on gadrooned circular bases, London 1808, 11½in (29cm) wide, 124.5oz.
£2,000–2,200
$2,900–3,200 ⚒ CSK

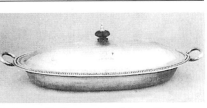

A George III silver entrée dish, by Charles Hougham, the cover with turned wood finial and beaded borders, the base engraved with crests, London 1783, 14¾in (37.5cm) wide.
£1,100–1,300
$1,600–1,900 ⚒ DN

◀ **A set of four George III silver entrée dishes,** by Thomas Robins, with detachable handles to the similar lids, engraved with a crest to both sides of the lid, all parts numbered, London 1809, 11½in (29cm) wide, 295oz.
£5,500–6,500
$8,000–9,500 ⚒ L

▶ **A set of four George III silver entrée dishes and covers,** by William Burwash and Richard Sibley I, detachable handles with foliate decoration, on two-handled warming stands raised on scroll and acanthus leaf bracket feet, terminating in pairs, London 1810, 15in (38cm) wide, 688oz.
£30,000–35,000
$43,000–51,000 ⚒ Bon

◄ **A matched pair of George III silver entrée dishes and covers,** by T. and J. Guest and Joseph Cradock, with gadrooned edging, engraved with a coat-of-arms and decorated with fruit, flowers and scrolling foliage, detachable handles, London 1810, one cover by another maker, marks worn, London 1813, 98.5oz.
£1,500–1,800
$2,200–2,600 🔨 Bea

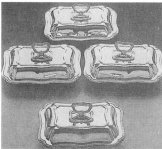

A set of four George III silver entrée dishes and covers, by Thomas Robinson, with gadrooned borders and detachable foliate ring handles, the covers engraved with crests, 1812, 11¾in (30cm) wide, 237oz.
£6,000–6,500
$8,700–9,500 🔨 P

► **A Victorian silver entrée dish and cover,** by Benjamin Smith III, the dish with an oak leaf and acorn chased border, the cover engraved with armorials, the base with a liner, London 1847, 16in (40.5cm) wide, 73.5oz, with a plated stand.
£2,000–2,200
$3,000–3,200 🔨 DN

◄ **A mid-Victorian silver entrée dish,** by Martin Hall & Co, with cover and detachable handle, with bead cast borders, the cover engraved with two oval panels, one engraved 'T' within foliate strapwork, Sheffield 1863, 12in (30.5cm) wide, 52.5oz.
£600–700
$850–1,000 🔨 HSS

A pair of late Victorian silver entrée dishes, by Atkin Brothers, the covers engraved with monograms, with detachable handles, Sheffield 1896, 11in (28cm) long, 113.5oz.
£1,600–1,800
$2,300–2,600 🔨 WW

A set of four Victorian silver entrée dishes, by Harrison Bros and Howson, with shaped reeded and foliate borders, the covers with detachable handles, Sheffield 1895, 11in (28cm) wide, 208oz.
£3,000–3,500
$4,500–5,000 🔨 AG

◄ **A George V-style silver entrée dish,** by James Deakin & Sons, with gadrooned edging, the cover with detachable handle, Sheffield 1918, 12in (30.5cm) wide, 60.5oz.
£550–650
$800–950 🔨 Bea(E)

A pair of silver entrée dishes, by W. H. P., with covers and handles, London 1908, 10in (25.5cm) wide, 80oz.
£1,100–1,200
$1,600–1,800 🔨 SWO

Sweetmeat Dishes

► **A silver sweetmeat dish,** pierced overall with geometric and floral designs, applied floral and scrolled edge, Chester 1895, 4⅛in (11.5cm) wide, 4.5oz.
£200–220
$300–320 🔨 GAK

Cross Reference
See Colour Review
(page 65–66)

An Edward VII silver sweetmeat dish, with rococo-style chased floral and diaper-pierced border, marked 'TL & EM', Chester 1903, 8in (20.5cm) wide, 8oz.
£200–240
$300–350 🔨 PFK

► **A silver sweetmeat dish,** c1910, 10¼in (26cm) wide.
£220–250
$320–360 ⊞ WeH

Dressing Table Accessories

A silver travelling shaving brush, Birmingham 1804, 11in (28cm) long, in a leather case.
£180–200
$250–300 ⊞ HUM

A silver pin tray, by William Comyns, London 1891, 8in (20.5cm) long.
£100–120
$150–175 ⚲ GAK

► **A silver eyebrow brush,** Birmingham 1913, 4in (10cm) long.
£35–45
$50–65 ⊞ ABr

A silver topped rouge pot, Birmingham 1915, 1½in (4cm) high.
£35–40
$50–60 ⊞ PSA

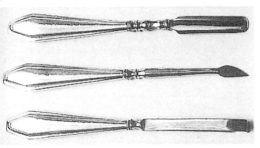

A silver nail file, with decorated handle, Birmingham 1919, 6in (15cm) long.
£22–25
$30–35 ⊞ ABr

◄ **A set of three manicure tools,** with silver handles, Birmingham 1917, 4¾in (12cm) long.
£15–18
$20–25 each ⊞ ABr

Clothes Brushes

A silver-backed clothes brush, Birmingham 1930, 5¼in (13.5cm) long.
£20–25
$30–35 ⊞ ABr

A silver-backed clothes brush, London 1910, 7in (18cm) long.
£20–30
$30–45 ⊞ ABr

◄ **A silver-backed clothes brush,** by Walker and Hall, Sheffield 1955, 6¼in (16cm) long.
£24–28
$35–40 ⊞ ABr

A silver-backed clothes brush, Birmingham 1932, 5¼in (13.5cm) long.
£20–25
$30–35 ⊞ ABr

Dressing Table Sets

► **A George II silver toilet service,** by John White, comprising ten pieces, each piece either engraved with arms or a crest, flat chased with shells, rocaille and diaper, later parts by Edward Farrell, London 1734, casket 10½in (26.5cm) wide, 227oz.
£180,000–200,000
$260,000–290,000 ⚲ S

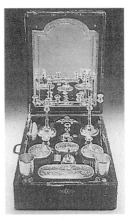

► **An Austrian silver dressing table set,** by J. C. Klinkosch, comprising 27 pieces, engraved with scrolling foliage around monogrammed initials 'ATH', Vienna c1870, inscribed 'J. C. Klinkosch', 23in (58.5cm) wide, in a fitted leather-bound wood case.
£7,000–8,000
$10,500–11,500 ⚲ S(G)

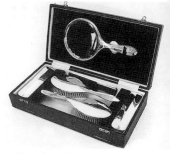

◀ **A Liberty Cymric silver dressing table set,** comprising a hand mirror, hairbrush, clothes brush and a comb, some marks worn, marked 'L&Co', Birmingham 1904, mirror 11in (28cm) long
£600–700
$850–1,000 ⚲ P

A William Hutton and Sons six-piece silver dressing table set, designed by Kate Harris, comprising a hand mirror, two clothes brushes, two hair brushes and a tray, stamped in relief with a young woman in modest nightclothes, framed by stylized lilies, stamped marks, London 1901–02.
£1,800–2,000
$2,600–2,900 ⚲ CSK

Items in the Dressing Table Accessories section have been arranged in date order within each sub-section.

▶ **A silver-gilt dressing table set,** comprising 23 pieces, chased and engraved in the chinoiserie style, each fully marked and engraved 'Callow of Mount Street, London W.', 1914, Britannia standard, mirror 25in (63.5cm) high, 97oz.
£6,500–7,200
$9,500–10,500 ⚲ C

A five-piece silver-backed dressing table set, comprising hand mirror, two clothes brushes and two hair brushes, Birmingham 1928–29, 15in (38cm) wide, in original case.
£150–180
$220–260 ⚲ GAK

Dressing Table Tidies

A rococo silver, silver-gilt, porcelain and polished steel-mounted Girl in a Swing dressing table casket, surmounted by an arched triple looking glass with folding doors, opening to reveal the crimson velvet lined fitted interior, perhaps from the St James's factory of Charles Gouyn, some slight damage, c1755, casket 10½in (26.5cm) wide, contained in a padded pale blue cotton lined wood box covered in black cotton.
£365,000–375,000
$530,000–540,000 ⚲ C
The recent discovery of this magnificent casket adds significantly to the knowledge of the productions currently attributed to the Girl in a Swing factory. It was undoubtedly a special commission, and a *tour de force* of the jeweller's craft. The presence of the hitherto unrecorded Girl in a Swing rococo plaques made specifically for it, and the contents including Girl in a Swing scent bottles and *étui*, strongly point to Charles Gouyn of Bennet Street, St James's, London, as the assembler. Very little is known about the Girl in a Swing factory, except that it existed from 1749–54 and was probably located in London.

A silver dressing table tidy, London 1895, 7½in (19cm) long.
£350–375
$500–560 ⊞ WN

A silver and glass bottomed dressing table tidy, c1903, 3in (7.5cm) long.
£60–80
$90–120 ⊞ WN

A Continental enamelled dressing table box, import mark for London 1904, 3½in (8.5cm) long.
£800–1,000
$1,200–1,500 ⚲ Bea

▶ **A silver dressing table box,** the top pierced with floral and foliate designs, Chester 1910, 6in (15cm) wide.
£320–360
$450–550 ⚲ GAK

A silver dressing table tidy, Birmingham 1902, 5½in (14cm) long.
£250–300
$350–450 ⊞ WN

A pair of silver and glass bottomed dressing table boxes, Birmingham 1903, 4in (10cm) long.
£120–140
$170–200 ⊞ WN

An Edwardian silver dressing table box, by H. Matthews, the hinged cover with a tortoiseshell panel decorated with ribbons and festoons, Birmingham 1909, 5in (12.5cm) wide.
£300–325
$450–475 ⚲ Bea

Hair Brushes & Combs

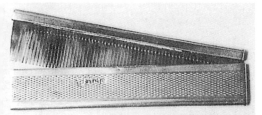

◄ **An engine-turned silver comb and holder,** Birmingham 1927, 3½in (9cm) long.
£35–40
$50–60 ⊞ ABr

A Victorian baby's silver-backed brush, by C. Saunders and F. Shepherd, Birmingham 1900, 3½in (9cm) wide
£50–60
$75–90 ⊞ BEX

► **A silver hairbrush,** by Wilson and Sharpe, with yellow enamel back, Edinburgh 1931, 9in (23cm) long.
£50–60
$75–90 ⊞ JACK

A silver-backed hairbrush, Birmingham 1933, 9½in (24cm) long.
£15–20
$20–30 ⊞ ABr

◄ **A pair of silver hair brushes,** with green enamel backs, Birmingham 1934, 9in (23cm) long.
£90–110
$130–160 ⊞ JACK

A silver-backed tortoiseshell comb, by Walker and Hall, Sheffield 1955, 6¾in (17cm) long.
£30–40
$45–60 ⊞ ABr

Nail Buffers

◄ **Three silver nail buffers,** marked Birmingham 1899, 1904 and 1910, largest 3½in (9cm) long.
£40–50
$60–75 each ⊞ VB

A silver nail buff with handle, Birmingham 1919, 3½in (9cm) long.
£35–45
$50–65 ⊞ ABr

An engine-turned silver nail buff, Birmingham 1930, 4in (10cm) long.
£30–35
$45–50 ⊞ ABr

Dressing table sets

Dressing table sets, sometimes fitted in wooden travelling cases, were made throughout the late 19th and early 20th centuries. They succeeded the earlier lavish toilet sets that from the late 17th century were essential luxuries for noblewomen and very often presented to them by their husbands on their marriage or on the birth of an heir. Most comprised a silver-backed hand mirror and hairbrushes, and often contained scent bottles with silver mounts, clothes brushes, combs and shoehorns. Larger sets could also include eye-baths, jewel-caskets, and pomade jars. The items were engine-turned, enamelled or embossed, and most were engraved. Some elaborate examples featured secret compartments. Prices vary according to the number of items in a set, the extent of the decoration and the condition.

◄ **An engine-turned silver nail buff,** with Art Deco design, Birmingham 1934, 3½in (9cm) long.
£22–26
$30–35 ⊞ ABr

Egg Stands

A silver egg stand, Sheffield 1818, 9in (23cm) high.
£1,000–1,200
$1,500–1,800 ⊞ DIC

A George IV silver egg stand, by Edward Barton, with central foliate carrying handle and pierced leaf spoon holders, 1829, the spoons of Fiddle pattern engraved with crests, by William Troby, 1828, 8in (20.5cm) diam, 30oz.
£700–800
$1,000–1,200 ⚒ P(EA)

A four-piece silver egg stand, Sheffield 1901, 7½in (19cm) high.
£350–400
$500–600 ⊞ PSA

> **Miller's is a price GUIDE not a price LIST**

Goblets & Cups
Cups

A Charles II silver tumbler cup, by Thomas Mangy, York 1677, 2in (5cm) high, 4oz.
£4,000–4,500
$5,800–6,500 ⚒ P(L)

A William and Mary silver tumbler cup, by Robert Timbrell, with engraved initials, 1700, 2½in (6.5cm) diam, 2.75oz.
£3,200–3,500
$4,500–5,000 ⚒ P

A Queen Anne silver cup, by John Rand, with cast scroll handle, marked with initials, London 1708, 3¼in (8.5cm) high, 8.5oz.
£4,000–4,500
$5,800–6,500 ⚒ HAM

> ## Tumbler cups
> Tumbler cups are beaten and raised from thick gauge silver with most of the weight in the base so that the cups return to an upright position when put on their side. Because they are so solid they are almost impossible to damage. Most date from the late 17th century, but they were also made throughout the 18th century. Early cups tend to be short and very broad in relation to their height; later examples are taller and thinner. Most are of plain design, but because they are very tactile objects they are popular with collectors today.

◄ **A George II Provincial two-handled silver cup,** by John Langlands and John Goodrick, with leaf-capped scroll handles, engraved with a coat-of-arms within a rococo cartouche, on moulded circular foot, Newcastle 1755, 7in (18cm) high, 31oz.
£1,800–2,200
$2,600–3,200 ⚒ C
The arms are those of Cookson impaling another.

A George III silver cup, by John Payne, with reeded girdle and scroll handles with heart-shaped terminals, London 1762, 5¼in (13.5cm) high, 11.25oz.
£280–320
$400–450 ⚒ Bea(E)

> **Cross Reference**
> See Colour Review (page 113)

A silver stirrup cup, by Tudor and Leader, modelled as a fox's head, gilt interior, Sheffield 1777, 5in (12.5cm) long.
£3,200–3,500
$4,500–5,000 ⚒ S(S)

A George III silver cup, by Hester Bateman, with a moulded girdle, later initials 'JAM' within a wreath, on a moulded spreading base, London 1782, 6½in (16.5cm) high, 12.5oz.
£500–550
$700–800 ⚒ DN

A set of 12 Victorian silver tumbler cups, by Arthur Sibley, engraved with the arms of Wakeham of Coton Hall, Co. Salop, 58oz, retailed by Gilliam, Serle St, London, London 1853, in a fitted baize-lined oak case.
£9,000–10,000
$13,000–14,500 ⚒ WW

A silver presentation three-handled loving cup, by Edward Barnard & Sons, with chased strapwork and raised on three ball feet, maker's mark, London 1873, 8in (20.5cm) high, 41oz.
£600–700
$870–1,000 ⚒ AH

Stirrup cups

These are drinking vessels in the form of an animal's head, without a handle or base, used by riders before hunting. They were first made in the 1770s, usually in the shape of a fox's head but from the 1780s onward appeared in the form of the head of a boar, foxhound, greyhound or stag.

▶ **A German silver stirrup cup,** modelled as a fox's head, c1880, 6in (15cm) high.
£1,300–1,500
$1,900–2,200 ⊞ SFL

Covered Cups

A William III silver two-handled cup and cover, by Matthew West, the lower body gadrooned and fluted, with decorative stamped leaves and stylized flowerheads, fully marked, London 1699, 5¾in (14.5cm) high, 18.75oz.
£4,500–5,000
$6,500–7,250 ⚒ S(NY)

An American silver spout cup and cover, by Samuel Vernon, the wide baluster body with slender swan-neck spout swelling at the base, scroll handle, moulded rim and raised foot, stepped domed cover with baluster finial, base engraved with initials 'M*B' and 'A' above 'C*B', Newport, RI, c1730, 6¼in (16cm) high, 14.5oz.
£52,000–60,000
$75,000–87,000 ⚒ S(NY)

◀ **An silver covered cup,** the cover and sides with pebbled decoration, engraved with foliage and floral cartouches, and an associated Egyptian saucer, Ottoman Empire, early 20thC, 5in (12.5cm) high.
£400–500
$600–700 ⚒ P

A Queen Anne silver cup and cover, London 1712, 9½in (24cm) high, 40oz.
£3,000–3,500
$4,000–5,000 ⚒ HYD

Auction or dealer?

All the pictures in our price guides originate from auction houses and dealers. Look for the symbol at the end of each caption to identify the source.

When buying at auction, prices can be lower than those of a dealer, but a buyer's premium and VAT will be added to the hammer price. Equally, when selling at auction, commission, tax and photography charges must be taken into account. Dealers will often restore pieces before putting them back on the market.

Both dealers and auctioneers will provide professional advice, so it is worth researching both sources before buying or selling your antiques.

Goblets

A silver-mounted ostrich egg goblet, indistinct maker's mark on rim, probably early 17thC, 11½in (29cm) high.
£11,000–13,000
$16,000–19,000 ⚒ C

A silver-mounted coconut goblet, by Matthew Boulton and John Fothergill, Birmingham 1776, 7½in (19cm) high.
£1,000–1,200
$1,500–1,800 ⊞ AMH

A George III goblet, by Henry Chawner, with bands of etched lines and a monogram within a cartouche, on round reeded foot, inscribed beneath 'MB to TB', London 1792, 5.5oz.
£500–550
$700–800 ⚒ DN

A George III silver goblet, plain urn-shaped bowl, on a raised circular foot with a beaded border, crested, maker's mark of William Brockwell, London 1781, 5½in (14cm) high, 7oz.
£550–600
$800–870 ⚒ Bon
The crest is that of Cove of Herefordshire.

A silver-mounted coconut wine goblet, on a hollow trumpet base, maker's mark 'H' over 'T', 18thC, 5in (12.5cm) high.
£500–550
$700–800 ⚒ TMA

A silver-mounted carved coconut goblet, London 1802, 6in (15cm) high.
£900–1,000
$1,300–1,500 ⊞ DIC
Items such as this would probably have been imported by sailors who carved the coconut shells themselves. The cups would then be mounted in silver and sold in the UK.

▶ **A pair of George III silver goblets,** by Robert and Samuel Hennell, with part-fluted bowls and gilt interiors, on gadrooned foot-rims, London 1806, 6½in (16.5cm) high, 17.75oz.
£700–800
$1,000–1,150 ⚒ P(S)

A pair of George III silver goblets, by Thomas Wallis and Jonathan Hayne, the ogee bowls part lobed and fluted below moulded girdles and rims, with threaded stems gilt interiors, engraved monogram, 1816, 6½in (16.5cm) high, 18oz.
£1,000–1,200
$1,500–1,800 ⚒ P(S)

A pair of silver goblets, by Robert Hennell, the sides embossed with a gamekeeper, hounds and pheasants, 1860, 7in (18cm) high, 23.25oz.
£1,700–2,000
$2,500–3,000 ⚒ P

A William IV silver-gilt goblet and stand, the bell-shaped cup applied with flowers and thistles, on a moulded base, the shallow dish-shaped stand with a border of trailing vine leaves, maker's mark of John Bridge, London 1830, stand with maker's mark of William Bateman for Rundell Bridge & Co, London 1836, 15½in (39.5cm) high, 106oz.
£3,600–4,200
$5,200–6,000 ⚒ Bon

◀ **A mid-Victorian silver goblet,** the bowl supported by an ivy leaf and branch stem, on a raised circular base with beaded border, maker's mark of Stephen Smith, London 1869, 8in (20.5cm) high, 10.5oz.
£550–650
$800–950 ⚒ Bon

Inkstands

A George II silver inkstand with three divisions, by Paul Crespin, engraved with armorials, with reeded border, supporting a cylindrical pounce pot and inkwell and central combination bell/taperstick/seal, each engraved with a crest, the seal with armorial intaglio, the bell without maker's mark, the taper sconce unmarked, the seal and clanger with lion passant only, London 1728, 12in (30.5cm) wide, 48oz.
£8,000–10,000
$11,600–14,500 ⚒ Bea
The arms and crest are those of Cary.

A George III silver partners' inkstand, by Richard Morton & Co, with blue cut-glass bottles, two with pierced silver covers, the third engraved with a crest above a motto, Sheffield 1775, 9½in (24cm) wide, 12oz.
£800–1,000
$1,200–1,500 ⚒ WW

A George III silver inkstand, by John and Thomas Settle, Sheffield c1818, 5in (12.5cm) wide.
£1,200–1,400
$1,800–2,000 ⊞ WELD

A Victorian silver inkstand, by Yapp and Woodward, the border stamped with trailing flowers, the two amber glass pots with flower embossed covers, on oak leaf bracket feet, damaged, Birmingham 1846, 8in (20.5cm) wide.
£700–800
$1,000–1,200 ⚒ DN

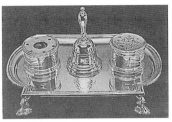

A George II silver inkstand, by Thomas Farren, engraved with the arms of King with a crescent for difference, on volute and pad feet, fitted with inkwell, pounce pot and bell, the fittings unmarked, London 1733, 12½in (32cm) wide, 62oz.
£16,000–18,000
$23,000–26,000 ⚒ S
The arms of King are for Peter King (1709–54), second son of Lord Chancellor King.

A George III silver inkstand, by John Emes, with two pen wells, on anthemion cast scrolling feet, three original cut-glass and silver topped bottles for pounce, quills and ink, London 1806, 10in (25.5cm) wide, 20oz.
£1,100–1,200
$1,600–1,800 ⚒ J&L
Pounce is a fine powder used for drying ink.

A silver inkstand, by William Elliott, with pierced panels of urns flanked by lions and bacchic heads, the top with two pen trays, engraved with arms and motto, on paw feet, marked, London 1819, 12¼in (31cm) wide, 103oz.
£13,000–15,000
$19,000–22,000 ⚒ S(NY)

A George IV silver partners' inkstand, by Samuel Roberts and George Cadman & Co, the base on winged foliate paw feet, Sheffield 1822, 11½in (29cm) wide, 30oz.
£1,400–1,600
$2,000–2,300 ⚒ WW

A George III silver inkstand, by Samuel Herbert, London 1765, 10in (25.5cm) wide.
£1,700–1,900
$2,500–2,800 ⊞ TGa

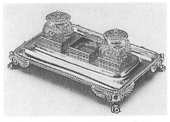

A George III three-division silver inkstand, by Thomas and Joseph Guest and Joseph Cradock, with gadrooned edging, on four winged paw feet, supporting three basketwork frames and two silver topped cut-glass wells, date letter removed, London c1809, 10in (25.5cm) wide, 26.5oz.
£550–750
$800–1,100 ⚒ Bea

A George IV silver standish, by Rebecca Emes and Edward Barnard, on four leaf-scrolled feet, with two pots for ink and pounce, together with taperstick, snuffer and stand, London 1821, 9¾in (25cm) wide, 25oz.
£1,300–1,500
$1,900–2,200 ⚒ J&L

A George IV silver inkstand, by John and Thomas Settle, the bold gadrooned borders with flowerhead and acanthus angles, two pen depressions and two silver mounted hobnail-cut glass wells, the central wafer box with taperstick and conical extinguisher, crested, on shell and acanthus paw feet, Sheffield 1821, 12in (30.5cm) wide, 54oz.
£2,400–2,600
$3,500–3,800 ⚒ N

A Victorian parcel-gilt inkstand, by Henry Wilkinson, the base with foliate and scroll border, on four pierced scroll feet, raised centre section for the shaped square silver-mounted bottles flanking the central melon-shaped wafer box, supporting a taperstick with double scroll handle and extinguisher and detachable nozzle, Sheffield 1846, 13½in (34.5cm) wide, 36.5oz without ink bottles.
£2,200–2,500
$3,200–3,600 ↗ L

A Victorian silver partners' inkstand, by Charles T. and George Fox, with a pierced fretwork crested gallery, a shaped gadrooned edge, three pierced fret tapering inkwells, engraved hinged covers, one crested, fitted with blue star-cut base glass liners, the corners with cast leaf spray knurled feet, London 1851, 11in (28cm) wide, 29oz.
£1,300–1,500
$1,900–2,200 ↗ WW

A silver inkstand, by George Fox, with original cut-glass bottles, London 1882, 9½in (24cm) wide.
£2,200–2,450
$3,200–3,500 ⊞ THOM

A Victorian silver-mounted tortoiseshell inkstand, with foliate pierced gallery, two silver-mounted glass inkwells with central box and a silver-mounted tortoiseshell paper knife, engraved with monogram, the stand engraved 'Asprey & Sons' 166 New Bond Street', 1885, 9in (23cm) wide.
£1,800–2,000
$2,600–2,900 ↗ C

A Victorian silver boat-shaped inkstand, engraved with a mermaid crest, with two pen trays and two moulded globular glass inkwells with silver covers, the central pierced container holding a cranberry glass jar and surmounted by an embossed taperstick with extinguisher, Birmingham 1846, 13½in (34.5cm) wide, 21oz.
£1,700–2,000
$2,500–3,000 ↗ P(EA)

A silver presentation inkstand, the tray engraved with scrolls, with two silver-mounted faceted glass inkwells with hinged lids and a taperstick, damaged, London 1856, 10in (25.5cm) wide.
£300–350
$450–500 ↗ GAK

A silver inkstand, by Richard Hennell, with engraved foliate scroll decoration and initials, two silver-mounted cut-glass inkwells and a taperstick, maker's mark 'R.H.', London 1869, 8½in (21.5cm) wide, 9oz.
£425–500
$600–700 ↗ MCA

A Victorian silver inkstand, by Henry Wilkinson & Co, with two silver-mounted cut-glass pots and a central chamber taperstick with scroll handle and snuffer, on bracket feet, London 1891, 10½in (26.5cm) wide, 16.25oz.
£1,600–1,800
$2,300–2,600 ↗ DN

A Victorian silver inkstand, in the shape of a scallop shell with mermaid figure handle, shell finial and rocky base, London 1848, 5in (12.5cm) wide.
£1,450–1,650
$2,100–2,500 ↗ RBB

A silver inkstand, by Henry Wilkinson & Co, the base pierced with scrolls and diaper, with two silver-mounted faceted glass bottles and a taperstick, Sheffield 1860, 9½in (24cm) wide, 17oz.
£320–385
$450–570 ↗ P(L)

A silver inkstand, by William Smily, engraved with a border of C-scrolls, acanthus leaves and stylized motifs, with two silver-mounted faceted glass bottles and detachable taperstick, 1865, 11¾in (30cm) wide, 31.25oz.
£1,300–1,500
$1,900–2,200 ↗ P

A silver inkstand, with two cut-glass and silver-mounted bottles, base probably originally a snuffer's tray, marked, c1890, 8¾in (22cm) wide.
£275–325
$400–470 ↗ L

Condition

The condition is absolutely vital when assessing the value of an antique. Damaged pieces on the whole appreciate much less than perfect examples. However a rare desirable piece may command a high price even when damaged.

A Victorian silver novelty inkstand, by Heath and Middleton, modelled as an envelope, the inkwell with clear glass liner and pen rests, a smaller rest holding a seal with uncut matrix, a match holder and a taper holder engraved 'The Gift of the Queen to William Boyd, Bishop of Ripon, Xmas 1893', also engraved with a patent registration number, Birmingham 1892, 7½in (19cm) wide, 16.75oz.
£750–850
$1,000–1,250 ⚱ CSK

▶ **A silver inkstand,** by Carrington, with two crystal inkwells, London 1893 and 1895.
£1,500–1,700
$2,200–2,500
⚱ LRG

A silver partners' inkstand, by Charles Stuart Harris, with gadrooned borders, pierced foliage scroll border motifs, a central sealing wax box, the cover as a taperstick with extinguisher, flanked by two glass ink bottles with hinged silver covers, on ball feet, London 1898, 9½in (24cm) wide, 26oz.
£1,200–1,400
$1,800–2,000 ⚱ WW

An Edwardian silver standish, by Walker and Hall, with a cast openwork three-quarter gallery of foliate scrolls, monogammed cartouche and an inscription, with silver-mounted cut-glass inkwells and scroll pen holder, Sheffield 1901, 12¾in (32.5cm) wide, 43oz.
£1,350–1,500
$2,000–2,200 ⚱ P(C)

A silver inkstand, by Gibson and Langman, with pierced fret gallery, a pair of cut-glass inkwells on a satin-wood base with chased panel feet, London 1896, 12in (30.5cm) wide.
£620–680
$900–1,000 ⚱ WW

An Edwardian silver desk standish, by Martin Hall & Co Ltd, on four pad feet, Sheffield 1908, 14in (35.5cm) wide, 36oz.
£600–700
$870–1,000 ⚱ HSS

A silver presentation inkstand, the stamp box flanked by square cut-glass ink bottles, on ball-and-claw feet, London 1913, 11in (28cm) wide, 13oz.
£620–680
$900–1,000 ⚱ AH

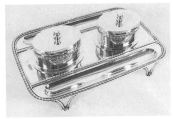

An Edwardian silver inkstand, by The Goldsmiths & Silversmiths Co, the two inkwells with clear glass liners between two depressions for pens, London 1903, 8½in (21.5cm) wide, 19oz.
£600–720
$870–1,000 ⚱ GAK

▶ **A George V silver inkstand,** with two silver-mounted cut-glass inkwells, inscribed, maker's mark 'B.B SLs', Birmingham 1935, 8¾in (22cm) wide, 13oz.
£350–420
$500–600 ⚱ Bea(E)

An 18thC-style silver ink standish, by The Goldsmiths & Silversmiths Co, on lion's paw feet, with central swing handle, one hinged cover engraved with the monogram of King George V with a crown above, the other with the Royal Armorial and motto within a garter cartouche with crown surmount, fitted with a cut-glass inkwell and a pierced pounce box, London 1931, 11in (28cm) wide, 71oz.
£1,800–2,100
$2,600–3,000 ⚱ CSK
A contemporary newspaper clipping suggests that this inkstand was presented to Lord Rothschild, chairman of the Royal Commission on Gambling. The other members of the Commission were given scarlet or black leather covered despatch boxes, each bearing the Royal Cypher.

Silver inkstands

Seventeenth-century inkstands were rectangular caskets containing an inkpot, pounce-pot (for pounce or sand used to dry ink) and a wafer-pot (containing wax disks for sealing letters). By the 18th century most inkstands consisted of a rectangular silver tray on four feet, usually with an inkpot and pounce-pot, together with a taperstick for melting sealing wax, or a small handbell. They were generally plain, except for the moulded scroll and shell or beaded rims and decorative feet. Glass pots with detachable silver mounts came into fashion from the mid-18th century, along with rectangular trays with pierced galleries to hold the pots. Many inexpensive inkstands were mass-produced in thin-gauge silver and Sheffield plate in the late 18th and 19th centuries.

Inkwells

A silver novelty inkwell, in the shape of an Infantry officer's seal-skin cap, the hinged top with applied filigree bullion, a detachable pen forming the plume, the sides and front embossed with bugle motifs and cap lines or cords, buckled chin strap, and glass liner with hinged cover, 3½in (9cm) high, 4oz.
£1,400–1,600
$2,000–2,300 ⚒ S(S)

A silver scallop-shaped inkwell, by Pairpoint Brothers, in the shape of a James I spice box, the cover with chased decoration and egg-and-dart flange border, engraved with initials, on shell feet, overstruck by D. and J. Wellby, London 1922, 5in (12.5cm) wide, 20.25oz.
£500–600
$700–870 ⚒ WW

A Victorian early 18thC-style silver inkwell, by Edward Barnard & Sons, with a pewter capstan-shaped well and a ring of quill holders, London 1890, 2in (5cm) high.
£300–350
$450–500 ⊞ HofB

A silver inkwell, by Edward Ker Reid, the lozenge-faceted glass bottle with floral embossed domed cover, London 1856, 7in (18cm) wide.
£375–425
$550–600 ⊞ WeH

A Victorian silver inkwell, with gadrooned borders, embossed with birds, foliate scrolls, flowers and two moustached masks, the hinged lid engraved with a monogram, marked with a lion and date letter only on the bar restraining the cut-glass jar, 4½in (11.5cm) diam, 4.5oz.
£300–340
$450–500 ⚒ P(EA)

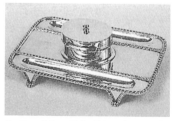

A silver inkwell, by Edward Barnard & Sons, with gadrooned edge, London 1905, 5in (12.5cm) wide.
£750–825
$1,100–1,200 ⊞ THOM

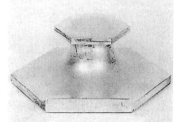

A silver capstan inkwell, by Walker and Hall, the front curved for a pen rest, with a hinged cover, Sheffield 1926, 10½in (26.5cm) wide.
£250–300
$350–450 ⚒ P(EA)

A Victorian silver inkwell, London 1894, 2in (5cm) high.
£325–375
$450–550 ⊞ TGa

Prices

The price ranges quoted in this book reflect the average price a purchaser might expect to pay for a similar item. The price will vary according to the condition, rarity, size, popularity, provenance, colour and restoration of the item, and this must be taken into account when assessing values. Don't forget that if you are selling it is quite likely that you will be offered less than the price range.

A Victorian silver inkwell and sunk centred tray, by Francis Boone Thomas, all on three scrolling bracket feet, marked London 1886, 9½in (24cm) diam, 14oz.
£600–700
$870–1,000 ⚒ DA

A silver-mounted glass inkwell, by J. C. Vickery, the cover with inset watch, the front with aperture for calendar cards, London 1906, 4½in (11.5cm) square.
£500–550
$700–800 ⚒ S(S)

Jewellery

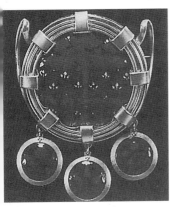

A silver-gilt and enamel ornament, by George Frampton, with bright green trees and flowers on a blue ground, for use as a buckle, pendant or brooch, 1898, 3¼in (8.5cm) diam.
£10,000–12,000
$14,500–17,500 ⚒ C

> Items in the Jewellery section have been arranged in date order within each sub-section.

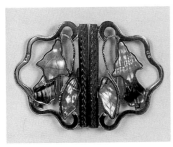

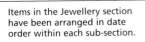

A silver pierced and engraved buckle, by Marshall Brothers, inset with purple, yellow and cream mother-of-pearl, Birmingham 1910, 3½in (9cm) wide.
£300–325
$450–470 ⊞ TC

◄ A pair of silver and foiled rose diamond openwork panel drop earrings.
£800–1,000
$1,200–1,500
⚒ CSK

► A silver and steel teddy tie pin, by Adie and Lovekin, Birmingham 1909, 3in (7.5cm) long.
£145–165
$200–250 ⊞ BEX

A pair of silver and paste drop earrings, late 1920s, 3in (7.5cm) long.
£225–250
$320–360 ⊞ JSM

► A silver ball tongue stud, from the mouth of Scary Spice, 1990s, 1in (2.5cm) long, with a letter of authenticity on 'The Spice Girls Ltd' headed paper.
£300–350
$450–500 ⚒ Bon

Five silver charms, for fitting to a bracelet, 20thC, largest ¾in (2cm) high.
£12–20
$15–30 each ⊞ TAC

Bracelets

A Victorian silver-gilt bracelet.
£200–250
$300–350 ⊞ AnS

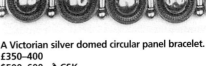

A Victorian silver domed circular panel bracelet.
£350–400
$500–600 ⚒ CSK

A Victorian silver-gilt bracelet, c1880, 6½in (16.5cm) long.
£550–600
$800–870 ⊞ WIM

◄ A Victorian silver bangle, with gold inlay, engraved with flowers, c1870, 1¾in (4.5cm) wide.
£300–350
$450–500 ⊞ WIM

A Victorian silver bangle, with gold-inlaid circles engraved with birds, c1870, 1¼in (3cm) high.
£270–300
$400–450 ⊞ WIM

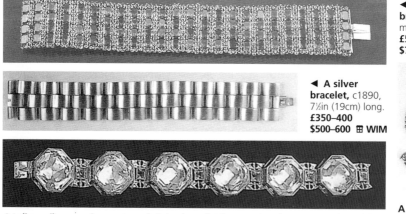

◄ **A Victorian garnet bracelet,** with silver-gilt mount, repaired.
£525–575
$750–850 ✗ SK

◄ **A silver bracelet,** c1890, 7½in (19cm) long.
£350–400
$500–600 ⊞ WIM

A Lalique silver, smoky quartz and citrine bracelet, impressed mark, c1908, 8¼in (21cm) long.
£12,000–13,000
$17,500–19,000 ✗ S(NY)
Articulated bracelets by René Lalique are rare.

A silver charm bracelet, with six charms including two opening caravans, 1950s–60s.
£40–50
$60–75 ⊞ BGA

Brooches

◄ **A Celtic revival silver-gilt pin brooch,** c1860, 2½in (6.5cm) diam.
£350–450
$500–650
⊞ WELD

A Victorian silver-gilt and cabochon garnet five-stone Huntingdon brooch, the reverse signed 'Waterhouse & Company, Dublin'.
£350–450
$500–650 ✗ CSK

Three silver name brooches, Annie, Pollie and Eliza, c1880, 1½in (4cm) diam.
£45–65
$65–95 each ⊞ FMN

A silver and Cairngorm plaid brooch, c1880, 4½in (11.5cm) diam.
£250–300
$350–450 ⊞ BWA

Four silver name brooches, Marian, Christina, Sissie and Dinah, 1880–1900, 1¼in (3cm) diam.
£40–50
$60–75 ⊞ EXC
Name brooches were made for nannies and maids to wear on their uniforms so that the family knew their name. A tremendous number were produced in silver, some with initials in a gold overlay.

Two silver name brooches, Katie and Lizzie, 1880–1920, 1½in (4cm) wide.
£45–65
$65–95 ⊞ FMN

A silver cricket bat brooch, with agate handle, Birmingham 1900, 1½in (4cm) high.
£225–250
$300–360 ⊞ BEX

Two Victorian silver name brooches, Polly and Isabel, largest 1¾in (4.5cm) wide.
£35–40
$50–60 each ⊞ SPE

◄ **Two Victorian silver brooches,** Good Luck and Mother, largest 1¾in (4.5cm) wide.
£40–50
$60–75 each ⊞ SPE

A sterling silver wing brooch, naturalistically fashioned with detailed plumage, marked with 'B', wings motif and 'Sterling', probably American, c1900, 4in (10cm) long.
£110–130
$160–190 ⚒ P

▶ **Four Victorian silver brooches,** largest 1¾in (4.5cm) wide.
£35–40
$50–60 each
⊞ SPE

A Victorian silver name brooch, Kate, 1¾in (4.5cm) wide.
£65–75
$90–100 ⊞ FMN

A silver-gilt floral spray brooch, by Dorrie Nossiter, set with sapphires, kunzite, emeralds, amethyst and seed pearls, c1900.
£1,750–2,000
$2,500–2,900 ⚒ SK

Four silver name brooches, Lizzie, Lily, Pollie and Louie, 1900–20, 1½in (4cm) wide.
£40–50
$60–75 each ⊞ EXC
Prices for name brooches depend on how popular the name is today, and with the current resurgence of Edwardian names, Lilly, Rose, etc, these brooches are once again in demand.

A Calcutta Scottish silver plaid brooch, c1920, 4in (10cm) wide.
£180–200
$260–290 PC

A silver-plated name brooch, Janey, 1920s, 2in (5cm) wide.
£30–40
$45–60 ⊞ FMN

A French silver paste-set plaque brooch, 1930s, 3in (7.5cm) wide.
£180–200
$260–290 ⊞ JSM

A silver, gold leaf and black Bakelite cicada brooch, 1930s, 3in (7.5cm) long.
£30–35
$45–50 ⊞ LBe

A marcasite and silver leaf flying insect brooch, 1930s, 3in (7.5cm) long.
£30–35
$45–50 ⊞ LBe

A sterling silver butterfly brooch, set with red stones, signed 'Valsran Brody-Baiardi', late 1940s, 4in (10cm) wide.
£130–150
$190–220 ⊞ LBe

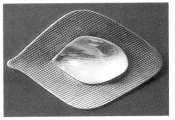

A Norwegian sterling silver brooch, designed by Grete Prytz Kittelsen, c1950, 2¾in (7cm) wide.
£100–120
$150–175 ⊞ DID

◀ **A Mikela Naur oxydized silver and 14ct gold pin,** for Anton Michelsen, 1970s, 4in (10cm) wide.
£100–150
$150–220 ⊞ DID

A silver spider brooch, with banded agate body, 1940s, 3in (7.5cm) long.
£85–95
$120–140 ⊞ LBe

An amoebic sterling silver brooch, by Karen Strand for Aage Drasted, c1955, 2¼in (5.5cm) wide.
£170–200
$250–290 ⊞ DID

Cufflinks

A pair of Victorian silver cufflinks, in the shape of shamrocks, set with green agate.
£70–80
$100–120 ⊞ SPE

A pair of silver cufflinks, c1900.
£30–40
$45–60 ⊞ JBB

A pair of Indian silver cufflinks, with painted ivory miniatures under glass, c1900.
£125–150
$180–220 ⊞ JBB

LOCATE THE SOURCE

The source of each illustration in Miller's can be found by checking the code letters below each caption with the Key to Illustrations, pages 311–314.

A pair of silver cricketing cufflinks, 1930s.
£120–150
$175–220 ⊞ JBB

A pair of Hans Hansen sterling silver cufflinks, hallmarked, 1940s.
£100–120
$150–175 ⊞ DID

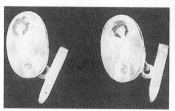

A pair of silver hand-painted cufflinks, depicting pin-up girls, 1950s.
£350–400
$500–600 ⊞ JBB
The term 'pin-up' derives from WWII when servicemen would 'pin-up' girlie pictures in their quarters. Pin-up material, especially from the 1940s–50s, is highly collectable today and the more unusual items such as these cufflinks can fetch high prices.

◄ **A pair of Hans Hansen sterling silver cufflinks,** c1940s.
£100–120
$150–175 ⊞ DID

Necklaces

A French rococo-style silver and paste necklace, with *ésprit* pendant drop, 19thC.
£150–180
$220–260 ⋌ PFK

A Victorian silver engraved locket and chain, c1880, 16in (40.5cm) long.
£240–260
$350–380 ⊞ DAC

▶ **A sterling silver torque,** by Bent Gabrielsen Pedersen for Hans Hansen, Denmark, the pendant set with black enamel, c1970.
£200–250
$290–360 ⊞ DID

A gilt and silver torque, by Bent Gabrielsen Pedersen for Hans Hansen, 1960s, 14in (35.5cm) long.
£500–550
$700–800 ⊞ DID

◄ **A Danish chalcedony and sterling silver necklace,** by N. E., c1960, 15in (38cm) long.
£300–350
$450–500 ⊞ DID

Pendants

A Greek silver coin, depicting Larissa, 5thC BC, intact, in modern setting as a pendant, ¾in (2cm) diam.
£250–300
$350–450 ⊞ HEL

A Charles I silver heart-shaped locket, inscribed, enclosing a plaque decorated in relief with a portrait of the King, 1¼in (3cm) high, in a black shagreen case.
£1,200–1,400
$1,800–2,000 ⚒ F&C

An enamelled silver pendant, by André Fernand Thesmar, c1900, 2¾in (7cm) long.
£2,800–3,200
$4,000–4,500 ⚒ S(NY)

An Edwardian silver and paste pendant, set with a peridot, 2in (5cm) high.
£60–70
$90–100 ⊞ DAC

An enamel and silver pendant, by Norman Grant, Edinburgh, c1960.
£150–200
$220–290 ⊞ DID

An Edwardian silver openwork pendant, set with sapphires and diamonds.
£370–400
$550–600 ⚒ WL

A Tapio Wirkkala sterling silver kinetic pendant and chain, by KultaKesus oy Hämeenlinna, Finland c1970, pendant 4¾in (12cm) high.
£750–850
$1,100–1,300 ⊞ DID

◄ **A Krud V. Anderson starburst sterling silver pendant and chain,** for Anton Michelsen, 1960s, pendant 2¼in (5.5cm) wide.
£180–200
$260–290 ⊞ DID

Insurance values

Always insure your valuable antiques for the cost of replacing them with similar items, regardless of the original price paid. Both dealers and auctioneers will provide a valuation service for a fee.

Rings

A silver ring, with plain elliptical band and domed glass stone covering paste stones of red, blue, green and orange, late 16thC.
£220–250
$300–350 ⊞ ANG

A rock crystal and silver kinetic ring, by Kapittaan Kulta, with a cornelian bead rolling around under the crystal, 1960s.
£220–250
$300–350 ⊞ DID

A sterling silver and gold-stone ring, by Elis Kauppi for Kupittaan Kulta, 1970.
£150–200
$220–290 ⊞ DID

A sterling silver and cabochon amethyst ring, by Just Andersen, import marks, 1973.
£220–250
$300–350 ⊞ DID

Jugs & Ewers

A French silver ewer and basin, both engraved with foliate cartouches on an engine-turned ground, the ewer with a forked rustic handle capped by a spray of buds and leaves, ewer 15½in (39.5cm) high, basin 18in (45.5cm) diam, 133oz.
£3,000–3,500
$4,500–5,000 ⚹ S(NY)

A George III hot water urn, by John Scofield, the body with four repoussé chased sunflowers with ovals, with central engraved crest, London 1782, 20in (51cm) high, 87oz.
£1,600–1,800
$2,300–2,600 ⚹ SK

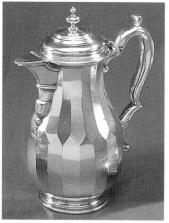

A Danish silver urn, with spiral fluted body, two cast flower and scroll handles and a cast dophin spigot with cockerel tap, Assayer's mark of C. Fabricus, Copenhagen 1767, 14½in (37cm) high, 40oz.
£1,450–1,650
$2,000–2,400 ⚹ DN

A George IV silver-gilt jug, the scroll handle formed as a vine tendril with slightly domed hinged cover with detachable running fox finial, chased with bands of foliage on a matted ground and engraved with inscription, maker's mark of John Bridge, marked on body, cover and finial, the base stamped 'Rundell Bridge et Rundell Aurifices Regis Londini', London 1829, 11in (28cm) high, 92oz.
£10,000–12,000
$14,500–17,500 ⚹ C

◀ **A Victorian silver jug and cover,** by Robert Hennell & Sons, the spout with hinged flap, London 1844, 8in (20.5cm) high, 24oz.
£3,000–3,500
$4,500–5,000 ⚹ S

A George II silver baluster-shaped jug, by Gabriel Sleath, the applied girdle above engraved armorials and crest, with scroll handle and thumb-piece, the stepped hinged cover with knop finial, on a spreading foot, 1731, 10in (25.5cm) high, 33oz.
£1,400–1,600
$2,000–2,300 ⚹ P(B)

A French silver hot milk jug, with domed hinged cover, knop finial and ebonized baluster side handle, on three scroll mounted hoof feet, engraved with a coat-of-arms, Paris, 19thC, 6in (15cm) high, 8oz.
£250–300
$350–450 ⚹ Bon

A coin silver water jug, by Gorham, the collar applied with classical portrait medallions, the handle with the figure of a draped nude maiden, marked and stamped '530', c1865, 10½in (26.5cm) high.
£1,350–1,500
$2,000–2,200 ⚹ NOA

French parcel-gilt ewer and basin, by Hénin and Cie, cast and chased with rocaille ornament, flowers and aquatic plants, Paris c1880, basin 18in (45.5cm) diam, 16.5oz.
£4,800–5,200
$7,000–7,500 ⚹ S

Further reading
Miller's Collecting Silver: The Facts At Your Fingertips, Miller's Publications, 1999

A silver ewer, the cover with castellated rim and foliate finial, and an associated metalware basin, Ottoman Empire, probably Egyptian, early 20thC, ewer 12½in (32cm) high.
£1,750–2,000
$2,500–3,000 ⚹ P

A Victorian silver punch jug, by Harrison Bros and Howson, with embossed rope and gadroon friezes and presentation inscription, Sheffield 1893, 9½in (24cm) high, 42oz.
£1,200–1,400
$1,750–2,000 ⚹ RBB

A silver jug, with reeded handle, on a stepped waisted socle and square foot, Sheffield 1910, 8in (20.5cm) high, 9oz.
£120–150
$180–220 ⚹ P(HSS)

A late Victorian silver jug-on-stand, with burner, lift-off swept cover, melon-fluted ebony finial and right-angled ebony handle, on a plain circular stand, engraved with a crest, maker's mark 'G.N.' over 'R.H.', Chester 1897, 13oz.
£600–700
$870–1,000 ⚹ HSS

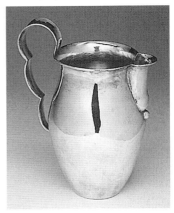

A Mexican sterling silver water jug, by William Spratling, with triple curve arched strap handle, Taxco c1940, 10in (25.5cm) high, 28.25oz.
£2,300–2,500
$3,500–3,600 ⚹ B&B

Beer Jugs

A George II silver beer jug, with repoussé decoration of a coursing scene, mark indistinct, London 1745, later decoration, 8¼in (21cm) high, 27.75oz.
£850–1,000
$1,200–1,500 ⚹ WW

A George III silver beer jug, by William Cripps, London 1762, 8in (20.5cm) high, 28oz.
£3,500–4,000
$5,000–5,800 ⊞ JSH

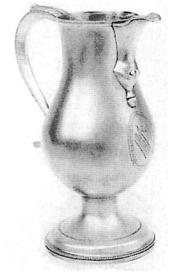

A George III beer jug, by John Kidder, the leaf-capped scroll handle with a heart-shaped terminal, on a spreading beaded edge foot, London 1786, 10½in (26.5cm) high, 31oz.
£5,500–6,500
$8,000–9,500 ⚹ WW

Cream Jugs

A George II Scottish cast silver cream jug, by John Main, chased with rococo scrolls and flowers above an applied girdle, with engraved dragon crest, gilt interior, Assay Master Archibald Ure, Edinburgh 1730, 4½in (11.5cm) high, 7.25oz.
£7,000–8,000
$10,000–11,500 ⚒ P
This cream jug attracted enthusiastic bidding because it is cast, Scottish, of early date and an unusual shape.

A George III silver cream jug, London 1779, 4in (10cm) high.
£300–350
$450–500 ⊞ TGa

A silver helmet-shaped cream jug, by John Bassingwhite, bright-cut with paterae and festoons, with a beaded edge, London 1790, 7½in (19cm) high, 3oz.
£600–700
$870–1,000 ⚒ WL

An early Georgian silver cream jug, with scroll handle, 3½in (9cm) high.
£320–360
$450–500 ⊞ PSA

A George IV provincial plain fluted silver cream jug, by J. Barber & Co, with scroll handle, on a circular foot, York 1821, 4½in (11.5cm) high, 9oz.
£2,500–3,000
$3,600–4,400 ⚒ C

A George III silver helmet-shaped cream jug, by Thomas Hallows, on a raised circular foot, 1783, 4¼in (11cm) high, 3oz.
£120–160
$180–230 ⚒ L

▶ **A George III silver cream jug,** with reeded rim, loop handle and base, London 1799, 10in (25.5cm) high, 3oz.
£230–280
$330–400 ⚒ AH

A George III silver cream jug, London 1760, 3½in (9cm) high.
£400–460
$600–650 ⊞ TGa

A repoussé silver cream pitcher, by R. and W. Wilson, with chased decoration, on hoof feet, Philadelphia 1825, 6½in (16.5cm) high, 8oz.
£220–250
$320–360 ⚒ SK(B)

A George III silver cream jug, on a square pedestal foot with applied beaded rim, London 1796, 4½in (11.5cm) high.
£180–250
$260–360 ⊞ PSA

Colour Review

A George IV silver-gilt toilet service, by Mary Ann & Charles Reily, London 1828, bottles 5in (12.5cm) high, 143oz.
€9,500–11,500
$13,500–16,500 ⚒ C

A silver-backed dressing table hand mirror, Birmingham 1902, 11in (28cm) long.
£120–140
$175–200 ⊞ ABr

A Victorian silver-backed hair brush, Birmingham 1894, 9½in (24cm) long.
£25–30
$35–45 ⊞ ABr

A silver-backed crumb brush, Birmingham 1904, 12½in (32cm) long.
£40–50
$60–75 ⊞ OBS

A silver nail buffer, c1910, 4½in (11.5cm) wide.
£30–40
$45–60 ⊞ VB

◀ **A silver and enamel hand mirror,** Birmingham 1934, 10in (25.5cm) wide.
£80–90
$115–130 ⊞ JACK

A 21-piece silver dressing table set, made for a 21st birthday, hallmarked, 1896, 21in (53.5cm) wide, in original silk-lined box.
£4,000–4,500
$5,500–6,500 PC

A pair of silver-backed clothes brushes, Birmingham 1932, 6in (15cm) long.
£30–40
$45–60 ⊞ ABr

A silver wine cup, the rim prick-engraved 'ETIH 55', maker's mark 'ET', c1655, 6in (15cm) high, 11oz.
£3,300–4,000
$4,800–5,800 ⚒ C

A Charles I silver goblet, marked R. W. Mullet, London 1634, 7in (18cm) high.
£7,500–8,500
$11,000–12,500 ⊞ PAY

◀ **A George II silver cup and cover,** by Charles Harfield, London 1732, 12in (30.5cm) high.
£10,000–12,000
$14,500–17,500
⊞ MHB

A Queen Anne silver cup, by J. Younghusband, scratched initials 'H' over 'AE', Newcastle 1712, 2in (5cm) high, 2oz.
£1,600–1,800
$2,300–2,600 ⚒ DN

A silver goblet, by James Stamp , London 1777, 6in (15cm) high.
£1,150–1,300
$1,500–2,000 ⊞ BEX

◀ **A George III silver wine goblet,** by Henry Chawner & John Emes, London 1797, 6in (15cm) high.
£800–900
$1,200–1,300 ⊞ BEX

A Victorian silver stirrup cup, by John S. Hunt, formed as a stag's head, gilt-lined, London 1864, 7in (18cm) long, 20oz.
£4,400–5,000
$6,500–7,500 ⚒ C

Items in the Colour Review have been arranged in date order within each sub-section.

A pair of Victorian silver goblets, by Stephen Smith, London 1870–72, 7in (18cm) high.
£1,000–1,250
$1,500–2,000 ⊞ PAY

A pair of Victorian silver goblets, by Frederick Elkington, London 1873, 5½in (14cm) high.
£900–1,000
$1,500–1,500 ⊞ PAY

A Victorian silver parcel-gilt goblet, by Elkington & Co, Birmingham 1878, 5½in (14cm) high.
£600–700
$850–1,000 ⊞ PAY

A George III silver inkwell, by William Abdy, London 1778, 4in (10cm) long.
£800–900
$1,200–1,300 ⊞ JBU

A George IV silver inkstand, by John & Thomas Settle, Sheffield 1821, 12in (30.5cm) wide.
£3,000–3,500
$4,000–5,000 ⚒ P(L)

A George IV silver and cut-glass inkstand, by Joseph Angell, London 1825, 9½in (24cm) long.
£2,500–2,750
$3,500–4,000 ⊞ PAY

A silver gallery pierced inkstand, by Charles & George Fox, London 1848, 7in (18cm) long.
£1,450–1,650
$2,100–2,400 ⊞ NOR

A George IV sterling silver inkstand, by Rebecca Emes & Edward Barnard I, the plain rectangular base with four scroll and shell feet, applied border decorated with flowers, shells and scrolls, pen depression on each side, family crest engraved on base, central taperstick has detachable nozzle and lifts off to reveal a sterling silver container for sealing wafers, contemporary cut-glass bottles mounted with a silver lift-off lid, one pierced for use with ink, the other with three holes for quills, London 1826, 12.5oz.
£1,600–1,800
$2,300–2,600 ⊞ SLI
The reverse of the base was engraved after WWII with 11 facsimile signatures and inscribed: 'Presented to Lt. Col. C. S. M. Heape, O.B.E., M.C., R.A. by the Military Advisers to the Press Censorship I.P.3. War Office in token of affectionate regard and in gratitude for his kindly understanding and guidance from 1939 to 1945.'

A silver gallery pierced inkstand, by Charles & George Fox, London 1848, 7in (18cm) long.
£800–900
$1,200–1,300 ⊞ JBU

A Victorian silver-gilt inkstand, by James Garrard, London 1891, 3½in (9cm) high.
£800–1,000
$1,200–1,500 ⊞ PAY

A silver inkstand, by Slater, Slater & Holland, copy of an earlier design, London 1900, 2in (5cm) high.
£1,400–1,600
$2,000–2,300 ⊞ JBU

▶ **A late Victorian silver inkstand,** with two cut-glass inkwells, c1900.
£130–160
$200–250 ⚒ G(B)

An Edwardian silver, enamel and glass inkstand, by J. Grinsell & Sons, Birmingham 1907, 3¼in (8cm) high.
£500–600
$700–870 ⊞ BEX

A silver inkstand, Birmingham 1909, 2½in (6.5cm) high.
£500–600
$700–870 ⊞ NOR

A silver-gilt Victorian inkwell, by John Figg, inset with mother-of-pearl and cornelian stones, London 1841, 6in (15cm) high.
£1,300–1,500
$2,000–2,200 ⊞ JBU

A Victorian inkwell, by Charles & George Fox, modelled as an owl, London 1845–46, 4in (10cm) high.
£3,500–4,000
$5,000–5,800 ⊞ NS

An Edwardian silver inkstand, by Elkington & Co, the base fitted with a two-tier pen rest and a square inkwell, the hinged lid engraved with a crest, Birmingham 1907, 12½in (32cm) wide.
£550–650
$800–950 ⚒ RTo

A Victorian silver and glass inkwell, by John S. Beresford, modelled as a ball, London 1883, 5in (12.5cm) high.
£450–500
$650–700 ⊞ BEX

A Victorian silver and glass inkwell and letter holder, by E. Finley & H. Taylor, modelled as a shell, London 1886, 5in (12.5cm) wide.
£700–800
$1,000–1,200 ⊞ BEX

A Victorian silver inkwell, modelled as a gnome, 1892, 4½in (11.5cm) high.
£1,650–1,850
$2,400–2,700 ⊞ BEX

A Victorian garnet and silver inkwell, by John Kirwan, Birmingham 1894, 2in (5cm) high.
£150–175
$200–250 ⊞ PAY

An Edwardian silver and glass 'diamond' inkwell, by Stokes & Ireland Ltd, Chester 1899, 4¾in (12cm) high.
£425–475
$600–700 ⊞ BEX

► **Two Victorian silver-gilt and glass inkwells,** by Charles Fox, London 1895, 2in (5cm) high.
£375–425
$550–600 ⊞ BEX

A Victorian silver and glass inkwell and pen rest, by L. Bennett & Co, Birmingham 1900, 3¾in (9.5cm) high.
£550–625
$800–900 ⊞ BEX

A Danish silver 'owl' inkwell, by P. Hertz, Copenhagen 1902, 7in (18cm) high.
£2,000–2,250
$3,000–3,500 ⊞ BEX

A silver inkwell, by The Guild of Handicraft, with blue enamelled lid and studded corners, with a green glass liner, 1906, 2¾in (7cm) high.
£1,600–1,800
$2,000–2,500 ⚒ G(B)

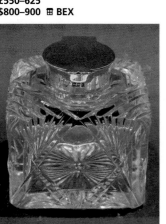

A silver and cut-glass inkwell, by Hawksworth, Eyre & Co, London 1914, 2¾in (7cm) high.
£320–355
$450–500 ⊞ BEX

A silver and cut-glass inkwell, by The Goldsmiths & Silversmiths Co, London 1920, 3¾in (9.5cm) diam.
£375–425
$550–600 ⊞ BEX

A silver travelling inkwell, by C. & R. C., London 1923, 1¼in (3cm) high.
£350–400
$500–580 ⊞ BEX

▶ **A silver-gilt dress pin,** with quatrefoil decoration, 16thC, 3½in (9cm) long.
£120–150
$175–220 ⚒ F&C

◀ **A silver and agate brooch,** in the form of a key, c1850, 3½in (9cm) long.
£500–600
$700–850 ⊞ BWA

A topaz and diamond openwork brooch, mounted in silver, silver-gilt and gold, c1720.
£2,300–2,500
$3,500–4,000 ⚒ P

A silver and marcasite set of earrings, bracelet, ring and pendant, inset with jade, 1920s, earrings 2in (5cm) long.
£230–260
$350–400 ⊞ DAC

A silver necklace, by Arthur & George Gaskin, set with turquoise, opal and pearl, c1910.
£1,000–1,200
$1,500–1,750 ⊞ JES

A silver beer jug, by
Thomas Mason, London
1739, 8½in (21.5cm) high,
38.5oz.
£10,000–11,000
$14,000–16,000 🔨 S

A George II silver-gilt ewer and basin,
by Aymé Videau, chased with floral swags
and grotesque masks, London 1746,
basin 15in (38cm) wide, 76oz.
£38,000–42,000
$55,000–61,000 🔨 S

A silver-mounted pottery jug,
by Thomas Law, London 1797,
7½in (19cm) high.
£1,100–1,300
$1,500–2,000 ⊞ NOR

A Victorian silver cream jug, by
C. Reily & E. Storer, London 1837,
6in (15cm) high.
£625–685
$900–1,000 ⊞ BEX

A Victorian silver cream jug, by
W. Aitkin, Chester 1900, 5in (13cm) high.
£240–265
$350–400 ⊞ BEX

A glass and silver overlay jug,
c1900, 7¼in (18.5cm) high.
£2,500–3,000
$3,500–4,500 ⊞ SFL

◄ **An Edwardian silver cream jug,**
by Thomas Bradbury & Sons, Sheffield
1901, 4in (10cm) high.
£200–225
$300–325 ⊞ BEX

► **An Edwardian silver cream jug,**
by Robert & William Sorley, London
1906, 3¼in (8.5cm) diam.
£250–300
$350–450 ⊞ BEX

**A George I silver tea
kettle on stand and lamp,**
maker's mark 'ED', c1718,
14in (36cm) high.
£10,000–12,000
$14,500–17,500 🔨 C

**A George I silver kettle
on stand,** maker's mark
of Gabriel Sleath, London
1726, 13½in (33.5cm) high.
£5,000–6,000
$7,000–9,000 🔨 Bon

**A Belgian silver hot
water kettle and
burner,** maker's mark
of Jean-Melchior Dartois,
Liège 1772, kettle
7½in (19cm) diam, 86.5oz.
£72,000–80,000
$104,000–116,000 🔨 C(G)

**A Queen Anne fluted
silver kettle,** by The
Goldsmiths & Silversmiths
Co, London 1907,
11in (28cm) high.
£650–700
$950–1,000 ⊞ JBU

A set of four Scottish silver place markers, by Hamilton
& Inches, Edinburgh 1886, 2¾in (7cm) wide.
£525–595
$750–900 ⊞ BEX

A set of four silver horse menu holders, Edinburgh
1895–96, 1¾in (4.5cm) high.
£850–950
$1,250–1,500 ⊞ NS

◀ A Victorian
silver name
place marker, by
William Comyns,
London 1896,
2½in (6.5cm) wide.
£150–165
$220–240 ⊞ BEX

A pair of Victorian silver menu holders, by Berthold
Muller, cast as Henry VIII and Queen Elizabeth, hinged strut
supports, London 1897, 4¾in (12cm) high, 5oz.
£450–550
$650–800 🔨 S(S)

A set of four silver and tortoiseshell menu holders,
by William Comyns, London 1906–10, 1¼in (3cm) high.
£700–800
$1,000–1,200 ⊞ BEX

A pair of Edwardian silver place markers, by Chrisford
& Norris, modelled as ducks, Birmingham 1909,
1¼in (3cm) high.
£300–345
$450–500 ⊞ BEX

▶ An Edwardian
silver place
marker, by
Stokes & Ireland,
Chester 1909,
1¼in (3cm) high.
£150–165
$200–250 ⊞ BEX

A set of six Edwardian silver coin place markers,
c1910, 1½in (4cm) diam.
£325–375
$500–550 ⊞ BEX

A set of four silver menu holders,
by G. Y. & Co, modelled as dogs,
Chester 1931, 1in (2.5cm) high.
£850–950
$1,250–1,500 ⊞ NS

▶ A set of four silver and piqué
menu holders, by William Comyns,
Birmingham 1909–10, 1½in (4cm) high.
£1,450–1,650
$2,000–2,500 ⊞ NS

A set of four silver and enamel
butterfly menu holders, Birmingham
1930, 2½in (6.5cm) high.
£1,250–1,450
$1,800–2,000 ⊞ NS

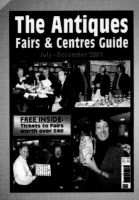

A Queen Anne silver miniature porringer, with hallmarks for London 1707, 2in (5cm) diam.
£750–850
$1,000–1,250 ⊞ NS

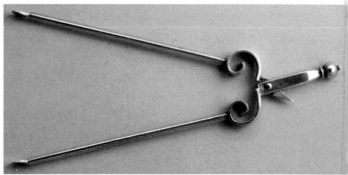

A pair of George I silver miniature fire irons, by David Clayton, of good gauge, hallmarked, London c1725, 4in (10cm) long.
£700–800
$1,000–1,200 ⊞ SLI
The 18th century was the peak period for the production of toys in England. David Clayton made only silver toys and his work was extremely prolific and of a consistently high quality.

A Queen Anne/George I silver miniature snuffer stand with scissors, c1710–15, 4in (10cm) high.
£2,850–3,250
$4,000–4,500 ⊞ NS

A silver miniature dust pan, by William van Strant, Amsterdam c1730, 2in (5cm) long.
£450–495
$650–700 ⊞ BEX

A silver miniature fireplace brush, not marked, c1750, 2¼in (5.5cm) long.
£350–495
$500–700 ⊞ BEX

A pair of Dutch silver miniature candlesticks, c1760, 2in (5cm) high.
£1,650–1,850
$2,400–2,700 ⊞ BEX

A set of Old English pattern silver miniature teaspoons, by John Taylor & John Robertson, Newcastle c1790, 2¾in (7cm) long.
£850–950
$1,250–1,500 ⊞ NS

A silver miniature basket, not marked, c1780, 1¾in (4.5cm) high.
£325–375
$500–550 ⊞ BEX

◀ **A Dutch silver miniature chandelier,** c1818, 7in (18cm) high.
£1,650–1,850
$2,500–3,000 ⊞ BEX

▶ **A Victorian silver miniature cradle,** by T. Wilkinson, chased and engraved, Birmingham 1883, 7in (18cm) high.
£4,200–4,700
$6,000–6,500 ⊞ PAY

A pair of Victorian silver miniature planters, by S. Blanckensee & Sons, Birmingham 1886, 1¼in (3cm) high.
£400–445
$600–650 ⊞ BEX

A Victorian silver miniature chair, London import mark for 1898, 1¼in (3cm) high.
£220–245
$300–350 ⊞ BEX

An Edwardian silver miniature chair, London import mark for 1903, 2in (5cm) high.
£220–245
$300–350 ⊞ BEX

A Victorian silver and glass miniature scent bottle, Birmingham 1900, 1¼in (3cm) high.
£300–350
$450–500 ⊞ BEX

A Dutch silver miniature cart and two bulls, London import mark for 1902, 4¼in (11cm) long.
£525–600
$750–900 ⊞ BEX

A silver miniature tea service, by J. Maxfield, comprising 12 pieces including spoons and tongs, Sheffield 1902–04, tray 5in (12.5cm) long.
£800–900
$1,000–1,300 ⊞ PAY

An Edwardian silver miniature cat, by H. C. Davis, Birmingham 1905, 2¾in (7cm) long.
£350–395
$500–550 ⊞ BEX

A pair of Edwardian silver miniature candlesticks, by James & William Deakin, Birmingham 1906, 2in (5cm) high.
£580–645
$850–950 ⊞ BEX

An Edwardian silver miniature baby's bath, by H. Williamson & Sons, Birmingham 1908, 3¼in (8.5cm) high.
£300–345
$450–500 ⊞ BEX

A Dutch silver miniature quaich, pseudo marks for Amsterdam, c1910, 2¼in (5.5cm) wide.
£200–235
$300–350 ⊞ BEX

A silver miniature photograph frame, by C. P. B., Birmingham c1910, 1½in (4cm) high.
£130–145
$200–225 ⊞ BEX

▶ **A silver stamp box,** by J. & R. G., Chester 1918, 3½in (9cm) high.
£650–700
$950–1,000 ⊞ NOR

An Edwardian silver-mounted mirror, by Walker & Hall, Birmingham 1901, 18in (45.5cm) high.
£1,300–1,450
$1,800–2,000 ⊞ BEX

An Edwardian silver-mounted mirror, by H. Matthews, Birmingham 1904, 10¼in (26cm) high.
£675–750
$950–1,100 ⊞ BEX

A silver-mounted mirror, by Charles S. Green & Co, Birmingham 1929, 15⅛in (39cm) high.
£1,000–1,150
$1,500–1,700 ⊞ BEX

A George III silver nutmeg grater, rectangular form with canted corners, the hinged lid engraved with foliate borders surrounding engraved amoeba work around a central initialled cartouche, the sides and base engraved with floral decoration, maker's mark of Joseph Taylor, Birmingham 1790, 2¼in (5.5cm) wide.
£900–1,100
$1,300–1,600 ⚒ Bon

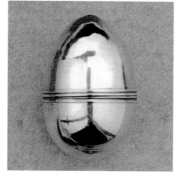

A George III silver nutmeg grater, egg form, the screw-off cover revealing a circular grater, with a reeded girdle, maker's mark of Thomas Meriton, London 1800, 1¾in (4.5cm) high.
£400–450
$600–650 ⚒ Bon

A George III silver nutmeg grater, by Reid & Sons, oval form with floral engraved bands, Newcastle 1829, 1½in (4cm) wide.
£800–1,000
$1,200–1,500 ⚒ P(L)

▶ **A pair of cast-silver photograph frames,** London 1892, 8in (20.5cm) high.
£2,000–2,250
$2,900–3,300 ⊞ NOR

A pair of silver frames, by William Comyns, 1893, 4in (10cm) wide.
£650–750
$900–1,100 ⊞ AMH

A Russian silver and lapis lazuli frame, c1900, 3½in (9cm) high.
£2,000–2,200
$2,900–3,200 ⊞ SHa

A silver photograph frame, by J. & W. Deakin, Chester c1902, 8½in (21.5cm) high.
£550–600
$800–850 ⊞ THOM

A silver photograph frame, by Saunders & Mackenzie, Birmingham 1918, 10in (25.5cm) high.
£425–485
$650–700 ⊞ BEX

A George III silver brazier, by S. Herbert & Co, for the American market, London 1765, 6¾in (17cm) diam, 17oz.
£2,000–2,400
$2,900–3,500 ⚒ S

A Napoleon III silver jardinière, on four scroll and foliage feet, with plated liner, probably French, c1860, 25½in (65cm) wide, 96oz.
£6,500–7,000
$9,500–10,000 ⚒ C(G)

▶ **A silver and tortoiseshell bookmark,** by Grey & Co, Birmingham 1906, 4½in (11.5cm) high.
£280–320
$400–450 ⊞ THOM

◀ **A Continental** *historismus* **silver nef,** the elaborately rigged vessel applied with figures and canons, the stern with English Royal arms, detachable base chased with a band of foliage, dolphin rudder and four wheel supports, probably German, c1925, London import marks for 1929, 19in (48.5cm) long, 101oz.
£4,000–4,500
$5,800–6,500 ⚒ S

A silver pincushion, in the shape of a shod horse's hoof, maker's mark indistinct, London 1893, 2in (5cm) wide.
£200–240
$300–350 ⚒ P(WM)

A silver pincushion, modelled as a lady's high-heeled shoe, decorated with a bow and scrolling foliage, Birmingham 1896, 3in (7.5cm) long.
£180–220
$250–350 ⚒ GH

A Victorian silver pincushion, by C. Saunders & F. Shepherd, modelled as a canoe, Birmingham 1899, 3½in (9cm) wide.
£300–345
$450–500 ⊞ BEX

An Edwardian silver pincushion, by Adie & Lovekin, modelled as a shoe, Birmingham 1904, 1¼in (3cm) high.
£400–455
$600–650 ⊞ BEX

l. A silver pincushion, by Levi & Salaman, in the form of a pig, Birmingham 1904, 1in (2.5cm) high.
£260–290
$350–400
r. A silver pincushion, by Adie & Lovekin, in the form of a bull, Birmingham 1908, 1½in (4cm) high.
£500–550
$700–800 ⊞ THOM

An Edwardian silver hedgehog pincushion, by Levi & Salaman, Birmingham 1904, 1¾in (4.5cm) high.
£550–650
$800–1,000 ⊞ NS

▶ **An Edwardian silver pincushion,** by Adie & Lovekin, modelled as a pig, Birmingham 1905, 2in (5cm) long.
£300–345
$450–500 ⊞ BEX

An Edwardian silver pincushion, by C. Saunders & F. Shepherd, modelled as a pig, Birmingham 1905, 2½in (6.5cm) long.
£265–295
$400–450 ⊞ BEX

An Edwardian silver pincushion, modelled as a pug dog, Birmingham 1906.
£450–550
$650–800 ✤ G(B)

An Edwardian silver pincushion, by Adie & Lovekin, modelled as a bulldog, Birmingham 1906, 2in (5cm) high.
£750–850
$1,200–1,500 ⊞ NS

A silver pincushion, by Gordes Vale, in the form of a rabbit, Birmingham 1907, 2½in (6.5cm) long.
£750–825
$1,000–1,200 ⊞ THOM

An Edwardian silver pincushion, by C. Saunders & F. Shepherd, modelled as a frog, Birmingham 1907, 1½in (4cm) long.
£650–750
$900–1,100 ⊞ NS

An Edwardian silver pincushion, modelled as a hedgehog, Birmingham 1907, 1½in (4cm) high.
£240–280
$350–400 ✤ G(B)

A silver pincushion, by A. & L. L., in the form of an elephant, Birmingham 1909, 2¾in (7cm) long.
£170–200
$250–300 ✤ GH

An Edwardian silver pincushion, by Adie & Lovekin, modelled as a polar bear, Birmingham 1909, 1in (2.5cm) high.
£900–1,100
$1,300–1,600 ⊞ NS

A silver pincushion, in the form of a frog, Birmingham 1909, 2¼in (5.5cm) long.
£400–460
$580–675 ✤ Bon(G)

A silver pincushion, by Adie & Lovekin, modelled as an emu, Birmingham 1909–10, 1½in (4cm) high.
£900–1,100
$1,300–1,600 ⊞ NS

▶ **A silver pincushion,** by W. J. M. & Co, in the form of a floating swan, Birmingham 1910, 2¾in (7cm) wide.
£200–240
$300–350 ✤ P(WM)

A silver pincushion, by Adie & Lovekin, modelled as a donkey, Birmingham 1909–10, 1¼in (3cm) high.
£800–900
$1,200–1,500 ⊞ NS

A George V silver pincushion, by Levi & Salaman, modelled as a robin with golf club, Birmingham 1910, 4½in (11.5cm) high.
£1,500–1,750
$2,200–2,500 ⊞ NS

A silver pincushion, Chester 1912, 5in (12.5cm) long.
£150–200
$200–300 ⚒ SWO

A George V silver pincushion, by S. & W., modelled as a chick, Birmingham 1910, 1in (2.5cm) high.
£800–900
$1,200–1,300 ⊞ NS

A George V silver pincushion, by Adie & Lovekin, modelled as an elephant, Birmingham 1910–11, 1½in (4cm) high.
£350–450
$500–650 ⊞ NS

▶ **A Victorian silver rattle,** by William Summers, London 1887, 4in (10cm) long.
£1,150–1,300
$1,700–1,900
⊞ BEX

A George V silver pincushion, by Crisford & Norris, modelled as a lizard, Birmingham 1922, 4¼in (11cm) long.
£900–1,100
$1,300–1,600 ⊞ NS

A George IV silver-gilt rattle, hallmarked, Birmingham 1827, 5in (12.5cm) long.
£1,000–1,250
$1,500–1,800 ⊞ NS

A George II baby teether, unmarked, 1740, 4¾in (12cm) long.
£1,100–1,250
$1,600–1,800 ⊞ NS

A Victorian silver-gilt and coral rattle, by Charles Rawlings and William Summers, in a fitted case, London 1838, 6¼in (16cm) long.
£800–1,000
$1,200–1,500 ⚒ GTH

A silver rattle, by Hilliard & Thompson, Birmingham 1887, 4½in (11.5cm) long.
£420–500
$600–700 ⊞ NOR

A child's silver and coral rattle, c1860, 6in (15cm) long.
£400–450
$600–650 ⊞ DIC

Auction or dealer?

All the pictures in our price guides originate from auction houses and dealers. Look for the symbol at the end of each caption to identify the source.

When buying at auction, prices can be lower than those of a dealer, but a buyer's premium and VAT will be added to the hammer price. Equally, when selling at auction, commission, tax and photography charges must be taken into account. Dealers will often restore pieces before putting them back on the market.

Both dealers and auctioneers will provide professional advice, so it is worth researching both sources before buying or selling your antiques.

An Elizabeth I silver chalice and paten, maker's mark 'IP' in a shield, London 1573, 6½in (16.5cm), 5oz.
£7,000–8,000
$10,000–11,500 ⚹ S

A Dutch silver crucifix, by L. Van de Bergh, Schoonhoven c1860, 3¾in (9.5cm) long.
£500–565
$700–800 ⊞ BEX

An Elizabeth I silver chalice, maker's mark 'G' above 'IV', late 16thC, 7½in (19cm) high, 9oz.
£3,400–3,800
$5,000–5,500 ⚹ S

A silver, amethyst and agate monstrance, c1880, 21in (53.5cm) high, in original box.
£300–350
$450–500 ⊞ BWA

An Elizabethan silver communion cup and cover, the bowl incised with two bands of stylized foliage, the cover similarly incised and with capstan finial, maker's mark hand grasping hammer between HC, London 1576, 7¾in (19.5cm), 11oz.
£4,500–5,500
$6,500–8,000 ⚹ S(S)

A pair of parcel-gilt silver Torah finials, with tapering shafts rising to baluster bodies inscribed in Hebrew and chased with scrolling foliage on ring matting below chains, pendants and fluted finials with pointed terminals, probably Chinese work, c1850, 7½in (19cm) high, 9oz.
£12,000–14,000
$17,000–20,000 ⚹ S

> Items in the Colour Review have been arranged in date order within each sub-section.

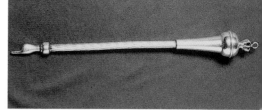

A European silver Torah pointer, c1890, 11in (28cm) long.
£650–750
$900–1,100 ⊞ SHa

A silver salver, unmarked, c1720, 17¼in (44cm) diam.
£1,500–1,800
$2,200–2,600 ⚹ DN

A George II silver salver, the border chased with alternating scale and shell motifs, the centre engraved with an armorial, London 1744, 10in (25.5cm) diam, 22.5oz.
£26,000–30,000
$37,500–43,500 ⚹ S

A silver salver, by John Langlands, Newcastle 1759, 12in (30.5cm) diam.
£2,500–2,800
$3,500–4,000 ⊞ JBU

A pair of silver salvers, by Edward Jay, London 1785, 8in (20.5cm) diam.
£4,000–4,500
$5,500–6,500 ⊞ MCO

◀ **A George III silver salver,** by Elizabeth Jones, London 1789, 20in (51cm) diam.
£6,250–6,750
$9,000–10,000 ⊞ MCO

A silver salver, by William Eaton, engraved with coat-of-arms, London 1816, 11¾in (30cm) diam, 44oz.
£2,500–3,000
$3,500–4,500 ⚒ C

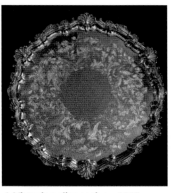

A Victorian silver salver, 1847, 21in (53.5cm) diam, 120oz.
£6,000–6,600
$8,500–9,500 ⊞ BEX

A pair of George II waiters, by William Williamson, Dublin 1885, 6½in (16.5cm) diam.
£5,000–5,500
$7,000–8,000 ⊞ NS

◄ An Indian sterling silver salver, c1900, 9¾in (25cm) diam.
£275–325
$400–450 ⊞ BEX

Miller's is a price GUIDE not a price LIST

Two silver-mounted scent bottles, c1860, largest 8¼in (21cm) long.
£600–650
£850–950 each ⊞ Som

A double-ended silver-topped scent bottle, blue glass overlay with waisted centre, c1890, 5¾in (14.5cm) wide.
£130–150
$200–220 ⚒ MED

A Victorian silver-mounted scent bottle, unmarked, 1880, 4in (10cm) high.
£650–750
$900–1,100 ⊞ NS

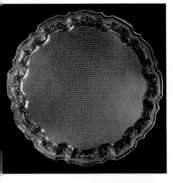

A Victorian silver-mounted scent bottle, with original glass body of oblong shape with faceted shoulders, the lid engraved 'Toilet Vinegar' and lined with cork, 1850, 3½in (9cm) high, with suede lined brown leather box.
£315–350
$450–500 ⊞ SLI

A Victorian silver and enamel scent bottle, by Saunders & Shepherd, London 1885, 1¾in (4.5cm) high.
£850–950
$1,200–1,500 ⊞ NS

A pair of silver-topped glass scent bottles, Birmingham 1896, 6½in (16.5cm) high.
£700–800
$1,000–1,200 ⊞ THOM

◄ A Victorian silver and enamel scent bottle, in the shape of a life buoy, Chester 1890, 2½in (6.5cm) diam.
£2,000–2,250
$3,000–3,500 ⊞ NS

A silver dish cross, by William Plummer, London 1758, 13in (33cm) square.
£3,200–3,500
$4,600–5,000 ⊞ MCO

A pair of George II silver-gilt cast rococo sugar nips, with shell decoration on the bowls and central pin, leaf decoration on the arms and finger grips, unmarked, c1740, 5in (12.5cm) long, 1.25oz.
£275–325
$400–450 ⊞ SLI

The earliest sugar nips date from about 1715 when they replaced the andiron type of sugar tong. By the 1770s sugar nips were being rapidly replaced by sugar tongs but were reintroduced in the mid-19thC. Mid-18thC sugar nips were often made to go with sets of teaspoons, and rococo sugar nips of various forms were often unmarked, as were also the teaspoons.

A French silver-gilt confiturier, maker's mark 'LJMH', Paris 1789, 10½in (26.5cm) high, 27oz.
£2,000–2,200
$2,900–3,200 ⚒ C(G)

◄ **A set of Victorian silver-gilt serving spoons and sifter,** by Thomas Smily, London 1873–74, in a fitted case, case 10in (25.5cm) wide.
£400–445
$550–650 ⊞ BEX

A silver fish or serving implement, by Henry Chawner, London 1791, 12in (30.5cm) long.
£500–600
$700–850 ⊞ MCO

A silver fish slice, by John Emes, London 1798, 11½in (29cm) long.
£450–500
$650–700 ⊞ MCO

► **Two silver-gilt and agate serving spoons,** by Francis Higgins, London 1884, in a box, 10 x 5in (25.5 x 13cm).
£600–650
$850–950 ⊞ MHB

A Victorian silver part dinner service, maker's mark of Martin Hall & Co, London 1882, largest dish 25in (63.5cm) wide, 834oz.
£22,000–25,000
$32,000–36,000 ⚒ C

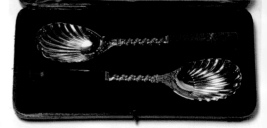

A set of silver fruit serving spoons and grape scissors, partial gilt, maker's mark J A/TS, possibly Joseph & Thomas Savory, London 1884, in a box, 10½ x 11in (26.5 x 28cm).
£1,000–1,200
$1,500–1,750 ⊞ MHB

A set of four silver serving spoons, Old English pattern, 1895.
£80–100
$100–150 ⚒ SWO

► **A pair of silver sugar nips,** by Cohen & Charles, modelled as a peg doll, some damage to face, London 1924, 3½in (9cm) high.
£550–625
$800–900 ⊞ JBU

A Georgian silver cream jug, with prickwork scroll panel, c1800, 5½in (14cm) wide.
£230–280
$330–400 ⊞ **PSA**

A George III silver cream jug, London 1805, 3½in (9cm) high.
£240–280
$350–400 ⊞ **TVA**

A George III silver cream jug, with scroll and acanthus handle, on a pedestal foot, London 1799, 5in (12.5cm) high.
£250–280
$350–400 ⊞ **PSA**

A Dutch .934 Standard silver cow creamer, modelled with its tail curled to form the handle, a hinged lid with an insect knop and bead eyes, export marks, London import marks for 1891, 11in (28cm) long.
£2,000–2,400
$2,900–3,500 ↗ **DN**

A silver cow creamer, late 19thC, 3.75oz.
£1,000–1,200
$1,500–1,800 ⊞ **DAD**

▶ **A Dutch silver cow creamer,** with red glass eyes, her tail raised to brush off the fly applied to the cover, c1900, 11in (28cm) long, 17.5oz.
£1,750–2,000
$2,500–2,900 ↗ **P**

A George III silver cream jug, with prickwork engraving, 4in (10cm) high.
£200–240
$290–350 ⊞ **PSA**

Hot Water Jugs

◀ **A George III silver hot water jug,** by John Scofield, with hinged cover and ebonized handle, engraved with the coat-of-arms of George III, surrounded by the Garter motto and a crown, maker's mark 'I.S.', London 1787, 11in (28cm) high, 23oz.
£1,600–2,000
$2,300–2,900 ↗ **MCA**

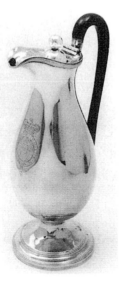

A George III silver hot water jug, by Charles Wright, crested and with gadrooned edging, the hinged cover with reeded finial, London 1770, 10½in (26.5cm) high, 21oz.
£400–450
$600–650 ↗ **Bea**

A George III silver hot water jug, by John Scofield, applied with classical medallions above fluting, London 1781, 12in (30.5cm) high, 22oz.
£1,200–1,400
$1,800–2,000 ↗ **S**

▶ **A George III silver hot water jug,** by Henry Chawner, fluted at the angles, with engraved initial 'B' below a baron's crest with drapery cartouche below a foliate band, the pedestal base with a single band of foliage, with hinged cover, ball button, and carved ivory handle, London 1795, 12½in (32cm) high, 28oz.
£1,300–1,500
$1,900–2,200 ↗ **S**

Items in the Jugs & Ewers section have been arranged in date order within each sub-section.

A George III silver hot water jug, by John Page, with ivory knop, chased shell oak leaf and gadrooned border and fruitwood handle, London 1814, 8in (20.5cm) high, 18oz.
£320–400
$450–600 ⚘ DN

A Regency silver hot water jug, by William Burwash, with gadrooned rim and treen handle, probably London 1816, 4½in (11.5cm) high, 24oz.
£220–250
$320–360 ⚘ GAK

A silver hot water jug, chased and embossed with floral garlands and ribbon ties and with reeded band, Birmingham 1892, 7in (18cm) high.
£145–175
$200–250 ⚘ GAK

▶ **An Edward VII silver hot water jug,** by Elkington & Co, with spiral fluting and leaf-shaped spout, London 1910, 8in (20.5cm) high, 17oz.
£200–240
$300–350 ⚘ Bea(E)

A silver hot water jug, by Martin, Hall & Co, engraved in Greek revival taste with a figural frieze, masks and festoons, with Greek helmet finial and gilt interior, engraved with crest and motto, London 1877, 13in (33cm) high, with fitted case.
£1,700–1,850
$2,500–2,700 ⚘ S

A Victorian silver hot water jug, by C. S. Harris, with reeded and fluted lower body, beaded edging, leaf spout, wrythen finial and wood scroll handle, on spreading base, marked on base, London 1886, 9in (23cm) high, 13oz.
£600–680
$870–1,000 ⚘ Bea

Pitchers

An American silver water pitcher, of Liverpool pottery type, the plain barrel-shaped body with short spout rising from three diminishing beads, the partly faceted slender hollow scroll handle with strut support, marked on base 'Pittman', Providence, Rhode Island c1800, 9in (23cm) high, 22oz.
£6,000–6,800
$8,700–9,900 ⚘ S(NY)

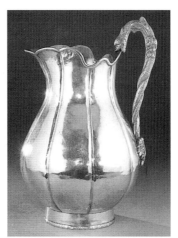

A South American silver pitcher, the branch handle entwined with a serpent, probably Bolivian, mid-19thC, 13¼in (33.5cm) high.
£1,400–1,600
$2,000–2,300 ⚘ S(NY)

An American silver water pitcher, by Tiffany & Co, flat chased in low relief with a band of griffins, urns and foliage, classical mask at the base of the handle, engraved with contemporary monogram, 550 Broadway, New York, c1865, 9in (23cm) high, 40oz.
£3,500–4,500
$5,000–6,500 ⚘ S(NY)

Kettles

A Dutch silver kettle, by H. N. H., with fixed wood scroll handle, on a stand with three leaf scroll supports, on paw and bun feet, with burner, Amsterdam c1735, re-assayed in 1822, 14½in (37cm) high, 66oz.
£3,200–3,600
$4,650–5,220 ⚒ DN

A George III silver kettle-on-stand, by Andrew Fogelberg and Stephen Gilbert, with later armorial engraving below handle, London 1785, 12in (30.5cm) high, 51oz.
£800–1,000
$1,200–1,500 ⚒ S

A Victorian silver kettle-on-stand, by Garrard & Co, with ivory and double-scrolled handle, London 1860, 15¾in (40cm) high, 68oz.
£1,300–1,500
$1,900–2,200 ⚒ B&L

A silver kettle-on-stand, by William Kidney, with cane covered scrolled loop handle, scroll decorated spout and chased rococo scroll and cartouche decoration, the stand with scrolled legs and pierced mask and flower decorated frieze, London 1739, 14in (35.5cm) high, 70.5oz.
£3,400–3,700
$5,000–5,500 ⚒ AH

▶ **A Dutch silver vase-shaped urn,** with spool-shaped cover and finial, two loop handles, silver-mounted wooden tap, on trumpet-shaped stem with bayonet mount and base, with bun feet, maker B. N., Amsterdam 1785, 17in (43cm) high, 89oz.
£2,600–3,000
$3,800–4,400 ⚒ DN

A George III silver tea kettle, the urn-shaped double lamp with detachable cover, the partly fluted kettle with reeded spigot terminating in a lion's mask with a carved ivory anthemion tap, a gadrooned shell and scroll rim, ivory and silver double serpent scroll handle and domed cover with wrythen bud finial, engraved twice with a coat-of-arms and with crests, maker's mark of Paul Storr, London 1808, 14in (35.5cm) high, 182oz.
£12,000–14,000
$17,500–20,500 ⚒ C
The arms are those of O'Callaghan impaling Ormonde for Cornelius, 1st Viscount Lismore of Shanbally, Co Tipperary, 1775–1857.

A George II rococo kettle-on-stand, by David Willaume II, decorated with flowers, scrolls, shells and molluscs, with two vacant cartouches, 1739, 14¼in (36cm) high, 87.5oz.
£7,000–8,000
$10,200–11,600 ⚒ P

A George III silver tea kettle, by William Plummer, with leather covered swing scrolling foliate handle, the kettle engraved with an armorial, the stand and lamp engraved with crests, London 1789, 15in (38cm) high, 88.25oz.
£2,000–2,400
$3,000–3,500 ⚒ CSK

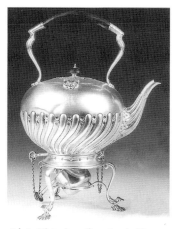

A late Victorian silver tea kettle, stand and burner, the stand on three scroll and shell feet, maker's mark of Hamilton and Inches, London 1892, 11½in (29cm) high, 37oz.
£400–500
$600–700 ✗ P(Ed)

An Edwardian silver kettle-on-stand, with gadroon and shell borders, fluted girdle and domed hinged lid, the stand with four scroll legs, shell feet and a burner, maker's mark of Nathan and Hayes, Chester 1908, 13½in (34.5cm) high, 46oz.
£500–600
$700–870 ✗ Bon

A Victorian silver tea kettle, stand and burner, by John Bodman Carrington, London 1893, 14in (35.5cm) high, 43oz.
£1,200–1,500
$1,750–2,200 ✗ P(S)

A silver tea kettle, stand and burner, by Mappin & Webb, Sheffield 1911, 11in (28cm) high, 38oz.
£800–1,000
$1,200–1,500 ⊞ CoHA

A silver kettle-on-stand, by G. H., with gadrooned border, part ebonized handle, the stand with four tapered legs and claw feet, Sheffield 1904, 12½in (32cm) high, 43oz.
£350–400
$500–600 ✗ P(E)

A silver kettle-on-stand, with central girdle, raised mounted ebony carrying handle and pull-off cover with knop finial, the stand of wirework form, on four legs with a burner, maker's mark of Martin Hall & Co, Sheffield 1916, 31oz.
£350–400
$500–600 ✗ Bon

Knife Rests

A pair of silver knife holders, modelled as tricycles, with slatted seats, London 1893–94, 5in (12.5cm) high, 9oz.
£620–680
$900–1,000 ✗ P(NE)
The knives would slide through the slats in the seat.

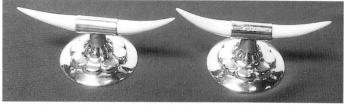

A pair of Edwardian silver and ivory knife rests, by T. Wooley, Birmingham 1903, 3½in (9cm) long.
£225–265
$300–380 ⊞ BEX

LOCATE THE SOURCE
The source of each illustration in Miller's can be found by checking the code letters below each caption with the Key to Illustrations, pages 311–314.

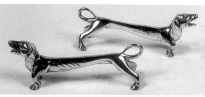

A pair of silver Dachshund knife rests, by William Hutton & Sons, Sheffield 1908, 3¼in (8.5cm) long.
£350–400
$500–600 ⊞ TC

Medals & Badges

A Gunpowder Plot silver medal, showing the snake of sedition gliding among lilies and roses, unsigned, inscription on reverse, 1605.
£100–120
$150–175 ⊞ EIM

A silver medal commemorating the marriage of Princess Mary and William of Orange, by J. Blum, 1641.
£750–850
$1,100–1,250 ⊞ BAL

A silver medal, commemorating the death of Charles I, by T. Rawlins, with a draped bust of Charles with long hair and a salamander amid flames on the reverse, 1649.
£320–350
$450–500 ⊞ BAL
The salamander on the reverse is used as an emblem of fortitude and patience under suffering.

A silver medal, commemorating the Embarkation at Scheveningen, by Peter van Abeele, with a bust of Charles II, Fame with trumpet over the fleet on the reverse, 1660.
£775–850
$1,100–1,300 ⊞ BAL

A silver medal, marking the execution of the Duke of Monmouth, showing the head of the Duke spouting blood, unsigned, 1685.
£180–220
$260–320 ⊞ EIM

A silver medal, commemorating the victories of Anne over Louis XIV, by P. H. Müller, the reverse with a tower besieged, the edge inscribed 'Dominus Tradidit Eum In Manus Foeminae Iudith XVIc', 1706.
£200–225
$290–330 ⊞ BAL
The imagery of this medal is designed to satirize Louis XIV for calling himself Magnus while at the same time being defeated by a woman, so making Anne 'greater'.

◄ **A Captain Cook Investigator of Oceans silver medal,** by L. Pingo, 1780.
£300–400
$450–600 ⊞ EIM

A silver medal, by J. Croker, commemorating the Act of Union Between England and Scotland, with a crowned bust and a statue of Anne as Pallas on the reverse, 1707.
£220–250
$320–360 ⊞ BAL

Insurance values

Always insure your valuable antiques for the cost of replacing them with similar items, regardless of the original price paid. Both dealers and auctioneers will provide a valuation service for a fee.

A silver medal marking the Death of the Earl of Effingham, by J. Milton, with Britannia seated on a globe on reverse, 1791.
£100–120
$150–180 ⚒ DNW

A silver satirical medal, Order of the Gorgomans, with a bust of Chin Quan, the sun in splendour on the reverse, c1800.
£220–250
$320–360 ⚒ DNW

A Waterloo silver medal, 1815.
£600–650
$870–1,000 ⚒ WAL
Awarded to Thomas Novis, 1st Reg Dragoon Guards, who was wounded at Waterloo.

A Dublin York Club silver ticket, by I. Parkes, with a bust of the Duke of York and bar loop for suspension inscribed 'Honi Soit Qui Mal y Pense', 1825.
£145–165
$200–250 ⊞ BAL

A Victorian silver Royal Sussex 1st Vol Battalion helmet plate.
£120–140
$170–200 PC

◀ **A South Africa silver medal,** 1877–79.
£450–500
$650–720 ⚒ WAL
Awarded to 1098 Pte H. Cooper, 2nd Dragoon Guards.

An Ally Sloper's silver medal for valour, the reverse inscribed 'To William J. Osborn for his Courageous Conduct at the Fire at Coast Guard Station, Castle Townshend, Co Cork, 7 July 1888', fitted with small ring for suspension.
£280–320
$400–450 ⚒ DNW
Ally Sloper was a favourite Victorian cartoon character and this medal was awarded by *The Sloperies* magazine to a reader who had saved some children from a fire.

▶ **The Gallantry Fund Award silver medal,** the reverse inscribed 'James Rowley, Decr. 15. 1894', in fitted case of issue.
£400–450
$600–650 ⚒ DNW
This medal was awarded by *Today* magazine in 1894 to a reader who had saved four people from drowning.

A silver medal, by J. McKay, commemorating the Highland Society of Scotland, to Gilbert McBlain, with an engraving of a plough and furrows on the reverse, Edinburgh hallmark and 'J.M.', 1833.
£140–160
$200–230 ⚒ DNW

A Baltic silver medal, 1854–55.
£60–80
$90–120 ⊞ RMC

A Brighton Aquarium Cat Show silver medal, by J. Restall, depicting three cats on face and inscribed to reverse, 1885.
£60–80
$90–120 ⊞ EIM

A silver province medal, commemorating the institution of the Royal Caledonian Curling Club on 25th July 1838, with a curling scene on the reverse, the suspension formed by thistles and a crown.
£80–90
$120–130 ⚒ DNW

A silver medal, commemorating the Zoological Society of London 1826, with various birds, edge engraved 'To Mr Abraham Dee Bartlett in Acknowledgement of Services Rendered to the Society 5th November 1872', in original Wyon case.
£1,250–1,450
$1,800–2,000 ⊞ BAL
The Wyons were a famous family of medal makers who came to England from Cologne in the 18th century and continued trading throughout the 19th century.

Miller's is a price GUIDE not a price LIST

A silver medal, commemorating Leith Academy 1889–1900, engraved with the facade, to Margaret I. Johnson, Edinburgh hallmark and for Hamilton and Inches.
£110–130
$160–190 ⚒ DNW

A silver medal, commemorating the Dublin Brewers and Distillers Exhibition, 1894, by Vaughton, with a large statue.
£230–260
$330–380 ↗ DNW

A silver prize medal, inscribed on reverse 'The Cat Club Won by Mrs H. V. James, "Blackwell Jogram" for the Best Long-Haired Male Smoke Cat, Jan 9th & 10th 1900, St Stephen's Hall Westminster', 1900.
£120–150
$170–220 ⊞ BAL

▶ **A silver medal,** by John Boyd Glasgow, commemorating Sandyford Burns Club instituted 1883, with two dogs, the reverse 'John Bruce 1902', inset with a portrait of Burns surrounded by floral and scroll mount, 1902.
£200–220
$290–320 ↗ DNW

A silver medal, commemorating the Aberdeenshire Bee Keepers' Association, with a bee in high relief, inscribed 'Association show 1919, awarded to W. M. Kennedy, 1st prize for display of honey and bees wax' on the reverse, 1919.
£220–250
$320–360 ↗ DNW

The Pluck silver medal for heroism, the reverse scroll inscribed 'Sgt Beisly', marked 'Birmingham 1897', with ring suspension and ribbon bar inscribed 'Special Service'.
£350–380
$500–550 ↗ DNW
Pluck **magazine was established in 1895 to counteract the influence of the 'Penny Dreadful' and celebrate the adventures of British heroes. Like other journals of the period, it awarded its own medals for brave and exceptional deeds.**

A silver and green enamel commemorative lapel badge, entitled 'Easter Rising 1916', the reverse with lapel stud fitting.
£160–180
$230–260 ↗ DNW

A silver medal, commemorating the National Pig Breeders' Association, founded 1886, by Restall, c1900.
£55–65
$80–95 ⊞ BAL

An Art Deco silver medal, by P. M. Dammann, depicting a female head, with a female figure and the reverse with Paris, 1907.
£200–220
$290–320 ↗ DNW
The 1907 date on the medal is that of the founding of the Compagnie Pour La Diffusion d'Electricité. The medal is thought to have been struck to mark an anniversary, either the 20th in 1927 or the 25th in 1932.

A silver challenge medal, for the Stockbridge (Edinburgh) Draughts Club, by R H.& B. Kirkwood, with black enamel squares, 1901.
£100–120
$150–180 ↗ DNW

A silver prize medal, commemorating the British Empire Games, England, 1934, inscribed 'Swimming 100 Yds Back 2nd' on the reverse.
£120–140
$170–200 ↗ DNW

A King George VI Coronation silver medal, signed by P. Metcalfe, with Queen Elizabeth, the Queen Mother on reverse, 1937.
£10–15
$15–20 ⊞ EIM

▶ **A silver-gilt medal,** a prize from Cowes Royal Southern Yacht Club, Isle of Wight, with a view of the club house with flag flying, 1937.
£55–65
$80–95 ⊞ BAL

Menu Holders

A pair of Chinese silver menu holders, modelled as dragons, c1880, 5in (12.5cm) long.
£575–650
$850–950 ⊞ BEX

A silver menu holder, Birmingham 1893, 3½in (9cm) wide.
£70–80
$100–120 ⊞ PSA

A set of four silver artist's palette menu holders, by Martin Hall & Co, Birmingham 1904, 1½in (4cm) high.
£475–525
$700–750 ⊞ TC

◄ **A set of eight Edwardian silver menu holders,** each with fox hunting trophy, Birmingham 1906, 2½in (6.5cm) wide, 3oz.
£650–750
$950–1,100 ⚒ AH

A set of four silver owl menu holders, with amber-coloured eyes, damage to one eye, Chester 1908, 1½in (4cm) high.
£650–750
$950–1,100 ⊞ JBU

A pair of silver lobster claw menu holders, by Sampson Mordan & Co, Chester 1907, 1¾in (4.5cm) high.
£300–350
$450–500 ⊞ BEX

A pair of Edwardian silver duck menu holders, by Crisford & Norris, Birmingham 1909, 1½in (4cm) wide.
£325–365
$450–550 ⊞ BEX

Miniatures

◄ **A silver miniature teapot,** engraved with leaves and ferns, with a wooden handle and finial, London 1881, 4in (10cm) high.
£325–375
$450–550 ⊞ DIC

► **A Dutch silver miniature tea caddy,** die stamped with three vignettes of gardeners, putti at play and a horse and figures in a landscape, c1885, 3½in (9cm) high.
£300–350
$450–500 ⊞ HofB

A Victorian silver miniature bowl, import marks for Sheffield 1894, 2in (5cm) diam.
£120–140
$170–200 ⊞ TVA

◄ **A Dutch silver miniature watering can,** with scrolled handle and central carrying handle, embossed with images of men and women sowing and watering seeds within scroll borders, importer's mark of Edwin Thompson, import marks for London 1896, 2½in (6.5cm) high, 1.5oz.
£140–180
$200–260 ⚒ Bon

◄ **An Edward VII silver miniature model of a sofa,** with chased and pierced decoration and padded velvet cushion, together with five miniature chairs and a footstool, Birmingham 1901, sofa 3½in (9cm) long.
£750–850
$1,100–1,250 ✗ Bea

A silver model of a parasol, with turned handle, Sheffield 1899, 4in (10cm) long.
£130–150
$190–220 ✗ AH

▶ **A silver model of fairies seated at a table,** marked, Chester 1900, 2in (5cm) wide, 1.25oz.
£270–300
$400–450 ✗ HCC

A Continental silver group of a barrel organ player, 1930s, 4in (10cm) wide.
£90–120
$130–170 ⊞ TAR

Mirrors

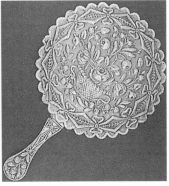

A Dutch or German silver hand mirror, with lobed border, embossed with a wicker basket filled with peonies and strawberries within a ribbon tie and laurel wreath border, the hinged handle with strawberries and ribbon ties, slight damage, with Turkish turgha import mark, 9½in (24cm) diam.
£550–650
$800–950 ✗ DN

A embossed silver mirror-back, with a continuous band of flowers and scrolls, encircling 16 petal-shaped lappets radiating from a central floral boss, Tughra marks, Ottoman Empire, 19thC, 12½in (32cm) diam.
£160–200
$230–290 ✗ P

A German silver dressing mirror, probably by H. Gladenbeck and Söhne, Berlin, decorated with rocaille ornament, engraved with monogram 'MR', c1860, 26¼in (66.5cm) high.
£1,700–1,850
$2,450–2,680 ✗ S(Am)

A Victorian cast silver-gilt dressing table mirror, by Hunt and Roskell, with a monogrammed cartouche flanked by children, 1881, 14½in (37cm) wide.
£7,000–8,000
$10,200–11,600 ✗ P

Condition

The condition is absolutely vital when assessing the value of an antique. Damaged pieces on the whole appreciate much less than perfect examples. However a rare desirable piece may command a high price even when damaged.

◄ **A Victorian silver-mounted mirror,** by William Comyns, the pierced surround decorated with cherubs, masks, birds and foliage, London 1887, 14¾in (37.5cm) high.
£360–400
$520–580 ✗ Bea

A silver-framed mirror, by John Septimus Beresford, embossed with stylized chinoiserie decoration, engraved with a monogram of Princess Adelaide, London 1889, 26½in (67.5cm) high.
£3,000–3,500
$4,400–5,000 ⚲ B&L

A late Victorian silver-mounted easel mirror, the foliate pierced and embossed frame with two cartouches, one depicting two young ladies being serenaded in a classical garden, the other of a classical terrace and garden, Birmingham 1900, 18¾in (47.5cm) high.
£800–900
$1,100–1,300 ⚲ P(S)

A pierced silver mirror, London 1901, 16½in (42cm) high.
£230–260
$350–400 ⚲ DOC

A late Victorian silver framed mirror, by William Comyns, decorated in repoussé with masks, birds, snakes and foliage, London 1896, 13in (33cm) high.
£650–750
$950–1,100 ⚲ LT

A Viennese silver mirror, with star beaded edge, c1900, 18½in (47cm) high.
£500–550
$700–800 ⚲ DORO

A silver mirror, by William Comyns, the frame decorated with scrolls, flowers and foliage, London 1900, 22in (56cm) high.
£400–500
$600–700 ⚲ Bea(E)

A silver-framed mirror, with central cartouche, pierced and embossed with scrolling foliage, Birmingham 1901, 18in (45.5cm) wide.
£1,800–2,200
$2,600–3,200 ⚲ TEN

Cross Reference
See Colour Review (page 122)

◄ **A French rococo-style silver-mounted dressing table mirror,** by Walker and Hall, stamped and pierced with scrolling foliage, enclosing a cartouche with engraved initials, on a velvet-backed easel stand, Sheffield 1901, 18in (45.5cm) high.
£750–850
$1,100–1,300 ⚲ C(S)

Auction or dealer?

All the pictures in our price guides originate from auction houses and dealers. Look for the symbol at the end of each caption to identify the source.

When buying at auction, prices can be lower than those of a dealer, but a buyer's premium and VAT will be added to the hammer price. Equally, when selling at auction, commission, tax and photography charges must be taken into account. Dealers will often restore pieces before putting them back on the market.

Both dealers and auctioneers will provide professional advice, so it is worth researching both sources before buying or selling your antiques.

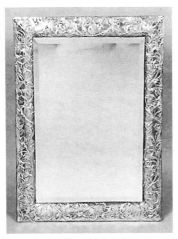

A silver dressing table mirror, decorated in repoussé with flowering tendrils, London 1901, 23in (58.5cm) high.
£500–600
$700–870 ✤ HYD

An Edwardian silver mounted easel mirror, by H. Matthews, the foliate and trellis pierced and embossed frame with vacant cartouche, Birmingham 1902, 11in (28cm) high.
£250–300
$350–450 ✤ P(S)

An Edwardian silver-mounted dressing table mirror, decorated with floral rococo scrolls, cartouche and covered in blue velvet, with strut, London 1907, 16in (40.5cm) high.
£450–550
$650–800 ✤ MAT

An Edwardian 17thC-style silver dressing table mirror, by The Goldsmiths & Silversmiths Co, the pierced frame decorated with cherubs among floral scrollwork, mounted on velvet, 1902, 27½in (70cm) high.
£1,750–2,000
$2,500–2,900 ✤ L

An Edwardian silver mirror, the embossed scrolling foliate frame with a central scrolling cartouche, on strut support, London 1903, 22in (56cm) high.
£500–550
$700–800 ✤ AH

An Edwardian silver-framed mirror, pierced with scrolling flowers and foliage, with a central cartouche, Birmingham 1903, 15½in (39.5cm) wide.
£550–650
$800–950 ✤ DN(H)

An Edwardian silver dressing table mirror, by William Comyns, with heart-shaped glass, the frame pierced and embossed with putti, masks, birds and scrolls, with blue velvet easel back, London 1905, 11in (28cm) high.
£550–650
$800–1,000 ✤ GAK

A W. M. F. silver-plated hand-mirror, c1910, 10½in (26.5cm) long.
£50–70
$75–100 ⊞ PSA

A silver hand-mirror, depicting The Reynolds Angels, Birmingham 1955, 9in (23cm) long.
£120–150
$180–220 ⊞ PSA

A George V silver dressing table mirror, with bevelled glass and plain frame, maker's mark worn, Birmingham 1917, 18¼in (46.5cm) high.
£300–350
$450–500 ✤ Bea(E)

Models

A 16thC-style silver figure of Mercury, holding the remains of a caduceus in his right hand, Italian/Flemish, on a marble pedestal base, 6½in (16.5cm) high.
£600–700
$870–1,000 ⚒ S(NY)

A French silver statue of a Saint Bishop, the reverse engraved with *accolé* armorials beneath Marquis' coronet, maker's mark illegible, on a wooden base, possibly Provence, c1710, 13in (33cm) high.
£7,000–8,000
$10,000–11,500 ⚒ C(G)

A French silver group of the Virgin and Child, damaged and repaired, stamped with six hallmarks, on an ebony veneered and silver-mounted base, early 19thC, 13⅝in (34.5cm) high.
£2,000–2,300
$2,900–3,500 ⚒ L
The hallmarks indicate that the figure was made in Paris by Jean-Ange-Joseph Loque before 1809.

A Portuguese silver toothpick holder, in the form of a soldier, mono-grammed, maker's mark worn, the base with pierced and embossed foliate decoration, on three paw feet, c1850, 8⅝in (22cm) high, 12oz.
£1,000–1,200
$1,500–1,800 ⚒ Bon

A silver figure of a slave, by John Hunt, on a marble base, c1860, 13¼in (33.5cm) high.
£2,250–2,500
$3,300–3,600 ⊞ SFL

A silver deer, by Edward Barnard & Sons, with Victorian duty stamp, pre-1891, 3½in (9cm) high.
£145–165
$200–250 ⊞ WeH

▶ **A German silver equestrian model of Albert, King of Saxony,** in military uniform, on a plinth, with trophies and banners at the angles, initialled 'A' below the crown, cast and chased with the arms of Saxony and inscribed 'Albert König von Sachsen 28 April 1828–19 Juni 1902', Elimeyer, Dresden, c1902, 13in (33cm) high, 86oz.
£3,400–3,600
$5,000–5,500 ⚒ S(G)

A silver model of a red deer stag, realistically cast and chased, London import marks for B. H. Muller, 1912, 20½in (52cm) high, 100oz.
£10,500–11,500
$15,000–16,500 ⚒ C

A silver model of an elephant, realistically modelled as a charging tusker, tusk detached, import marked, London 1924, 9in (23cm) high, 28oz.
£1,800–2,000
$2,600–3,000 ⚒ S

A silver figure of Morse Code, by The Goldsmiths & Silversmiths Co, on a textured base, set on a wooden plinth with an inscribed silver plate, London 1938, 12½in (32cm) high overall, 98oz.
£2,800–3,200
$4,000–4,500 ⚒ L

Mugs

A George I silver mug, by John Elston, with reeded girdle and scroll handle, Exeter 1716, 3¼in (8.5cm) high, 4.75oz.
£600–720
$870–1,000 ⚒ Bea(E)

A George II baluster mug, by Thomas Whipham, with later allover fluted decoration and engraved initials, with leaf-capped scroll handle, on spreading base, London 1743, 5in (12.5cm) high, 12oz.
£350–450
$500–650 ⚒ Bea

▶ **A silver quart mug,** with reeded upper and lower bands and fluted scroll handle, maker's mark 'RG', London 1770, 6¼in (16cm) high, 23oz.
£850–950
$1,300–1,500 ⚒ HAM

A George III baluster mug, by John King, with later presentation inscription, leaf-capped double scroll handle and spreading foot, London 1767, 4¾in (12cm) high, 10oz.
£250–280
$350–400 ⚒ Bea(E)

A George I mug, by John Farnell, with scroll handle, initialled on thumbpiece, London 1717, 4in (10cm) high, 7.5oz.
£1,000–1,200
$1,500–1,800 ⚒ Bea

A George II silver baluster mug, with leaf-capped scroll handle, c1745, 4¾in (12cm) high, 11oz.
£300–360
$440–520 ⚒ P(WM)

A silver pint mug, by Thomas Farren, with moulded rim, leaf-capped scroll handle, on a moulded spreading foot, the base inscribed with initials, London 1741, 7in (18cm) high, 11.5oz.
£550–600
$800–870 ⚒ WW

A George III silver baluster mug, later chased with a hunt scene, maker's mark 'I.S.', possibly for John Swift, London 1759, 12oz.
£500–600
$700–870 ⚒ Bea

A silver pint mug, with acanthus leaf scrolled handle, maker's mark 'IK' for John Kentenber, London 1771, 5in (12.5cm) high, 14oz.
£600–650
$870–1,000 ⚒ MCA

◀ **A George III plain silver baluster mug,** with leaf-capped double scroll handle, on spreading base, maker's mark 'I.K.', possibly for John King, London 1775, 5in (12.5cm) high, 10oz.
£550–600
$800–870 ⚒ Bea

A George III silver mug, by Hester Bateman, with moulded rim and leaf-capped double scroll handle, later chased, engraved with a monogram within a C-scroll cartouche, the underside later engraved with a retailer's name and address, London 1783, 5in (12.5cm) high, 11oz.
£300–340
$450–500 ⚒ CSK

A George III silver mug, by Peter, Ann and William Bateman, later chased with scrolls and foliage, with leaf-capped double scroll handle, London 1799, 5in (12.5cm) high, 10.5oz.
£260–300
$380–450 ⚒ Bea

> **Cross Reference**
> See Tankards (page 195)

A George IV silver mug, by William Bateman, with reeded bands, inscribed 'Arundel Christmas Market 1828 ... 10 Fat South Down Ewes', and initials, engraved with a bird of prey, London 1828, 5in (12.5cm) high, 15oz.
£500–550
$700–800 ⚒ DN

A George III silver mug, by Langlands and Robertson, with applied rib band, scroll handle and rim foot, Newcastle 1784, 6in (15cm) high, 17oz.
£800–900
$1,200–1,300 ⚒ AG

A George III silver mug, with reeded staves, the base with later inscription, maker's mark poorly struck, 1800, 4½in (11.5cm) high, 11.5oz.
£280–320
$400–450 ⚒ L

▶ **A William IV silver christening mug,** the campana-shaped mug on a spreading circular foot with foliate decoration and gilt interior, maker's mark rubbed, London 1832, 3½in (9cm) high.
£300–350
$450–500 ⚒ L

A William IV silver christening mug, by Reily and Storer, the body embossed and engraved with flowers within double-reeded reserve, with acanthus scroll handle, London 1833, 5in (12.5cm) high, 6oz.
£230–270
$330–400 ⚒ EH

A George III silver mug, by Peter and Ann Bateman, decorated with horizontal bands of reeding and with a bracket handle, the front engraved with a vignette of a running fox with an inscription 'Success to Newton Hunt and the Lancashire Fox Hounds', London 1792, 3½in (9cm) high, 6.75oz.
£650–750
$950–1,100 ⚒ CSK

A George IV child's silver mug, by William Sharp, London 1826, 3in (7.5cm) high.
£325–350
$470–500 ⊞ BEX

A Victorian silver christening mug, by Edward Barnard & Sons, London 1838, 3¼in (8.5cm) high.
£350–400
$500–600 ⊞ BEX

A Victorian silver christening mug, by F. D. Dexter, embossed with figures, a cartouche with monograms, on scroll feet, London 1844, 3¾in (9.5cm) high.
£320–360
$465–520 ↗ DN

A Victorian silver christening mug, by Roberts and Briggs, the body embossed and engraved with a parrot among vine leaves, on a rocaille base, with scroll handle, London 1857, 6in (15cm) high, 5oz.
£240–280
$350–400 ↗ EH

A silver christening mug, by Josiah Williams & Co, engraved with ferns, Exeter 1878, 6½in (16.5cm) high, 4oz.
£160–175
$230–250 ↗ P(NE)

A Victorian silver christening mug, by Martin Hall & Co, embossed with leaf scrolls and fruits, with scroll handle and shell-chased foot, Sheffield 1855, 5in (12.5cm) high, 5oz.
£300–340
$450–500 ↗ DN

A Victorian silver christening mug, by G. Richards and E. Brown, London 1864, 3¼in (8.5cm) high.
£250–300
$350–450 ⊞ BEX

◄ **A silver-gilt christening mug,** by Charles Fox, decorated with foliate bands and beaded edging, with an angular handle, 1870, 4½in (11.5cm) high.
£250–300
$350–450 ↗ Bea(E)

A silver mug, by Robert Hennell, with leaf-capped scroll handle and engraved floral decoration, London 1872, 4¾in (12cm) high.
£300–340
$450–500 ↗ Bea(E)

▶ **A Victorian silver mug,** by William Hunter, with engraved bird and geometric decoration, monogrammed 'H', London 1879, 4in (10cm) high, 6oz.
£280–300
$400–450 ↗ SLN

A Victorian octagonal silver mug, by George Angell, engraved with panels of scrolls and flowers and 'Lucy', with shaped borders and scroll handle, London 1856, 4in (10cm) high.
£220–240
$300–350 ↗ DN

A Victorian silver christening mug, the sides panelled with embossed bulrushes and a cartouche, with beaded scroll handle and circular foot, Birmingham 1862, 3½in (9cm) high, 3oz.
£100–130
$150–200 ↗ DN

An Egyptian-style silver-gilt christening mug, by R. M. E. H., London 1873, 3½in (9cm) high.
£600–680
$870–1,000 ⊞ DIC

A Victorian silver 'Exeter' pint mug, by Josiah Williams & Co, engraved with stylized Holbeinesque decoration, butterfly and foliate panels, within beaded borders, inscribed, Exeter 1882, 5½in (14cm) high, 8.75oz.
£240–280
$350–400 ⚒ P(E)

A Victorian child's silver mug, by Holland, Aldwinckle and Slater, the bell-shaped body decorated with applied foliate strapwork in early 18thC-style, engraved with the cyphers of Prince Edward of York, further engraved with inscription 'From VRI 23 June 1895', London 1893, 3½in (9cm) high, on an ebonized wood plinth.
£7,700–8,500
$11,000–12,500 ⚒ S(NY)
This mug was given to Prince Edward of York on his first birthday, 23 June 1895, by his great-grandmother Queen Victoria.

A Victorian silver christening mug, by Edward Barnard & Sons, London 1886, 3½in (9cm) high.
£300–330
$450–480 ⊞ BEX

A silver christening mug, Birmingham 1898, 3in (7.5cm) high.
£80–100
$120–150 ⊞ PSA

A silver mug, commemorating the coronation of George V and Queen Mary, marked, Sheffield 1910, 3¼in (8.5cm) high.
£500–550
$700–800 ⊞ SHa

LOCATE THE SOURCE
The source of each illustration in Miller's can be found by checking the code letters below each caption with the Key to Illustrations, pages 311–314.

◄ **A silver christening mug,** by Mappin & Webb, London 1927, 3½in (9cm) high.
£250–300
$360–450 ⊞ BEX

► **A silver half pint christening mug,** by William Hutton & Sons, Birmingham 1932, 3½in (9cm) high.
£220–250
$320–360 ⊞ BEX

A Victorian silver christening mug, by Edward Barnard & Sons, London 1890, 3½in (9cm) high.
£200–225
$300–330 ⊞ BEX

A Victorian silver christening mug, by Harry Atkin, engraved with flowers and leaves, Sheffield 1899, 3in (7.5cm) high.
£220–250
$320–360 ⊞ BEX

A silver christening mug, with Georgian-style handle, hallmarked 1924, 8in (20.5cm) high.
£90–120
$130–180 ⊞ SnA

Napkin Holders

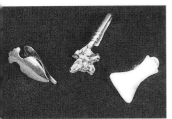

◄ A set of four silver napkin holders, by John William Kirwan, with enamelled bands in red, blue and green, Birmingham 1896, 2in (5cm) high.
£750–825
$1,100–1,200 ⊞ JBU

Three silver napkin clips, c1910, largest 1½in (4cm) long.
£85–95
$125–140 each ⊞ BEX
Napkin clips were used by gentlemen to pin their napkins to their shirts or ties.

A pair of silver napkin rings, by G. Angell, London 1860, 1½in (4cm) high.
£200–250
$300–350 ⊞ WELD

◄ A silver napkin ring, Birmingham 1926, 1½in (4cm) high.
£80–100
$120–150 ⊞ MRW

A silver napkin ring, egg cup and spoon, by Harry Atkin, Sheffield 1937–39, egg cup 2½in (6.5cm) high.
£200–225
$300–325 ⊞ BEX

Nutmeg Graters

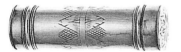

A Queen Anne silver cylindrical nutmeg grater or tobacco rasp, by Thomas Kedden, with detachable rasp, the case fully marked around the rim and engraved with a band of hatched and diaper-engraved lozenges, the pull-off cap engraved with a stylized flower motif, the base engraved with initials '*RL*', the pull-off cap with lion's head erased and maker's mark 1703.
£3,800–4,200
$5,500–6,000 ⚒ P

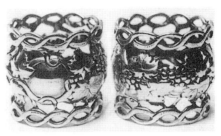

A George III silver nutmeg grater, by Matthew Linwood, Birmingham 1786, 1½in (4cm) wide.
£1,075–1,175
$1,500–1,700 ⊞ BEX

A George III silver nutmeg grater, modelled as a barrell, 1789, 1¼in (3.5cm) high.
£875–975
$1,300–1,500 ⊞ BEX

A George III silver nutmeg grater, by Thomas Willmore, London 1801, 1in (2.5cm) high.
£875–975
$1,300–1,500 ⊞ BEX

A George III silver nutmeg grater, by T. and J. Phipps and E. Robinson II, London 1815, 2in (5cm) high.
£1,175–1,295
$1,700–1,900 ⊞ BEX

A cylindrical silver nutmeg grater, by Mary Anne and Charles Reily, with side opening, London 1826, 3in (7.5cm) long.
£550–650
$800–1,000 ⊞ TC

Oddities

◀ **A silver-mounted frosted glass biscuit barrel,** by Martin Hall & Co, Sheffield 1867, 7in (18cm) high.
£900–1,100
$1,300–1,600 ⊞ TC

A cast silver clockwork table bell, by Joseph Braham, modelled as a tortoise, activated by the head or tail, 1903, 6¼in (16cm) long, 14oz.
£2,200–2,600
$3,200–3,800 ↗ TEN

◀ **A pair of silver-mounted ash billiard cues,** hallmarked London 1896.
£700–800
$1,000–1,200 ↗ S

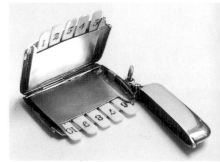

A silver butt marker, London 1925, 2in (5cm) wide.
£1,800–2,000
$2,600–2,900 ⊞ JBU

A silver table bell, by J. H. S., London 1935, 4½in (11cm) high.
£500–550
$700–800 ⊞ TC

An Indian Mughal dagger and silver-mounted scabbard, the jade hilt inlaid on either side with a ruby-set foiled crystal, 18thC, 16¾in (42.5cm) long.
£3,200–3,500
$4,500–5,000 ↗ S

A silver sauce bottle coaster, London 1907, 1½in (4cm) high.
£80–100
$120–150 ⊞ HEI

A silver and glass spirit flask, with silver-gilt cap, Chester 1887, 6½in (16.5cm) high.
£250–275
$350–400 ⊞ JAS

▶ **A Victorian silver-mounted conical glass spirit flask,** with leather carrying case and straps, Birmingham 1894, 10in (25.5cm) long.
£180–200
$250–300 ↗ AAV

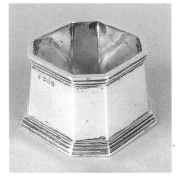

▶ **A pair of late Victorian silver glove stretchers,** by George Heath, modelled as a duck's head, with glass eyes, realistically engraved with feathers, marked, London 1887, 8in (20.5cm) long.
£300–350
$450–500 ↗ Bon

◀ **A silver gorget,** by Irvine of Fermanagh, engraved with a royal coat-of-arms, c1765, 4½in (11.5cm) wide.
£800–900
$1,200–1,300
⊞ WELD

A French silver three-piece jardinière set, by Bointaburet, with sterling silver liners, c1860, largest 15½in (39.5cm) wide.
£13,500–15,000
$19,500–21,500 ⊞ SFL
Bointaburet pieces are usually of very fine quality and very heavy. The fact that this is a set also enhances the price.

A Continental silver .930 standard rococo-style jardinière, with silver-plated liner, import marks for Mappin & Webb, London 1898, 22in (56cm) wide.
£3,500–4,000
$5,000–5,800 ↗ B&B

A French silver watch/key ring, in the shape of a rifle, c1910, 2in (5cm) long.
£275–325
$400–470 ⊞ BEX

A Spanish silver library lamp, by Domingo Estrada, for two lights, cast, chased and applied with leaves and foliage, the silk-fitted sliding screen surmounted by a dove, laurel leaf finial, marked on base and sconces, Zaragosa c1780, 26in (66cm) high, 50.5oz.
£2,000–2,250
$3,000–3,300 ↗ S(G)

A silver-mounted magnifying glass, by William Comyns, 1887, 9in (23cm) long.
£140–160
$200–230 ⊞ HUM

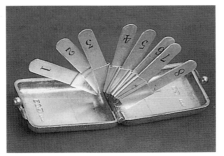

A silver butt marker, with hinged lid, containing eight numbered silver pegs, hallmarked, c1920, 2½in (6.5cm) high.
£1,700–1,850
$2,500–2,800 ↗ Bon

A pair of miniature Royal Worcester plaques, with contemporary pierced silver surrounds, each signed 'Raymond Rushton', date code for 1912, 4in (10cm) diam.
£900–1,000
$1,300–1,500 ⊞ TVA

A silver butt marker, by J. C. Vickery, the hinged and sprung case opening to reveal ten ivory numbered markers, London 1912, 2½in (6.5cm) high.
£1,600–1,800
$2,300–2,600 ↗ S(S)
This device was used to determine in a gentlemanly fashion where each member of the shooting party was to stand. The markers were placed in the case with the numbers pointing downwards, and then each person selected one, in the manner of drawing straws.

Auction or dealer?

All the pictures in our price guides originate from auction houses and dealers. Look for the symbol at the end of each caption to identify the source.

When buying at auction, prices can be lower than those of a dealer, but a buyer's premium and VAT will be added to the hammer price. Equally, when selling at auction, commission, tax and photography charges must be taken into account. Dealers will often restore pieces before putting them back on the market.

Both dealers and auctioneers will provide professional advice, so it is worth researching both sources before buying or selling your antiques.

◀ **A silver-gilt trumpet-shaped posy holder,** with folding tripod support, engraved with foliate anthemions and decorated with chain festoons set with turquoises, maker's mark 'W.N.', London 1864, 4½in (11.5cm) high.
£700–800
$1,000–1,200 ⚒ **Bea**

> **Miller's is a price GUIDE not a price LIST**

▶ **A silver-mounted tripod posy holder,** with folding supports and cut blue glass bowl, engraved with foliage, the beaded lip decorated with festoons of chains, maker's mark of Thomas Stapleton, London 1874, 5in (12.5cm) high.
£1,000–1,200
$1,500–1,800 ⚒ **Bea**

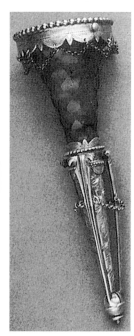

A mother-of-pearl posy holder, with silver-gilt mounts, the bowl applied at lip and base with chased sprays of flowers, the handle curved and similarly set with chain and pin, 5in (12.5cm) high, in contemporary fitted case, with label 'Parkes/12 Vigo Street/Regent Street/W', and incised maker's mark.
£2,500–3,000
$3,500–4,500 ⚒ **Bea**

A silver-gilt purse, with plaques depicting dead game, c1820, 3in (7.5cm) wide.
£325–375
$470–560 ⊞ **MB**

▶ **A silver purse,** Birmingham 1915, 3in (7.5cm) wide.
£130–140
$190–200 ⊞ **PSA**

A Victorian silver and steel shoehorn, c1884, 7½in (19cm) long.
£20–25
$30–35 ⊞ **OBS**

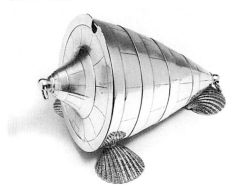

A Victorian silver spoon warmer, by Archer, Machin and Marsh, modelled as a buoy, decorated to simulate wood bound with metal bands, with gilded interior, Sheffield 1871, 8in (20.5cm) wide, 16.5oz.
£1,500–1,650
$2,200–2,500 ⚒ **P**

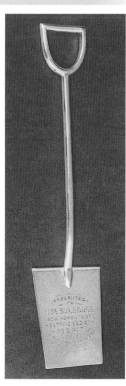

A silver novelty ship's ventilator, by S. Jacob, London 1911, 4¼in (11cm) high.
£300–350
$450–500 ⊞ **TC**

◀ **A silver commemorative spade,** by J. R., inscribed 'A Memento of Cutting Sod of No. 3 Pit from Welsh Colliery', Glasgow 1919, 8in (20.5cm) high.
£350–400
$500–600 ⊞ **BEX**

Photograph Frames

A silver photograph frame, by William Comyns, London 1892, 6½in (16.5cm) wide.
£420–460
$600–650 ⊞ THOM

A Victorian silver photograph frame, slight damage, 6½in (16.5cm) high.
£65–75
$95–110 ⊞ Q2

A silver photograph frame, by Saunders and Shepherd, Birmingham 1892, 6¾in (17cm) high.
£600–650
$870–950 ⊞ THOM

▶ **A pair of late Victorian silver easel photograph frames,** the borders pierced with acanthus leaves, fruit, floral garlands and masks of musical cherubs, with a monogrammed cartouche, London 1894, 8½in (21.5cm) high.
£800–1,000
$1,200–1,500 ⚒ HYD

A silver photograph frame, by L. Emmanuel, Birmingham 1893, 8in (20.5cm) high.
£400–450
$600–650 ⊞ THOM

Cross Reference
See Colour Review (page 122)

◀ **A silver and enamel photograph frame,** by Hutton & Sons, embossed with entwined plant forms heightened with blue/green enamels, stamped maker's marks, London 1903, 4in (10cm) high.
£600–700
$870–1,000 ⚒ P

A late Victorian embossed silver-mounted photograph frame, Birmingham 1899, 8in (20.5cm) high.
£250–300
$350–450 ⚒ GAK

▶ **A silver photograph frame,** embossed in bold relief with chrysanthemums and poppies, with J. W. Benson retailer's stamp, maker's marks for Chester 1904, 13½in (34.5cm) high.
£700–800
$1,000–1,200 ⚒ P

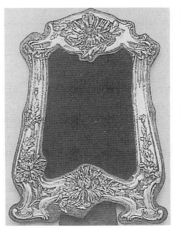

A silver photograph frame, Birmingham 1904, 6in (15cm) high.
£325–375
$450–550 ⊞ THOM

A silver photograph frame, by
William Comyns, London 1905,
7¼in (18.5cm) high.
£450–500
$650–700 ⊞ THOM

▶ A silver photograph frame,
by R. Pringle, Birmingham 1908,
5in (12.5cm) high.
£200–235
$300–350 ⊞ THOM

An Edwardian silver photograph
frame, Chester 1908,
6½in (16.5cm) high.
£225–250
$300–350 ⊞ ATQ

A silver photograph frame, by
A. and J. Zimmerman, Birmingham
1913, 4½in (11.5cm) high.
£180–200
$260–300 ⊞ THOM

A silver photograph frame, by
W. J. Myatt & Co, Chester 1905,
8in (20.5cm) high.
£300–350
$450–500 ⊞ THOM

A silver photograph frame, by
J. and W. Deakin, Sheffield 1916,
7in (18cm) high.
£300–340
$450–500 ⊞ THOM

A silver photograph frame, by
H. Matthews, Birmingham 1907,
6½in (16.5cm) high.
£320–360
$460–520 ⊞ THOM

A silver photograph frame, by
Richard Cooper, Birmingham 1911,
5½in (14cm) high.
£200–220
$300–320 ⊞ THOM

A silver photograph frame, with
two scroll feet and an oak back and
strut, Chester 1918, 9in (23cm) high.
£130–170
$190–250 ⊞ PSA

◀ A silver travelling photograph
frame, with a push-button clasp
opening to reveal a central hinged
frame with an oval aperture, maker's
mark of The Goldsmiths & Silversmiths
Co Ltd, London 1922, 3in (7.5cm) high.
£300–360
$450–520 ✗ Bon

Pincushions

A silver shoe pincushion,
Birmingham 1890, 3¼in (8.5cm) long.
£200–240
$300–350 ⊞ PSA

A silver pincushion, modelled as a
jockey's cap, marked 'CS.FS',
Birmingham 1891, 2½in (6.5cm) wide.
£200–225
$300–325 ⚒ GH

A Victorian silver pincushion, by
M. and W., modelled as a rocking
cradle, registered No. 291605,
Sheffield 1896, 2¼in (5.5cm) long.
£220–270
$320–390 ⚒ GH

An Edwardian silver pincushion,
modelled as a leopard, inscribed on
the collar 'Coronation 1902', the fore
paw stamped 'No. 24', London 1902,
7in (18cm) long.
£550–600
$800–870 ⚒ AH

A silver pincushion, by Levi and
Salaman, modelled as a hedgehog,
Birmingham 1903, 1½in (4cm) high.
£480–520
$700–750 ⊞ THOM

A silver pincushion, by S. & Co,
modelled as a standing pig, Birmingham
1904, 3¼in (8.5cm) long.
£130–150
$190–220 ⚒ GH

A silver pincushion, modelled as a
pig, c1905, 3¼in (8.5cm) long.
£350–375
$500–550 ⊞ HAN

An Edwardian silver pincushion,
by Adie and Lovekin, modelled as
an elephant, Birmingham 1905,
2in (5cm) long.
£250–280
$360–400 ⊞ HofB

A silver pincushion, by Saunders and
Shepherd, modelled as a camel,
Birmingham 1906, 2¼in (5.5cm) long.
£500–650
$700–1,000 ⊞ THOM

A silver pincushion, by S. M. & Co,
modelled as a fledgling bird, Chester
1905, 2in (5cm) long.
£140–170
$200–250 ⚒ GH

A silver pincushion by Crisford and
Norris, modelled as a duck, cushion
replaced, Birmingham 1906,
2½in (6.5cm) high.
£375–425
$560–620 ⊞ THOM

◄ **A silver pincushion,** by A. & L.,
modelled as a standing bulldog,
Birmingham 1906, 2¾in (7cm) long.
£370–420
$500–600 ⚒ GH

Prices

The price ranges quoted in this
book reflect the average price a
purchaser might expect to pay
for a similar item. The price will
vary according to the condition,
rarity, size, popularity,
provenance, colour and
restoration of the item, and this
must be taken into account
when assessing values. Don't
forget that if you are selling it
is quite likely that you will be
offered less than the price range.

A silver pincushion, modelled as a stag, import mark for Chester 1907, 3½in (9cm) high.
£650–700
$950–1,000 🔨 **FHF**

A silver pincushion, by A. and L. Ltd, modelled as a camel, Birmingham 1907, 2½in (6.5cm) long.
£320–360
$460–520 🔨 **GH**

A silver pincushion, by C. and K., modelled as a swan, Birmingham 1907, 3in (7.5cm) long.
£300–325
$450–470 🔨 **GH**

Miller's is a price GUIDE not a price LIST

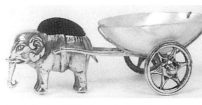

◀ **A silver and mother-of-pearl pincushion,** modelled as an elephant and cart, Birmingham 1909, 3½in (9cm) long.
£550–650
$800–1,000 ⊞ **AMH**

A silver pincushion, by Adie and Lovekin, modelled as a hedgehog, Birmingham 1908, 2in (5cm) wide.
£320–370
$450–500 🔨 **GH**

A silver pincushion, modelled as a dog with a mother-of-pearl cart, Birmingham 1909, 4¾in (12cm) long.
£500–600
$700–870 🔨 **RBB**

A silver pincushion, by C. and N., modelled as a roller skate, Birmingham 1909, 2½in (6.5cm) long.
£220–250
$320–360 🔨 **GH**

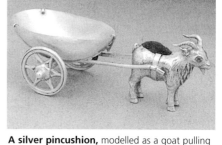

A silver pincushion, by A. and L., modelled as a goat pulling a mother-of-pearl cart, Birmingham 1909, 6½in (16.5cm) long.
£320–360
$450–500 🔨 **GH**

A silver pincushion, modelled as a goat pulling a cart, the goat set with red glass eyes, the mother-of-pearl cart mounted on two silver wheels, maker's mark of Adie and Lovekin, Birmingham 1910, 3½in (9cm) long.
£440–480
$650–700 🔨 **Bon**

A silver pincushion, modelled as a teddy bear, with original velvet, maker's mark rubbed, Chester 1927, 1½in (4cm) high.
£550–600
$800–870 🔨 **FHF**

Auction or dealer?

All the pictures in our price guides originate from auction houses and dealers. Look for the symbol at the end of each caption to identify the source.

When buying at auction, prices can be lower than those of a dealer, but a buyer's premium and VAT will be added to the hammer price. Equally, when selling at auction, commission, tax and photography charges must be taken into account. Dealers will often restore pieces before putting them back on the market.

Both dealers and auctioneers will provide professional advice, so it is worth researching both sources before buying or selling your antiques.

Rattles

A silver rattle and whistle, by Thomas Tearle, engraved with acanthus leaves and initials 'SH', with coral teething stick, c1740, 6¼in (16cm) long.
£575–625
$850–900 ⚒ P

A George II child's silver rattle and whistle, engraved with a crest and motto, with coral teething stick, marked, probably E.L., c1740, 4½in (11.5cm) long.
£900–1,000
$1,300–1,500 ⚒ P

A baby's silver rattle and whistle, faceted baluster form, alternative engraved panels, two tiers of bells, replacement mother-of-pearl teether, maker's mark only, probably J. F., 18thC, 5¼in (13.5cm) high.
£150–180
$220–260 ⚒ Bon

▶ **A George III child's silver rattle and whistle,** by Peter and Ann Bateman, with eight bells dependent in two tiers, bright-cut engraved with foliage and prick-dot wrigglework, with coral teething stick, 1797.
£1,100–1,200
$1,600–1,800 ⚒ P

A silver rattle and whistle, in the shape of four bells suspended from a lion and a chain, probably Dutch, 18thC, 2¾in (7cm) long, 2oz.
£1,500–1,650
$2,200–2,500 ⚒ S(Am)

A silver rattle and whistle, with engraved decoration, coral teether and carrying ring, maker's mark of W. T., late 18thC, 6in (15cm) long.
£700–850
$1,000–1,250 ⚒ Bea(E)

Insurance values

Always insure your valuable antiques for the cost of replacing them with similar items, regardless of the original price paid. Both dealers and auctioneers will provide a valuation service for a fee.

▶ **A George III silver rattle and whistle,** by Peter and Ann Bateman, engraved with floral and foliate swags and monogram, with coral teether, London 1804, 5in (12.5cm) high.
£800–1,000
$1,200–1,500 ⚒ Bon

A George III silver rattle and whistle, by Joseph Taylor, bright-cut engraved latticework and foliate decoration, with two rows of three dependent bells, with coral teething bar, repaired, Birmingham c1800, 4½in (11.5cm) long.
£225–275
$300–400 ⚒ P(O)

◀ **A George III silver rattle and whistle,** engraved with stylized vertical banding, two of the eight bells and teething piece missing, London 1811, 4¼in (11cm) long.
£150–180
$220–260 ⚒ P(E)

A George III silver rattle and whistle, by Theodosia Ann Atkins, the frill with six dependent bells, integral loop and fitting and coral teething bar, 1816, 4¾in (12cm) long.
£450–550
$650–800 ✂ P(O)

A silver-gilt rattle, by Charles Rawlings, in the shape of a pagoda, hung with bells, coral teething piece, one bell missing, London 1824, 6in (15cm) long.
£2,300–2,500
$3,300–3,600 ✂ HAM
The unusual design of this rattle accounts for the high value.

A Victorian sterling silver and mother-of-pearl rattle and whistle, 4in (10cm) long.
£100–140
$150–200 ⊞ RRA

A Victorian silver rattle and whistle, with ivory teething ring, 7in (18cm) long.
£80–90
$120–130 ⊞ EKK

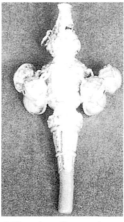

A Victorian silver and coral rattle, by George Unite, Birmingham 1843, 4in (10cm) long.
£500–600
$700–870 ⊞ BEX

A silver rattle, with ivory teething ring, Chester 1892, 3in (7.5cm) long.
£140–180
$200–260 PC

▶ **A silver rattle and whistle,** c1910, 4in (10cm) long.
£220–250
$320–360 ⊞ BaN

A silver baby's rattle, by George Unite & Sons, with ivory teething ring, Birmingham 1920, 5in (12.5cm) long.
£360–400
$500–580 ⊞ BEX

◀ **A silver baby's rattle,** depicting faces of the moon, with ivory teething ring, c1912, 3in (7.5cm) long.
£140–180
$200–260 ⊞ BaN

▶ **A silver and mother-of-pearl rattle,** by Crisford and Norris, depicting Father Christmas, Birmingham 1929, 5in (12.5cm) long.
£550–650
$800–950 ⊞ THOM

A Victorian silver rattle and whistle, knopped form, with embossed floral roundel decoration, two rows of dependent bells, integral loop fitting, coral teething bar, mouthpiece damaged, Birmingham 1860, 4½in (11.5cm) long.
£180–220
$260–320 ✂ P(O)

Religious

An Italian silver holy water bucket, the scalloped swing handle rising from satyrs' masks, repaired, engraved with date '1662', 17thC, 7½in (18.5cm) diam, 19.5oz.
£2,000–2,400
$3,000–3,500 ⚒ S(NY)

A silver devotional pendant, with the Virgin and Child, a crucifixion scene on the reverse, in red, green, blue and white watercolour on vellum, possibly southern Germany, c1700, 3in (7.5cm) high.
£270–300
$400–450 ⊞ JSM

A Canadian silver chalice and paten, by Peter Nordbeck, Halifax, Nova Scotia, early 19thC, chalice 9in (23cm) high.
£4,000–4,500
$5,800–6,500 ⚒ RIT

A Belgian silver miniature holy water font, by Berthold Müller, c1840, 8in (20.5cm) high.
£350–400
$500–600 ⊞ EXC

◄ **A silver-cased jug,** possibly for ecclesiastical use, of clear glass ovoid form, central band flat-chased with quatrefoil motifs and set with chysoprase as the cover, terminating in a spread circular foot, engraved with clover motifs, the base engraved around the rim 'Presented to Captain J.R. Walters on his 21st Birthday 3-2-1871', maker's mark of 'JR' in a shaped rectangular punch, 1870, 8¼in (21cm) high.
£700–800
$1,000–1,200 ⚒ P(Ba)

A Victorian silver chalice, by J. H, the bowl half decorated with floral designs, on pricked ground, the six-sided stem with Gothic-style knop, on spreading shaped foot, London 1891, 9in (23cm) high, 27.5oz.
£600–700
$870–1,000 ⚒ L

> **Cross Reference**
> See Colour Review
> (page 126)

A silver St Christopher dashboard plaque, enamelled in green and white, Birmingham 1936, 2¼in (5.5cm) wide.
£100–120
$150–175 ⚒ S

Salvers

A George I silver salver, the centre later engraved with a coat-of-arms within a rococo cartouche, the reverse engraved with a presentation inscription, on eight shaped bracket feet, maker's mark of Benjamin Pyne, London 1718, Britannia standard, 15½in (39.5cm) diam, 56oz.
£30,000–35,000
$43,500–50,500 ⚒ C

A George I silver-gilt salver, engraved with a band of rosettes and diaperwork, the centre with a lozenge-of-arms within a cartouche, the reverse with later presentation inscription on four bracket feet, maker's mark of Abraham Buteau, London 1723, 12¼in (31cm) square, 45oz.
£12,500–15,000
$18,200–21,800 ⚒ C

A silver salver, with chased decoration, initialled 'CWB', maker's mark 'DL', London 1735, 6in (15.5cm) diam.
£1,100–1,200
$1,600–1,800 ⚒ Bon(G)

A George II silver salver, by Joseph Sanders, London 1743, 6in (15cm) diam.
£500–560
$700–800 ⊞ TGa

A George II silver waiter, by John Langlands, with moulded shell and scroll border, on three hoof feet, Newcastle c1756, 7in (18cm) diam.
£650–750
$900–1,000 ⚒ C(S)

A pair of early George III silver salvers, by Ebenezer Coker, engraved with the arms of Sir John Lambert in each centre, moulded and gadrooned borders, on fluted pad feet, marks for London 1767 and 1769, 15in (38cm) diam.
£1,200–1,700
$1,700–2,500 ⚒ AG

A George III silver salver, by Richard Sibley, with gadrooned border and engraved crest, on three leaf scroll and paw feet, London 1817, 9in (23cm) diam, 16.75oz.
£600–700
$870–1,000 ⚒ DN

A George II silver salver, by William Peaston, with rococo rim, the centre with an armorial capped by a bull's head crest, on lion paw feet, 1746, 7in (18cm) diam, 10oz.
£520–580
$750–850 ⚒ P

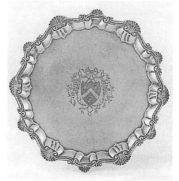

A late George II silver salver, by Ebenezer Coker, engraved with an armorial within a flower wreath and ribbon-tied cartouche, within a shell and C-scroll border, on hoof feet, London 1756, 10¾in (27.5cm) diam, 18oz.
£1,000–1,200
$1,500–1,800 ⚒ DN

A George III silver salver, by John Scofield, with beaded borders and an engraved shield-shaped armorial, on four anthemion chased feet, London 1778, 14in (35.5cm) diam, 41oz.
£1,800–2,000
$2,600–3,000 ⚒ DN

▶ **A William IV silver salver,** with a raised shell and leaf scroll border and a wide band flat chased with shells, C-scrolls and flowers, engraved with a presentation inscription, on four leaf-chased claw-and-ball feet, sponsor's mark 'RG' untraced, Sheffield 1832, 21in (53cm) diam, 121oz.
£2,000–2,300
$3,000–3,300 ⚒ DN

A George II silver salver, the moulded border with a shell and scroll edge, engraved with an armorial within a band of scrolls, flowers and foliage, with three leaf scroll feet, maker probably George Methuen, London 1754, 15in (38cm) diam, 48oz.
£1,200–1,500
$1,800–2,200 ⚒ P(S)

A George III silver waiter, by Elizabeth Cooke, with shell and scroll border, on three feet, London 1763, 6½in (16.5cm) diam, 6.25oz.
£500–600
$700–870 ⚒ DN

A George III silver salver, by Robert Ross, London 1785, 6¾in (17cm) diam.
£700–800
$1,000–1,200 ⊞ CoHA

A Victorian silver salver, the body engraved with arabesque and rocaille scrolls enclosing a vignette of hounds, inscribed 'Ballybourney Coursing Meeting', maker's mark of William K. Reed, London 1845, 18in (45.5cm) diam, 80oz.
£1,000–1,100
$1,500–1,600 ⚒ EH

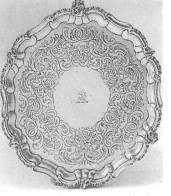

A Victorian silver salver, by Charles Rawlings and George Summers, the centre engraved with a crest within a band of scrolling foliage, the raised moulded border with a rococo scroll edge, on panel feet, 14½in (37cm) diam, 41oz.
£750–850
$1,000–1,200 ⚒ WW

A pair of Victorian silver salvers, by John Hunt, each engraved with a band of flowers and an armorial, on four cast scroll feet, London 1847, 10in (25.5cm) diam, 42oz.
£650–750
$900–1,000 ⚒ DN

A Victorian silver salver, crested above presentation monogram and dated '1860', within a surround of scrolling foliage and chased scroll and acanthus border, on three shell and acanthus feet, London 1856, 14in (35.5cm) diam, 41.5oz.
£600–700
$870–1,000 ⚒ Bea

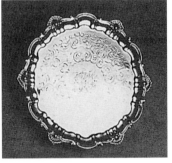

A silver salver, by H. W., flat-chased with scrollwork enclosing a monogram, on three panelled feet, London 1862, 7in (18cm) diam.
£120–150
$180–220 ⚒ HYD

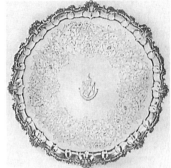

A Victorian silver salver, by John Hunt and Robert Roskell, with a raised piecrust, shell and scroll decorated border with engraved scrolling flower and leaf inner decoration and coat-of-arms, on four scroll leaf feet, stamped 'Hunt and Roskell late Storr and Mortimer 5018', London 1868, 25¼in (64cm) diam, 196oz.
£2,700–3,000
$4,000–4,500 ⚒ P(Ch)

◄ **A Victorian silver salver,** with beaded rim, pierced wavy border and foliate motifs, the centre engraved with swags and scrolls, on three bun feet, Sheffield 1894, 12in (30.5cm) diam, 30oz.
£450–500
$650–700 ⚒ WL

A Victorian silver salver, by Robert Garrard II, with a presentation inscription, London 1882, 23in (58.5cm) diam, 136oz.
£2,600–3,600
$3,800–5,200 ⚒ WW

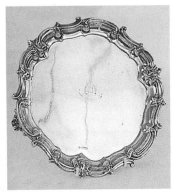

Sets/pairs
Unless otherwise stated, any description which refers to 'a set' or 'a pair' includes a guide price for the entire set or the pair, even though the illustration may show only a single item.

◄ **A George II-style silver salver,** with foliate and scrolled rim and three cast acanthus feet, Sheffield 1910, 10½in (26.5cm) diam.
£170–200
$250–300 ⚒ GAK

An Edwardian silver salver, by Charles Stuart Harris, with central armorial, on four plain feet, London 1903, 8¼in (21cm) square, 14oz.
£170–200
$250–300 ⚒ DN

A silver salver, by W. and S. S., with scroll and pie-crust border, on four scrolled feet, Sheffield 1915, 17¾in (45cm) diam, 68.5oz.
£700–800
$1,000–1,200 ⚒ WL

Cross Reference
See Trays (page 126)

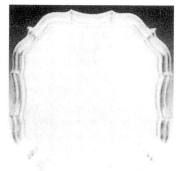

A George V silver salver, on four hoof feet, maker's mark of B.B.S., Birmingham 1928, 17¾in (45cm) square, 66oz.
£600–660
$870–1,000 ⚒ Bea

▶ **An Elizabeth II silver salver,** by Emile Viner, with concave corners, four volute feet, centred by the letter 'P', Sheffield 1963, 16½in (42cm) square, 63oz.
£600–700
$870–1,000 ⚒ DA

A silver salver, with Chippendale-style border, standing on three short scrolling feet, Birmingham 1937, 14in (36cm) diam.
£400–480
$600–700 ⚒ Mit

Sauce Boats

A George II silver cream boat, by Stephen Buckle, with wavy rim and hoof feet, York 1745, 5¼in (13.5cm) wide.
£450–500
$650–700 ⚒ P
The York Assay Office ceased in 1716 and, until its re-opening in about 1776, local makers were obliged to use other assay offices. Stephen Buckle of Spurriergate, York, registered his distinctive mark at the Newcastle Assay Office in 1738. By 1761, he had taken over his father's business in York where he traded until 1774.

A George II silver sauce boat, by George Wickes, with double scroll acanthus leaf-capped handle, with a crest beneath the spout, on three legs ending in claw-and-ball feet with lion mask terminals at top, London 1742, 5¾in (14.5cm) high, 19oz.
£1,300–1,500
$1,900–2,200 ⚒ B&B

▶ **A later George II silver cream boat,** with card-cut rim, leaf-capped flying scrolled handle, later embossed with foliate design, standing on three shell and hoof feet, London 1758, 5in (12.5cm) long.
£100–110
$150–160 ⚒ GAK

A Georgian silver sauce boat, on three shell feet, later embossed with floral design, maker 'SM', later decoration, London 1753, 6in (15cm) long, 4oz.
£200–250
$290–360 ⚒ GAK

A pair of George III silver sauce boats, by Daniel Smith and Robert Sharp, engraved with an armorial, London 1765, 8¾in (22cm) wide, 29oz.
£2,500–2,750
$3,500–4,000 ⚒ S

A pair of early George III plain silver gravy boats, by William Sampel, with gadrooned borders, double C-scroll handles with acanthus leaf heads, on shell cast scroll legs with leaf feet, London marks for 1761, 6½in (16.5cm) wide, 26oz.
£1,900–2,200
$2,700–3,200 ⚒ AG

A pair of George III silver sauce boats, by Elizabeth Munns, with punched beaded borders, a flying leaf-capped scroll handle on applied shell legs with hoof feet, London 1768, 7¼in (18.5cm) long, 15.5oz.
£1,600–1,800
$2,300–2,600 ⚒ WW

Facts in brief

The earliest English and American sauce boats date from the reign of George I. At first they had simple waved borders, but soon acquired gadrooned edges that predominated until the 1770s, when punched or beaded borders appeared. With the turn of the century and the onset of Regency influence the sauce boat became more elaborate with massive borders and feet, and the handles became a major feature, as they occasionally were in the mid-18th century. Design stagnated during the 19th century and later examples follow the style of their predecessors. Sauce boats were usually made in pairs and single ones are, therefore, less desirable.

A pair of George III silver sauce boats, by Daniel Smith and Robert Sharp, engraved with a crest, moulded shaped gadrooned edge, on cast shell appliqué scroll legs to shell feet, London 1769, 6in (15cm) wide, 24.25oz.
£2,200–2,500
$3,200–3,600 ⚒ WW

A pair of George III silver sauce boats, by Wm Skeen, London 1769, 5¼in (13.5cm) wide.
£1,000–1,200
$1,500–1,800 ⊞ AMH

A silver sauce boat, London 1769, 3¼in (8.5cm) high.
£400–450
$600–650 ⊞ AMH

A pair of George III silver sauce boats, by William Grundy, with gadrooned borders and acanthus leaf-capped double scroll handle, on shell feet, engraved on one side with armorial shield, 1770, 8¾in (22cm) long.
£2,000–2,500
$3,000–3,600 ⚒ P

A pair of Britannia standard Georgian-style silver sauce boats, with crinkle rims, scroll handles, bulbous bodies and hoof supports, London 1901, 4¾in (12cm) long.
£180–230
$260–330 ⚒ DDM

A pair of Edwardian silver sauce boats, by Elkington & Co, each with a rising scroll handle, engraved with crest and motto, on three hoof feet, Birmingham 1902 and 1903, 7in (18cm) long, 11oz.
£750–800
$1,100–1,200 ⚒ C(S)

A George II-style silver sauce boat, with heavy gadrooned rim and three shell and hoof feet, London 1902, 7in (18cm) wide, 9oz.
£170–200
$250–300 ⚒ GAK

▶ A pair of 18thC-style silver sauce boats, by William Comyns, engraved with a crest, on shell feet, London 1913, 9in (23cm) wide, 30oz.
£750–825
$1,000–1,200 ⚒ WW

◀ A silver sauce boat, Birmingham 1911, 6¾in (17cm) wide.
£110–140
$160–200 ⊞ SnA

◀ A pair of Edwardian silver-gilt shell-shaped sauce boats, with bird handles and moulded spreading feet, 8½in (21.5cm) wide, with a pair of matching ladles with trailing vine moulded handles, London 1906, 69.8oz.
£2,000–2,200
$3,000–3,200 ⚒ AH

◄ **A pair of double-lipped silver sauce boats,** by William Comyns and Sons, of early Georgian design, the moulded oval bodies with shaped rims and flared lips, spreading bases, each with two cast scroll handles, London 1925, 7¾in (19.5cm) wide 29oz.
£1,000–1,200
$1,500–1,800 ➚ S

A pair of George III-style silver sauce boats, on three feet, 1931, 6¼in (16cm) wide, 8oz.
£240–280
$350–400 ➚ L

A silver sauce boat, marked 'Dysons of Windsor', Chester 1937, 6in (15cm) wide.
£300–350
$450–500 ⊞ CoHa
This piece was produced for the Coronation of 1937.

A pair of silver sauce boats, with scroll handles, on reeded oval bases, Chester 1938, 7in (18cm) wide, 4oz, with fitted case.
£240–280
$350–400 ➚ Bon(C)

Scent Bottles

A Continental silver-gilt Pilgrim flask-shaped scent bottle, chased in relief with chinoiserie figures on both sides, possibly French, c1720, 3¾in (9.5cm) high.
£600–700
$870–1,000 ➚ P

A Continental silver-gilt scent bottle, embossed with figural scenes and scroll borders, unmarked, 18thC, 4¼in (11cm) high, 3oz.
£400–500
$600–700 ➚ Bon

A German silver and enamel scent bottle and stopper, with tall neck engraved with buildings, the body inset on both sides with a circular enamel plaque painted in bright colours with a flowerspray, within an engraved border of swags, the stopper attached by a chain, 18thC, 2¾in (7cm) long.
£400–440
$600–650 ➚ P

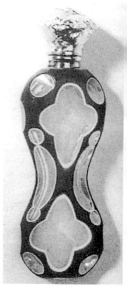

A silver-mounted glass scent bottle, with blue and white double overlay on a waisted clear body, c1860, 4in (10cm) high.
£380–430
$570–630 ⊞ Som

◄ **l. A green overlay glass scent bottle,** with embossed silver mount, c1860, 3½in (9cm) long.
£350–400
$500–600
r. A brick-red Lithyalin scent bottle, with silver mount, c1850, 2¾in (7cm) long.
£400–500
$600–700 ⊞ Som

A barrel-shaped scent bottle, diamond cut blue glass, with silver mount, c1860, 3¼in (8.5cm) long.
£300–350
$450–500 ⊞ Som

An embossed silver-mounted glass scent bottle, with red body and cut white overlay decoration, c1860, 3¾in (9.5cm) high.
£380–440
$570–650 ⊞ Som

An embossed silver-mounted Bohemian red-flashed glass scent bottle, engraved with deer in landscapes, c1860, 6¼in (16cm) high.
£550–600
$800–870 ⊞ Som

A mid-Victorian silver-gilt and cobalt blue glass scent bottle, maker's mark of Abraham Brounett, London 1864, 3¼in (8.5cm) high.
£450–500
$650–700 ➴ Bon

A light blue opaline glass scent bottle, with chased silver cage, chain and finger ring, c1870, 2¼in (5.5cm) high.
£400–450
$600–650 ⊞ Som

A lime green double-ended scent bottle, with engine-turned silver mounts, c1870, 5½in (14cm) long.
£300–360
$450–500 ⊞ Som

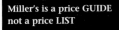
Miller's is a price GUIDE not a price LIST

A French enamelled silver scent bottle, decorated in pastel shades with figures in a landscape, c1870, 4in (10cm) high.
£1,200–1,400
$1,800–2,000 ⊞ BHa

A Clichy scent bottle, with silver top and inner stopper, c1870, 3in (7.5cm) high.
£450–520
$650–750 ⊞ BHa

An amethyst shaded glass toilet water bottle, with diamond and fan-cut decoration, silver mount marked, Birmingham c1880, 6¾in (17cm) high.
£500–600
$700–870 ⊞ Som

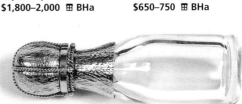

A glass scent bottle, in the shape of a champagne bottle, with hallmarked silver-gilt top, c1880, 2½in (6.5cm) high.
£250–300
$350–450 ⊞ ALiN

A French silver and blue enamel scent bottle, decorated with the figure of a child in pink, green and white, slight restoration, c1880, 2½in (6.5cm) high.
£1,200–1,400
$1,800–2,000 ⊞ THOM

◄ **top. A double-ended scent bottle,** the clear waisted body with green overlay, embossed silver mounts, c1870, 5½in (14cm) long.
bottom. A double-ended scent bottle, the clear glass engraved overall with floral sprays, a printy cut band round the centre, one silver-gilt plain cap engraved '18 March 1880', monogram on the other, c1880, 5in (12.5cm) long.
£400–450
$600–650 each ⊞ Som

A silver-gilt and cut-glass scent bottle, in the shape of a cross, c1880, 4½in (11.5cm) high.
£1,600–1,800
$2,300–2,600 ⊞ THOM

A silver-topped cut-glass scent bottle, by T. Stockwell, 1884, 4in (10cm) high.
£2,200–2,600
$3,200–3,800 ⊞ THOM

A silver scent bottle and stopper, repoussé-decorated, the screw cover engraved with a flower, on a circular foot, London 1890, 2¾in (7cm) high.
£280–320
$400–450 ⚒ P

A silver-topped scent bottle, Birmingham 1882, 2in (5cm) high.
£50–60
$75–90 ⊞ DAC

An enamelled silver scent bottle, with hinged cover, painted on one side with a condor eagle perched on a grassy rock, in shades of brown and grey, maker's mark 'H & A', Birmingham 1884, 4¼in (11cm) long.
£700–800
$1,000–1,200 ⚒ P

A cut-glass scent bottle, by J. Gloster & Sons, the silver cover decorated with flutes, reeds and foliage, Birmingham 1891, 6¼in (16cm) high.
£230–260
$330–380 ⚒ Bea(E)

A Victorian silver scent bottle, enamelled on the front with a spray of dog roses in pink and white, maker's mark 'H & A', Birmingham 1882, 4in (10cm) high, in original fitted case.
£900–1,100
$1,300–1,600 ⚒ P

▶ **A pair of silver-mounted glass dressing table scent bottles,** of faceted square form, the glass with lozenge decoration, with hinged tops and stoppers, maker's mark 'H & A', Birmingham 1885, 5¼in (13.5cm) high.
£600–700
$870–1,000 ⚒ Bon

A clear glass two-compartment heart-shaped bottle, with silver-gilt mounts and stoppers, c1882, 3¼in (8.5cm) high.
£620–680
$900–1,000 ⊞ Som
One compartment in a double bottle was often used for scent and the other for smelling salts.

A double-ended scent bottle, with cranberry overlay, silver mounts, c1885, 4in (10cm) long.
£320–360
$450–500 ⊞ THOM

A green glass flute-cut double perfume bottle, with moulded silver tops, c1890, 4in (10cm) long.
£80–90
$120–130 ⚒ MED

Prices

The price ranges quoted in this book reflect the average price a purchaser might expect to pay for a similar item. The price will vary according to the condition, rarity, size, popularity, provenance, colour and restoration of the item, and this must be taken into account when assessing values. Don't forget that if you are selling it is quite likely that you will be offered less than the price range.

A Victorian silver triple loop twist scent bottle, Birmingham 1899, 5in (12.5cm) long.
£300–350
$450–500 ⊞ AAV

A hobnail cut-glass ovoid scent bottle, by Mappin Bros, with hinged heavily figured silver top inscribed 'Katherine 1900', hallmarked London 1899, 4in (10cm) high.
£90–100
$130–150 ⚒ MED

A late Victorian silver scent bottle, with hinged cover and glass stopper, some damage, maker's mark 'H & A', Birmingham 1893, 4¼in (11cm) high.
£320–360
$450–500 ⚒ Bon

A ruby red overlay glass scent bottle, with lozenge decoration, the hinged silver cover embossed with foliate scrolls, maker's mark of Hilliard and Thomason, Birmingham 1897, 6in (15cm) long.
£320–360
$450–500 ⚒ Bon

A French cut-glass scent bottle, with silver screw top, c1900, 5in (12.5cm) long.
£140–160
$200–230 ⊞ LBr

A glass scent bottle, modelled as a lemon, with damaged silver top, 19thC, 2¾in (7cm) high.
£320–350
$450–500 ⊞ GH

◄ A Stourbridge cameo glass scent bottle, with violets and a butterfly, silver top and inner stopper, c1904, 3½in (9cm) long.
£1,000–1,250
$1,500–1,800 ⊞ BHA

A cut-glass scent bottle, with silver top, Birmingham 1902, 3in (7.5cm) high.
£60–80
$90–120 ⊞ PSA

◄ A cut-glass scent bottle, with silver ring, Birmingham 1907, 5½in (14cm) high.
£60–80
$90–120 ⊞ DAC

A waisted cylindrical decanter, the silver mount with a tricorn spout, London 1909, 13in (33cm) high.
£270–300
$400–450 ⊞ WeH

◄ A cut-glass scent bottle, with silver and blue enamel top, London 1927, 8in (20.5cm) high.
£145–155
$210–225 ⊞ DAC

Serving Implements

A Queen Anne silver two-pronged fork, 8in (20.5cm) long.
£350–400
$500–600 ⊞ TGa

A Georgian silver punch ladle, with twisted whalebone
handle, probably Scottish, 7½in (19cm) long.
£80–120
$120–175 ⊞ TAC

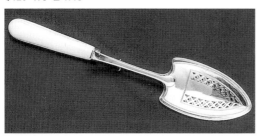

A George III silver chop server, by William Eley I, with
pierced and sprung spade-shaped blades and plain ivory
grip, London 1796, 12in (30.5cm) long.
£350–400
$500–600 ⊞ HofB

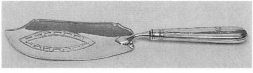

A George III silver fish slice, London 1804,
11½in (29cm) long.
£220–250
$320–360 ⊞ TGa

A silver ladle, with turned marine ivory stem, crested,
maker's mark 'WT', London 1831, 17in (43cm) long.
£265–300
$400–450 ↗ S(S)

A silver marrow scoop, by George Adams, with thread
edge, London 1843, 9in (23cm) long.
£150–170
$220–250 ↗ TC
Used for extracting the marrow from cooked bones,
these implements came with a large scoop at one end
and a smaller one at the other. Marrow scoops can
also be found on the handle end of spoons.

▶ **A silver Fiddle pattern fish slice,** by Benori Stephens,
pierced and engraved fish design, London 1835,
12¼in (31cm) long.
£300–325
$440–470 ↗ TC

A German silver cake slice, by Gottfried Johan Boden,
the blade pierced and engraved, the scroll handle with
rocaille decorated terminal, c1740, 11in (28cm) long, 6.5oz.
£3,000–3,300
$4,500–4,800 ↗ S(G)

A silver serving trowel, maker's mark probably of William
Plummer, London 1772, 11in (28cm) long.
£1,250–1,400
$1,800–2,000 ↗ Bon

A silver and ivory travelling apple corer, c1804,
4in (10cm) long.
£150–180
$220–260 ⊞ PSA

**A pair of George III silver-
gilt Fiddle, Thread and
Shell pattern salad
servers,** by Eley, Fearn and
Chawner, 1808–09,
9in (23cm) long, 11oz.
£800–1,000
$1,200–1,500 ↗ P

**A set of Victorian silver
figure utensils,** probably
by Francis Higgins, spoon
1815, knife and fork
handles 1856, blade 1857,
tines 1849, knife 8in (20cm)
long, 6.5oz.
£400–460
$600–650 ↗ L

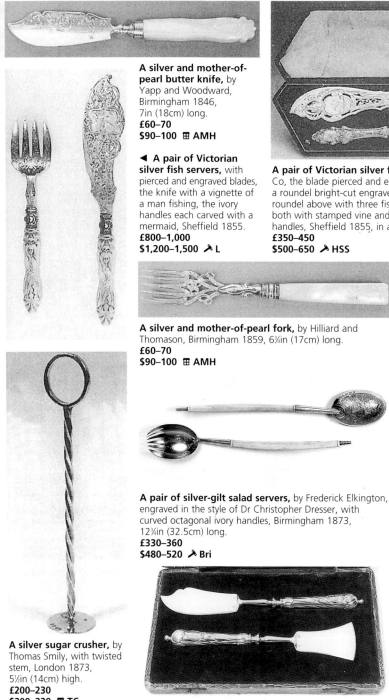

A silver and mother-of-pearl butter knife, by Yapp and Woodward, Birmingham 1846, 7in (18cm) long.
£60–70
$90–100 ⊞ AMH

◀ **A pair of Victorian silver fish servers,** with pierced and engraved blades, the knife with a vignette of a man fishing, the ivory handles each carved with a mermaid, Sheffield 1855.
£800–1,000
$1,200–1,500 ⚒ L

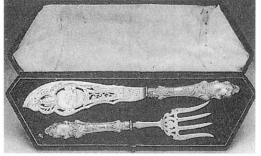

A pair of Victorian silver fish servers, by Martin, Hall & Co, the blade pierced and engraved with foliage enclosing a roundel bright-cut engraved with a swan and a smaller roundel above with three fish, the tines similarly decorated, both with stamped vine and pendant husk decorated handles, Sheffield 1855, in a fitted case.
£350–450
$500–650 ⚒ HSS

A silver and mother-of-pearl fork, by Hilliard and Thomason, Birmingham 1859, 6¾in (17cm) long.
£60–70
$90–100 ⊞ AMH

A pair of silver-gilt salad servers, by Frederick Elkington, engraved in the style of Dr Christopher Dresser, with curved octagonal ivory handles, Birmingham 1873, 12¾in (32.5cm) long.
£330–360
$480–520 ⚒ Bri

A pair of Scottish silver harlequin sugar nips, Edinburgh c1870, 4½in (11.5cm) long.
£400–445
$600–650 ⊞ BEX

◀ **A pair of French silver servers,** c1885, 9in (23cm) wide, in a fitted case.
£100–110
$150–160 ⊞ ASAA

A silver sugar crusher, by Thomas Smily, with twisted stem, London 1873, 5½in (14cm) high.
£200–230
$300–330 ⊞ TC

A Victorian silver and steel muffin fork, mark erased, c1890, 11in (28cm) long.
£60–70
$90–100 ⊞ OD

A silver cake knife, by L. E. and S, Sheffield 1898, 10½in (26.5cm) long.
£200–225
$300–330 ⊞ BEX

◀ **A Victorian silver pickle fork,** with ivory handle, Sheffield 1898, 7in (18cm) long.
£40–50
$60–75 ⊞ TAC

A pair of silver-handled nut crackers, Birmingham 1899, 4½in (11.5cm) long.
£170–200
$250–300 ⊞ CoHA

▶ **A silver 'saw' cake knife,** by Martin, Hall & Co, Sheffield 1921, 11in (28cm) wide, in a fitted case.
£1,100–1,250
$1,600–1,800 ⊞ BEX

A silver King's pattern cheese scoop, by The Goldsmiths & Silversmiths Co, London 1925, 8¼in (21cm) long.
£300–330
$450–500 ⊞ TC

◀ **A silver orange peeler,** by Tom Marshall, 1998, 1¾in (4.5cm) long.
£70–80
$100–120 ⊞ STG

An American sterling silver orange peeler, by Gorham & Co, c1900, 6in (15cm) long.
£220–250
$320–360 ⊞ BEX

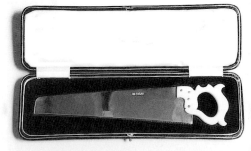

A silver lemon juice extractor, by Adie Bros, Birmingham 1930, 3¼in (8.5cm) long.
£150–170
$220–250 ⊞ BEX

Grape Scissors

A pair of silver grape scissors, by George Unite, Birmingham 1882, 7in (18cm) long.
£475–525
$700–750 ⊞ BEX

A pair of silver grape scissors, by George Adams, London 1864, 7in (18cm) long.
£425–475
$600–700 ⊞ BEX
George Adams worked for Chawner & Co, one of the major 19th-century manufacturers of table silver.

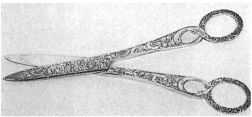

A pair of Victorian silver-gilt grape scissors, London 1889, 6¾in (17.5cm) long.
£400–460
$600–675 ⊞ TGa

▶ **A pair of Edwardian silver grape scissors,** by Elkington, Birmingham 1903, 7in (18cm) long.
£425–475
$600–700 ⊞ BEX

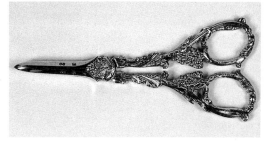

A pair of silver grape scissors, by William Hutton & Sons, London 1888, 6¼in (16cm) long, 4oz.
£530–585
$750–850 ⊞ TC

Sifter Spoons

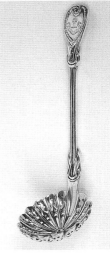

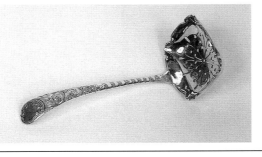

A William IV silver sugar sifter, by George Adams, London 1845, 6in (15cm) long.
£90–100
$130–150 ⊞ **ASAA**

A silver sifter spoon, by Hilliard and Thomason, with vine leaf decoration, Birmingham 1881, 5in (12.5cm) long.
£200–225
$290–325 ⊞ **AMH**

A silver sifter spoon, by Lias, London 1854, 5½in (14cm) long.
£200–220
$290–320 ⊞ **AMH**

◄ **A silver sifter spoon,** Sheffield 1900, 4¾in (12cm) long.
£120–140
$175–200 ⊞ **AMH**

Sugar Tongs

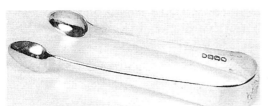

A pair of silver sugar tongs, with maker's mark 'SR', c1781, 3½in (9cm) long.
£35–45
$50–65 PC

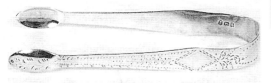

A pair of silver sugar tongs, London 1793–94, 3½in (9cm) long.
£45–65
$65–95 PC

A pair of silver sugar tongs, Birmingham 1890, 3½in (9cm) long.
£40–50
$60–75 PC

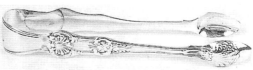

A pair of silver bright-cut sugar tongs, by Hester Bateman, London c1784, 5in (12.5cm) long.
£100–130
$150–200 ⊞ **DIC**

A pair of silver sugar tongs, by Peter and Ann Bateman, London 1801, 5½in (14cm) long.
£60–70
$90–100 ⊞ **DIC**

A pair of silver sugar tongs, London 1828, 3½in (9cm) long.
£35–45
$50–65 PC

Condition

The condition is absolutely vital when assessing the value of an antique. Damaged pieces on the whole appreciate much less than perfect examples. However a rare desirable piece may command a high price even when damaged.

Sewing Accessories

A silver needle holder, 1870, 2½in (6.5cm) long.
£30–35
$45–50 ⊞ VB

A silver pin tray, London 1895,
4½in (11.5cm) long.
£80–100
$120–150 ⊞ PSA

A silver thimble and cotton-reel holder,
c1920, 2in (5cm) high.
£100–120
$150–200 ⊞ MRW

▶ An Edwardian silver-topped
glass pin jar, the silver cover by Levi
and Salaman, mounted with a pin
cushion in the form of a bird,
Birmingham 1907, 4¼in (11cm) high.
£140–160
$200–230 ⚘ CGC

Smoking Accessories

A silver cigar cutter, Birmingham
1892, 1¼in (3cm) long.
£50–60
$75–90 ⊞ EMC

Cross Reference
See Colour Review (page 178)

◀ A Qajar silver-mounted ostrich
egg ghalian, the figural cartouches
with calligraphic details, the bowl and
shaft with a wood support, Persia
19thC, 24½in (62cm) high.
£2,300–2,600
$3,500–3,800 ⚘ S
It is unusual to find a ghalian
incorporating an ostrich egg.

A silver regimental table lighter, by Joseph
Braham, with horn handle, engraved with the
cipher of the Royal Artillery Regiment and
presentation inscription, 1905, 2½in (6.5cm) long.
£320–360
$450–500 ⚘ DN

A Fabergé silver and gold cigarette holder,
decorated with a hound pursuing a wild boar,
the two-colour gold tip chased with leaf tips,
St Petersburg c1910, 3½in (9cm) long.
£2,000–2,200
$3,000–3,200 ⚘ S(NY)

A Rowenta silver-cased pocket
lighter, Germany 1930s–40s,
2in (5cm) high.
£70–80
$100–120 ⊞ FAM

A Dunhill silver and black
enamel bridge top
lighter, with a clock,
import marks for London
1929, 2in (5cm) high.
£1,400–1,900
$2,000–2,800 ⚘ AAV

A silver table cigar lighter, by Mappin &
Webb, of navette form raised on an oval foot
with two foliate embossed handles flanking a
central flame and two removable matches, with
bell-shaped gadrooned finials, London 1925,
3½in (9cm) high, 5.75oz.
£160–200
$230–290 ⚘ CGC

Cigar Boxes & Cases

A silver cigar box, in the shape of a panel fronted coffer, London 1939, 7in (18cm) wide, 21oz.
£550–650
$800–950 ⚒ GAK

A silver three-cigar case, by Hilliard and Taylor, Birmingham 1863, 5in (12.5cm) long.
£325–375
$450–550 ⚒ DIC

A silver presentation cigar box, inscribed 'To Harry F. Homer "Marksman" from the Directors of Arsenal Football Club...7th May 1949', with fitted interior, 9½in (24cm) wide.
£475–525
$700–750 ⚒ S
Harry Homer was known to thousands of Arsenal fans as the organizer of the Arsenal Club Enclosure which he founded in 1936. It is said that he never missed an Arsenal match and as 'Marksman' he contributed famous articles in the club's match programmes. As an Oxford MA he was a senior English professor, and later taught English in Spain.

◀ An Edwardian silver cigar case, curved rectangular shape, engraved with foliate designs, monogrammed and dated 1906 within a cartouche, 4½in (11.5cm) long, in original velvet-lined and fitted case.
£150–200
$220–290 ⚒ GAK

▶ A silver cheroot case, by Yapp and Woodward, engraved with a hunting scene, Birmingham 1845, 4¾in (12cm) long.
£600–675
$870–1,000 ⚒ TC

A silver castle-top cigar case, with a view of Windsor Castle within foliate scroll decoration, maker's mark of Nathaniel Mills, Birmingham 1839, 5in (12.5cm) long, 2.25oz.
£600–700
$870–1,000 ⚒ Bon

Cigarette Boxes & Cases

A silver double cigar and cigarette box, by John Newton Mappin, monogrammed in one corner and enamelled in dark blue 'Cigars' and 'Cigarettes', with cedarwood lining, 1894, 9½in (24cm) wide.
£1,300–1,500
$1,900–2,200 ⚒ P

▶ A silver cigarette case, with an enamelled scene of a scantily-draped lady inside the lid, London 1896, 3in (7.5cm) wide.
£2,000–2,250
$3,000–3,300 ⊞ SHa

LOCATE THE SOURCE
The source of each illustration in Miller's can be found by checking the code letters below each caption with the Key to Illustrations, pages 311–314.

◀ A silver and enamel cigarette case, with oval painted picture, c1900, 3½in (9cm) long.
£800–1,000
$1,200–1,500 ⊞ SFL

A silver and enamel cigarette case, decorated with a picture of Leda and the Swan, c1900, 3½in (9cm) long.
£1,800–2,000
$2,600–2,900 ⊞ SFL

An Austrian silver cigarette box, c1900, 4¾in (12cm) wide.
£2,200–2,500
$3,200–3,600 ⊞ SFL

A silver cigarette case, Birmingham 1904, 2¾in (7cm) long.
£130–150
$200–220 ⊞ GIO

◀ **A Norwegian silver cigarette box,** rectangular form, incurved sides, spot hammered decoration, slightly domed cover with a melon finial and stylized decoration, on four scroll bracket feet, wood lined, inscribed, 8¾in (22cm) long.
£400–500
$600–700 ➹ Bon

A silver cigarette box, engraved with sailing ships, c1930, 6½in (16.5cm) wide.
£400–450
$600–650 ⊞ SFL

Tobacco Boxes

A Dutch silver tobacco box, with squeeze-action sides, engraved with scenes from Abraham's attempted sacrifice of Isaac, maker's mark only, c1700, 3½in (9cm) long.
£4,000–4,500
$5,800–6,500 ➹ P

A George II tobacco box, by Edward Cornock, the stepped and moulded cover engraved with an armorial within a foliate cartouche, maker's mark, London 1727, 4in (10cm) long.
£3,700–4,200
$5,300–6,200 ➹ DN

A Dutch silver tobacco box, by Jan Buysen, engraved with an undulating scroll border, with detachable cover, Amsterdam 1800, 6in (15cm) high.
£3,800–4,200
$5,500–6,200 ➹ S(Am)

An Edwardian silver tobacco box, by Horton and Allday, the hinged cover engraved with partridges, the reverse with pheasants, gilt interior, Birmingham 1901, 1½in (4cm) diam.
£350–420
$500–600 ➹ WW

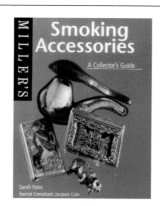

Soup Tureens

A pair of early George III silver soup tureens, by George Methuen, with gadrooned borders and domed covers, pomegranate finials, on rococo scroll feet, engraved with crests and armorials, 1760, 17in (43cm) wide, 194.5oz.
£11,000–13,000
$16,000–19,000 ⚒ P

▶ **A Georgian silver crested Adam-style oval tureen,** by Henry Greenway, the domed lid with urn finial, reeded loop handles, oval base and beaded edging, London 1779, 9in (23cm) long, 18.25oz.
£700–800
$1,000–1,200 ⚒ AH

A George III silver two-handled oval half-fluted soup tureen, on an oval foot with gadrooned borders, finial repaired, maker's mark 'J.S.' for John Schofield, London 1789, 9in (23cm) high, 66oz.
£2,700–3,000
$4,000–4,500 ⚒ MCA

A George III silver tureen dish, with domed cover, reeded cross-over handle, engraved coat-of-arms with motto 'Habere et Dispertire', and a crest, maker's mark 'P.S.' for Paul Storr, on a Sheffield plate two-handled covered warming base, with bun feet, London 1800, 66.5oz.
£4,000–4,500
$5,800–6,500 ⚒ MCA
The arms are those of Heathcote.

A George III silver tureen, by Solomon Hougham, with part fluted sides, the cover with crescent finial, bull's head drop ring handles, nulled borders, on four cloven hoof feet, London 1805, 6¼in (16cm) high, 18oz.
£1,000–1,400
$1,500–2,000 ⚒ DN

A George III silver soup tureen, by William Fountain, with nulled border, two lion mask ring handles, on bird claw feet, (lacking the cover), London 1806, 12in (30cm) high, 77oz.
£2,000–2,400
$3,000–3,500 ⚒ DN

A pair of George III silver soup tureens, covers and liners, with leaf-capped reeded lion's mask scroll handles, later engraved with coats-of-arms, crests and coronets, maker's mark of Paul Storr, London 1812, 15in (38cm) wide, 372oz.
£52,000–60,000
$75,000–87,000 ⚒ C

A pair of William IV silver soup tureens, covers and stands, maker's mark of Benjamin Smith, London 1830, stands 23in (58.5cm) wide, 629oz.
£65,000–70,000
$94,000–101,000 ⚒ C

A Victorian silver soup tureen, with later cover and stand, the tureen by D. and C. Houle, London 1843, finial by Robert Garrard, London c1835, stand and cover by Sydney Bellamy Harman, London c1916, stand 26in (66cm) wide, 318oz.
£11,000–13,000
$16,000–19,000 ⚒ S

▶ **A German silver tureen and cover,** by Bruckmann and Söhne, of ribbed form with a broad band of scrolling foliage, the cover with bud finial, cover stamped No. 12–9438, Heilsbronn c1890, 19in (48.5cm) high.
£2,500–2,750
$3,500–4,000 ⚒ S(G)

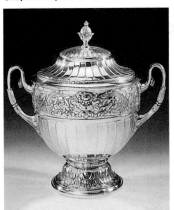

A silver 18thC-style tureen, by Crichton Bros, with bright-cut borders, London 1913, 8¾in (22cm) wide, 14.5oz.
£500–550
$700–800 ⚒ S(S)
Crichton Brothers (c1890–1940) were noted for their fine reproductions of silverware from the 17th and 18th centuries.

Spoons

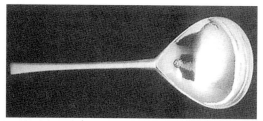

A Henry VII silver slip-top spoon, engraved with Gothic initial 'M', London 1506, 6¾in (17cm) long, 1oz.
£6,000–6,600
$8,500–9,500 ⚷ C(NY)
The unique uninterrupted system of marking silver in London since 1478 at Goldsmiths' Hall ensures that the buyer of a spoon like this knows that it was made in 1506. However, because silver was melted down in times of crisis and with changes of fashion, the few early examples which have survived have done so because of their fairly low silver value. Nevertheless today they are highly prized by specialist collectors, and spoons of Henry VII's reign are very rare.

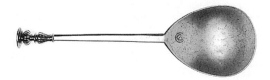

An Elizabeth I silver-gilt seal-top spoon, by Christopher Easton, the bowl later prick-dot engraved with '1641' over 'T.I.', Exeter, c1590, 6in (15cm) long.
£2,000–2,200
$3,000–3,200 ⚷ P

▶ **A James I silver seal-top spoon,** by Daniel Cary, prick-engraved with ownership initials, London 1606,
7in (18cm) long.
£1,400–1,600
$2,000–2,300 ⚷ PFK

An Elizabeth I *lion séjant* silver spoon, with deep fig-shaped bowl and tapering stem, the finial parcel gilt, the reverse of the bowl engraved 'WB', marked in bowl and on reverse of stem, London 1592, 6½in (16.5cm) long.
£2,800–3,200
$4,000–4,500 ⚷ C

A James I silver apostle spoon, St Matthew, provincial c1620, 7¼in (18.5cm) long.
£2,200–2,500
$3,000–3,500 ⚷ S

A Henry VIII silver *lion séjant affrontée* spoon, by William Simpson, London 1503, 6¾in (17cm) long.
£21,000–23,000
$30,000–33,000 ⚷ S
This spoon is very early, and therefore rare, and has the added distinction of coming from the singer Roger Whittaker's collection. Spoons that come from known collectors have been selling extremely well.

A Henry VIII silver maidenhead spoon, by William Simpson, the terminal bearing traces of gilding, London 1543, 6in (15cm) long.
£2,300–2,750
$3,500–4,000 ⚷ S

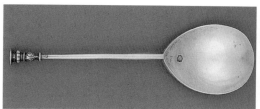

Apostle spoons

Apostle spoons first appeared during the reign of Henry VIII and for many people were the only item of silver they possessed. Large quantities were made in both London and the provinces.
They are so-named because the finials are headed by apostles and saints, each one identifiable by the emblems they hold in their right hand, although these can be difficult to discern. Very few full sets of Christ and all the apostles survive; they should all be made by the same maker in the same year. Production of London apostle spoons ceased in the reign of Charles I, but provincial spoons continued to be made for another 20 years.

from top left: St Matthias, St James the Greater, St Jude, St Matthew, St Andrew, St Simon, St Thomas, St John, St Peter, St James the Less, St Philip and St Bartholomew

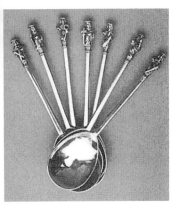

Seven James I silver apostle spoons, by Daniel Covey.
£3,000–3,500
$4,500–5,000 ⚖ AAV

> **Miller's is a price GUIDE not a price LIST**

A Charles I silver slip-top spoon, by Edward Hole, the finial engraved with initials, London 1633, 5in (12.5cm) long.
£850–1,000
$1,250–1,500 ⚖ RBB

▶ **Two Charles I silver stump-top spoons,** by David Cary, with tapering octagonal stems and curved fig-shaped bowls, 1635, 7in (18cm) long, 3.5oz.
£9,500–11,000
$13,800–16,000 ⚖ P

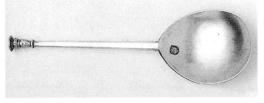

A Charles I silver seal-top spoon, by Richard Crosse, London 1636, 6½in (16.5cm) long.
£700–800
$1,000–1,200 ⚖ S

A Charles I silver apostle spoon, St Bartholomew, London 1636, 7¼in (18.5cm) long.
£1,400–1,600
$2,000–2,300 ⚖ S

A Charles I silver seal-top spoon, the fluted and foliate baluster seal with traces of gilding, the terminal engraved with 'pricked' initials 'AB AW', London 1638, 6in (15cm) long.
£500–600
$700–870 ⚖ P

A silver trefid spoon, by Katherine Mangey, Hull 1675–1700.
£900–1,100
$1,300–1,600 ⚖ DDM

A Charles II silver lace-back trefid spoon, with flared terminal, the back of the stem engraved with prick-dot initials 'ME', the bowl with ribbed rat-tail, West Country c1680, 7¾in (19.5cm) long.
£550–600
$800–870 ⚖ P

Miller's Compares

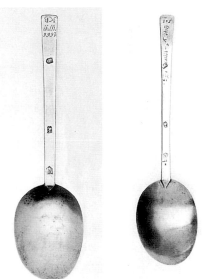

I. A Charles II puritan spoon, by John King, London 1666.
£1,600–1,750
$2,300–2,500 ⚖ P

II. A Charles II puritan spoon, by John King, with a baptismal inscription on stem, 1666.
£900–1,100
$1,300–1,600 ⚖ P

These two spoons are very similar in design and made in the same year, but Item I fetched considerably more in the auction room because the hallmarks are extremely clear. The marks on Item II are considerably worn and it was therefore a less desirable piece.

A James II silver trefid spoon, the oval bowl with a plain rat-tail, repaired, maker's mark probably Wm Mathew, London 1685, 7½in (18.5cm) long, 1oz.
£300–340
$450–500 ✎ Bon

A James II silver trefid spoon, by Edward Hulse, prick-dot engraved on front of stem, maker's mark 'EH', London 1685.
£500–550
$700–800 ✎ P

A James II silver trefid spoon, by John Smith, the bowl with a plain rat-tail, worn, London 1688, 7¼in (18.5cm) long, 1oz.
£280–320
$400–450 ✎ Bon

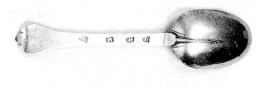

A William and Mary silver trefid spoon, the handle end with engraved initials, the bowl with beaded rat-tail, maker's mark 'WM', 1689, 7½in (19cm) long.
£850–1,000
$1,250–1,500 ✎ L

A silver mote spoon, the plain oval bowl with narrow rat-tail, pierced with holes, maker's mark 'AH' with crown above and cinquefoil below, c1690, 5in (12.5cm) long.
£400–500
$600–700 ✎ P
A mote spoon was used for straining tea leaves.

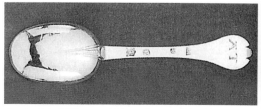

A set of six William and Mary silver trefid tablespoons, by Jonathan Bradley, engraved with contemporary initials 'AT', London 1694, 9oz.
£1,600–1,800
$2,300–2,600 ✎ S(NY)

A William III silver Hanoverian pattern spoon, by Geo Cox, c1698, 8in (20.5cm) long.
£160–200
$230–290 ⊞ CoHA

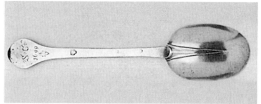

A William III provincial silver trefid spoon, with rounded terminal, ribbed rat-tail bowl, the front of the stem decorated with foliate scrolls, the reverse engraved '*S*G*' above '1699', maker's mark stamped twice 'C A', 8½in (21.5cm) long.
£350–400
$500–600 ✎ P

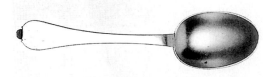

A William III silver trefid spoon, by Isaac Davenport, with ribbed rat-tail, 1700, 7½in (19cm) long.
£350–400
$500–600 ✎ P
This spoon is interesting as it demonstrates the transitional period between trefid and wavy end spoons.

A Queen Anne silver dog nose spoon, by Isaac Davenport, 1703, 7½in (19cm) long.
£130–150
$190–220 ✎ P(EA)

◀ **A Queen Anne silver trefid spoon,** scratch initialled to reverse of bowl, 'A*H' over 'H*C 1705', crested to front, 7in (18cm) long, 1oz.
£220–250
$320–360 ✎ Bon

A Queen Anne silver trefid spoon, by John Elston, Exeter 1706, 8in (20.5cm) long.
£370–400
$550–600 ⚒ S(S)

Seven silver dog-nose tablespoons, with rat-tail bowls, engraved with wing and coronet crests, London 1701 and c1720, 17.5oz.
£820–900
$1,200–1,300 ⚒ DN

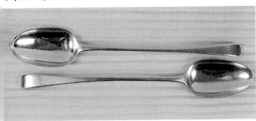

A pair of George II silver Old English pattern serving spoons, each engraved with a crest, maker's mark possibly that of Thomas and William Chawner, London 1750, 5.25oz.
£500–550
$720–800 ⚒ JAd

A George II silver basting spoon, by Richard Gosling, with shell motif back, London 1753, 12¼in (31cm) long, 5.25oz.
£250–275
$350–400 ⚒ DD

A George III silver Hanoverian pattern teaspoon, the bowl decorated with a bird and cage and 'I Love Liberty' in relief, engraved letters 'T.H.I' to terminal, date marks rubbed, maker's mark unclear, c1770.
£110–130
$150–200 ⚒ AG
This spoon refers to the celebrated case of John Wilkes, the English agitator and reformer, who secured the great reforms of the abolition of general warrants, the freeing of the press and the freedom of choice for the electors. Support of Wilkes' cause became national after his imprisonment in 1768 and on his discharge in 1770, the same symbol being found on Wilkes' seals and glasses.

A provincial silver trefid spoon, by George Trowbridge, the stern pricked with initials 'ES/TS' and dated '1724', Exeter 1711.
£300–350
$450–500 ⚒ Bea(E)

A George I silver Hanoverian pattern basting spoon, by Thomas Mann, engraved on the underside with a coat-of-arms, 1718, 14¼in (36cm) long.
£900–1,100
$1,300–1,600 ⚒ L
By the end of the 18th century serving and basting spoons were often included in services, but in the early part of the century they were produced individually.

A Dutch silver dog-nose spoon, by Adriaan Stratenius, Rotterdam 1735, 7¾in (19.5cm) long.
£100–120
$150–180 ⚒ S(AM)

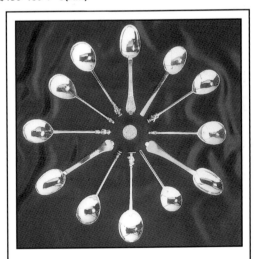

A silver feather-edged gravy straining spoon, London 1775, 12in (30.5cm) long.
£400–500
$600–700 ⊞ DIC

A George III silver spoon, with later embossed decoration, London 1794, 9in (23cm) long.
£60–80
$90–120 ⊞ ASAA

▶ **A set of six George III silver Old English and Thread pattern dessert spoons,** by George Smith and William Fearne, crested above motto, London 1795, 7oz.
£150–180
$220–260 ⚲ Bea

A George III silver stuffing spoon, by William Eley and William Fearn, London 1816, 12in (30.5cm) long.
£140–180
$200–260 ⊞ TVA

A George IV silver basting spoon, by John, Henry & Charles Lias, London 1825, 12in (30.5cm) long.
£200–235
$300–350 ⊞ BEX

A George IV silver Fiddle pattern soup ladle, by John Pringle, Perth c1827, 8oz.
£450–550
$650–800 ⚲ DN

Miller's is a price GUIDE not a price LIST

◀ **A pair of Queen Victoria Diamond Jubilee silver spoons,** the handles set with coins of Victoria, the stems twisted, the bowls engraved '1837–97', above repoussé work of roses, thistles and clovers, monogrammed to back, 7in (18cm) long, 3oz, with fitted case.
£200–250
$300–350 ⚲ SK

A set of six sterling silver teaspoons, entitled 'Monarch of the Century, 1837–1937', made for the Coronation 1937, in a fitted case 7½ x 6in (19 x 15cm).
£130–145
$190–210 ⊞ WeH

▶ **An early Victorian silver spoon,** c1841, 9in (23cm) long.
£30–35
$45–50 ⊞ SnA

Cross Reference
See Colour Review (page 180)

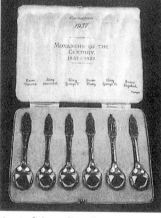

A silver sifter spoon, by Lias, London 1845, 6in (15cm) long.
£200–230
$300–330 ⊞ AMH

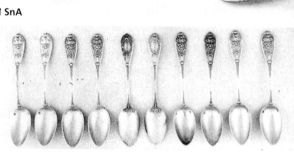

A set of ten French silver-gilt crested teaspoons, the handles chased with baskets of flowers, ribbon ties and beading, maker's mark 'PQ' flanking an axe head, retailer Odiot, Paris marks, c1850, two unmarked.
£200–250
$300–350 ⚲ DN

Colour Review

A silver bodkin, 17thC, not marked.
£550–650
$800–1,000 ⊞ BEX

A James II silver needle case, not marked, London c1685.
£600–700
$870–1,000 ⊞ BEX

◄ **A silver bodkin,** engraved with crosses and chevrons, late 17thC, 5½in (14cm) high.
£100–160
$150–250 ⚹ P(WM)

► **A silver bodkin,** stamped 'M.M.', late 17thC, 5½in (14cm) high.
£250–300
$350–450 ⚹ P(WM)

A Georgian silver needle case, engraved with flowers, 1½in (4cm) high.
£30–40
$45–60 ⚹ P(WM)

A silver filigree tape measure, with domed cover and twisted handle, tape within, 1in (2.5cm) high.
£130–160
$200–250 ⚹ P(WM)

A French silver niello needle case, not marked, c1850, 3in (7.5cm) high.
£280–320
$400–465 ⊞ BEX

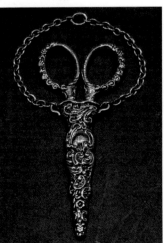

A Victorian pair of silver and steel scissors with case, by Levi & Salaman, Birmingham 1897, 3¼in (8.5cm) long.
£300–345
$450–500 ⊞ BEX

A French silver tape measure, with coffee grinder-style handle and leaf engraved decoration, 19thC, 1in (2.5cm) high.
£120–150
$175–220 ⚹ P(WM)

An Edwardian silver tape measure, by William Comyns, Sheffield 1905, 3in (7.5cm) diam.
£600–800
$870–1,200 ⊞ NS

A silver ribbon threader, by Samuel Mordan & Co, in the shape of a slipper, with floral engraving, London 1905, 2in (5cm) long.
£120–140
$175–200 ⚹ P(WM)

A silver and enamel cigarette case, depicting a view of Windsor Castle, hallmarked London 1886, 3½in (9cm) long.
£1,350–1,500
$2,000–2,200 ⊞ SHa

An Austrian silver and enamel cigarette case, c1900, 3½in (9cm) long.
£1,100–1,200
$1,600–1,750 ⊞ SHa

A silver-mounted glass match striker, Birmingham 1905, 2in (5cm) high.
£280–325
$400–470 ⊞ HCA

A Continental silver cigarette case, with concealed enamel nude scene, c1910, 3¾in (9.5cm) wide.
£3,000–3,400
$4,400–5,000 ⊞ THOM

A Victorian silver lighter, by Aldred Fuller, London 1896–97, 2in (5cm) high.
£2,000–2,250
$2,900–3,300 ⊞ NS

An Austrian 800 silver, enamel and diamond case, by George Anton Scheid, Vienna c1900, 3½in (9cm) long.
£2,200–2,500
$3,200–3,600 ⊞ BEX

An Edwardian silver cigar cutter, by Charles Boyton & Sons, in the shape of a lock, Birmingham 1905, 1¾in (4.5cm) high.
£550–600
$800–870 ⊞ BEX

A Continental silver cigar case, with an enamel portrait of a naked lady on the lid, 1920, 5in (13cm) high.
£800–900
$1,200–1,300 ⊞ PT

Items in the Colour Review have been arranged in date order within each sub-section.

A Victorian silver and steel cigar cutter/penknife, by J. A., Birmingham 1892, 1¾in (4.5cm) long.
£175–195
$250–280 ⊞ BEX

A silver and enamel cigarette case, decorated with reclining nude with a fan, c1900, 3¼in (8.5cm) wide.
£1,000–1,200
$1,500–1,750 ⊞ SFL

A Russian silver and enamel cigarette case, by Kurlikov, the cover with an enamlled panel painted with a bearded gentleman with embroidered coat and fur cloak, town background, within embossed scrolls and set with a blue gem, red gem thumbpiece, signed, Moscow 1908–17, 4in (10cm) long.
£350–400
$500–600 🔨 S(S)

A silver-mounted ruby glass match striker, Birmingham 1923, 2½in (6.5cm) high.
£300–350
$450–500 ⊞ HCA

A George II silver soup tureen and cover, by William Cripps, with shell cartouche and scroll supports, the cover with crescent and sun crest below the motto 'Major Virtus Quam Splendor', 18½in (47cm) long, 136oz.
£14,000–16,000
$20,500–23,500 ⚒ S
The crest is that of Baillie of Jerviswood, Lanarkshire and Mellerstain, Kelso, Roxburghshire.

A George II silver soup tureen and cover, by Edward Wakelin, on quilted and fluted rococo supports, with shell centred side handles and gadroon rim, the raised cover with fruit finial, numbered I, London 1759, 16in (40.5cm) wide, 101oz.
£14,500–16,500
$21,000–24,000 ⚒ S

A Regency silver soup tureen and cover, by Mackay, Edinburgh 1810, 15in (38cm) wide, 123oz.
£3,000–3,500
$4,500–5,000 ⚒ WW

A pair of silver tureens, maker's mark of Thomas Robins, London 1803, 7in (18cm) high.
£6,300–7,000
$9,000–10,500 ⊞ MCO

A Victorian silver soup tureen and cover, by Benjamin Smith III, London 1840, 17¼in (44cm) wide.
£5,000–5,500
$7,000–8,000 ⚒ S

A Portuguese silver tureen and cover, in the shape of a duck, with cross-feather handle to cover, 20thC, 14¾in (37.5cm) long, 54oz.
£2,500–3,000
$3,500–4,500 ⚒ S(NY)

A French silver-gilt soup tureen, cover and liner, by Marc-Augustin Lebrun, with applied armorials between cornucopia handles and beaded and anthemion decorated foot, the cover with basket of fruit finial, Paris 1819–38, 10in (25.5cm) diam, 101oz.
£14,000–16,000
$20,500–23,500 ⚒ S
The arms are those of Bülow, Barons von Bülow.

Prices

The price ranges quoted in this book reflect the average price a purchaser might expect to pay for a similar item from a similar source. The price will vary according to the condition, rarity, size, popularity, provenance, colour and restoration of the item, and this must be taken into account when assessing values. Don't forget that if you are selling it is quite likely that you will be offered less than the price range.

▶ **A Victorian silver soup tureen,** by Stephen Smith & William Nicholson, London 1857, 14in (35.5cm) wide.
£4,300–4,800
$6,000–7,000 ⊞ PAY

A Spanish soup tureen and cover, with lion mask ribbon tied reeded handles, shell and gadroon border and central girdle, engraved with two coats-of-arms, the pull-off cover with a flute girdle and dragon finial, maker's mark of Duran, 16¾in (42.5cm) wide, 128oz.
£1,800–2,200
$2,600–3,200 ⚒ Bon

A knop stemmed silver Christening spoon, decorated with a fish, cockerel and lion, early 12thC, 7in (18cm) long.
£3,500–4,000
$5,000–5,800 ⚒ **CSK**

A James I silver maidenhead spoon, by William Frend, London 1613, 6in (15cm) long.
£17,000–20,000
$24,500–29,000 ⚒ **CSK**
Ex-Roger Whittaker collection. It is rare to find such a spoon in good condition.

A George III silver Old English pattern basting spoon, by Charles Houghan, London 1788, 12in (30.5cm) long.
£220–260
$300–380 ⊞ **CoHA**

▶ **A set of six Victorian silver and gilt apostle spoons, tongs and tea strainer,** London 1896, in a fitted case, case 6¼in (16cm) long.
£155–185
$225–270 ⊞ **HEI**

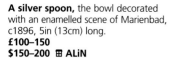

A silver spoon, the bowl decorated with an enamelled scene of Marienbad, c1896, 5in (13cm) long.
£100–150
$150–200 ⊞ **ALiN**

A set of eight Edwardian silver and enamel spoons, with decorative tops and crests celebrating various towns, events and views, 4¾in (12cm) long.
£15–20
$20–30 ⊞ **VB**

A set of silver teaspoons and sugar nips, Sheffield 1902, box 10¼in (26cm) wide.
£90–110
$130–160 ⊞ **ABr**

A set of six silver apostle spoons, with twist stems, Birmingham 1900, 3¾in (9.5cm) long.
£70–90
$100–130 ⊞ **PSA**

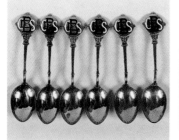

A set of six silver and enamel teaspoons, Birmingham 1924, 4¼in (11cm) long.
£110–130
$160–200 ⊞ **CoHA**

A set of silver and enamel coffee bean spoons, retailed by T. & J. Perry, Birmingham 1936, in original case, 6 x 5in (15 x 12.5cm).
£200–225
$300–325 ⊞ **JACK**

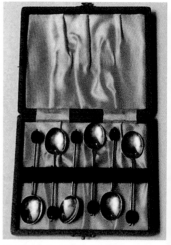

A set of six coffee spoons, Birmingham 1938, 3½in (9cm) long.
£50–60
$75–90 ⊞ **ABr**

A German silver-gilt tankard, marked on base rim 'IS' and with later Austrian control marks, c1565, 5½in (14cm) high, 18oz.
£10,000–12,000
$14,500–17,500 ➶ S(NY)

A pair of silver-gilt flagons, attributed to Roger Stevens, London 1638, 13½in (34.5cm) high.
£62,000–67,000
$90,000–97,000 ➶ S

◀ **A silver tankard,** by Robert Cooper, with presentation inscription, London 1697, 6½in (16.5cm) high, 22oz.
£5,300–5,800
$7,500–8,500 ➶ C

A parcel-gilt tankard, maker's mark 'O' in a shield, possibly Austrian, c1640, 8in (20.5cm) high, 22.4oz.
£7,500–9,000
$11,000–13,000 ➶ S(G)

A Scandinavian silver tankard, c1690, 6¼in (16cm) high, 17oz.
£3,500–3,800
$5,000–5,500 ➶ C

A George II silver tankard, by Thomas Whipham, London 1746, 6in (15cm) high, 31oz.
£1,600–1,800
$2,300–2,600 ➶ HAM

A William III silver tankard, by Samuel Dell, London 1695, 7in (18cm) high.
£5,700–6,200
$8,000–9,000 ⊞ JBU

An American silver tankard, engraved with 'A*Z*S', maker's mark of Joseph Clark, Danbury, Connecticut, c1780, 8½in (21.5cm) high, 30oz.
£5,000–5,500
$7,000–8,000 ➶ CNY

A silver parcel-gilt tankard, by George Angell, probably chased by Frederick Courthope, London 1866, 12¾in (32.5cm) high, 71.5oz.
£8,000–10,000
$11,500–14,500 ➶ S(NY)

▶ **A silver tankard,** by William Shaw II and William Priest, domed cover, London 1752, 7½in (19cm) high, 29oz.
£1,800–2,000
$2,600–2,900
➶ DN

◀ **A George III silver tankard,** London 1809, later decoration, 2¾in (7cm) high.
£120–140
$175–200 ➶ SWO

A pair of George II silver tea caddies, by John Jacobs, with sliding bases, chased at the shoulders with flowers and scrolls, the sliding covers flat-chased below hinged shell handles, London 1752, 4in (10cm) long, 32oz.
£7,000–7,500
$10,000–11,000 ⚒ S

A set of three Dutch silver tea canisters, by Rudolph Sondag, in contemporary silver and mother-of-pearl-mounted case, damage to case, Rotterdam 1768, canister 4½in (11.5cm) wide.
£8,500–9,500
$12,500–13,500 ⚒ S

A silver tea caddy, Birmingham 1890, 5in (12.5cm) high.
£350–400
$500–600 ⊞ CoHA

A silver caddy spoon, by J. Snatt, modelled as a hand, London 1805, 2¾in (7cm) long.
£800–1,000
$1,200–1,500 ⊞ NOR

A George III silver caddy spoon, by Richard Crossley, London 1781, 3¾in (9.5cm) long.
£310–345
$450–500 ⊞ BEX

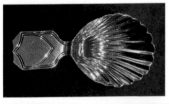

◄ **A George III silver caddy spoon,** by Elizabeth Morley, London 1803, 2¾in (7cm) long.
£330–365
$500–550 ⊞ BEX

A Victorian silver caddy spoon, by William Eaton, London 1843, 4¼in (11cm) long.
£295–325
$400–450 ⊞ BEX

A Victorian silver caddy spoon, by George Unite, Birmingham 1848, 3½in (9cm) long.
£200–225
$300–325 ⊞ BEX

A silver and agate caddy spoon, by J. Cook & Son, Birmingham 1923, 4in (10cm) long.
£240–265
$350–385 ⊞ BEX

A bullet-shaped silver teapot, by A. Nelme, Britannia mark, London 1720.
£12,000–15,000
$17,000–21,750 ⚒ S&S

◄ **A Queen Anne silver coffee pot,** by Richard Green, engraved with the arms of St John, London c1700, 10in (25.5cm) high.
£9,000–10,000
$13,000–14,000 ⊞ PAY

A George I silver coffee pot, by Isaac Cookson, Newcastle 1722, 12in (30.5cm) high, 30oz.
£2,200–2,500
$3,200–3,600 ⚒ P(NE)

A George III silver coffee pot,
by John Swift, London 1764,
11in (28cm) high.
£2,000–2,200
$2,900–3,200 ⊞ JBU

A silver engraved coffee pot,
by W. & J. Priest, London 1766,
11½in (29cm) high.
£2,800–3,200
$4,000–4,600 ⊞ DIC

A Belgian parcel-gilt coffee pot,
attributed to Guillaume Dengis, Liège
1768, 13¾in (35cm) high, 57oz.
£40,000–45,000
$58,000–65,000 ⚷ S(G)

**A George III drum-shaped silver engraved
teapot,** by John Denziloe, London 1775,
4in (10cm) high.
£2,800–3,200
$4,000–4,600 ⊞ PAY

A Maltese silver coffee pot,
maker's mark 'MC', c1770,
10½in (26.5cm) high, 28oz.
£3,200–3,600
$4,600–5,000 ⚷ C(G)

A George III silver coffee pot, by
Benjamin Gignac, London 1796,
10½in (26.5cm) high.
£3,600–4,000
$5,200–5,800 ⊞ MHB

A George IV silver teapot, by William Elliot,
1825, 4¾in (12cm) high.
£850–950
$1,250–1,500 ⊞ PAY

◀ **An American silver coffee pot,** by Jacob
Kuchler, with monogram 'EGL', Philadelphia
c1805, 15in (38cm) high, 48oz.
£12,000–14,000
$17,500–20,500 ⚷ S(NY)

**A George IV silver
teapot,** by William Elliot,
1825, 4¾in (12cm) high.
£850–950
$1,250–1,500 ⊞ PAY

A silver teapot, with inscription, 1882,
5in (12.5cm) high.
£400–450
$580–650 PC

**An Edwardian silver coffee biggin
on stand,** by Walter, John, Michael
& Stanley Barnard, London 1901,
9¾in (25cm) high.
£2,200–2,450
$3,200–3,500 ⊞ BEX

A George III silver three-piece tea service, by William Burwash & Richard Sibley, London 1811, teapot 5in (12.5cm) high.
£2,000–2,250
$2,900–3,300 ⊞ **PAY**

A George IV silver three-piece tea service, by J. Barber & Co, York 1824, sugar 4in (10cm) high.
£3,200 3,500
$4,600–5,000 ⊞ **MHB**

▶ **A silver three-piece tea service,** by Robert Hennel, London 1831, teapot 5in (12.5cm) high, with case.
£1,300–1,500
$1,900–2,200
⊞ **HCA**

A German silver nine-piece tea and coffee service, maker's marks of Anton Georg Eberhard Bahlsen & Carl Becker, c1840 and 1905, kettle and stand 16in (40.5cm) high, 293oz.
£8,000–9,500
$11,600–13,800 ⚒ **C**

◀ **A silver four-piece tea and coffee service,** by Hayne & Cater, London 1850, largest 11in (28cm) high.
£2,000–2,200
$2,900–3,200
⊞ **JBU**

An Austrian silver three-piece tea set, by Mayerhofer & Klinkosch, Vienna 1840, teapot 8½in (21.5cm) high, 77oz.
£2,000–2,500
$2,900–3,600 ⚒ **S(G)**

A silver three-piece tea service and biscuit barrel, by Robert Hennell, London 1861, 84oz.
£3,000–3,500
$4,500–5,000
⚒ **PFK**

An Imperial Austrian silver travelling breakfast service, by E. & T. Schiffer, Vienna 1864, case 20¼in (51.5cm) wide, 150oz.
£7,000–8,000
$10,200–11,600 ⚒ **S(G)**

A Victorian silver five-piece tea and coffee service, made by W. S., Birmingham 1875, coffee pot 12½in (32cm) high, 101oz, in an oak travelling case.
£1,600–2,000
$2,300–2,900 ⚒ **P(E)**

▶ **A silver three-piece tea service,** by Hukin & Heath, after a design by Christopher Dresser, all pieces fit inside the teapot, London 1883, teapot 3½in (9cm) high.
£1,000–1,250
$1,500–1,800 ⊞ **SHa**

A German silver tea and coffee service, by Wollenweber, Munich 1880, tray 34in (86.5cm) wide, 204.75oz, with oak case
£8,000–9,000
$11,500–13,000 ⚒ **S**

A late Victorian silver four-piece tea service, by C. S. Harris, London 1899, 10¼in (26cm) high, 65oz.
£1,000–1,200
$1,500–1,750 ⚒ HAM

An Aesthetic Movement silver tea service, by Elkington & Co, Birmingham 1901, coffee pot 8¾in (22cm) high.
£2,000–2,300
$2,900–3,500 ⊞ MHB

An Edwardian silver three-piece tea service, by James & William Deakin, Sheffield 1903–04, teapot 6¼in (16cm) high.
£900–1,000
$1,300–1,500 ⊞ BEX

A silver four-piece tea and coffee service, by Mappin & Webb, Sheffield 1929, coffee pot 8¼in (21cm) high.
£900–1,000
$1,300–1,500 ⊞ MHB

◀ **A silver three-piece tea service,** by Suckling, Birmingham 1934–35, teapot 7in (18cm) high.
£700–800
$1,000–1,200 ⊞ BEX

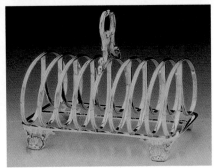

◀ **A George III silver six division toast rack,** on reeded supports, London 1799.
£550–600
$800–870 ⊞ GLa

A Victorian nine division toast rack, by Richard Sibley, on four shell bracket feet, with retailer's stamp for Makepeace, London 1840–44, 5in (13cm) high, 13oz.
£700–800
$1,000–1,200 ⊞ NS

▶ **A pair of George III silver oblong snuffer trays,** by John Green & Co, Sheffield 1800, 9in (23cm) long.
£2,000–2,400
$2,900–3,500
⊞ NS

◀ **A French silver-gilt tray,** attributed to Jean-Charles Cahier, on lion's paw feet, the underside with wood panelling, Paris 1819–38, 33in (84cm) wide.
£22,000–26,000
$32,000–37,700 ⚒ C(G)

A silver tray, by Atkin Bros, Sheffield 1926, 27in (68.5cm) long.
£1,800–2,000
$2,600–2,900 ⊞ MHB

A George III silver cup and domed cover, by Thomas Whipham & Charles Wright, London 1763, 14in (35.5cm) high, 63oz.
£3,400–3,800
$4,900–5,500 ⚷ DN

A Dutch silver parcel-gilt trophy, in the shape of a drinking horn, 1867, 19¾in (50cm) high, 164oz.
£6,000–7,000
$8,500–10,000 ⚷ Bon

A silver-gilt polo challenge cup trophy, by Robert Hennell, engraved with winners' names 1890–98, 1871, 19in (48cm) high, 138oz.
£3,200–3,500
$4,600–5,000 ⚷ C(S)

A silver two-handled vase and cover, by Benjamin Smith, for Rundell, Bridge & Rundell, London 1807, 15¼in (39cm) high, 115oz.
£19,000–22,000
$27,500–32,000 ⚷ S

A silver-mounted vase, by Dalpayrat, with green ground, c1895, 8in (20.5cm) high.
£1,200–1,400
$1,750–2,000 ⊞ SUC

A pair of silver vases, by The Goldsmiths & Silversmiths Co, London 1900–01, 8in (20.5cm) high.
£550–650
$800–950 ⊞ JBU

A silver-gilt cup and cover, by S. & Co, raised on a plinth, London 1913, 24½in (62cm) high, 200oz.
£5,000–6,000
$7,250–8,700 ⚷ B

A Victorian silver and enamel vesta case, maker SM, London 1886, 2in (5cm) high.
£1,300–1,500
$1,900–2,200 ⚷ GH

A Victorian silver vesta case, retailed by W. J. H., Birmingham 1876–77, 2in (5cm) high.
£325–375
$470–560 ⊞ NS

◀ **A silver and enamel vesta case,** 1903, 2in (5cm) high.
£450–500
$650–720 ⊞ HCA

▶ **A silver vesta case,** Chester 1903, 2in (5cm) high.
£70–85
$100–115 ⊞ HCA

A silver and enamel vesta case, decorated with a match and inscribed 'A match for any man', maker D. & F., Birmingham c1887, 1½in (4cm) high.
£340–360
$500–550 ⚷ GH

A late Victorian silver and enamel vesta case, rounded upright rectangular shape, the front enamelled with an image of a horse's head, with a dependent loop, maker's mark of T. A. & Co, Birmingham 1894, 1¾in (4.5cm) high.
£400–500
$580–720 ⚷ Bon

An Edwardian silver vesta case, enamelled with the vices of drinking, gambling and smoking, maker's mark possibly Richard Culver, Birmingham 1908, 2in (5cm) high.
£180–220
$260–320 ↗ Bon

A George V silver and enamel vesta case, by F. J. C. & Co, Birmingham 1917, 2in (5cm) high.
£325–375
$450–550 ⊞ NS

A silver vesta case, inset with gold flowerheads and a shield, Birmingham 1920, 1¾in (4.5cm) high.
£120–150
$175–220 ↗ GH

A lady's silver and enamelled vesta case and cigarette case, Birmingham 1933, 6 in (15cm) wide.
£150–175
$220–260 ⊞ JACK

A Charles II silver wine taster, maker's mark 'RM', London 1662, 3¾in (9.5cm) wide, 3oz.
£2,200–2,500
$2,900–3,600 ↗ HAM

A French silver wine taster, inscribed 'P. Auriacombe', 1838.
£160–195
$230–280 ↗ G(B)

A French 1st Standard wine taster, with twist fluted and reverse punched beading, engraved 'J. Chavernoz', c1838, 4in (10cm) diam.
£360–400
$550–580 ⊞ GLa

◄ **A Continental** *tastevin,* Paris c1845, 4in (10cm) diam.
£550–650
$800–950 ⊞ HEB

► **A French silver wine taster,** inscribed 'Noirot Nuits', 1811.
£150–180
$220–260 ↗ G(B)

A silver punch ladle, by George Bulman, Newcastle 1732, 14in (35.5cm) long.
£1,000–1,100
$1,500–1,600 ⊞ MCO

A pair of James II silver flasks, inscribed 'Ex-Dono Jacobus II', unmarked, c1685, 5in (12.5cm) high, 33oz.
£6,000–7,000
$8,700–10,200 ↗ S

A silver punch ladle, by A. S., with whale bone handle, Glasgow 1832, 17in (43cm) long.
£500–550
$720–800 ⊞ MCO

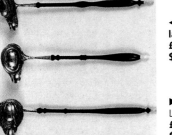

◄ **Three Danish silver punch ladles,** 19thC, 17in (43cm) long.
£400–450
$580–650 ⊞ AEF

► **A silver whisky tot,** by J. Goodwin, London 1729, 2¼in (5.5cm) high.
£1,500–1,700
$2,200–2,500 ⊞ NOR

A pair of silver wine labels, by Joseph Willmore, Birmingham 1832.
£200–225
$290–325 each ⊞ MCO

A silver wine label, Birmingham 1843.
£120–140
$175–200 ⊞ DIC

A silver port bottle label, London 1873.
£65–75
$95–110 ⊞ PSA

◀ **A George III sterling silver brandy warmer,** by William Justis, with plain bowl-shaped body on a wide stepped and reeded foot, with turned wood handle, hallmarked, London 1761, 7½in (19cm) long, 5.75oz.
£2,000–2,400
$2,900–3,500 ⊞ SLI

A George III sterling silver brandy warming pan, by Richard Ferris, with curved handle, engraved with a contemporary family crest, hallmarked, Exeter c1800, 3¾in (9.5cm) high, 6.25oz.
£1,600–1,800
$2,300–2,600 ⊞ SLI

A William IV silver claret jug, chased with bacchanalian processions on a matted vine-strewn ground below acanthus girdle, leafy claw handle springing from a moustachioed mask, crested spreading foot with foliate border, engraved 'D C Rait Fecit', London 1834, 12¾in (32.5cm) high, 39oz.
£3,800–4,200
$5,500–6,000 ⋋ S

A silver-gilt-mounted glass claret jug, by Reily & Storer, London 1842, 12in (30.5cm) high.
£6,000–7,000
$8,700–10,200 ⋋ S(G)

A Victorian silver claret jug, by William George Sissons, with oriental-style engraving, London 1875, 9in (23cm) high.
£1,550–1,750
$2,200–2,500 ⊞ PAY

A Victorian silver-mounted cut-glass claret jug, by Charles Edwards, with trailing flower girdle, etched in aesthetic style with a butterfly and stork among prunus, openwork and engraved neck mount of foliage, the spreading support with lotus leaf border, London 1882, 11¼in (29cm) high.
£4,200–4,600
$6,000–6,600 ⋋ S

◀ **A silver-mounted claret jug,** by Harry Atkin, the glass cut with fans and hobnails, the mount with chased fuiting vines and gadrooned cap, Sheffield 1884, 9½in (24cm) high.
£950–1,100
$1,400–1,600 ⋋ TEN

◀ **A Victorian silver-mounted claret jug,** by James Dixon, hallmarked, Sheffield 1887, 10in (25.5cm) high.
£900–1,200
$1,300–1,750 ⊞ CoHA

A Victorian silver-mounted cut-glass claret jug, by Finlay & Taylor, London 1890, 9in (23cm) high.
£2,000–2,200
$2,900–3,200 ⊞ PAY

A Victorian silver-mounted glass claret jug, by Charles Edwards, London 1898, 15in (38cm) high.
£9,900–11,000
$14,000–16,000 ⊞ BEX

An Edwardian silver-mounted cut-glass claret jug, by The Goldsmiths & Silversmiths Co, London 1904, 12¼in (31cm) high.
£6,750–7,500
$9,800–10,900 ⊞ BEX

An Edwardian silver-mounted cut-glass claret jug, by William Hutton & Sons, London 1904, 10in (25.5cm) high.
£1,650–1,850
$2,375–2,675 ⊞ PAY

Miller's is a price GUIDE not a price LIST

A silver-mounted glass claret jug, by Mappin & Webb, Sheffield 1913, 7¼in (18.5cm) high.
£1,100–1,250
$1,600–1,800 ⊞ BEX

A pair of silver coasters, c1768, 5in (12.5cm) diam.
£2,900–3,200
$4,200–4,600 ⊞ DIC

A pair of George III pierced silver wine coasters by William Davies, Edinburgh 1771–72, 4½in (11.5cm) diam.
£4,000–4,500
$5,800–6,500 ⊞ NS

Two silver wine coasters, London c1807, 6in (15cm) diam.
£2,500–2,750
$3,600–4,000 ⚒ S(S)

A set of four William IV coasters, by Henry Wilkinson & Co, pierced with bacchanalian masks and urns between fruiting grape vines below leaf wrapped reeded rims, with turned wood bases centred by cockerel and roaring lion crests, 6in (15cm) diam.
£4,200–4,700
$6,000–6,800 ⚒ S

An Edwardian silver-mounted glass decanter, by J. Heath & J. Middleton, in the shape of a tyre, Birmingham 1906, 9½in (24cm) high.
£2,400–2,650
$3,500–3,900 ⊞ BEX

A pair of silver–mounted glass 'glug-glug' decanters, by Hukin & Heath, Birmingham 1921, 11in (28cm) high.
£1,350–1,480
$1,950–2,100 ⊞ BEX

◄ **A George III four bottle silver decanter frame,** the reeded, leaf-capped handle issuing from four scallops above four acanthus leaf straps, the frame with narrow vertical fluting and applied with four stopper holders, the base with fluted band and gadroon border with leaf and shell corners, on foliate bracket feet, crested, the supports of the frame with lion masks above overlapping trefoils, complete with four cut-glass decanters with hobnail and fluted decoration, waisted wavy-edged necks and matching stoppers, complete with a set of four wine labels incised Port, Rum, Wiskey (sic) and Brandy, the frame by Philip Rundell, 1819, three of the wine labels by J. W. Story & William Elliot, 1812, and one by Reilly & Storer, 1837, the box with brass retailer's plaque engraved 'Lambert, Coventry St. Silversmiths', in original fitted box, 12¼in (31cm) high, 53.25oz.
£4,200–4,700
$6,000–6,800 ⚒ P

A Victorian silver wine ewer, by Edward Barnard & Sons, London 1868, 11¾in (30cm) high.
£3,450–3,850
$4,900–5,500 ⊞ BEX

A matched pair of Victorian Renaissance-style Cellini pattern silver ewers, by Stephen Smith, 1869–71, 11½in (29cm) high, 51oz.
£3,400–4,000
$5,000–5,800 ⚒ P(B)

A silver Armada wine ewer, Sheffield 1887, 12½in (32cm) high.
£2,000–2,400
$3,000–3,500 ⊞ MHB

A Victorian silver wine ewer with stopper, by Walker & Hall, Sheffield 1896, 14½in (37cm) high.
£1,800–2,000
$2,600–3,000 ⊞ AMH

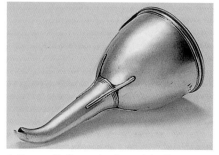

A George III silver wine funnel, by Thomas Meriton, of plain circular shape with reed edge borders, London 1800, 6in (15cm) high, 5oz.
£400–600
$580–870 ⚒ P(L)

A George III silver wine funnel, by Eames & Barnard, with gadrooned rim, 1814.
£400–475
$580–690 ⚒ G(B)

A George III silver wine funnel, with detachable rim, 5in (12.5cm) high.
£750–850
$1,100–1,200 ⊞ HEB

A pair of George III silver wine coolers, by Daniel Smith & Robert Sharp, armorial engraved between ram's head handles, the rim and foot with applied beaded borders, Sheffield plate covers and liners, London 1782–83, 10¼in (26cm) high, 127oz excluding liners.
£35,000–40,000
$51,000–58,000 ⚒ S

A pair of silver campana-shape ice pails, each chased to the front and back with a coat-of-arms, with reeded and shell-capped scroll handles, maker's mark of Paul Storr, London 1818, 10in (25.5cm) high, 235oz.
£40,000–45,000
$58,000–65,000 ⚒ Bon

◄ **A George III silver wine cooler,** by Robert Garrard, liner missing, London 1818, 10in (25.5cm) high.
£9,000–10,000
$13,000–14,500 ⚒ S

A pair of George IV silver wine coolers, with detachable collars and liners, engraved with a crest, maker's mark of Philip Rundell, London 1821, 11in (28cm) high, 221oz.
£25,000–30,000
$36,000–43,000 ⚒ C

A pair of George IV silver-gilt wine coolers, by Benjamin Smith, applied twice with a coat-of-arms, London 1826, 10½in (26.5cm) high, 302oz.
£65,000–70,000
$94,000–101,000 ⚲ C

► A pair of George IV silver wine coolers, by Thomas Blagdin, Thomas Hodgson, Samuel Kirkby, Joseph Elliott & Jonathon Woollin, Sheffield 1829, 10½in (26.5cm) high.
£13,000–15,000
$19,000–22,000 ⚲ S(S)

A pair of French silver wine coolers, maker's mark of Pierre-Francois Turquet, Paris, 1838–55, 10in (25.5cm) high, 186.5oz.
£6,000–7,000
$8,700–10,200 ⚲ S(S)

A pair of German silver wine coolers, by Georg Roth, after Meisonnier design, with mermaid handles holding serpents, chased with panels of mythological scenes, flowers and the Bourbon armorials, c1890, 11in (28cm) high, 159oz.
£6,500–7,500
$9,500–10,500 ⚲ S

A French silver wine cooler and metal liner, maker's mark of Maison Odiot, Paris c1920, 13¼in (33.5cm) high, 107.5oz.
£5,000–5,600
$7,250–8,250 ⚲ S(G)

A George III silver pounce pot, by Rebecca & William Emes.
£280–320
$400–460 ⊞ CoHA

A silver-sided paperweight, with cut corners, brown agate top, 1840, 3¼in (8.5cm) long.
£280–325
$400–470 ⊞ TC

► A Victorian silver pencil, modelled as a pistol, c1870, 2½in (6.5cm) long.
£325–375
$470–560 ⊞ BEX

A silver seal, with ivory handle, France c1860, 4½in (11.5cm) high.
£1,000–1,200
$1,500–1,750 ⊞ SHa

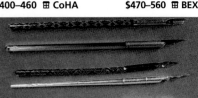

A selection of pens, with Tunbridge ware, cranberry glass, tartanware, silver and mother-of-pearl handles, 1870–1910, largest 7½in (19cm) long.
£30–135
$45–195 ⊞ VB

► A silver seal, with hollow handle and hinged lid, London 1875, 3in (7.5cm) high.
£230–260
$330–380 ⊞ HUM

► A silver-mounted ivory letter opener, c1880, 13in (33cm) long.
£450–550
$650–800 ⊞ SHa

A Victorian silver slide-action pencil, with 18ct gold decoration, set with diamonds, emeralds and rubies, the top surmounted by a Royal crown with red enamel decoration and a band set with emeralds and rubies, the body bears Prince of Wales feathers rising from a crown above a band of old cut diamonds above blue enamel lettering 'Ich Dien', presented by the Prince of Wales to an Indian Prince, c1885, 4in (10cm) long.
£5,000–5,500
$7,250–8,000 ⊞ NS

A silver and mother-of-pearl sealing wax set, Birmingham 1899, 5in (12.5cm) wide.
£325–375
$470–560 ⊞ AMH

A silver seal, with carved ivory handle, 19thC, 4in (10cm) high.
£1,200–1,400
$1,750–2,000 ⊞ SHa

Postal equipment

Before the advent of the gummed envelope, all types of postal equipment were used for completing and dispatching letters and documents. Wax or thin stickers (wafers) were used for sealing, usually marked with the crest of the sender. The vast range of equipment available to collectors includes seals, tapers and other wax-melting devices, sealing-stick holders, wafers and stamp holders.

A silver and enamel half and one penny stamp envelope, Birmingham 1903, 1½in (4cm) wide.
£500–550
$700–800 ⊞ THOM

▶ **A silver stamp case,** Birmingham 1910, 1¼in (3cm) long.
£50–65
$75–95 ⊞ PSA

A silver sealing wax holder, modelled as Mr Punch, Birmingham 1905, 3in (7.5cm) high.
£300–350
$450–500 ⊞ PSA

A set of silver postal scales, hallmarked, 3½in (9cm) high.
£300–350
$450–500 ⊞ SFL

A silver engraved stamp case, Birmingham 1914, 1¾in (4.5cm) wide.
£80–90
$115–130 ⊞ PSA

A silver paper knife, in the shape of a basket-hilted broadsword, maker's mark of J. W. K., Edinburgh 1912, 8in (20.5cm) long.
£250–300
$350–450 ✗ P(Sc)

◄ **Two pairs of silver salt spoons,** Birmingham 1852 and 1879, largest 4¼in (11cm) long.
£180–200
$260–290 each pair ⊞ AMH

► **Four silver salt spoons,** with twisted handles, London 1861, 2¾in (7cm) long.
£90–100
$130–150 ⊞ AMH

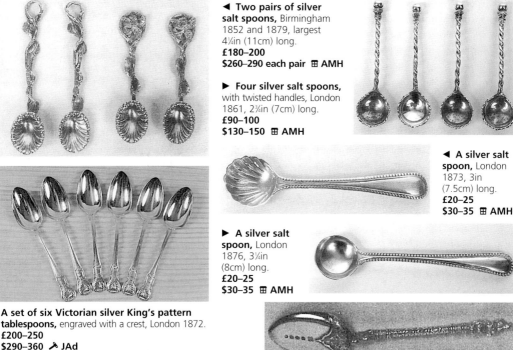

◄ **A silver salt spoon,** London 1873, 3in (7.5cm) long.
£20–25
$30–35 ⊞ AMH

► **A silver salt spoon,** London 1876, 3¼in (8cm) long.
£20–25
$30–35 ⊞ AMH

A set of six Victorian silver King's pattern tablespoons, engraved with a crest, London 1872.
£200–250
$290–360 ✗ JAd

A silver spoon, by Hilliard and Thomason, Birmingham 1876, 5in (12.5cm) long.
£250–300
$350–450 ⊞ AMH

Six silver ice cream spoons, by Aldwinckle and Slater, London 1880–81, 5in (12.5cm) long.
£180–200
$260–290 ⊞ AMH

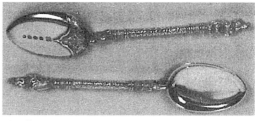

A silver salt spoon, London 1885, 3½in (9cm) long.
£25–30
$35–45 ⊞ AMH

A silver jam spoon, Sheffield 1898, 6in (15cm) long.
£60–65
$90–95 ⊞ AMH

A Liberty Cymric silver preserve spoon, by Archibald Knox, commemorating the Coronation of Edward VII, the bowl inscribed 'AD1902 EVII', the stem with a ball spacer, stamped marks, Birmingham 1901, 4¼in (11cm) long.
£200–225
$290–325 ⊞ DAD

A set of six silver teaspoons, by William Comyns, with pierced and foliate terminals, London 1901, 4½in (11.5cm) long, 2oz.
£220–260
$320–380 ✗ Bon

◄ **Two Liberty Cymric silver spoons,** one possibly designed by Oliver Baker, with egg-shaped bowl, 7½in (19cm) long, and an enamelled silver spoon, with circular bowl, half enamelled in blue, the slender handle having a ball knop with scale pattern, 4½in (11.5cm) long, both marked 'L&Co.', 'Cymric', Birmingham 1901 and 1902 respectively.
£700–800
$1,000–1,200 ✗ P

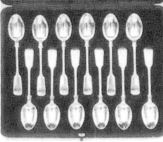

▶ **A pair of silver spoons,** with scroll engraved and pierced handles and bowls, marked 'W. B. & S.', Sheffield 1905, in a fitted case.
£140–170
$200–250 ⚒ GTH

A pair of silver spoons, commemorating the Coronation of Edward VII, c1902, 10in (25.5cm) long, in original silk-lined case.
£180–190
$260–275 ⊞ DAC

A pair of silver teaspoons, the terminals decorated with crossed tennis racquets, inscribed 'S.G.L.T.C.', c1910, 7in (18cm) long.
£80–100
$120–150 ⊞ WaR

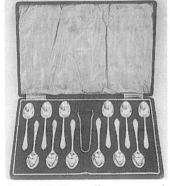

A set of 12 Edward VII silver Fiddle pattern coffee spoons, by J. Round & Son, initialled 'G', Sheffield 1908, 6oz, in a fitted case.
£200–220
$290–320 ⚒ Bea

A set of six silver Liberty teaspoons and sugar tongs, the design attributed to Archibald Knox, the handles cast in relief with stylized Honesty, Birmingham 1923, in original fitted case.
£400–500
$600–700 ⚒ CSK

A set of 12 silver coffee spoons and a pair of sugar tongs, by Walker and Hall, Sheffield 1910, 11in (28cm) long, in a fitted case.
£220–250
$320–360 ⊞ TVA

Sets/pairs

Unless otherwise stated, any description which refers to 'a set' or 'a pair' includes a guide price for the entire set or the pair, even though the illustration may show only a single item.

A silver cranberry spoon, with ivory handle, Sheffield 1918, 7¼in (18.5cm) long.
£40–60
$60–90 ⊞ TAC

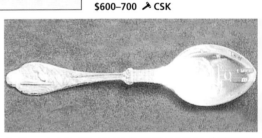

A silver christening spoon, by Docker & Burn, depicting a stork holding a baby in its wings, the bowl engraved with a pendulum clock, 1928, 6in (15cm) long.
£75–85
£110–125 ⊞ BEX
The child's date of birth can be engraved on the clock face.

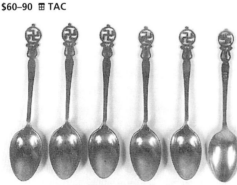

◀ **A set of six silver spoons,** the handles with traditional good luck symbol, marked for 1934, 3½in (9cm) long.
£50–60
$75–90 ⊞ CHe

◀ **A silver spoon and pusher,** by E. V., Sheffield 1940, 4in (10cm) long, in original case.
£60–70
$90–100 ⊞ BEX

A silver golfing spoon, inscribed 'Coxmoor 1969', 4½in (11.5cm) long.
£20–30
$30–45 ⊞ WAB

Tankards

An Elizabeth I silver-gilt tankard, with scroll handle, hinged domed cover, winged demi-figure thumbpiece and fluted baluster finial, engraved with a coat-of-arms within a shaped cartouche, maker's mark of a rose slipped, London 1578, 7in (18cm) high, 14oz.
£35,000–40,000
$50,000–58,000 ⚘ C
The chased decoration of strapwork panels, fruits and foliage on this tankard are typical of Elizabethan ornament.

A William III silver three pint tankard, by John Sutton, the flat moulded top with corkscrew thumbpiece, the body engraved with armorials, on a moulded foot, London 1686, 7in (18cm) high, 29oz.
£10,000–12,000
$14,500–17,500 ⚘ P(G)

A Charles II silver tankard, the cover with a cast scroll thumbpiece, engraved with a coat-of-arms, possibly by George Day, London 1664, 4¼in (11.5cm) high, 8.5oz.
£3,200–3,600
$4,500–5,200 ⚘ Bon

A Charles II silver tankard, engraved with a coat-of-arms within a laurel wreath, the scroll handle engraved with initials, maker's mark 'R.H.', crowned, London 1680, 6in (15cm) high, 24oz.
£7,000–7,600
$10,000–11,000 ⚘ MAT
This piece is in excellent condition with original armorials, full marks on body and cover, maker's mark on the handle, and is clearly a first rate piece.

Cross Reference
See Colour Review (page 181)

◄ **A Norwegian silver peg tankard,** with engraved foliate decoration, the lid set with a coin, inscribed, maker's mark of Suder Meyer, c1697, 8in (20.5cm) high, 30oz.
£3,400–3,750
$5,000–5,500 ⚘ Bon

► **A William III silver tankard,** with applied girdle, moulded spreading foot rim and scroll handle, the flat stepped cover with a cast duck thumbpiece, engraved with an armorial within foliate mantling, maker's mark 'SM' beneath a coronet, not traced, London 1697, 7in (18cm) high, 33oz.
£5,500–7,500
$8,000–11,000 ⚘ DN

A parcel-gilt silver tankard, with detachable cast scroll handle and leaf-capped bearded mask thumbpiece, the body with detachable sleeve finely pierced and chased, the hinged cover with detachable mount similarly pierced and chased and with central flowerhead, the rim later engraved with a crest, the interior of the cover later engraved with the Royal crest, probably by Jacob Bodendick, c1670, 8in (20.5cm) high, 54oz.
£42,000–45,000
$61,000–65,000 ⚘ C
The crest on the rim is that of Savory for Thomas Field Savory, 1779–1847, the Royal crest is for HRH the Duke of Sussex, 1773–1843.

A Charles II silver tankard, engraved with a contemporary lady's armorial, marked 'MK', London 1681–82, 5¼in (13.5cm) high, 13oz.
£5,500–6,500
$8,000–9,500 ⚘ PFK

A Queen Anne silver tankard, by Benjamin Pyne, the hinged cover with chair-back thumbpiece, the body engraved with a coat-of-arms, London 1709, 8¾in (22cm) high, 48oz.
£8,500–9,000
$12,300–13,000 ⚹ P(NE)

A George II silver tankard, by Richard Gurney & Co, with engraved armorial, London 1741, 8½in (21.5cm) high, 42oz.
£3,200–3,700
$4,500–5,500 ⚹ DN

A silver tankard, by Langlands and Goodrich, handle initialled, cover possibly replaced, Newcastle 1756, 7¼in (18.5cm) high, 23oz.
£1,300–1,600
$1,900–2,300 ⚹ MJB

A George I silver tankard, by Jonathan Newton, slightly tapering form, with a moulded girdle, domed lid, chair-back thumbpiece and lappet pendant to the hinge, the scrolling handle terminating in a shield, stepped base, London 1722, 8in (20.5cm) high, 29oz.
£1,800–2,200
$2,600–3,200 ⚹ HCC

A George II silver tankard, by Richard Gurney & Co, engraved with armorials above a reeded girdle, the domed hinged cover with scroll thumbpiece, the scroll handle with heart-shaped terminal, London 1744, 7½in (19cm) high, 27oz.
£2,000–2,400
$2,900–3,500 ⚹ Bea

A George II plain silver baluster tankard, the domed lid with pierced thumbpiece attached to a scroll handle, the body with moulded girdle and engraved armorial with motto and crest, stepped base, marker's mark 'PE' (Peter Elliott), Exeter 1759, lid maker JK (John Kidder), London 1786, 7½in (19cm) high, 27oz.
£900–1,100
$1,300–1,600 ⚹ PFK

A George II silver provincial tankard, with scroll handle, open-work scroll thumbpiece and hinged domed cover, maker's mark 'R.F.', Exeter 1736, 7in (18cm) high, 24oz.
£3,000–3,400
$4,500–5,000 ⚹ C

An American silver tankard, by Thomas Edwards, now altered to a jug, marked, Boston c1750, 8½in (21.5cm) high, 26.25oz.
£1,400–1,750
$2,000–2,500 ⚹ B&B

A George III silver tankard, with domed lid, maker's mark 'I.S.', London 1760, 26oz.
£850–950
$1,200–1,400 ⚹ JH

A George III silver tankard, engraved with a monogram on the handle, probably by Jacob Marsh, London 1766–67, 7in (18cm) high, 22oz.
£1,200–1,400
$1,800–2,000 ⚒ SK(B)

A George III silver flagon, tapering circular form, with lower girdle and scroll handle, the domed hinged cover with a pierced shell thumbpiece, on a spread circular foot, monogrammed, maker's mark probably of Charles Wright, London 1771, 12¼in (31cm) high, 42oz.
£1,400–1,600
$2,000–2,300 ⚒ Bon

A silver tankard, by John Langlands I, with openwork chair-back thumbpiece, the handle with heart-shaped terminal, Newcastle 1774, 7½in (19cm) high, 26.75oz.
£2,500–2,750
$3,600–4,000 ⚒ B&B

A silver presentation tankard, the hinged domed cover with pierced thumbpiece and double scroll handle, later embossed with standing and firing rifle volunteers and a laurel wreath surrounding an inscription, maker's mark JS, possibly John Swift, London 1775, 7½in (19cm) high, together with two pewter quart tankards.
£1,000–1,200
$1,500–1,800 ⚒ S(S)

A George III silver quart tankard, with pierced thumbpiece, domed lid and scroll handle, engraved with initials 'L.T.A.', maker 'C.W.', London 1776, 9in (23cm) high, 27oz.
£1,400–1,600
$2,000–2,300 ⚒ RBB

A George III silver tankard, with a pierced scrollwork thumbpiece, engraved with presentation inscription, possibly by Thomas Chawner, London 1784, 8½in (21.5cm) high, 24oz.
£2,200–2,500
$3,200–3,600 ⚒ Bon

A silver tankard, the cover inscribed, marked, possibly by Jan Lotter, c1800, 6½in (16.5cm) high, 24oz.
£2,000–2,200
$2,900–3,200 ⚒ TEN

A George III silver baluster tankard, with double scroll handle, on a spreading base, with later spout and decoration, the base and hinged cover by Samuel Godbeher and Edward Wigan, London 1787, spout London 1845, 27.5oz.
£600–680
$850–950 ⚒ Bea

◄ **A silver tankard,** by Henry Green, London 1794, 7¾in (19.5cm) high.
£1,800–2,000
$2,600–2,900 ⊞ AMH

A Regency silver quart tankard, by Rebecca Emes and Edward Barnard I, the hinged flat cover with a reeded band to the serpentine edge, with gilt interior and pierced chair-back thumbpiece to the hollow scroll handle, on a base moulding, engraved with an initial, London 1818, 7in (18cm) high, 28.5oz.
£1,200–1,400
$1,800–2,000 ⚒ WW

A William IV silver-gilt tankard, by William Eaton, the body applied with an oval plaque depicting a horse race within a leaf and berry surround, the part-fluted detachable cover cast with matted acanthus and detachable finial in the form of acorns, London 1832, 12¼in (31cm) high, 122oz.
£8,000–10,000
$11,500–14,500 ⚒ S

Miller's is a price GUIDE not a price LIST

A silver wine flagon, by Stephen Smith and William Nicholson, with a fawn finial, the body engraved with swags and palmette frieze, London 1864, 14¼in (36cm) high, 58oz.
£1,250–1,400
$1,800–2,000 ⚒ P(NW)

Tea Caddies

A Belgian tea caddy, the pull-off cover with a knop finial, gadrooned borders, traces of gilding, maker's mark of Pieter van Sychen, Bruges c1710, 5¼in (13cm) high, 8.5oz.
£9,000–10,000
$13,000–14,500 ⚒ Bon

A Dutch silver tea caddy, maker's mark 'H' with a figure and sword in shield, early 18thC, 4in (10cm) high, 4oz.
£1,500–1,700
$2,200–2,450 ⚒ S(Am)

A Dutch silver tea caddy, the sides chased with sunflowers and acorns, Leeuwarden 1711, 5¼in (13cm) high, 7oz.
£4,000–4,500
$5,800–6,500 ⚒ S(Am)

A George I Britannia standard silver tea caddy, with canted corners, slide off cover and pull off domed cover with knop finial, later engraved foliate decoration, central cartouche, on a rectangular foot with canted corners, maker's mark of John Farnell, London 1715, 5in (12.5cm) high, 6oz.
£800–900
$1,200–1,300 ⚒ Bon

◄ **A pair of George II silver tea caddies,** by John Newton, with sliding bases and domed caps, London 1739, 5in (12.5cm) high, 16.5oz.
£3,200–3,500
$4,500–5,000 ⚒ S(NY)

► **A George II silver tea caddy set,** by Elizabeth Godfrey, engraved with contemporary arms and crests, the bases with scratch weights, London c1744, 5½in (14cm) high, 46oz.
£23,000–25,000
$33,000–36,000 ⚒ S(NY)
The arms are those of Hoblyn of Bodrane and Nansahyden, Cornwall, with another in pretence.

A George II silver caddy set, by James Shruder, comprising a circular bowl and cover and two oblong caddies, each applied on either side with rococo cartouches enclosing the crest and armorials of King, also applied with shells, bulrushes, scrolls and flowers, London 1748, caddies 5¾in (14.5cm) high, 64oz.
£70,000–76,000
$101,000–110,000 ⚒ S
The arms of King are for Thomas King (1712–79), fourth son of Lord Chancellor King who succeeded his three elder brothers as fifth Lord King and Baron of Ockham in 1767.

▶ **A George II silver tea caddy,** by Charles Aldridge and Henry Green, with gadrooned edging and shell motifs, the detachable cover with artichoke finial, London 1759, 5½in (14cm) high, 10oz.
£900–1,100
$1,300–1,600
⚒ Bea

A George III silver caddy set, by Emick Romer, the domed lids with cast shell finials, the bases initialled 'AS', London 1767, 5¼in (13cm) high, 30.5oz, in a contemporary fitted mahogany box.
£6,000–7,000
$8,700–10,200 ⚒ S(NY)

A George III silver tea canister, by Albertus Schurman, 1760, 5¾in (14.5cm) high, 9.5oz.
£850–1,000
$1,250–1,500 ⚒ P

◀ **A George III silver tea caddy,** by Thomas Hemming, London 1772, 7in (18cm) high, 9.25oz, with original red velvet and braid lined shaped and fitted shagreen box.
£3,200–3,600
$4,500–5,200 ⚒ L

▶ **A George III silver tea caddy,** by Aldridge and Green, with urn finial, engraved with bright-cut borders of formal ornament and monogram, 1778, 4½in (11.5cm) high, 13oz.
£2,000–2,200
$2,900–3,200 ⚒ C(S)

A Dutch silver tea caddy, by B. Swierink, the cover applied with laurel swags and portrait medallions, swing handle, Amsterdam 1780, 5½in (14cm) long, 28.5oz.
£3,300–3,700
$4,800–5,500 ⚒ S(AM)

> **Cross Reference**
> See Colour Review (page 182)

A George III silver tea caddy, by John Carter, with Adam-style design, London 1773, 5in (12.5cm) high, 14oz.
£4,000–5,000
$5,000–7,000 ⚒ S

◀ **A George III silver tea caddy,** with urn-shaped finial, bright-cut engraved foliate detail, London 1786, 5¾in (14.5cm) wide, 13oz.
£700–800
$1,000–1,200 ⊞ WL

A George III silver tea caddy, by Henry Chawner and John Emes, decorated with bands of foliage, crested within a floral wreath, London 1796, 6in (15cm) high, 10.5oz.
£900–1,100
$1,300–1,600 ⚒ Bea

A George III silver tea caddy, by Thomas Wallis II, with tongue-and-dart edged wavy rim, domed cover with fruit finial, engraved with flowers and oval medallions above two wreath cartouches, one with initial 'C', on four ball feet, interior with fixed divider, complete with key, 1806, 6in (15cm) high, 20.75oz.
£1,550–1,650
$2,200–2,400 ⚒ P

A late Victorian ivory and silver-mounted tea caddy, by John Round & Son, with engraved crest, the part-fluted silver cover with an ivory finial, Sheffield 1890, 4¾in (12cm) high.
£550–600
$800–870 ⚒ P(E)

▶ **A silver tea caddy,** with domed top and fluted sides, c1909, 3in (7.5cm) high.
£400–450
$600–650 ⊞ GIO

A George III silver lobed tea caddy, by Henry Chawner and John Emes, with engraved cartouches, panels of shells and foliage, fixed overhead handle, two lidded compartments, two keys, London 1796, 6¼in (16cm) wide, 14.25oz.
£1,300–1,500
$1,900–2,200 ⚒ P(S)

A silver tea caddy, by William Comyns, the vase-shaped body chased and embossed with floral and foliate decoration, vacant cartouche to front, the concave hinged lid with engraved edge and plain top, complete with key, London 1889, 4½in (11.5cm) high.
£550–600
$800–870 ⚒ GAK

▶ **A Continental silver tea caddy,** with canted corners, embossed with C-scrolls and vignettes of a couple in a landscape, import marks for Samuel Boyle Landeck and Sheffield 1899, 6oz.
£220–250
$320–360 ⚒ P(WM)

A Portuguese silver tea canister and cover, engraved with a coat-of-arms, 19thC, 8in (20.5cm) high, 18oz.
£950–1,150
$1,400–1,700 ⚒ Bea(E)

A Victorian silver tea caddy, by Thomas Munday, with reeded sides and hinged cover, London 1890, 3½in (9cm) high, 9.5oz.
£700–800
$1,000–1,200 ⚒ Bea

A silver tea caddy, in the shape of a Georgian knife box, with hinged lid, Birmingham 1913, 3¼in (8.5cm) high.
£240–280
$350–400 ⚒ GAK

Tea Caddy Spoons

A silver caddy spoon, by Thomas Evans, London 1789, 3½in (9cm) long.
£300–340
$450–500 ⊞ AMH

A silver caddy spoon, London 1795, 2¼in (5.5cm) long.
£225–245
$320–350 ⊞ BEX

A silver caddy spoon, by Joseph Taylor, with a daisy bowl, Birmingham 1797, 2½in (6.5cm) long.
£200–220
$290–320 ⊞ STH

A silver caddy spoon, by Abraham Taylor, London 1797, 2½in (6.5cm) long.
£335–365
$480–550 ⊞ BEX

A George III silver caddy spoon, by George Nangle, 1800, 3½in (9cm) long.
£100–125
$150–180 ⊞ TGa

◀ **A George III silver caddy spoon,** by Joseph Taylor, the bowl pierced with quatrefoil motifs, the handle with a vacant cartouche, Birmingham 1799.
£250–275
$350–400 ⚒ P

A silver tea caddy spoon, by Thomas Robinson II and Samuel Harding, London 1809, 3½in (9cm) long.
£220–250
$320–360 ⊞ AMH

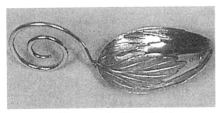

A silver caddy spoon, by Wardell and Kempson, Birmingham 1818, 3½in (9cm) long.
£440–480
$650–700 ⊞ AMH

A George III silver caddy spoon by Thomas James, with plain egg-shaped bowl, the handle engraved with a monogram, 1810.
£280–320
$400–460 ⚒ P

A George III silver caddy spoon, by Thomas James, the bowl engraved with a floral branch, the terminal with a vacant cartouche in the shape of a flowerhead, London 1813, 4¼in (11cm) long.
£600–675
$870–1,000 ⚒ Bon

A George IV Fiddle pattern silver caddy spoon, by Thomas James, the bowl engraved with foliate and flower decoration, the handle engraved with the initial 'H', 1822.
£500–550
$700–800 ⚒ P

◀ **A George IV Fiddle pattern silver caddy spoon,** by Joseph Taylor, the bowl with foliate and floral-engraved central panel, Birmingham 1822.
£175–200
$250–300 ⚒ P

LOCATE THE SOURCE
The source of each illustration in Miller's can be found by checking the code letters below each caption with the Key to Illustrations, pages 311–314.

◀ **A George IV silver caddy spoon,** by Powell and Coates, with fiddle handle, London 1822, 3in (7.5cm) long.
£190–210
$275–300 ⊞ STH

▶ **A silver caddy spoon,** by F. Higgins, London 1859, 4in (10cm) long.
£240–260
$350–380 ⊞ AMH

A silver caddy spoon, by Gervaise Wheeler, Birmingham 1834, 3¼in (8.5cm) long.
£250–275
$350–400 ⊞ BEX

◀ **A silver caddy spoon,** by John, Henry and Charles Lias, London 1874, 4in (10cm) long.
£30–35
$45–50 ⊞ BEX

Cross Reference
See Colour Review (page 182)

A silver caddy spoon, by Hilliard and Thomason, Birmingham 1881, 3½in (9cm) long.
£260–300
$400–450 ⊞ DIC

▶ **A silver caddy spoon,** with shovel handle, Birmingham 1895, 3½in (9cm) long.
£160–180
$230–260 ⊞ DIC

Tea, Coffee & Chocolate Pots

A James II silver chocolate pot, derived from Chinese porcelain, with swan-neck spout at right angles to the wood C-scroll handle, the cover attached by a chain and with sliding urn finial, the lower handle terminal engraved with contemporary initials 'ED' surrounded by mullets, engraved with later inscription above moulded base band, monogram mark '(?)PB', London 1686, 7½in (19cm) high, 21.25oz.
£38,000–42,000
$55,000–60,000 ⚒ S(NY)

A George I silver chocolate pot, by Pentecost Symonds, with partly faceted swan-neck spout, engraved with arms in baroque cartouche, sliding baluster finial, Exeter 1718, maker's mark, the base with scratch weight '32 13', 11in (28cm) high, 34.5oz.
£13,000–15,000
$19,000–22,000 ⚒ S(NY)
The arms are possibly those of Sanford.

◀ **A George I silver teapot,** by Francis Nelme, engraved with a contemporary armorial, with a wooden scroll handle, London 1724, 4½in (11.5cm) high, 12oz.
£10,500–11,500
$15,000–16,500 ⚒ S(S)

A George I silver teapot, the cover with part wood finial, the body engraved with a coat-of-arms within a foliate scroll cartouche, maker's mark 'JP' possibly for John Penfold, London c1720, 4¼in (11cm) high, 15oz.
£2,400–2,800
$3,500–4,000 ⚒ C

A George III silver coffee pot, by Thomas Farren, with panelled straight spout, domed hinged cover with turned finial and serpent carved wood scroll handle, London 1725, 10in (25.5cm) high, 25oz.
£3,800–4,200
$5,500–6,200 ⚒ Bea

An early George II silver teapot, by Edward Bennett, with a band of fine diaper and scroll engraving at the shoulder and lid rim, straight tapered spout, moulded foot, London 1728, 4¼in (11cm) high, 14oz.
£4,500–5,000
$6,500–7,000 ⚒ P(G)

A Belgian silver baluster-shaped teapot, by Petrus van Eesbeeck, the ribbed body, hinged cover and bird's head spout engraved with *Régence* strapwork husks and foliate latticework on matting, wood handle and rim foot, Brussels c1730, date letter illegible, 6¾in (17cm) high, 20oz.
£47,000–50,000
$68,000–72,500 ⚒ S(G)

A George II silver coffee pot, by Richard Beal, with domed lid, octagonal spout, engraved crest, stepped base, replaced wooden handle, London 1733, 9in (23cm) high, 24oz.
£2,500–3,000
$3,500–4,500 ⚒ HCC

A George II silver coffee pot, with scroll spout and wood handle, domed cover with spire finial, crested, 1735, 8½in (21.5cm) high, 23oz.
£2,600–2,900
$3,800–4,200 ⚒ N

A George II silver coffee pot, by Edward Pocock, crested with motto above monogram, flat domed hinged cover with turned finial, leaf-capped panelled spout and wood scroll handle, London 1735, 9in (23cm) high, 24.5oz.
£2,200–2,400
$3,200–3,500 ⚒ Bea

◀ **A George II silver coffee pot,** with ebony scrolled handle, London 1738, 7½in (19cm) high, 15oz.
£1,200–1,400
$1,750–2,000 ⚒ AH

A George II silver coffee pot, by John Pero, moulded swan-neck spout, hinged bun cover with turned finial, hardwood scroll handle, London 1737, 9in (23cm) high, 25.5oz.
£1,000–1,200
$1,500–1,800 ⚒ WW

A George II silver teapot, by Richard Gurney & Co, with chased rocaille scroll and foliage scalework to the top and wooden scroll handle, incised initials, London 1748, 6½in (16.5cm) high, 18oz.
£1,750–2,000
$2,500–3,000 ⚒ WW

A George II silver coffee pot, with scroll chased cut-card borders to spout and handle, domed cover with spire finial, on spreading base, Newcastle 1740, 9in (23cm) high, 30oz.
£3,000–3,400
$4,500–4,500 ⚒ N

A George II silver baluster-shaped coffee pot, by Daniel Piers, richly chased and embossed with flowerheads and foliage, with partly fluted curved spout, reverse scroll handle with acanthus thumbpiece, hinged cover with further foliage decoration and pine cone finial, on spreading base, the base with later presentation inscription, 1748, 12¼in (31cm) high, 56oz.
£2,300–2,700
$3,500–4,000 ⚒ C(S)

A George II silver teapot, by John Rowe, with rococo swan neck spout, the shoulder engraved with a band of strapwork, marked on base and cover, London 1750, 5in (12.5cm) high, 12.5oz.
£1,800–2,000
$2,600–2,900 ⚺ S(NY)

A George II silver teapot, by Gabriel Sleath, the body engraved with a band of scrollwork and masks and contemporary monogram, 1752, 5in (12.5cm) high, 15oz.
£1,600–2,000
$2,300–2,900 ⚺ L

A George II silver chocolate pot, by Peter Archambo II and Peter Meure, with turned finial, subsequently fixed to cover, wood scroll handle on spreading base, marks worn, London c1753, 9in (23cm) high, 20.75oz.
£1,250–1,500
$1,800–2,200 ⚺ Bea

A George II silver coffee pot, by John Wirgman, embossed with shells and a crest, the hinged domed lid with pineapple finial, London 1755, 10in (25.5cm) high, 31oz.
£1,600–1,800
$2,300–2,600 ⚺ P(G)

An Italian silver pear-shaped coffee pot, with S-shaped spout terminating in a bird's head, wood harp-shaped handle, the hinged cover fluted with scroll thumbpiece rising to a flower-shaped finial, plain spreading reeded foot, marked on base and cover, Genoa 1757, 10½in (26.5cm) high, 33oz.
£18,000–20,000
$26,000–29,000 ⚺ C(G)

A George II silver coffee pot, by Robert and Albin Cox, the hinged cover with turned finial, wood scroll handle, on a spreading base, London 1759, 10in (25cm) high, 23.5oz.
£2,200–2,500
$3,200–3,600 ⚺ Bea

Insurance values

Always insure your valuable antiques for the cost of replacing them with similar items, regardless of the original price paid. Both dealers and auctioneers will provide a valuation service for a fee.

A George II silver coffee pot, with wood scroll handle, the detachable domed hinged cover secured by a pin, with detachable finial, on spreading base, maker's mark worn, London 1759, 11in (28cm) high, 23.5oz.
£2,000–2,300
$2,900–3,500 ⚺ Bea

▶ **A Belgian silver coffee pot,** with conforming foot, the cover with scroll finial and carved ivory handle, Liège 1764, 8¼in (21cm) high, 17oz.
£8,600–9,000
$12,450–13,000 ⚺ HAM
Belgian silver of this period is rarer than German or Dutch silver. The Belgian market for antiques is also currently very strong.

A George III silver baluster-shaped coffee pot, by Francis Crump, the cover with spiral reeded finial, leaf-chased spout, wood handle and round moulded foot, London 1764, 10¾in (27.5cm) high, 30.5oz.
£1,800–2,000
$2,600–2,900 ⚺ DN

A George III silver baluster coffee pot, with a crest within a surround of scrolls, flowers and foliage, with later decoration, maker's mark 'T.E.', London 1774, 9¼in (23.5cm) high, 26oz.
£500–550
$700–800 ⚒ Bea(E)

A George III silver bullet-shaped teapot, with wooden handle and knop, 4in (10cm) high.
£1,200–1,600
$1,800–2,300 ⊞ PSA

A George III silver teapot, by William Vincent, with reeded bands, wavy edge and hinged cover, fruitwork handle and finial, maker's mark 'W.V.', London 1788, 5½in (14cm) high, 15.5oz.
£320–350
$450–500 ⚒ MCA

A George III silver coffee pot, by Daniel Smith and Robert Sharp, the domed lid with urn finial, embossed with drapes and tassels and engraved with a crest, leaf-capped spout, later loop handle and spreading foot with beaded edging, London 1775, 13in (33cm) high, 35oz.
£3,000–3,500
$4,500–5,000 ⚒ AH

A Dutch silver teapot, by Jan de Wal II, with ivory scroll handle and finial, hinged cover, four leaf supports, Leeuwarden 1784, 15in (38cm) high, 14.5oz.
£3,700–4,200
$5,300–6,000 ⚒ S(Am)

A George III silver teapot, with hinged domed cover and matched finial, loop handle and ivory insulators, engraved with initials 'W.A.W.' within a surround, handle repaired, on a matching stand with four feet, maker's mark 'C.A.' for Charles Aldridge, London 1788, 7in (18cm) long, 19.5oz.
£1,000–1,200
$1,500–1,800 ⚒ MCA

◀ **A George III silver reeded coffee biggin,** by Henry Chawner and John Emes, with polished wood scroll handle, domed detachable cover with acorn finial, on a stand with curving supports with a burner, each component engraved with the same crest, London 1796, 12in (30.5cm) high, 33.25oz.
£1,400–1,600
$2,000–2,300 ⚒ CSK

A George III silver tea urn and matching coffee urn, engraved twice with a coat-of-arms and crest, maker's mark of John Romer, London 1777, largest 22in (56cm) high, 141oz.
£10,000–12,000
$14,500–17,500 ⚒ C
The arms are those of Willis.

A George III engraved silver teapot, by William Plummer, London 1785, 5½in (14cm) high, 15.25oz.
£1,800–2,000
$2,600–2,900 ⊞ TC

LOCATE THE SOURCE
The source of each illustration in Miller's can be found by checking the code letters below each caption with the Key to Illustrations, pages 311–314.

A George III silver coffee pot and matching teapot, by Robert Sharp, of quadrangular urn form with incurved angles, bright-cut collars of grapes, acorns and fruit, reel-shaped cover with ball finial, both monogrammed 'JMY', London 1796, teapot lacks finial, coffee pot 13½in (34.5cm) high, 63oz.
£1,900–2,200
$3,000–3,500 ⚒ S(NY)

A George III silver coffee pot, by Wakelin and Garrard, with tapering sides and scalloped leaf-capped spout with shell motif at base, engraved with crest of Henderson, 1797, 11½in (29cm) high, 39.5oz.
£2,700–3,000
$3,900–4,500 ⚒ P

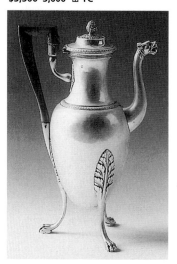

A George III silver urn-shaped coffee pot, by Richard Cooke, London 1800, 11½in (29cm) high, 32.5oz.
£2,250–2,500
$3,300–3,600 ⊞ TC

A silver teapot, by George Smith and Thomas Hayter, with bright-cut panelled decoration, London 1797, 4in (10cm) high.
£1,500–1,800
$2,200–2,600 ⊞ DIC
Bright-cutting was popular at the end of the 18th century. It employs the same method as engraving, but uses a burnished steel tool to cut the metal, which polishes the silver as it cuts, producing a sharp design which reflects the light.

A George III silver monogrammed coffee pot, by Peter, Anne and William Bateman, with thread edging, ivory finial and scroll handle, on spreading pedestal base, with presentation initials under the base, London 1800, 10in (25.5cm) high, 25.75oz.
£1,400–1,600
$2,000–2,300 ⚒ Bea

A George III silver coffee pot, monogrammed below a bright-cut band with flowers, foliage and acorns, the hinged cover with urn-shaped finial, wood scroll handle, on a spreading pedestal base, maker's mark 'I.M.' possibly for John Mince, London 1799, 10½in (26.5cm) high, 26oz.
£1,700–1,900
$2,500–2,800 ⚒ Bea

A George III silver coffee pot, by Peter, Anne and William Bateman, with thread edging, wood scroll handle and finial, on a spreading pedestal base, London 1800, 10½in (26.5cm) high, 23.25oz.
£1,600–1,800
$2,300–2,600 ⚒ Bea

A George III part-fluted silver teapot, by Solomon Royes and John East Dix, with shell and scroll border, silver knob and handle with cornucopia, on shell and scroll bracket and paw feet, London 1818, 23.25oz.
£600–700
$870–1,000 ⚒ DN

A George IV silver teapot, by William Traies, London 1822, 10in (25.5cm) wide.
£600–650
$870–1,000 ⊞ TVA

A French silver coffee pot, with pineapple finial, scrolled spout with lion-mask moulded terminal, on three paw feet, early 19thC, 12¼in (31cm) high, 36oz.
£800–900
$1,200–1,300 ⚒ B&L

A Regency silver coffee pot, by Joseph Angell, with repoussé rococo floral scroll chasing, engraved with an armorial in a cartouche, a chased moulded leaf-capped swan-neck spout, the domed cover with an asparagus finial, the wood handle with dolphin head terminal, London 1816, 10½in (26.5cm) high, 25.5oz.
£1,400–1,500
$2,000–2,200 ⚒ WW

A George IV silver pear-shaped teapot, with hinged cover, leaf-capped spout, scrolling wood handle with knop, on cast scroll feet, London 1822, 8in (20.5cm) high, 25.25oz.
£450–500
$650–700 ⚒ L&E

A George IV silver coffee pot, by George Burrows II and Richard Pearce, with gadrooned border, leaf-chased handle and spout, on a circular foot, London 1826, 7in (18cm) high, 27.5oz.
£700–800
$1,000–1,200 ⚒ DN

A George IV silver teapot, with half-fluted decoration, gadrooned rim and foot, leaf-capped scrolled handle, London 1827, 4¾in (12cm) high, 20oz.
£360–400
$500–600 ⚒ GAK

A George IV silver coffee pot, by Emes and Barnard, with lobed body and melon finial, 1828, 8¾in (22cm) high, 28oz.
£600–700
$870–1,000 ⚒ L

A German silver-gilt lined coffee pot, with polished wood scroll handle and flattened rising cover with foliate baluster finial, one side engraved with a monogam, 19thC, 6in (15cm) high, 17.5oz.
£600–700
$870–1,000 ⚒ CSK

A William IV silver coffee pot, with embossed panels of foliate decoration on a matted ground, maker's mark 'E.B.', 10in (25.5cm) high, 36oz.
£800–1,000
$1,200–1,500 ⚒ Bon

A William IV silver teapot, embossed with panels of flowers and leaves, the domed cover with cast flower finial, leaf-chased handle and spout, on four feet, probably by Edward Barton, London 1833, 5in (12.5cm) high, 28.5oz
£650–720
$900–1,000 ⚒ DN

An early Victorian silver teapot, maker's mark 'IM&S', London 1839, 6in (15cm) high.
£1,000–1,200
$1,500–1,800 ⊞ SHa

◄ **A Dutch silver coffee pot** by Bennewitz and Son, the partly ribbed spout ending in a panther's head, with later fitted burner, Amsterdam 1834, 13¼in (33.5cm) high, 34.5oz.
£2,000–2,200
$2,900–3,200 ⚒ S(Am)

A Victorian silver teapot, with richly embossed decoration, on four mask and scroll feet, 9½in (23.5cm) high, 30oz.
£750–850
$1,000–1,200 ⚒ LF

A Victorian pear-shaped silver teapot, by Edward Barnard & Sons, the hinged lid with flower finial, London 1839, 6in (15cm) high, 22oz.
£350–400
$500–600 ⚒ P(NE)

A Victorian melon-shaped silver teapot, by Edward Barnard & Sons, on a foliate foot with similar spout and handle, floral finial, London 1840, 6½in (16cm) high, 26oz.
£1,800–2,000
$2,600–2,900 ⚒ L

A Victorian silver coffee pot,
by Robert Gray & Son, with leaf-capped scroll handle and spout, on spreading base, Glasgow 1843, 11in (28cm) high, 32.5oz.
£1,000–1,200
$1,500–1,800 ⚒ Bea

A Victorian silver teapot, by McKay and Chisholm, decorated with scrolls, flowers and scalework, Edinburgh 1848, 7in (18cm) high.
£330–400
$500–600 ⚒ Bea(E)

An Austro-Hungarian silver lobed coffee pot, the domed cover with cast flower knob with a simulated ivory handle, on four leaf-chased feet, Vienna 1856, 6½in (16.5cm) high.
£380–420
$550–600 ⚒ DN

A silver coffee pot, by John and George Angell, with reeded decoration, engraved with shells and foliage, London 1847, 11½in (29cm) high, 29oz.
£500–600
$700–870 ⚒ E

A Victorian silver coffee pot, by Robert Garrard, engraved with a crest, London 1854, 6¾in (17cm) high, 20oz.
£550–650
$800–1,000 ⚒ WW

A Victorian silver teapot, by J. M., of octagonal baluster form, with wavy rim, hollow scrolled handle, engraved with panels of flowers and vacant cartouches, octagonal foot, floral finial to lid, Glasgow 1857, 7in (18cm) high, 25oz.
£370–420
$550–600 ⚒ GAK

> **Cross Reference**
> See Colour Review (page 182)

◄ **A late Victorian silver coffee pot,** of waisted form with half-lobed decoration, maker S. W. S., 1896, 6in (15cm) high, 13.5oz.
£180–220
$260–320 ⚒ L

A Victorian silver coffee pot, with urn-shaped finial to hinged lid, beaded decoration and engraved body, on pedestal base, 10in (25.5cm) high, 24oz.
£550–650
$800–1,000 ⚒ LF

A Victorian silver coffee pot by William Hunter, engraved with hatched scrolling and vacant cartouches, London 1855, 11in (28cm) high, 24oz.
£450–550
$650–800 ⚒ WW

A Victorian silver teapot, by J. McKay, embossed and chased with C-scrolls and floral design around a cartouche, engraved with a crest and motto, Edinburgh 1858, 12¼in (31cm) long, 26oz.
£400–500
$600–700 ⚒ AG

A pair of silver George II-style *café au lait* pots, by Tessier, domed covers with baluster finials and fruitwood scroll handles, engraved with a crest, 1915, 8in (20.5cm) high, 33oz.
£900–1,000
$1,300–1,500 ⚒ C(S)

Tea & Coffee Services

A George III silver four-piece coffee and tea service, by John Emes, with bright-cut border and cartouche engraved with a crest, London 1798, 52oz.
£1,600–2,000
$2,300–2,900 ✒ L&T

▶ **A Dutch silver two-piece tea service,** by Pierre Hyacinthe la Ruelle, the teapot with wood handle and knop finial, Amsterdam 1806, cream jug 5½in (14cm) high, 17.5oz.
£1,300–1,500
$1,900–2,200
✒ S(Am)

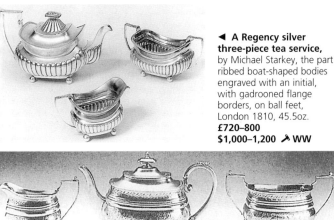

A George III silver three-piece tea service, of compressed vase shape, vertically lobed, crested, comprising teapot, by Burwash and Sibley, creamer and sugar bowl, by Emes and Barnard, London 1808–09, teapot 4in (10cm) high, 39oz.
£800–900
$1,200–1,300 ✒ S(NY)

◀ **A Regency silver three-piece tea service,** by Michael Starkey, the part ribbed boat-shaped bodies engraved with an initial, with gadrooned flange borders, on ball feet, London 1810, 45.5oz.
£720–800
$1,000–1,200 ✒ WW

A George III silver three-piece tea service, with floral and leaf engraving, on ball feet, makers S. H. and I. T., London 1814.
£820–900
$1,200–1,300 ✒ RBB

A George III silver three-piece tea service, by George Hunter, initialled above reeded lower bodies, London 1817, 49.75oz.
£900–1,000
$1,300–1,500 ✒ Bea

A George IV silver teapot and matching milk jug, by T. Johnson, with fluted and reeded lower bodies, leaf-capped scroll handles and spreading bases, London c1822, 29oz.
£550–750
$800–1,000 ✒ Bea

▶ **A George IV silver teapot and matching two-handled sugar basin,** by William Eley II and William Fearn, London c1823, 41.5oz.
£700–800
$1,000–1,200 ✒ DN

◀ **A George IV composite silver three-piece tea service,** the melon fluted bodies chased with panels of matted foliage, the teapot with leafy collar and flower embossed circular foot, the others with leaf-capped scroll handles, on leaf chased shaped circular bases, teapot by William Hunter, London 1823, the others Thomas Ballam, London 1821, teapot 7½in (19cm) high, 52oz gross.
£920–1,100
$1,300–1,600 ✒ S(S)

LOCATE THE SOURCE

The source of each illustration in Miller's can be found by checking the code letters below each caption with the Key to Illustrations, pages 311–314.

A George IV silver three-piece tea service, by Charles Fox, engraved with flowers and scrolls, crested, London 1826, 34oz.
£1,100–1,200
$1,600–1,800 ✗ F&C

A George IV silver four-piece coffee and tea service, by Rebecca Emes and Edward Barnard, of panelled and globular form, embossed with foliage and flowers, on leaf and shell cast feet, London 1826, 82.5oz.
£2,200–2,500
$3,200–3,600 ✗ P(HSS)

A William IV silver teapot, cream jug and sugar basin, by Edward Farrell, chased with flowers, scrolls and foliage, engraved with a crest, 1833, teapot 6in (15cm) high, 46oz.
£800–1,200
$1,200–1,800 ✗ C

A William IV silver four-piece coffee and tea service, by John Fraser, with acanthus leaf-capped scroll handles and flower finials, foliate scroll feet and stylized stiff leaf borders, engraved with armorials, c1835, 83.5oz.
£1,800–2,200
$2,600–3,200 ✗ P

A William IV silver four-piece coffee and tea service, by Edward Barnard & Sons, of compressed segmented form, with leaf-capped shoulders, handle and spout, on scroll bracket feet, 1836, 77.5oz.
£1,700–2,000
$2,500–2,900 ✗ P(C)

A matched silver four-piece coffee and tea service, the teapot, milk jug and sugar basin by Jonathan Hayne, London 1827, the coffee pot, sugar basin lid and milk jug lid by Samuel Hayne and Dudley Cater, London 1836, 90.5oz.
£2,000–2,700
$2,900–3,900 ✗ Bea

A silver four-piece coffee and tea service, by John Edward Terrey, with all over repoussé decoration, the cartouches to the teapot and coffee pot engraved with a boar's head crest, London 1844, 75oz.
£1,300–1,500
$1,900–2,200 ✗ WW

A Victorian silver four-piece coffee and tea service, by Joseph II and Albert Savory, London c1838, 73oz.
£1,600–2,000
$2,300–2,900 ✗ WW

A Victorian silver Melon pattern three-piece tea service, by Joseph and Albert Savory, monogrammed, London c1845, 49.25oz.
£1,200–1,700
$1,800–2,500 ⚘ Bea

A Victorian silver three-piece tea service, by Edward Barnard & Sons, London 1847, and a pair of bright-cut sugar tongs, 48.5oz.
£800–1,000
$1,200–1,500 ⚘ Bea

A southeast Asian silver three-piece tea set, each piece with an anthropomorphic cover with antlers, the body worked in low relief with *shou* characters, 19thC, teapot 6in (15cm) high, 41oz gross.
£250–300
$350–450 ⚘ P(E)

A Victorian silver four-piece coffee and tea service, by Robert Hennell, the circular bodies with fluted divisions and engraved scroll leaf and trailing flower decoration, all with leaf-capped scroll handles and scroll feet, London 1847, 68.5oz gross.
£1,250–1,450
$1,800–2,200 ⚘ P(Ch)

A silver three-piece tea service, by Thomas Smily, embossed with flowers and leaves, London 1858, teapot 6in (15cm) high, 45oz.
£600–700
$870–1,000 ⊞ CCG

A Victorian silver four-piece coffee and tea service, sugar bowl handle loose, maker 'R.G.', Edinburgh 1851 and 1853, 78oz.
£2,000–2,500
$2,900–3,600 ⚘ DN

An early Victorian silver four-piece coffee and tea service, of circular baluster form, with engraved decoration, on scroll feet, Birmingham 1860, 90oz.
£1,100–1,300
$1,600–1,900 ⚘ JAd

A Victorian George II-style silver five-piece coffee and tea service, by William Smily for A. B. Savoy & Sons, London 1864, 77.5oz.
£1,300–1,500
$1,900–2,200 ⚘ CGC

A Victorian silver four-piece tea service, the two pots with fruitwood handles and wooden finials to the oval flush hinged lids, straight spout to teapot, foliate and bright-cut engraving overall, all crested, maker's mark rubbed, Sheffield 1864, teapot 5in (12.5cm) high, 48oz.
£1,400–1,800
$2,000–2,600 ⚘ L

◄ **A Dutch silver four-piece tea service,** by Jacob D. Arnoldi, on vine leaf supports, with double-scroll handles, Amsterdam 1865, teapot 6¾in (17cm) high, 52oz.
£850–950
$1,250–1,400 ⚘ S(Am)

A Victorian silver four-piece coffee and tea service,
by Smith, Nicholson & Co, decorated with Cellini pattern,
initialled, London 1866, 77oz, in a fitted oak case with
carrying handles.
£2,300–2,600
$3,400–3,800 ⚒ S(S)

A Victorian silver six-piece coffee and tea service,
maker's mark of Stephen Smith, London 1866 and 1867, 168oz
£3,600–4,000
$5,200–5,800 ⚒ Bon

A Victorian silver four-piece coffee and tea service,
by Edward Barnard & Sons, the sides engraved with foliate
panels divided by vertical bands of beading, the covers with
acorn finials, 1872, 70oz, in a fitted wooden case.
£1,100–1,300
$1,600–1,900 ⚒ P(B)

A late Victorian silver matching four-piece tea service,
bright-cut engraved with wreathed oval shields, with leaf
motif borders, coffee pot and cream jug with maker's mark
'H.H.', probably for Henry Holland, London 1878, teapot
and sugar bowl with maker's mark 'J.A.J.S.', London 1881,
63.25oz gross, in a lined oak case.
£1,800–2,000
$2,600–2,900 ⚒ MCA

A Victorian silver-gilt three-piece tea service, by Robert
Harper, embossed with flowers, scroll and diaper panels,
the teapot with a domed cover and rose finial, cast bird's
head spout with a bearded mask, on mask and scroll feet,
1879, 27.5oz.
£680–780
$1,000–1,200 ⚒ DN

A Victorian silver four-piece tea service, with engraved
foliate decoration throughout, maker's stamp 'T.W'.,
London 1879, 62oz.
£800–900
$1,200–1,300 ⚒ Mit

A silver four-piece coffee and tea service, by J. R. Callwell
& Co, with butterfly finials, c1880.
£1,600–1,800
$2,300–2,600 ⊞ SFL

A silver four-piece coffee and tea service, by Frederick
Elkington, with lozenge and floral borders, chased and
engraved with a monogram, with bamboo moulded
handles, 1880, in a burr-walnut and ebony box,
29in (73.5cm) wide.
£1,250–1,500
$1,800–2,200 ⚒ P(EA)

A Victorian silver four-piece coffee and tea service, by James Dixon & Son, engraved with a crest within bright-cut medallions, the tea kettle and jug with inscription, stiff leaf chased borders and handles embellished with rams' masks, Sheffield 1880, 205oz.
£4,500–5,000
$6,500–7,000 ✇ S

▶ **A Victorian silver four-piece coffee and tea service,** by Henry Stratford, the oval bodies engraved with sprays of ferns, with bead edges, the milk jug and sugar basin with gilt interiors, Sheffield 1882, 66oz gross.
£1,250–1,500
$1,800–2,200 ✇ WW

▶ **A Victorian silver three-piece tea service,** engraved with stylized swags and strapwork, with beaded acanthus handles, Sheffield 1883, 34oz.
£450–550
$650–800 ✇ P(NE)

◀ **A silver four-piece coffee and tea service,** with monogram 'J.B.', teapot by Richard Cooke, London c1800, coffee pot, creamer and sugar basin, London c1884, 64oz.
£850–950
$1,250–1,400 ✇ SK

◀ **A silver four-piece tea service,** by Joshua Vander, with half-reeded design, London 1892, 70oz.
£700–800
$1,000–1,150 ✇ P(Ed)

A Victorian silver four-piece circular tapered half fluted coffee and tea service, by Elkington & Co, the covers with ivory insets, on rim feet, engraved monograms, Birmingham marks 1884–86, pattern No. 10699, 69oz, with an oak baize-lined travelling case, 12½in (32cm) wide.
£1,200–1,600
$1,800–2,300 ✇ AG

A Victorian silver four-piece tea service, by C. E. & Co, with half-reeded design, the tea and coffee pots with pearwood handles, Sheffield 1894–99, 59oz.
£600–700
$870–1,000 ✇ PFK

A silver coffee and tea service, London c1895, milk jug London 1809, teapot 7in (18cm) high.
£1,450–1,650
$2,300–2,400 ⊞ TGa

A four-piece silver coffee and tea service, by Gibson and Langman for The Goldsmiths & Silversmiths Co, the swirl-fluted bodies on gadrooned bases, the flared collars pierced with arabesques, tea and coffee pots with carved horn angular handles, London 1894, coffee pot 9¼in (23.5cm) high, 79oz gross.
£2,000–2,200
$2,900–3,200 ✇ S

A Victorian silver seven-piece coffee and tea service, by Mappin & Webb, each lobed and embossed with cartouches within flowers, scrolling foliage and shells, with an engraved crest, on paw feet, ivory handles and finials, Sheffield 1898, 237.75oz.
£6,500–7,500
$9,500–11,000 ✇ P(S)

◀ **A silver three-piece tea service,** with vertical fluting and reeded body bands, Chester 1900, 33oz.
£350–400
$500–600 ✇ GAK

A German silver five-piece coffee and tea service, by
Deyhle, with bone fitted loop handles and hinged covers,
c1900, 86oz.
£880–1,000
$1,300–1,500 ⚒ S(Am)

An Edwardian silver four-piece tea service, decorated
with scrolling foliage, water jug 8in (20.5cm) high, 54oz.
£700–850
$1,000–1,250 ⚒ Mit

An Edwardian silver three-piece tea service, by The
Goldsmiths & Silversmiths Co, with half-reeded design,
London 1902, 32oz.
£350–420
$500–600 ⚒ Bea(E)

A silver five-piece tea service and tray, each piece on
four leaf-and-scroll supports, maker's mark J.F., Glasgow 1908.
£2,000–2,400
$2,900–3,500 ⚒ P(Ed)

A Victorian silver four-piece coffee and tea service, by
C. S.Harris, with gadrooned, shell and acanthus edging,
engraved with flowers and scrolling foliage, London 1900, 80oz.
£950–1,100
$1,400–1,600 ⚒ Bea(E)

An Edwardian silver four-piece tea service, London
1901, teapot 10½in (26.5cm) wide, 74oz.
£900–1,200
$1,300–1,800 ⚒ AH

An Edwardian silver three-piece tea service, by W. Hutton
& Sons, the teapot with a winged lion finial, on fluted
pedestal bases, 1902, 61.5oz.
£1,000–1,200
$1,500–1,800 ⚒ P(E)

An Edwardian silver four-piece tea service, the teapot
and hot water jug each with foliate cast finial and ebony
loop handle, embossed with scrolling foliage, London
1903–04, 68oz.
£1,100–1,200
$1,600–1,800 ⚒ AH

◄ **An Edwardian silver five-piece tea service,** by The
Goldsmiths & Silversmiths Co, engraved with stylized flowers
and foliage, London 1907, kettle Sheffield 1908, 99oz.
£800–1,000
$1,200–1,500 ⚒ P(F)

A George III-style silver three-piece tea service, by Walker and Hall, each piece with shell-capped curved legs, Sheffield c1908, 40oz.
£500–600
$700–870 ↗ MEA

A George V silver four-piece tea service, with thread edging on four bun feet, maker's mark 'H.A.', Sheffield 1918, 56oz.
£500–600
$700–870 ↗ Bea(E)

A George V silver four-piece tea service, by The Goldsmiths & Silversmiths Co, each circular body with vertical reeding and textured foliate borders, London 1926, 69oz.
£680–740
$950–1,000 ↗ Bea(E)

A silver four-piece oblong-shaped tea service, the teapot and hot water jug with compressed handles and knobs, Sheffield 1932, 56oz gross.
£750–950
$1,100–1,380 ↗ DN

An Edward VIII silver four-piece coffee and tea service, with maker's mark 'S' and 'W', Sheffield 1936, 54.5oz.
£750–950
$1,100–1,400 ↗ Bea

A silver three-piece tea service, with gadrooned edges, the teapot with ebonized handles and knop, the sides with half gadrooning, early 20thC, 35oz.
£300–330
$450–500 ↗ TRL

A George V silver four-piece coffee and tea service, by James Dixon & Sons, together with a pair of sugar tongs, Sheffield c1918, 56.6oz, in a fitted mahogany case.
£900–1,200
$1,300–1,800 ↗ Bea

An early 18thC-style silver four-piece coffee and tea service, by Walker and Hall, Sheffield 1932, coffee pot 9¾in (25cm) high.
£1,000–1,200
$1,500–1,800 ↗ CGC

A George V silver three-piece globular tea service, on stepped circular bases, maker's mark 'B & S', Sheffield 1935, 34oz.
£400–450
$600–650 ↗ Bea(E)

A silver four-piece half-fluted boat-shaped tea service, by Walker and Hall, the teapot and hot water jug with domed covers, ivory button finials, angular scroll handles, gadroon and shell borders, on ball feet, Sheffield 1936, 70oz.
£1,400–1,600
$2,000–2,300 ↗ WL

Toast Racks

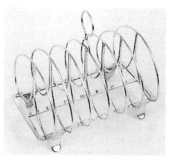

A George III silver six-division toast rack, by Thomas Hatter, London 1813, 5½in (14cm) long.
£300–350
$450–500 ⊞ PSA

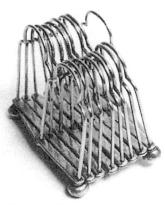

A Georgian silver extending toast rack, 3½in (9cm) long closed.
£600–650
$870–1,000 ⊞ CRA

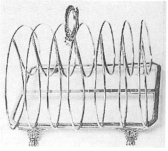

A George III silver toast rack, by W. Summers, London 1816, 6in (15cm) long.
£400–450
$600–650 ⊞ SnA

A Victorian silver six-division toast rack, by Edward Barnard & Sons, with four cast acanthus feet, with centre ringlet carrying handle, London 1846, 6in (15cm) long.
£260–300
$375–450 ➴ GAK

A Victorian silver toast rack, by William Spooner, Birmingham 1849, 6½in (16.5cm) long.
£280–320
$400–450 ⊞ TGa

A Victorian silver toast rack and egg cruet, by Edward Barnard & Sons, engraved with contemporary monogram, London 1850, with four later spoons by George Adams, London 1862, 8¾in (22cm) long, 20oz.
£1,100–1,200
$1,600–1,800 ⊞ PAY

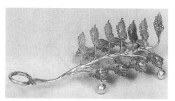

A silver toast rack, by Aldwinckle and Slater, Birmingham 1861, 8¼in (21cm) long.
£350–400
$500–600 ⊞ AMH

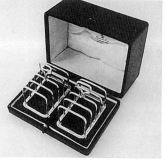

A silver articulated toast rack, designed by Dr Christopher Dresser for Hukin & Heath, c1884, 6in (15cm) long.
£500–600
$720–870 ⊞ MoS

A pair of silver toast racks, Sheffield 1911, each 2½in (6.5cm) long, in original case.
£120–140
$175–200 ➴ GAK

A four-division silver toast rack, Birmingham 1932, 3¼in (8.5cm) wide, 4oz.
£450–500
$650–700 ⊞ PAY

A silver toast rack, by Mappin & Webb, Sheffield 1938, 4in (10cm) wide.
£60–65
$90–95 ⊞ ASAA

A silver toast rack, by E. V., Sheffield 1937, 5in (13cm) wide.
£65–70
$95–100 ⊞ WAC

Trays

A George III silver two-handled tea tray, by William John Fisher, engraved with armorials within scrolls, flowers, foliage and fruit on a matted ground, the border with thread edging, London 1797, 25in (63.5cm) wide, 86oz.
£1,400–1,600
$2,000–2,300 ⚲ Bea

A George III silver tea tray, by John Watson, engraved with a coat-of-arms, the handles chased with flowers and acanthus leaves, shell, acorn and gadrooned border, Sheffield 1817, 19¼in (49cm) long, 81.5oz.
£2,400–2,800
$3,500–4,000 ⚲ P(Sc)

An early Victorian silver tray and salver service, the tray decorated with engraved armorials, motto, trellis, baskets of fruits and foliate scrolls, with chased, fluted, floral and leaf border and C-scroll handles, with two matching salvers on fluted scroll feet, all inscribed on bases 'B. Smith, Duke Street, Lincoln's Inn Fields', London 1844, tray 23¾in (60.5cm) long, 181oz, in original oak baize-lined box.
£4,500–5,000
$6,500–7,250 ⚲ AG

A silver tray, London 1870, 7in (18cm) diam.
£300–340
$440–500 ⊞ THOM

A Victorian silver two-handled tray, by Henry Wilkinson & Co, with pellet border, engraved with fruiting vine decoration, within a scroll border, on four squat foliate feet, London 1891, engraved with cypher dated '1894', 28in (71cm) long, 116oz.
£2,200–2,600
$3,200–3,800 ⚲ L

A Victorian silver gallery tray, by Mappin & Webb, Sheffield 1896, 115oz.
£1,400–1,800
$2,000–2,600 ⚲ AAV

A late Victorian silver twin-handled tray, by Daniel and John Wellby, bright-cut engraved with harebell festoons, leafy scrolls and anthemion motifs, on bun feet, Sheffield 1896, 27½in (70cm) long, 170oz.
£3,000–3,300
$4,400–4,800 ⚲ P(WM)
The unusual design of the handles and pierced octagonal borders contributed to the high price achieved.

A late Victorian silver tray, by Elkington & Co, the raised moulded borders with rococo leaf sprays and scrolls, London 1899, 31in (78.5cm) wide, 162oz.
£1,500–1,800
$2,200–2,600 ⚲ WW

◄ **A late Victorian silver two-handled tray,** with leaf-capped handles, gadroon and shell border, the centre with engraved decoration and crest, maker's mark of William Gibson and John Langman, London 1898, 29¼in (74.5cm) wide, 172oz.
£2,200–2,500
$3,200–3,600 ⚲ Bon

Insurance values

Always insure your valuable antiques for the cost of replacing them with similar items, regardless of the original price paid. Both dealers and auctioneers will provide a valuation service for a fee.

◄ **A silver tea tray,** by Harrison Brothers and Howson, initialled 'H', Sheffield 1898, 20in (51cm) long, 106oz.
£750–900
$1,100–1,300 ⚲ Bea(E)

A two-handled silver tray, with tied reeded border, on four bun feet, Sheffield 1910, 23in (59cm) long, 83oz.
£800–1,000
$1,200–1,500 ⚒ L

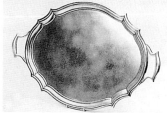

A George V silver tea tray, by The Goldsmiths & Silversmiths Co, of oval barbed outline with ogee moulded rim and scroll handles, 1920, 29in (73.5cm) long, 141oz.
£1,200–1,400
$1,750–2,000 ⚒ P(G)

◀ **A two-handled silver tray,** by Mappin & Webb, with shaped reeded border and dated cypher, Birmingham 1935, 22in (55.5cm) long, 81.5oz.
£1,200–1,600
$1,750–2,300 ⚒ L

A two-handled silver tea tray, by Mappin & Webb, the edges gadrooned and with foliate and shell moulding at the corners, the handles moulded with foliage, shells and fruiting vines, the centre engraved within an elaborate rectangular cartouche with the arms of Sir Charles Johnston and a presentation inscription to Lady Johnston, by the Members of the Corporation of London, Sheffield 1915, 146oz.
£2,000–2,400
$2,900–3,500 ⚒ P(S)

Trophies

A George II silver-gilt cup and cover, by John White, with applied armorials of King on either side, floral swags above with sea monsters and figures below, the shaped square foot cast with shells and rocaille, foliate double scroll handles, the unmarked domed cover cast with the crest of King, London 1737, 14in (35.5cm) high, 110oz.
£54,000–60,000
$78,000–87,000 ⚒ S

A George III silver two-handled cup and cover, leaf-capped scroll handles, pull-off cover with gadrooned border and swirl finial, the whole on a raised circular foot with a gadrooned border, inscribed 'Ex Amicitia uetereque consuetudine ROSE PRICE Hoc poculum dono dedit CALVERTO TENNANT Augusti 7 die anno MDLCCLX', maker's mark of William Grundy, London 1760, 9in (23cm) high, 28oz.
£650–700
$950–1,000 ⚒ Bon

A George III silver cup, by Francis Crump, the cover with a fluted ovoid finial and gadrooned edge, the body engraved with an armorial shield within floral sprays, London 1770, 12¼in (31cm) high, 44.25oz.
£1,100–1,200
$1,600–1,800 ⚒ P(F)

Condition

The condition is absolutely vital when assessing the value of an antique. Damaged pieces on the whole appreciate much less than perfect examples. However a rare desirable piece may command a high price even when damaged.

▶ **A George III silver cup,** by Andrew Fogelberg, the domed part-fluted cover with fluted finial, with reeded scroll handles and a cartouche crest engraved with the arms of Hall of London and Warnham, Sussex, on a round gadrooned column and square pierced base with ball feet, London 1773, 15½in (39.5cm) high, 50oz.
£1,200–1,400
$1,800–2,000 ⚒ DN

A George III sterling silver cup and cover, engraved with a coat-of-arms, maker's mark for Charles White, London 1774, 14¼in (36cm) high, 52.5oz.
£1,300–1,500
$1,900–2,200 ⚒ LJ

A George III two-handled silver cup and cover, vase shape, angular scroll handles, engraved foliate and ribbon tied swag decoration, unmarked pull-off cover with engraved decoration and a fluted acorn finial, the whole on a raised circular foot, reeded borders, 13¾in (35cm) high, 38oz.
£700–800
$1,000–1,200 ⚒ Bon

A George III silver-gilt presentation Kiddush cup, by John W. Storey, the campana-shaped body applied with a collar of grapevine and chased with a band of lobes outlined by matting, engraved with inscription, pedestal foot with egg-and-dart border, London 1808, 8¾in (22cm) high, 32oz.
£20,000–24,000
$29,000–35,000 ⚒ S(NY)

A George IV silver campana-shaped standing cup, by C. B., with lower lobing and fruiting vine chasing to the upper rim, foliate decoration to the matted rim of the circular spreading foot, presentation inscription dated '1921', Edinburgh 1821, 8in (20.5cm) high, 20.5oz.
£500–600
$700–870 ⚒ L

A silver trophy, for Branksome Park Tennis Club Men's Singles, c1900, 9in (23cm) high.
£100–120
$150–175 ⊞ WaR

A Victorian silver two-handled campana-shaped trophy cup, by Robert Harper, decorated in high relief with flowers and foliage, with scrolling acanthus handle and knopped stem, London 1862, 83.5oz.
£1,000–1,400
$1,500–2,000 ⚒ Bea

A silver trophy, by Walker and Hall, for the Rodway Hill Golf Club Syston Challenge Cup, hallmarked, Sheffield 1910, on a base, 12½in (32cm) high, in original case.
£500–700
$700–1,000 ⚒ S

A Dunlop silver Hole in One trophy, on black base, 1930, 3in (7.5cm) high.
£55–65
$80–95 ⊞ WaR

> **Cross Reference**
> See Colour Review (page 186)

A silver tennis trophy, from Palace Hotel, Torquay, hallmarked, 1930s, 4in (10cm) high.
£50–60
$75–90 ⊞ WaR

A silver cup and cover, by Robert Garrard, London 1936, 8in (20.5cm) high.
£350–400
$500–580 ⊞ CoHA

A sterling silver two-handled trophy cup, by Black, Starr and Frost, engraved to one side '1937 Washington Handicap one mile and a quarter, Laurel, Maryland, Won by War Admiral', 11½in (29cm) high, 50oz.
£425–475
$600–690 ⚒ SK

Vases

◀ **A matched pair of Georgian silver vases and covers,** London 1777 and 1782, 14in (35.5cm) high.
£3,800–4,200
$5,500–6,000
🔨 HOLL

A pair of late Victorian silver vases, by Elkington & Co, cast in the shape of rams' masks with foliate cornucopiae on mossy plinths, with opaque glass shell-moulded liners, 12½in (32cm) high.
£1,800–2,000
$2,600–2,900 🔨 P(WM)

A Victorian silver campana-shaped vase, decorated with stylized foliate scrolls, maker's mark F. B.s, Sheffield 1896, 9in (23cm) high.
£200–240
$290–350 🔨 Bea(E)

A Victorian silver baluster-shaped vase, by Robert Hennell, with gadrooned rim, engraved with hatched motifs and bands including anthemions, forks, scrolls, vitruvian scroll and key pattern bands, London 1869, 18½in (47cm) high, 50oz.
£1,800–2,000
$2,600–2,900 🔨 P(S)

▶ **A pair of Continental baluster vases,** by William Moering, on tripod supports with hoof feet, import marks for London 1901, 11in (28cm) high, 34oz.
£550–800
$800–1,200 🔨 Bea

A pair of Dutch silver flower vases, the bodies chased with classical figures, with angel caryatid handles and crimped tops, c1880, 6in (15cm) high, 15oz.
£330–370
$470–550 🔨 GAK

A silver replica of the Warwick vase, by Edward Barnard & Sons, applied with lions' pelts below masks, vines and beaded tongue-and-dart rim, with bifurcated vine handles, London 1908, 8¼in (21cm) high, 62oz.
£3,200–3,600
$4,500–5,500 🔨 S(S)
The original Warwick vase, of massive size, was excavated in Italy in 1771 and was eventually sold to the then Earl of Warwick. It is now in the Burrell Collection in Glasgow. Silver versions took the form of wine coolers, cups and even a tea set is recorded. Paul Storr was a prolific user of this design, and there are also examples in Sheffield plate. This piece is modelled after the antique, and they always seem to attract brisk bidding.

A pair of silver neo-classical-style vases and covers, by Hutton & Sons, with ram's mask handles, Sheffield 1911, 11½in (29cm) high.
£1,600–1,750
$2,300–2,500 🔨 P(C)

▶ **An Italian silver vase,** by Gabriel de Vecchi, 1922.
£500–600
$700–870 ⊞ DID

A pair of silver-mounted glass vases, c1920, 6¾in (17cm) high.
£140–160
$200–230 ⊞ RUL

A pair of silver spill vases, with foliate rims, Birmingham 1926, 9½in (24cm) high.
£140–170
$200–250 🔨 G(B)

Vesta Cases

A silver vesta case, by H. J., with ribbed edge around a foliate and trellis engraved body, initialled, Birmingham 1885, 1¾in (4.5cm) long.
£40–60
$60–90 ✗ CGC

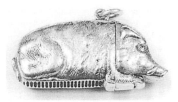

A Victorian silver vesta case, modelled as a recumbent wild boar, marked 'LE', Birmingham 1888, 2¼in (5.5cm) long.
£800–850
$1,200–1,250 ✗ GH

A silver vesta case, modelled as a water bottle in a basket, with a hinged cover, maker's mark of A. and L., Birmingham 1888, 2in (5cm) high.
£400–450
$600–650 ✗ Bon

◀ A Victorian silver and enamel cricketing vesta, by J. G., decorated with a batsman at the wicket, Birmingham 1892, 1½in (4cm) high.
£480–500
$700–720 ✗ GH

◀ A Victorian silver vesta case, by Nathan and Hayes, in the shape of a padlock, with engraved decoration, maker's mark worn, Birmingham 1888, 2½in (6.5cm) long.
£420–480
$600–700 ✗ Bea

A silver parcel-shaped vesta case, Birmingham 1894, 2in (5cm) wide.
£300–350
$450–500 ⊞ THOM

A silver dog vesta case, modelled as Toby, marked 'SML', Birmingham 1890, 2½in (6.5cm) high.
£700–750
$1,000–1,100 ✗ GH

A silver vesta case, enamelled with a chisel and inscribed 'Don't [chisel] me out of it', marked 'LE', Birmingham 1895, 1½in (4cm) long.
£400–450
$600–650 ✗ GH

Auction or dealer?

All the pictures in our price guides originate from auction houses and dealers. Look for the symbol at the end of each caption to identify the source.

When buying at auction, prices can be lower than those of a dealer, but a buyer's premium and VAT will be added to the hammer price. Equally, when selling at auction, commission, tax and photography charges must be taken into account. Dealers will often restore pieces before putting them back on the market.

Both dealers and auctioneers will provide professional advice, so it is worth researching both sources before buying or selling your antiques.

A silver vesta case, with gold circle, Birmingham 1898, 1½in (4cm) high.
£45–55
$65–80 ⊞ PSA

A silver vesta case, Birmingham 1901, 1¾in (4.5cm) high.
£50–70
$75–100 ⊞ PSA

A silver commemorative vesta case, by J. and C., with a portrait of Edward VII, c1901, 2in (5cm) high.
£140–180
$200–260 ⚒ GH

A silver vesta case and candle holder, London 1903, 1¾in (4.5cm) square.
£400–450
$600–650 ⊞ JBU

A silver vesta, modelled as a coffee pot, Birmingham 1905, 3¼in (8cm) high.
£300–350
$450–500 ⊞ AMH

An Edwardian silver combined vesta case and spirit lighter, modelled as a baluster coffee pot, the striking plate affixed below the handle, the spout with detachable cap attached to the finial of the cover by means of a chain, maker's mark indistinct, ? & Co, Birmingham 1905, 3¼in (8.5cm) high.
£250–300
$350–450 ⚒ P

▶ **An Edwardian silver table vesta case,** modelled as a miniature cigar box, the hinged lid set with a central scrolled handle and a miniature model of a dog, maker's mark of John Collard Vickery, London 1907, 2¼in (5.5cm) long.
£350–450
$500–650 ⚒ Bon

Prices

The price ranges quoted in this book reflect the average price a purchaser might expect to pay for a similar item. The price will vary according to the condition, rarity, size, popularity, provenance, colour and restoration of the item, and this must be taken into account when assessing values. Don't forget that if you are selling it is quite likely that you will be offered less than the price range.

A silver vesta case, by R. W., with a standing hound, Birmingham 1906, 1½in (3.5cm) diam.
£400–450
$600–650 ⚒ GH

An Edwardian silver combined vesta case and stamp box, the front set with a smaller rectangular compartment, the whole engraved with floral and foliate scrolls, maker's mark of W. L., Birmingham 1906.
£300–350
$450–500 ⚒ Bon

A silver vesta case, depicting a billiard game, maker's mark 'JF', Birmingham 1907, 1½in (4cm) diam.
£450–500
$650–700 ⚒ S(S)

Cross Reference
See Colour Review (page 186)

A silver vesta case, the lid inscribed 'His Masters Voice', with the dog and horn gramophone trade-mark, the interior inscribed 'With the Compliments of the Gramophone Company Ltd', marked 'SM & Co', Chester 1907, 1¾in (4.5cm) long.
£700–750
$1,000–1,100 ⚒ GH

Safety box

The vesta case is a small box used to carry wax vesta matches. There are two main types: freestanding for a desk or table, and pocket size. Following the invention of the safety match in 1855, the pocket vesta case became popular, and is the type most widely collected today. Enamelled vesta cases are particularly sought after by collectors, and are more expensive than plain, engraved or engine-turned cases. Known as matchsafes in the USA, they are usually 1½–3in (4–7.5cm) long, with sprung, hinged lids, and a serrated edge to form a striker for lighting the match.

► **A silver vesta case,** Birmingham 1908, 1¾in (4.5cm) long.
£50–70
$75–100 ⊞ PSA

Miller's is a price GUIDE not a price LIST

A silver caricature vesta of a WWI soldier, with pronounced nose and wearing a cap, maker A. W. H., London 1917, 3in (7.5cm) high.
£1,400–1,600
$2,000–2,300 ⚒ GH

◄ **A silver table matchbox,** by Asprey & Co, in the shape of a pagoda, with three engine-turned swivel doors, cylindrical columns on square base, London 1926, 7in (18cm) high.
£800–1,000
$1,200–1,500 ⚒ DN

A silver vesta case, by Walker and Hall, 1920s, 2¼in (5.5cm) high.
£80–100
$120–150 ⊞ FMN

Walking Sticks

◄ **A malacca walking stick,** the ivory and silver *piqué* handle with crossed 'Cs' design, with silver collar, c1690, 38in (96.5cm) high.
£850–950
$1,200–1,400 ⊞ MGe

A French malacca walking cane, with two-tone chased gold tau handle, c1780, 39in (99cm) high.
£2,600–2,900
$3,800–4,200 ⊞ MGe

A silver-capped walking stick, formed from the end section of a narwhal tusk, c1850, 35in (89cm) high.
£1,400–1,600
$2,000–2,300 ⊞ MGe

A Continental malacca silver-handled walking stick, c1790, 38in (96.5cm) high.
£600–700
$870–1,000 ⊞ MGe

A Victorian tiger's-eye walking cane, with silver neck ring, 35½in (90cm) high.
£100–125
$150–180 ⊞ SPU

◄ **A Folk Art walking cane,** with carved serpent handle and silver collar, c1860, 36in (91.5cm) high.
£440–480
$630–700 ⊞ MGe

LOCATE THE SOURCE
The source of each illustration in Miller's can be found by checking the code letters below each caption with the Key to Illustrations, pages 311–314.

Wine Antiques

A George III silver punch ladle, London 1775,
11½in (29cm) long.
£240–300
$350–450 ⊞ TGa

A Danish silver punch ladle, with wood and ivory handle,
19thC, 17in (43cm) long.
£575–625
$830–900 🔨 AEF

A silver-topped cork,
the top cast as a fawn or
doe, with a tree support,
hallmarked London 1827.
£220–280
$320–400 ⊞ CS

**A magnum-sized cast
silver-topped cork,** with
a bunch of grapes forming
the handle, maker's initials
for George Ivory, hallmarked
London 1856.
£180–200
$260–290 ⊞ CS

◀ **A silver-topped, leather-
cased hunting flask,**
c1920, 10in (25.5cm) high.
£250–275
$350–400 ⊞ RTh

▶ **A fitted tray of silver
cocktail accessories,** with
corkscrew, sugar tongs and
sifter spoons, Sheffield
and London 1931,
10in (25.5cm) wide, 21oz.
£300–350
$450–500 🔨 WL

Bottle Labels

▶ **A set of four silver
bottle labels,** by Thomas
Phipps and Edward Robinson
II, engraved Frontiniac, Sherry,
Port and Madeira, London
1792, 1½in (4cm) wide.
£600–650
$870–1,000 🔨 GAK

Two silver wine labels,
Champagne and Hock
c1790, 2in (5cm) wide.
£200–220
$290–320 ⊞ DIC

◀ **A set of five inscribed
silver bottle-collar
labels,** by Matthew Fenton
& Co, Sheffield 1794,
3½in (9cm) diam.
£750–800
$1,100–1,200 ⊞ DIC

◀ **Two silver wine labels,**
Port and Claret, c1820,
2½in (6.5cm) wide.
£40–50
$60–75 ⊞ CS

▶ **A silver shell and
foliate wine label,** London
1827, 2½in (6.5cm) wide.
£150–175
$220–255 ⊞ DIC

Two pairs of George IV silver wine labels, Sherry, Port, Marsala and Claret, maker's mark of William Eaton, London 1828, and maker's mark of Charles Reily and George Storer, London 1830, 2½in (6.5cm) wide.
£200–250
$290–350 ⚒ Bon

Items in the Wine Antiques section have been arranged in date order within each sub-section.

▶ **Six pierced silver vine leaf labels,** with chains, by Joseph Willmore, Birmingham 1827–32, 2in (5cm) wide.
£450–500
$650–700 ⚒ WW

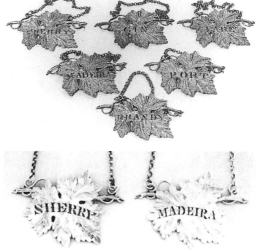

A silver vine leaf label, pierced with Madeira, London 1852, 2½in (6.5cm) wide.
£100–150
$150–220 ⊞ DIC

◀ **A silver gin label,** marked, London 1968, 1¾in (4.5cm) wide.
£40–50
$60–75 ⊞ JAS

Two matching silver cast leaf decanter labels, by Joseph Willmore, Sherry and Madeira, Birmingham 1841, and George Unite, 1854.
£180–220
$260–320 ⚒ DN

A silver brandy decanter label, Chester 1906, 1¼in (3cm) high.
£110–130
$150–200 ⊞ CoHA

Brandy Warming Pans

A George I silver brandy saucepan, with turned wood handle, the moulded circular lipped bowl engraved with an armorial and with a moulded rim, maker's mark indistinct, London 1725, 6in (15cm) wide, 5.5oz.
£800–900
$1,200–1,300 ✗ CSK

A George II silver brandy warming pan, of circular bellied form, bearing the Moody crest, with turned wooden baluster handle, maker's mark of Robert Lucas, London 1731, 7¼in (18.5cm) long, approx 4oz.
£600–700
$870–1,000 ✗ Bon

A George III silver brandy warming saucepan and cover, by Henry Chawner and John Emes, with engraved crest, hinged spout cover, stained ivory finial and turned wooden handle, London 1796, 6in (15cm) high, 10.5oz.
£800–900
$1,200–1,300 ✗ Bea

> **Miller's is a price GUIDE not a price LIST**

Claret Jugs

A Victorian silver claret jug, by Robert Gray & Son, the domed cover with grape bunch finial, vine bough loop handle, Glasgow 1840, 12in (30.5cm) high, 29oz.
£2,000–2,200
$2,900–3,200 ✗ S

A silver-mounted claret jug, with barley-twist handle, cut and engraved with flowers, with star-cut base, c1860, 9½in (24cm) high.
£1,500–1,800
$2,200–2,600 ⊞ CB

Cross Reference
See Colour Review
(page 188)

A Victorian silver-mounted and engraved glass claret jug, by John Figg, the hinged cover with crested shield and lion finial and presentation inscription, London 1860, 10½in (26.5cm) high.
£2,200–2,400
$3,200–3,500 ✗ Bea

A Victorian silver-necked glass claret jug, by George Richards and Edward Brown, the body with a swelling star-cut base and engraved florets within diapers, the similar repoussé silver neck with chased mounts of masks and bead edges to a short scroll spout, the hinged, domed cover inscribed as a prize, a rampant lion thumbpiece supporting a vacant shield and with a decorated scroll handle fixed to a beaded girdle, with traces of gilt, London 1863, 10½in (26.5cm) high.
£2,200–2,500
$3,200–3,600 ✗ WW

◄ **A fine Victorian silver-necked glass claret jug,** by Hirons, Plante & Co, having a circular foot to an engraved ovoid body decorated with diaper and bellflowers, with two sunburst cartouches, the slender silver neck engraved with a vacant oval cartouche to a bead edge rim, the domed hinged cover with a shell thumbpiece to a split scroll terminal handle, Birmingham 1864, 12in (30.5cm) high.
£1,500–1,700
$2,200–2,500 ✗ WW

◄ **A Victorian Mannerist-style silver-gilt and glass claret jug,** with lidded grotesque mask spout over acanthus and strapwork neck, the body engraved with flowers, bell-husk swags and maidenhair fern, with anthemion and grotesque mask scroll handle, Sheffield 1865, 12in (30.5cm) high.
£2,000–2,300
$2,900–3,400 ✗ EH

A Victorian silver-mounted claret jug, modelled as a seal, the central loop carrying-handle linking front and back flippers, 1881, 6½in (16.5cm) long.
£10,000–12,000
$14,500–17,500 ✗ Bri
This decanter is particularly desirable because the glass is original.

A Victorian silver-mounted claret jug, by Edward Charles Brown, the bulbous glass body etched with fruiting vine and grape decoration to the handle and fittings, with a shaped hinged lid, London 1871, 5in (12.5cm) high.
£1,700–1,900
$2,500–2,800 ✗ L

A French silver-mounted cut-glass claret jug, with domed cover and pomegranate finial, maker's mark 'H. Fres & Cie', c1880, 10in (25.5cm) high.
£1,800–2,000
$2,600–2,900 ✗ S

▶ A Victorian silver-mounted claret jug, the glass body etched with ivy leaves, with applied flower-chased silver collar, caryatid scroll handle, mask, spout and domed cover, with lion rampant and shield finial, maker's mark 'C.F.', Sheffield 1883, 11½in (29cm) high.
£2,800–3,200
$4,000–4,500 ✗ S

A silver-mounted glass claret jug, with etched floral sprays bordered by pierced scrolling silver overlay, the silver neck with lobed spout and dragon handle, maker's mark 'SS', London 1885, 14½in (37cm) high.
£1,400–1,700
$2,000–2,500 ✗ P(NE)

A Victorian silver-mounted glass claret jug, with star-cut tapering glass body, engraved 'Rangoon Boat Club Regatta, 1891', Sheffield 1890, 9in (23cm) high.
£700–800
$1,000–1,150 ✗ C(S)

◀ A Victorian silver-mounted glass claret jug, by John Grinsell & Sons, glass believed to be original, hallmarked Sheffield 1891, 8¼in (21cm) high including finial.
£1,800–2,000
$2,600–2,900 ⊞ PAY

A green glass and silver-mounted claret jug, with engraved thistle decoration, silver collar and lid with thumb rest, maker N. & W., marked for 1894, 8¾in (22cm) high.
£600–800
$870–1,200 ✗ P(B)

A late Victorian silver-mounted glass claret jug, by Gibson and Langman, the swirl-moulded body with a pierced repoussé silver-mounted flange and neck, decorated with flowers and rocaille scrolls on a trellis ground, a cast mask spout, the hinged domed cover with foliate scroll band and artichoke finial, and cast leaf-capped foliage-strewn scrolling handle, London 1896, 9in (23cm) high.
£1,100–1,400
$1,600–2,000 ✗ WW

A pair of silver-mounted claret jugs, the cut-glass bodies with hobnail decoration, scroll handles and plain hinged lid, some damage, Birmingham 1899, 8½in (21.5cm) high.
£500–600
$700–870 ✗ Bon(C)

A silver-mounted claret jug, the clear glass etched with flowers, possibly Portuguese, mid-20thC, 11½in (29cm) high.
£600–700
$870–1,000 ⊞ **WeH**

An Edwardian silver-mounted cut-glass claret jug, by Thomas Webb, with plain glass loop handle and silver spout, stopper and mount, London 1904, 8½in (21.5cm) high.
£600–700
$870–1,000 ⚒ **Bea(E)**

A pair of French silver-mounted glass claret jugs, by Bointaburet, Paris c1910, 9in (23cm) high, in a fitted box.
£2,500–2,750
$3,500–4,000 ⚒ **P**

A silver-mounted cut-glass claret jug, by The Goldsmiths & Silversmiths Co, with flower and leaf embossed mounts and presentation inscription, London 1916, 11in (28cm) high.
£1,700–1,900
$2,500–2,800 ⚒ **DN**

> Miller's is a price GUIDE not a price LIST

Coasters

A pair of George III silver wine coasters, by Robert Hennell I, with pierced and beaded galleries, on turned walnut bases, London 1776, 5in (12.5cm) diam.
£1,200–1,500
$1,800–2,200 ⚒ **DN**

A pair of George III silver wine coasters, of circular form, with pierced bodies and beaded borders, with central cartouche, crested, the wooden bases with central ivory buttons, maker's mark of Robert Hennell, London 1777, 12in (30.5cm) diam.
£2,400–2,800
$3,500–4,000 ⚒ **Bon**

◀ **Three George III silver wine coasters,** by William Burwash and Richard Sibley, crested at the centre, the rims and bases with gadrooned edging, London 1809, 5¾in (14.5cm) diam.
£2,500–3,000
$3,500–4,400 ⚒ **Bea**

◀ **A set of three George III silver wine coasters,** by William Stevenson, London 1780, 4¾in (12cm) diam.
£2,200–2,500
$3,200–3,600 ⊞ **TGa**

A pair of Victorian silver wine coasters, by Henry Wilkinson & Co, decorated in relief with grapes and vine leaves, with turned wood bases, Sheffield 1847, 9in (23cm) diam, 30oz.
£1,850–2,000
$2,700–2,900 ⚒ **Bea(E)**

A pair of George III silver wine coasters, of circular fluted bellied form with gadrooned borders, the wooden bases with central initialled buttons, marks rubbed, London, probably 1814, 6in (15cm) diam.
£1,000–1,200
$1,500–1,800 ⚒ **Bon**

A pair of George III parcel-gilt wine coasters, of circular form with fluted decoration and shaped gadrooned borders, with fluted silver-gilt centres, crested, on wooden bases, maker's mark of John Poynton & Co, Sheffield 1809, 6¼in (16cm) diam.
£2,200–2,500
$3,000–3,500 ⚒ **Bon**
The crest and motto is that of Plunket and Trotter of Scotland.

Decanters

A Victorian three-bottle decanter frame, by Henry Wilkinson & Co, the three faceted blue glass decanters with vine leaf spirit labels, pierced for Rum, Gin and Brandy, London 1839, 17in (43cm) high, 30oz.
£2,500–3,000
$3,500–4,500 ⚒ S(S)

▶ **A pair of silver overlay decanters,** 12in (30.5cm) high.
£400–450
$600–650 ⊞ SUL

A pair of silver-mounted clear glass dimple-type decanters, by Hukin and Heath, Birmingham 1921, 11in (28cm) high.
£280–320
$400–450 ⚒ CGC

Sets/pairs
Unless otherwise stated, any description which refers to 'a set' or 'a pair' includes a guide price for the entire set or the pair, even though the illustration may show only a single item.

Ewers

A German silver parcel-gilt baluster ewer, by Johann Mittnacht I, the body applied with a bearded mask, embossed and chased with acanthus and gadroons and with entwined handle, marked on body and foot, Augsburg 1690–95, 12in (30.5cm) high, 40oz.
£6,500–7,500
$9,500–11,000 ⚒ S(G)

LOCATE THE SOURCE
The source of each illustration in Miller's can be found by checking the code letters below each caption with the Key to Illustrations, pages 311–314.

▶ **A Renaissance-style silver wine ewer,** by James and Nathaniel Creswick, the lip and cover with masks, the handle formed as a female figure, London 1854, 12in (30.5cm) high.
£2,200–2,500
$3,200–3,600 ⚒ DN

A Victorian silver wine ewer, by William Smily, with a fruiting vine handle, engraved with oval panels, flowers and scrolling leaves, London 1856, 13¾in (35cm) high, 25oz.
£850–1,000
$1,300–1,500 ⚒ DN

A Victorian silver baluster ewer, on a rising foot and with applied scroll rim and handle, the body decorated with rococo flowers, foliage, C-scrolls, scale and trellis work, the front with a vacant cartouche, engraved above the shoulder within a garter cartouche, probably by John Mitchell, Glasgow 1854, 14in (35.5cm) high, 30.25oz.
£1,600–1,800
$2,300–2,600 ⚒ CSK

◀ **A silver ewer,** by Edward Barnard & Sons, the body with engraved scrolling decoration, the handle modelled as a vine with applied fruit and leaf detail, ivory insulators and leaf thumbpiece to the lid, London 1858, 14¼in (36cm) high, 24.5oz.
£750–850
$1,100–1,300 ⚒ P(Ed)

A Victorian silver baluster ewer, by John Hunt, engraved with a mermaid crest, with plain loop handle on spreading base, the base rim inscribed 'Hunt & Roskill, Late Storr and Mortimer', London 1863, 12in (30.5cm) high, 22oz.
£1,400–1,600
$2,000–2,300 ✗ Bea

▶ **A Renaissance-style French first standard silver ewer,** in the shape of a nautilus shell with wave-chased spout, the lid mounted with a conch shell finial, the handle cast and chased in the form of a horn-blowing triton, marked 'Puiforcat, France', c1915, 12½in (32cm) high, 38oz.
£2,800–3,200
$4,000–4,500 ✗ NOA

A silver wine ewer, the body with a band of reeding above scrolling foliage and two cartouches, London 1865, 12in (30.5cm) high, 17.5oz.
£620–750
$900–1,100 ✗ E

A Victorian silver ewer, by Robert Hennell, embossed with a scene of two huntsmen resting after the hunt, engraved with a crest and inscribed, London 1872, 11in (28cm) high, 38oz.
£2,000–3,000
$3,000–4,500 ✗ Bon

A silver Cellini ewer, 1879, 13in (33cm) high.
£1,500–1,700
$2,200–2,500 ⊞ DIC
The Cellini pattern ewer was a standard design of claret jug made throughout the second half of the 19th century. They are often gilded and tend to be relatively small, follow the same shape, and may have self-opening lids. Many Cellini jugs were made in Glasgow.

◀ **A Victorian silver Armada pattern ewer,** by Job Frank Hall, embossed with scrolls and masks, with applied beasts' heads and figures flanking vacant cartouches, the cover with articulated handle lever, London 1894, 12in (30.5cm) high, 28oz.
£2,000–2,200
$2,900–3,200 ✗ S

Funnels

A George III silver two-part wine funnel, by S. H., with beaded edges, London 1794, 6in (15cm) high.
£450–550
$650–800 ✗ GAK

▶ **A silver wine funnel,** by William Burwash, the detachable strainer with gadrooned edging, London 1814, 6in (15cm) high.
£600–700
$870–1,000 ✗ Bea(E)

▶ **A George III silver wine funnel,** London 1799, 6in (15cm) high.
£550–650
$800–1,000 ⊞ TGa

▶ **A George III silver two-part wine funnel,** the bowl of double ogee shape with gadrooned rim, London 1815.
£600–700
$870–1,000 ⊞ CS

A George III silver wine funnel, Sheffield 1803, 6in (15cm) high.
£1,250–1,500
$1,800–2,200 ⊞ SHa

Hip Flasks

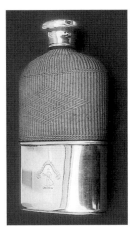

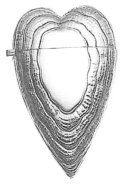

A Victorian silver and wicker hip flask, 6in (15cm) high.
£135–150
$200–220 ⊞ BCA

A Victorian silver-topped hip flask, the hobnail-cut glass body with gilt-lined integral cup, London 1885, 5½in (14cm) high.
£150–180
$220–260 ✗ EH

A cut-glass flask, with silver base and top, hallmarked, c1920, 5¼in (13.5cm) high.
£160–180
$230–260 ⊞ RTh

A Victorian heart-shaped silver double spirit flask, by C. H. Cheshire, decorated with a rock-like finish around a vacant central panel on each side, with two electroplated interior screw-on caps, Birmingham 1888, 5¼in (13.5cm) high.
£800–1,000
$1,200–1,500 ✗ P

Wine Coolers & Ice Buckets

A pair of Belgian silver-gilt wine coolers, by Joseph-Germain Dutalis, the foot rims inscribed, Brussels c1820, including original iron rods and braces.
£52,000–55,000
$75,000–79,000 ✗ S(NY)

Two silver-gilt wine coolers and liners, applied with cast trailing vines, vine tendril handles, plain collars and liners, engraved twice with coats-of-arms, the liners and collars with a crest of the Guelphic Order, maker's mark of William Eley II, London 1828–30, 11¾in (30cm) high, 325 oz.
£22,000–25,000
$32,000–36,000 ✗ C

A silver-mounted glass ice bucket, by The Goldsmiths & Silversmiths Co, with multi-faceted glass, Birmingham 1929, and a pair of silver tongs, Sheffield 1934, bucket 8½in (21.5cm) high.
£550–600
$800–870 ⊞ TC

Wine Tasters

▶ **A silver wine taster,** unmarked, c1660, 2½in (6.5cm) diam.
£1,650–1,850
$2,400–2,700 ⊞ BEX

A French silver wine taster, with fluted sides and reverse-punched beading, the serpent ring handle with scaled finish, inscribed around side 'J. Richards' and 'F. Cacussey', Paris 1750, 3in (7.5cm) diam, 3.5oz.
£800–900
$1,200–1,300 ✗ P

Cross Reference
See Colour Review (page 187)

◀ **A French provincial silver wine taster,** the sides chased with bunches of grapes, the ring handle formed by eagles' heads and terminating in an arrow head, inscribed 'Antoine Mouseron 1776', maker's mark, 2½in (6.5cm) diam, 3oz.
£700–800
$1,000–1,200 ✗ P

Writing

A silver-mounted leather and ivory notecase, by Yapp and Woodward, the silver covers engraved with Westminster Abbey, the reverse with a country church, the ivory leaves marked with the days of the week, with original silver twist pencil, Birmingham 1847, 3½in (9cm) long.
£500–550
$700–800 ✗ S(S)

An American silver paper knife and stamp container, c1880, 9½in (24cm) long.
£350–400
$500–600 ⊞ JBU

A silver-mounted paper knife, by Francis Higgins, with Albany-pattern handle and plain ivory blade, marked, London 1883, 14¼in (36cm) long.
£150–180
$220–260 ✗ Bon

A silver and tortoiseshell paper knife, Birmingham 1899, 14¾in (37.5cm) long.
£200–225
$300–330 ⊞ WeH

A collection of silver pencils, 1870–1910, longest 4½in (11.5cm) long.
£20–40
$30–60 each ⊞ VB

A silver ruler letter opener, London 1899, 8½in (21.5cm) long.
£340–375
$500–550 ⊞ SHa

A late Victorian silver and velvet blotter, of rectangular form, the blue velvet ground applied with silver floral and foliate C-scrolls and diaper panels, maker's mark 'W.C.', 9¼in x 11¾in (23.5 x 30cm).
£200–300
$300–450 ✗ P(WM)

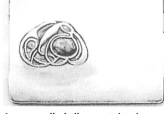

An enamelled silver notebook sleeve, by Liberty & Co, with Knox design motif, marked 'L & Co', Birmingham 1903, 2¾in (7cm) wide.
£300–350
$450–500 ✗ P

A silver letter balance, by G. Betjeman & Sons, the white onyx base with shaped cut-out silver frame, the ladder beam with a flat tray at each end, with a set of five brass weights, London 1918, 6½in (16.5cm) long.
£250–350
$350–500 ✗ CGC

◄ **A silver-gilt four-piece desk set,** each piece pavé set with small ruby-coloured stones and a split seed pearl with the Persian crescent moon and star, and comprising rocker blotter, seal, pen and small clear glass inkwell, stamped '935', c1928, in a cream and velvet lined and fitted case.
£550–650
$800–1,000 ✗ HSS

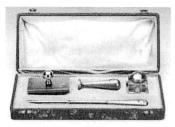

A silver Yard-O-Led Diplomat pencil, London 1948, 4¾in (12cm) long.
£60–70
$90–100 ⊞ ABr

A silver Yard-O-Lette lady's pencil, London 1948, 4in (10cm) long.
£40–50
$60–75 ⊞ ABr

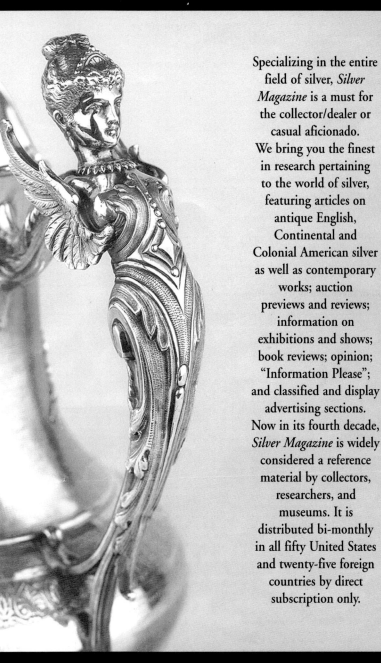

Decorative Arts

Silverware of the first half of the 20th century is now established as a modern classic. In Europe and America, groups of art lovers and individuals were encouraging new ideas and fresh looks away from traditional machine-made cheap copies of earlier 18th century designs, which were very popular with a growing affluent middle class. This resulted in the formation of various guilds and groups all in the pursuit of new design, sometimes emphasizing hand production, such as the Arts and Crafts movement in Great Britain. Thus New Art, now known collectively as Applied Arts/Decorative Arts, was created.

During the last 30 years of the 19th century, the then radical and revolutionary designs of Dr Christopher Dresser, which were manufactured by James Dixon and Elkington among others, could today be mistaken for 'avant garde' current design in a contemporary interior. Later in the 19th century Art Nouveau, based on naturalistic decorative ornaments applied to highly curvilinear objects, usually wrought in heavy gauge silver and often partially cast and hand chased was produced in Europe and America. Large manufacturing companies produced many die-stamped, cheap commercial items such as picture frames and toilette brushes for the gift market. Concurrently,

however, artist craftsmen of the newly formed Arts and Crafts movement, such as Omar Ramsden and Alwyn Carr, A. E. Jones, C. R. Ashby, and Archibald Knox at Liberty, were all producing their own style of Art Nouveau. It is now recognised that Ashby and Knox were icons of early 20th century design.

A separate movement was also developing, lead by Charles Rennie Mackintosh, whose Modernist designs, along with Ashbee's, were the prime factor in modern applied arts. In Vienna, Joseph Hoffmann and others at the Weiner Werkstätte were designing objects without ornamentation and made to order in the best quality. This was to become the foundation of 1930s Art Deco. Jean Emille Puiforcart, father of Art Deco silver, was preaching minimalism in 1920s Paris. His silver is always of the highest qualtiy and the designs very usable in today's interior. In Great Britain, new design was encouraged and a wealth of designers/silversmiths emerged, among these H. G. Murphy and Harold Stabler. Meanwhile Scandinavia, with its own distinctive look, was producing some of the best affordable domestic silver, notably by the successful firm of Georg Jensen of Denmark, who was employing many of the silversmiths of the time and thus introducing new designs on a regular basis.

Fay Lucas

Arts & Crafts

A Victorian silver picnic tea service, designed by Christopher Dresser for Hukin and Heath, London, comprising 11 silver pieces and four porcelain pieces, Sheffield 1894, 38oz, in a fitted leather case.
£5,000–5,500
$7,200–8,000 ⚒ S
The designer of this service, Christopher Dresser, became Art Advisor to Hukin and Heath around 1877. The Furniture Gazette noted in 1879 that 'the firm have secured the services of (Dr Dresser) in order to be reliable in point of design'.

Miller's is a price GUIDE not a price LIST

◀ **A silver pepperette,** by C. R. Ashbee, inlaid with five moonstones, London 1900, 3in (7.5cm) high.
£950–1,150
$1,400–1,700 ⚒ RID

A Victorian plain silver vase, by J. Wakely and F. C. Wheeler, of square form tapering to circular, and with four C-shaped handles, 1899, 5in (12.5cm) high, 11oz.
£320–380
$450–550 ⚒ MSW

A Liberty silver chalice, by Archibald Knox, the deep conical bowl above four slender interlocked stems, enclosing an onyx stone mounted on the broad circular foot, stamped maker's marks 'L&C°, R^D 37023', with Birmingham hallmarks for 1900, 9½in (24cm) high, 19.5oz.
£11,000–13,000
$16,000–19,000 ⚒ C

◀ **An Arts and Crafts silver punchbowl,** by West & Sons, the body chased and engraved with bands of Celtic motifs and roundels, applied with four plaques, Dublin 1901, 15in (38cm) high.
£2,500–3,000
$3,500–4,500 ⚒ JAd

A Guild of Handicraft silver bowl and spoon, by C. R. Ashbee, the hammered round bowl with reeded loop handle set with a green quartz cabochon, London 1902, 3in (7.5cm) diam.
£1,600–2,000
$2,300–2,900 ✦ HOLL

A silver buckle, by Archibald Knox for Liberty & Co, with green enamelled inserts, marked, London 1902, 3½in (9cm) wide.
£1,100–1,250
$1,600–1,800 ⊞ SHa

A silver photograph frame, by Rogers and Whitehouse, decorated with clover leaf pattern, Birmingham 1903, 4⅜in (12cm) diam.
£340–380
$500–550 ✦ THOM

A Guild of Handicraft silver box, enamelled with a mallard duck, some restoration, marked, London 1903, 5¼in (13.5cm) wide.
£650–700
$950–1,000 ✦ P

An Arts and Crafts silver bowl, by Florence and Louise Rimmington, the hammered body with three open leaf petal-embossed handles, London 1903, 4¼in (11cm) diam.
£220–250
$320–360 ✦ WW

A Liberty & Co silver cream jug, with plain looped handle and three ball feet, Birmingham 1904, 3in (7.5cm) high.
£280–320
$400–450 ✦ GAK

A Liberty & Co Cymric silver butter dish, by Archibald Knox, the domed cover with loop handle set with a turquoise cabochon, and a butter knife, marked 'L & Co', Birmingham 1904, butter dish 7½in (19cm) long.
£5,500–6,500
$8,000–9,500 ✦ P

An Arts and Crafts silver tyg, by Wakely and Wheeler, with hammered finish and three scroll handles, London 1905, 7½in (19cm) high.
£350–400
$500–600 ✦ CGC

An Arts and Crafts silver casket, by William Hutton & Sons, probably designed by Kate Harris, with shaped hinged straps, set with pink tourmaline cabochons, maker's mark for London 1905, 9½in (24cm) long.
£1,600–1,800
$2,300–2,600 ✦ P

Sets/pairs

Unless otherwise stated, any description which refers to 'a set' or 'a pair' includes a guide price for the entire set or the pair, even though the illustration may show only a single item.

A silver-plated fish knife and fork, designed by Charles Rennie Mackintosh for the Tea Rooms of Miss Cranston in Glasgow, with stylized trefid end pattern, the knife with rat-tail reverse, 1905, knife 8¼in (21cm) long.
£1,100–1,200
$1,600–1,800 ⊞ DAD

An Edwardian hammered silver bowl, by W. H. Haseler, with twin bifurcated loop handles, pierced with stylized flowerheads, Birmingham 1906, 5¼in (13.5cm) wide, 2.5oz.
£200–220
$290–320 ✦ S(S)

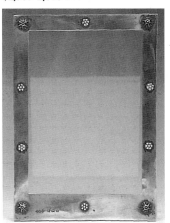

A Liberty & Co silver and enamel picture frame, Birmingham 1907, 7¼in (18.5cm) high.
£700–850
$1,000–1,300 ✦ RTo

A silver napkin ring, by Josef Hoffmann for Weiner Werkstätte, initialled, marked, 1908–10, 2in (5cm) diam.
£700–850
$1,000–1,300 ✗ DORO

▶ **A silver bowl,** by A. E. Jones, the body with a stud-work border and wirework tendril handles, Birmingham 1908, 8in (20.5cm) wide, 4oz.
£400–450
$600–650 ✗ S(S)

A hand-beaten silver belt buckle, by W. H. Haseler for Liberty & Co, with green and blue enamel inserts, stamped marks, Birmingham 1909, 3¼in (8.5cm) long.
£280–325
$400–470 ⊞ DAD

A silver rose bowl, the hammered sides decorated in relief with four female mask cartouches on a leaf frieze, supported by four winged female figures, stamped and scratched 'Lydia Cooper Lon. 1911', 11¼in (28.5cm) diam, 70oz.
£2,400–2,650
$3,500–3,900 ✗ P

An Arts and Crafts silver boat-shaped dish, by A. E. Jones, of hammered design, pierced at either end with a panel of lily pads, the sides and pedestal foot with stud decoration, Birmingham 1913, 11¾in (30cm) long.
£900–1,000
$1,300–1,500 ✗ P

A silver caddy spoon, by George Payne & Son, the stem terminating in four scrolls supporting a ball finial, Birmingham 1914.
£300–350
$450–500 ✗ P
A. E. Jones and Omar Ramsden both made articles for Payne & Son, jewellers and silversmiths of Oxford and Tunbridge Wells.

A German silver coffee pot, by Emmy Roth, the handle with two ivory bands and an ivory finial, signed and stamped, 1920s, 11½in (29cm) high.
£1,000–1,200
$1,500–1,800 ✗ P

A hammered silver-metal chalice, by Joseph Hoffman for the Wiener Werkstätte, embossed with a continuous frieze of fruiting vine motifs, the body embossed with small flowerheads within each central flute, raised on a spreading foot, marked, c1920–25, 6½in (16.5cm) high.
£4,000–4,500
$5,800–6,500 ✗ WDG

◀ **A set of four silver goblets,** by the Artificers' Guild, the bodies with ropework girdles and a frieze of fish in low relief, marked for 1923, 3in (7.5cm) diam, 19oz.
£2,000–2,200
$2,900–3,200 ✗ P

▶ **A Liberty silver comport,** with lightly beaten effect and Celtic inspired motifs, Birmingham mark 1927, 7in (17.5cm) high.
£450–500
$650–720 ✗ Mit

A silver caddy spoon, with stylized pierced scroll handle, marked, Birmingham 1924, 2¾in (7cm) long.
£200–240
$290–350 ✗ Bon

A Liberty & Co silver vase, with flat chased grape and vine decoration, on a loaded base, Birmingham 1936, 8¾in (22cm) high.
£1,500–1,700
$2,150–2,450 ⊞ PAY

Art Nouveau

A set of six Art Nouveau sterling silver buttons, c1895.
£250–300
$350–450 ⊞ SHa

A silver sugar bowl and sifter ladle, by Heath and Middleton, the bowl formed as a fluted flowerhead resting on an openwork leafy tendril base, the interior chased to simulate petals, the sifter ladle with budding sprig stem, stamped marks, London 1887, 4½in (11.5cm) diam.
£450–500
$650–700 ⊞ DAD

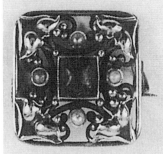

An Art Nouveau silver button hook, c1900, 8¼in (21cm) long.
£30–40
$45–60 ⊞ OBS

An Art Nouveau silver-framed dressing table clock, Birmingham 1898, 6½in (16.5cm) high.
£450–500
$650–750 ✗ Bea

An Art Nouveau silver brooch with turquoise, matrix and pearls, c1900, 1in (2.5cm) wide.
£130–160
$190–230 ⊞ GOO

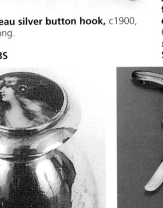

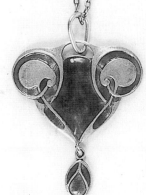

An Art Nouveau silver inkstand, with an enamelled portrait head, c1900, 2¾in (7cm) high.
£450–500
$650–700 ⊞ ASA

A silver-gilt, enamel and pearl brooch, the stem and bud with pale green *plique-à-jour* enamel leaves suspending two flowerhead drops, the petals of freshwater pearls, c1900.
£1,000–1,100
$1,500–1,600 ✗ P(Gen)

A silver and enamel pendant, by Murrle, Bennett & Co, set with blue stones, c1900, 1½in (4cm) wide.
£400–450
$600–650 ⊞ SHa

Five silver hatpins, by Charles Horner and Pearce and Thompson, c1900, largest 11in (28cm) long.
£35–60
$50–90 each ⊞ VB

A Schoonhoven silver buckle, designed by Gerrit Greup, stamped marks, c1900, 4in (10cm) long.
£270–325
$390–470 ✗ S(Am)

An Art Nouveau silver photograph frame, depicting a lady picking apples, c1900, 11in (28cm) high.
£400–450
$600–650 ✗ GAZE

◀ A silver buckle, the lower part in the form of a reclining lady, Birmingham, c1900, 3¼in (8.5cm) wide.
£300–350
$450–500 ⊞ SHa

A silver belt buckle, designed by Kate Harris, the central section with a girl holding a bowl and surrounded by flowers, retailed by W. G. Connell, mark worn, London 1901, 5½in (14cm) long, 2oz.
£200–240
$290–350 ⚒ Bon

◄ **A silver vase,** by The Goldsmiths & Silversmiths Co, London 1901, 8in (20.5cm) high.
£270–300
$400–450 ⊞ ANO

A pair of Art Nouveau silver flower vases, by Elkington & Co, on circular bases, Birmingham 1902, 6in (15cm) high.
£420–460
$600–700 ⚒ GAK

An Art Nouveau silver paperweight, by William Hutton & Sons, Birmingham 1902, 3½in (9cm) wide.
£220–250
$290–360 ⊞ Rac

An Art Nouveau silver photograph frame, c1902, 5in (12.5cm) square.
£400–450
$600–650 ⊞ ASA

An Art Nouveau silver photograph frame, decorated with Honesty motifs, Birmingham 1903, 6½in (16.5cm) high.
£550–650
$800–950 ⊞ SHa

A set of four Art Nouveau silver salts, by Elkington & Co, each with three scroll handles, fitted blue glass liners, three spoons missing, Birmingham 1903, 2in (5cm) high.
£300–340
$450–500 ⚒ RTo

A silver jam spoon, Sheffield 1903, 5½in (14cm) long.
£25–30
$35–45 ⊞ AMH

An Edwardian silver double photograph frame, by William Hutton & Sons, the top with green and blue enamelled panels, 1903, 11in (28cm) wide.
£2,500–3,000
$3,500–4,500 ⚒ P(B)

An Edwardian silver photograph frame, by Charles S. Green & Co, chased with a young woman picking apples, 1904, 6in (15cm) high.
£320–380
$450–550 ⚒ P

A silver-mounted green glass decanter, designed by C. R. Ashbee, Guild of Handicrafts, glass by James Powell, London 1904, 8½in (21.5cm) high.
£1,250–1,400
$1,800–2,000 ⊞ RUSK

◄ **An Art Nouveau silver belt,** by William Hutton & Sons, probably to a design by Kate Harris, composed of 15 shaped round plaques and a larger clasp, each depicting a young girl in profile, Birmingham 1905, 30in (76cm) long.
£450–500
$650–700 ⚒ DN

A silver casket, by Nathan and Hayes, the hinged cover repoussé-decorated with a portrait of a maiden, the interior cedar-lined for cigarettes, Chester 1906, 6¼in (16cm) wide.
£300–330
$450–475 🔨 WW

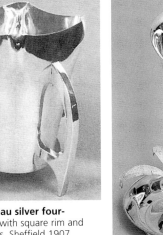

An Art Nouveau silver four-handled cup, with square rim and angular handles, Sheffield 1907, 6in (15cm) high.
£400–450
$600–650 ⊞ WeH

◀ A silver box, designed by Kate Harris, retailed by Liberty & Co, c1910, 4½in (11.5cm) wide.
£350–400
$500–600 ⊞ ASA

A silver lily-shaped vase, with beadwork leaves, marked, Birmingham 1907, 13½in (34.5cm) high.
£575–650
$850–950 ⊞ SHa

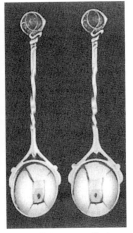

▶ A pair of silver spoons, by W. A. S. Benson, each handle with intertwined heart and flowerhead motifs, London 1911, 6¼in (16cm) long.
£650–700
$950–1,000 🔨 WDG

A set of six enamelled silver coffee spoons, by Liberty & Co, the twisted stems elaborately attached, circular green and blue enamelled tops, marked 'L&Co', Birmingham 1910, 4in (10cm) long, in original wooden fitted case.
£600–700
$870–1,000 🔨 P

An Art Nouveau hammered silver three-handled cup, maker's mark overstruck, 1910, 14½in (37cm) high.
£800–1,000
$1,200–1,500 🔨 Gam

A set of six Art Nouveau silver and enamel liqueur glasses, gilt lines, the base with blue enamel Tudor rose, Birmingham 1919, 3in (8cm) high, in original fitted case stamped 'JP'.
£500–560
$700–800 🔨 CSK

Art Deco

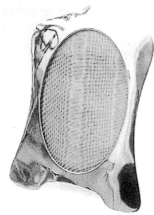

An Art Deco silver photograph frame, by L. Emmanuel, Birmingham 1915, 7¼in (18.5cm) high.
£350–390
$500–570 ⊞ THOM

A silver toast rack, marked 'MN & Co', Birmingham 1921, 6in (15cm) wide.
£80–120
$12–180 ⊞ WAC

A pair of French silver candle holders, by Puiforcat, with rose-pink quartz liners, c1930, 6¼in (16cm) high.
£4,000–5,000
$5,800–7,250 ⊞ SFL

An Art Deco four-piece silver tea service, by Alexander Clark Co, with scroll spouts, the teapot and hot water jug with ivory finials to the hinged covers and ivory scroll handles, on panel feet, Sheffield 1937, 53oz.
£1,500–1,700
$2,200–2,500 ⚒ WW

A pair of silver candlesticks, by A. E. Jones, with oak barley-twist columns, the drip pans and bases with hammered decoration, Birmingham 1919, 6in (15cm) high.
£600–700
$870–1,000 ⚒ RTo

A French silver marcasite plaque brooch, centred with synthetic blue spinel, 1930, 2in (5cm) wide.
£70–80
$100–120 ⊞ JSM

A silver tureen, by Evald Nielsen, with ivory handles, c1930, 11¼in (28.5cm) wide.
£3,400–3,750
$5,000–5,500 ⊞ SFL

▶ **An Art Deco silver three-piece tea service,** Birmingham 1937, 6½in (16.5cm) high.
£1,700–2,000
$2,500–2,900
⚒ SWO

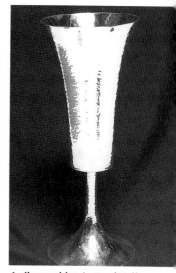

A silver goblet, by Josef Hoffmann for Wiener Werkstätte, c1920, 9in (23cm) high.
£4,300–4,800
$6,000–7,000 ⊞ ANO

A silver and paste brooch, 1925–35, 1¾in (4.5cm) long.
£200–240
$290–350 ⚒ DORO

A silver sweetmeat stand, by Charles Boyton, on a turned ivory stem, marked, London 1934, 4¾in, (12cm) diam.
£500–600
$700–800 ⚒ F&C

◀ **A faceted silver teapot,** designed by Wiwen Nilsson, 1930s, manufactured in Sweden 1947, 8½in (21.5cm) high.
£5,000–6,000
$7,200–8,700 ⚒ BUK

Colour Review

Three Arts and Crafts silver-gilt chased dishes, by W. J. Counell, London 1897, 9in (23cm) diam.
£3,250–3,750
$4,800–5,500 ⊞ PAY

A silver buckle, by C. R. Ashbee, with a turquoise at each corner, c1897, 3¼in (8.5cm) wide.
£4,000–4,500
$5,800–6,500 ➷ S

An Arts and Crafts turquoise and silver necklace, c1900.
£400–450
$600–650 ⊞ ASA

A silver tea caddy, with blue and green inserts, early 20thC, 3¾in (9.5cm) high.
£1,200–1,500
$1,800–2,200 ⊞ ASA

A silver and polychrome enamel vase, mark of Liberty & Co and Cymric, Birmingham 1902, 8¾in (22cm) high, 20oz.
£16,000–17,500
$23,500–25,500 ➷ Bon

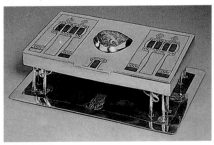

A silver and enamel cigarette box, by W. H. Haseler & Co, designed for Liberty & Co, minor loss to enamel, stamped maker's marks 'WHH', Birmingham 1904, 8in (20.5cm) wide.
£14,000–15,000
$20,500–22,000 ➷ C

An Arts and Crafts silver inkstand, by Joseph Ridge, London 1905, 7in (18cm) long.
£1,700–2,000
$2,500–3,000 ⊞ PAY

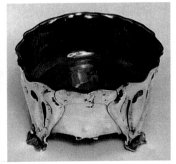

An Arts and Crafts silver serving bowl, by Middleton & Heath, London 1902, 10in (25.5cm) diam.
£5,000–5,500
$7,000–8,000 ⊞ SHa

> Miller's is a price GUIDE not a price LIST

A Guild of Handicrafts silver and enamel sugar bowl, cover and spoon, the design attributed to C. R. Ashbee, stamped maker's and London marks, bowl and cover 1906, spoon 1905, 5¾in (14.5cm) diam.
£1,800–2,200
$2,600–3,200 ➷ S(NY)

A Liberty & Co set of six silver and enamel teaspoons, designed by Archibald Knox, stamped and hallmarked, 1926, 4¼in (11cm) long.
£675–750
$990–1,100 ⊞ DAD

A hammered silver caddy spoon, by Henry George Murphy, the stem pierced and chased with Tree of Life motif, London 1929, 4in (10cm) long.
£550–600
$800–870 ⊞ DAD

▶ **A Swedish Art Nouveau silver and *plique-à-jour* enamel stemmed cup,** by C. G. Hallberg, faults, stamped, Stockholm 1899, 7in (18cm) high.
£2,750–3,250
$4,000–4,800 ➷ S(Am)

An Art Nouveau silver cigarette box, 3½in (9cm) square.
£420–460
$600–650 ⊞ ASA

▶ **An Art Nouveau Liberty silver and enamel cigarette box,** 6½in (16.5cm) wide.
£550–600
$800–870 ⊞ ASA

An Art Nouveau claret jug, with a silver mount, 12½in (32cm) high.
£1,200–1,600
$1,800–2,300 ⊞ ASA

An Art Nouveau silver cigarette case, by William Hutton.
£350–400
$500–600 ⊞ ASA

◀ **An Art Nouveau silver and cornelian buckle,** 4in (10cm) wide.
£380–430
$550–625 ⊞ ASA

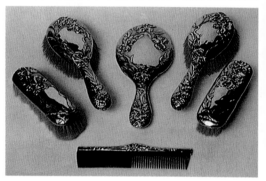

An Art Nouveau silver dressing table set, c1900.
£300–350
$450–500 ⊞ ASA

A French Art Nouveau silver pendant, set with moonstones and sapphires.
£550–650
$800–950 ⊞ ASA

A silver, enamel and pearl pendant, c1900, 19½in (49.5cm) long.
£900–1,000
$1,300–1,500 ⚒ P(Gen)

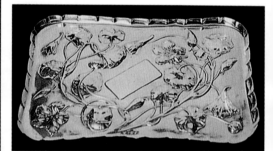

An Art Nouveau silver tray, c1900, 11in (28cm) wide.
£300–400
$450–600 ⊞ ASA

A silver, enamel and hardstone necklace, by L. Gaillard, stamped, c1900, 27½in (70cm) long.
£10,000–11,000
$14,500–16,000 ⚒ P(Gen)

▶ **A silver and enamel pot and cover,** by Thomas Latham & Ernest Morton and Laurent, maker's mark, Birmingham 1901, 3½in (9cm) high.
£1,200–1,400
$1,800–2,000 ⚒ S

A German silver rose bowl, by Friedrich Adler, c1902, 4½in (11.5cm) wide.
£800–900
$1,200–1,300 ⊞ SUC

▶ **A silver and enamel photograph frame,** by William Hutton & Son, London 1903, 8 x 5½in (20.5 x 14cm).
£2,300–2,650
$3,500–3,900 ⊞ THOM

A pair of Art Nouveau silver photograph frames, c1903, 13 x 10in (33 x 25.5cm).
£1,200–1,500
$1,800–2,200 ⊞ ASA

A pair of Art Nouveau silver vases, c1905, 4in (10cm) high.
£300–340
$450–500 ⊞ PSA

A silver dress clip, set with marcasite and amazonite, 1930s, 1in (2.5cm) long.
£35–40
$50–60 ⊞ JSM

A set of four Art Nouveau menu holders, by Henry Matthews, Birmingham 1905–06, 1½in (4cm) high.
£850–950
$1,300–1,500 ⊞ NS

◄ **A silver-overlaid cranberry glass vase,** by Alvin & Co, c1905, 10in (25.5cm) high.
£2,000–2,200
$2,900–3,200 ⊞ SFL

► **An Art Nouveau silver-fronted clock,** Birmingham 1910, 12in (30.5cm) high.
£750–850
$1,100–1,300 ⊞ SHa

An Art Deco silver five-piece tea and coffee service, by M. M. Boulenger, with rosewood handles and finials, Paris c1930, tray 23¼in (59cm) long, 149oz gross.
£5,000–6,000
$7,000–8,700 ⚒ S

An American five-piece silver tea and coffee service, maker's mark of Fletcher & Gardiner, Philadelphia c1813, coffee pot 11½in (29cm) high, 194oz.
£6,000–7,000
$8,500–10,500 ⚒ CNY

An American coin silver tea service, by Woodward & Grosjean, c1847, largest 8in (20.5cm) high.
£6,800–7,600
$10,000–11,000 ⊞ YAN

◄ **A pair of American sterling silver repoussé vegetable dishes,** by William Holmes, c1850, 10in (25.5cm) diam.
£4,800–5,200
$7,000–7,500 ⊞ YAN

A George I Irish silver bowl, by Thomas Bolton, Dublin 1716–17, 5in (12.5cm) diam.
£6,800–7,500
$10,000–11,000 ⊞ NS

A George II Irish silver bowl, by Robert Goble II, Cork 1735, 5½in (14cm) diam.
£12,000–14,000
$17,500–20,500 ⊞ NS

An Irish silver cream jug, by Robert Glaiville, Dublin 1740, 4in (10cm) high.
£2,400–2,900
$3,500–4,200 ⊞ NS

An Irish sterling silver sauce ladle, by Andrew Goodwin, with part wooden handle, maker's mark stamped in centre, marked Dublin 1740, 8¼in (21cm) long.
£600–700
$870–1,000 ⊞ SLI

An Irish silver loving cup, by William Homer, 1777, 6in (15cm) high.
£1,100–1,300
$1,600–1,900 ⊞ JBU

A pair of Irish silver beakers, by Terry Williams, Cork c1805, 3½in (9cm) high.
£8,000–9,000
$11,500–13,000 ⊞ NOR

A George III Irish sterling silver sauce boat, by James Le Bas, with reeded rim, on three cast shell and hoof feet, with flying scroll handle, hallmarked Dublin 1811, 4¼in (11cm) high, 7oz.
£1,550–1,800
$2,200–2,600 ⊞ SLI

An Irish silver mustard pot, by James Scott, Dublin 1815, 2½in (6.5cm) high.
£700–800
$1,000–1,200 ⊞ JBU

A pair of George I silver salt cellars, by Matthew Walker, Dublin 1725, 2¾in (7cm) diam.
£3,000–3,500
$4,500–5,000 ⊞ NS

A Victorian chased silver coffee pot, by J. Maloney, Dublin 1843, 10in (25.5cm) high.
£1,300–1,500
$1,900–2,200 ⊞ PAY

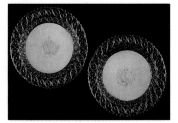

◄ **A pair of George III Irish silver salvers,** by James Graham, on three cast scroll panel supports, the centres engraved with armorials, Dublin c1770, 9in (23cm) diam, 32oz.
£16,000–18,000
$23,000–26,000 ⚒ S

A George II Irish silver pint mug, by Robert Calderwood, Dublin 1747, 4¾in (12cm) high.
£2,500–2,850
$3,500–4,000 ⊞ NS

A pair of George III Irish silver sauce boats, by Thomas Jones, with gadrooned rims, Dublin 1778, 26.5oz.
£2,800–3,200
$4,000–4,500 ⚒ JAd

A pair of Irish silver sauce boats, Cork c1780, 7in (18cm) long.
£4,500–5,000
$6,500–7,000 ⊞ NOR

◄ **A George III Irish silver sugar bowl,** by Thomas & Harmer, Cork 1785, 5½in (14cm) high.
£3,000–3,500
$4,500–5,000 ⊞ NS

► **A George III Irish silver basket,** engraved and pierced, probably by J. Moore, Dublin 1795, 14in (35.5cm) long.
£4,000–4,500
$5,800–6,500 ⊞ PAY

A Russian silver-gilt relic cross, inscribed with saints' names and containing relics, 16thC, 4in (10cm) high.
£2,400–2,800
$3,500–4,000 ⊞ ICO

A Russian silver-gilt pendant cross, inscribed on reverse, containing relics, 17thC, 3in (7.5cm) high.
£2,400–2,700
$3,500–4,000 ⊞ ICO

A Russian partially gilt silver beaker, maker's mark 'MW', St Petersburg c1735, 4in (10cm) high, 5.25oz.
£1,500–1,650
$2,220–2,400 ⚒ DORO

A Russian silver-gilt cross, inscribed on reverse as containing relic of a stone from Golgotha, c1800, 2in (5cm) high.
£1,200–1,300
$1,800–1,900 ⊞ ICO

Miller's is a price GUIDE not a price LIST

A Fabergé silver-mounted cut-glass decanter, the silver lid with pine cone finial and garland-draped thumbpiece, maker's mark below Imperial warrant, inventory No. 7682, Moscow pre-1896, 10½in (26.5cm) high.
£5,500–6,500
$8,000–9,500 ⚒ S

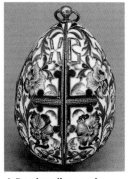

A Russian silver and enamel Easter egg, enclosing an icon, marked, c1900, 3½in (9cm) high.
£7,000–8,000
$10,000–11,500 ⚒ S(NY)

A pair of Fabergé silver, translucent enamel and bowenite table candlesticks, with the mark of workmaster Karl Gustav Hjalmar Armfelt, St Petersburg, c1900, 4¼in (11cm) high.
£30,000–35,000
$43,500–50,500 ⚒ S(NY)

A pair of Russian silver-gilt and cloisonné enamel water jugs, by Pawel Akimow Ovchinnikov, maker's mark below Imperial warrant, Moscow 1879, 10in (25.5cm) high, 88.5oz.
£4,000–4,500
$5,800–6,500 ⚒ S(Am)

◄ **A Fabergé cloisonné and silver-gilt kovsch,** signed below Imperial double-headed eagle, Moscow late 19thC, 3in (7.5cm) wide.
£900–1,000
$1,300–1,500 ⚒ Bon

A Georgian Scottish silver-mounted stag's horn vinaigrette, with original sponge, 2¼in (5.5cm) long.
£1,000–1,200
$1,500–1,800 ⊞ CoHA

A Scottish silver quaich, by Robert Innes, Inverness 1740, 5in (12.5cm) diam.
£6,500–7,500
$9,500–11,000 ⊞ NS

A pair of Scottish silver candlesticks, by John Kincard, Edinburgh 1746, 6½in (16.5cm) high, 22.25oz.
£3,200–3,850
S4,500–5,500 ➚ WW

A George II Scottish silver waiter, by Coline Allan, Aberdeen 1750, 6in (15cm) diam.
£7,500–8,000
$11,000–11,500 ⊞ NS

A Scottish silver sugar bowl, by William Dempster, Edinburgh 1763, 3½in (9cm) diam.
£1,150–1,250
$1,700–1,800 ⊞ JBU

A Scottish silver lemon strainer, by Pat Robinson, Edinburgh 1774, 6in (15cm) long.
£450–500
$650–700 ⊞ NOR

A set of six Scottish sterling silver teaspoons with matching mash spoon, by John Keith, the teaspoons with maker's mark, Banff c1800, mash spoon with additional mark, teaspoons 5in (12.5cm) long, 3oz.
£800–900
$1,200–1,300 ⊞ SLI

A Scottish silver reeded mug, by David Gray, Dumfries 1820, 3in (7.5cm) high.
£3,000–3,500
$4,500–5,000 ⊞ NS

A William IV Scottish chased silver coffee pot, by Elder & Co, Edinburgh 1833, 11in (28cm) high.
£1,400–1,600
$2,000–2,300 ⊞ PAY

A Scottish silver pin, inset with slate, c1850, 2in (5cm) diam.
£225–275
$300–400 ⊞ WIM

A Victorian Scottish sterling silver card case, by George Cunningham, both sides engine-turned to simulate tartan, the centre of one side with a vacant cartouche, maker's mark, Edinburgh 1855, 3¾in (9.5cm) high, 2.25oz in original leather box stamped 'Mackay, Cunningham & Co'.
£700–800
$1,000–1,200 ⊞ SLI

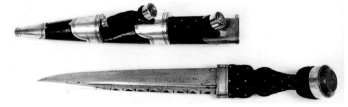

A Scottish silver and leather dirk, decorated with citrines, c1870, 18in (45.5cm) long.
£650–800
$1,000–1,200 ⊞ BWA

A silver marrow scoop, by Hester Bateman, London 1775.
£320–360
$450–520 ⊞ BEX

A pair of George III silver salt cellars, by Hester Bateman, London 1773–74, 2½in (6.5cm) diam.
£850–950
$1,300–1,500 ⊞ NS

A silver basket, by Hester Bateman, London 1774, 5in (12.5cm) high.
£1,200–1,400
$1,800–2,000 ⊞ AMH

A silver sugar vase, by Hester Bateman, London 1775, 7½in (19cm) high.
£2,500–2,850
$3,500–4,500 ⊞ MCO

A George III silver helmet-shaped cream jug, by Hester Bateman, London 1873–84, 7in (18cm) high.
£1,200–1,400
$1,800–2,000 ⊞ NS

A silver sugar sifter, by Hester Bateman, London 1784, 5½in (14cm) high.
£800–900
$1,200–1,300 ⊞ NOR

▶ **A silver pap boat,** by Hester Bateman, London 1788.
£700–800
$1,000–1,200 ⊞ NOR

◀ **A pair of George III silver pierced wine coasters,** by Hester Bateman, London 1790, 5in (12.5cm) diam.
£5,250–5,750
$7,500–8,500 ⊞ NS

A George III silver bright-cut tea caddy, by Hester Bateman, London 1786, 6in (15cm) high.
£5,500–6,500
$8,000–9,500 ⊞ NS

A George III silver cream jug, by Peter & Jonathan Bateman, London 1790, 6in (15cm) high.
£2,000–2,200
$2,900–3,200 ⊞ PAY

◀ **A George III silver bright-cut tea caddy,** by Peter & Ann Bateman, London 1793–94, 4in (10cm) high.
£4,000–4,500
$5,800–6,500 ⊞ NS

A pair of George III silver pierced salt cellars, by Peter & Ann Bateman, London 1797, 3in (7.5cm) wide.
£800–1,000
$1,200–1,500 ⊞ NS

▶ **A sterling silver sugar basket,** by Hester Bateman, without a handle, engraved with contemporary family crest, London 1811, 4in (10cm) high.
£1,700–2,000
£2,500–2,900 ⊞ SLI

An American sterling silver, copper and gold tea caddy, by Gorham, 1881, 4in (10cm) high.
£6,000–6,400
$8,700–9,300 ⊞ BEX

An American silver-gilt and cut-glass decanter, by Gorham, c1893, 14¾in (37.5cm) high.
£3,000–3,400
$4,500–5,000 ⚡ S(NY)

An American sterling silver and glass jam pot, by Gorham, c1920, 4¾in (12cm) high.
£200–225
$290–325 ⊞ BEX

An American silver Art Deco cocktail set, by Erik Magnussen for Gorham, comprising a cocktail pitcher and 12 martini goblets, marked on bases and numbered A14082 and 14083, the pitcher with 1930 date symbol, pitcher 12in (30cm) high, 92oz.
£3,400–3,800
$5,000–5,500 ⚡ S(NY)

A silver buckle, by Georg Jensen, designed as a pierced dragonfly, with a cabochon opal, c1895.
£3,000–3,300
$4,500–4,800 ⚡ S(Am)

A silver tea strainer, by Georg Jensen, import mark, 6in (15cm) long.
£225–275
$325–400 ⊞ MHB

A pair of silver candelabra, by Georg Jensen, 1918, 13½in (34.5cm) high.
£22,000–25,000
$32,000–36,000 ⊞ SFL

A silver beaker, by Georg Jensen, import mark, 3½in (9cm) high.
£500–550
$700–800 ⊞ MHB

A silver three-piece dressing table set, by Georg Jensen, 1925–33, hairbrush 8¾in (22cm) long.
£450–550
$650–800 ⚡ BUK

▶ **A pair of silver servers,** by Georg Jensen, c1930.
£400–600
$600–870 ⊞ ASA

A silver fish dish and cover, by Georg Jensen, signed 'Johan Rohde', c1930, 30in (76cm) wide.
£40,000–45,000
$58,000–65,000 ⊞ SFL

> Items in this section have been arranged in date order within each maker.

◀ **A silver Blossom four-piece tea service,** by Georg Jensen, comprising teapot and cover, hot water jug and cover, sucrier and cover and milk jug, the covers with flower bud finials, with lightly hammered decoration and ivory half-fluted pistol grip handles, on three paw feet, import marks for London 1935–36.
£4,500–5,000
$6,500–7,000 ⚡ TEN

A silver stemmed bowl, by Georg Jensen, 1930s, 4¼in (11cm) high.
£650–800
$950–1,200 ⊞ ASA

A silver tureen and cover, designed by Harald Nielsen for Georg Jensen, No. 547C, the stepped pull-off cover with stylized scroll finial, the body with two stepped ebony handles, on a circular foot, 1933–44, 11in (28cm) diam, 29oz.
£2,000–2,400
$2,900–3,500 ⚒ Bon

A silver centrepiece with cover, by Georg Jensen, c1945, 15in (38cm) wide.
£18,000–20,000
$26,000–29,000 ⊞ SFL

A silver mantel clock, designed by Johan Rohde for Georg Jensen, marked '333' on base, c1945, 12in (30.5cm) high.
£17,000–20,000
$24,500–29,000 ⚒ CNY

▶ **A pair of silver five-light candelabra,** by Georg Jensen, decorated with grapes and leaves, marked '383', post–1945, 10in (25.5cm) high, 186oz.
£17,000–20,000
$24,500–29,000 ⚒ CNY

A silver three-piece Pyramid pattern coffee set and matching two-handled tray, designed by Harald Nielsen for Georg Jensen, comprising coffee pot, creamer and covered sugar bowl, with oval tray, numbered 600A, 600B and 600V, engraved initial 'N' on bases, post-1945, coffee pot 10¼in (26cm) high, 119oz gross.
£12,000–14,000
$17,500–20,500 ⚒ S(NY)

A silver water pitcher, by Georg Jensen, with fluted handle, numbered 385D, post–1945, 8¼in (21cm) high, 25.5oz.
£2,800–3,200
$4,000–4,500 ⚒ S(NY)

A silver brooch, by Georg Jensen, with pierced and scrolled decoration of stylized leaves and flowers, marked 'Georg Jensen & Wendel A/S (1945–51)' and 'Sterling Denmark', c1947.
£300–340
$450–500 ⚒ P

A George I silver sugar caster, by Paul de Lamerie, engraved with a contemporary coat-of-arms of Treby quartering Grange for the Rt Hon George Treby, MP, with baluster finial, London 1719–20, 6in (15cm) high, 5.5oz.
£12,000–14,000
$17,500–20,500 ⊞ NS

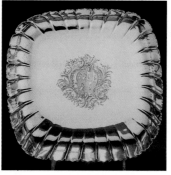

A silver strawberry dish, by Paul de Lamerie, engraved with rococo armorials, on a rim foot, initialled T.I.E. on underside, London 1715, 7in (18cm) square, 10oz.
£4,500–5,500
$6,500–8,000 ⚒ S
The arms are those of Baliney impaling Sorey.

▶ **A George II silver pint mug,** by Paul de Lamerie, London 1733–34, 4in (10cm) high.
£11,000–13,000
$16,000–19,000 ⊞ NS

A pair of Britannia Standard silver sauce boats, each with engraved coat-of-arms, maker's mark of Paul de Lamerie, London 1730, 7¾in (19.5cm) long, 30oz.
£50,000–60,000
$72,500–87,000 ⚒ C

A Victorian silver toothpick, by Sampson Mordan, modelled as a pistol, c1850, 1¾in (4.5cm) long.
£300–350
$450–500 ⊞ BEX

A Victorian silver-gilt double compartment scent bottle, by Sampson Mordan, 1870–71, 3½in (9cm) high.
£1,750–1,950
$2,500–2,900 ⊞ NS

A Victorian silver-mounted and ceramic Worcester scent bottle, by Sampson Mordan, London 1885–86, 2in (5cm) high.
£650–750
$950–1,100 ⊞ NS

A Victorian scent bottle, by Sampson Mordan, in the shape of a horseshoe, 1886–87, 2in (5cm) long.
£1,150–1,350
$1,700–2,000 ⊞ NS

A Victorian silver and agate scent bottle, by Sampson Mordan, London 1887, 1½in (4cm) high.
£400–475
$600–700 ⊞ BEX

A Victorian silver and enamel vesta case, by Sampson Mordan & Co, 1890–91, 2¼in (5.5cm) long.
£2,750–3,250
$4,000–4,700 ⊞ NS

◀ **A silver vesta case pencil hook penknife,** by Sampson Mordan & Co, London 1891, 3¼in (8cm) long.
£600–675
$870–1,000 ⊞ NOR

A silver sovereign case, by Sampson Mordan, in the shape of an oyster, hallmarks for London, 1887, 1½in (4cm) diam.
£1,150–1,250
$1,700–1,800 ⊞ NS

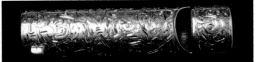

A Victorian silver vesta case, by Sampson Mordan & Co, in the shape of a whistle, engraved, hallmarked London, 1897–98, 2¾in (7cm) long.
£325–375
$470–560 ⊞ NS

◀ **A Victorian silver and ruby glass scent bottle,** by Sampson Mordan & Co, London 1892, 3in (7.5cm) high.
£300–350
$450–500 ⊞ BEX

A George V silver pincushion, by Sampson Mordan & Co, modelled as a fish, Chester 1913–14, 1½in (4cm) high.
£650–750
$950–1,100 ⊞ NS

A Victorian silver dip pen and pencil, by Sampson Mordan & Co, London 1898, 3¾in (9.5cm) long.
£150–165
$220–240 ⊞ BEX

◀ **A set of four silver menu holders,** by Sampson Mordan & Co, modelled as owls, Chester 1907, 1½in (4cm) high.
£1,100–1,200
$1,600–1,800 ⊞ NS

An Edward VII silver chalice, by Omar Ramsden & Alwyn Carr, inscribed on foot rim 'Omar Ramsden et Alwyn C.E. Carr Me Fecervnt', London 1904, 5in (12.5cm) high, 7.5oz.
£450–550
$650–800 ⋎ CAG

▶ **An Edward VII silver-backed lady's hand mirror,** by Omar Ramsden & Alwyn Carr, the moulded back embossed with three entwined roses, the twisted handles set with an oval turquoise, London 1907, 11½in (29cm) long.
£700–800
$1,000–1,200
⋎ CAG

A pair of silver mustard pots, by Omar Ramsden, London 1938, 5½in (14cm) high.
£2,250–2,500
$3,300–3,600 ⊞ MHB

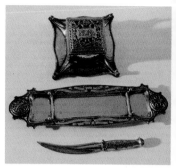

A George V desk set, by Omar Ramsden & Alwyn Carr, made for Nora Dunlop-Smith (1891–1979), comprising inkwell, pen tray and paperknife, the inkwell lid inscribed 'Nora', with green enamelled back, the pen tray with the initial 'N' and green enamelled backing, the paperknife handle inscribed 'Nora' and with green cabochon stone, engraved on inkstand and pen tray 'Omar Ramsden et Alwyn Carr Me Fecervnt MCMXIV', London 1913, pen tray 11in (28cm) long, 27oz gross.
£3,200–3,600
$4,500–5,000 ⋎ CAG

A silver string holder, by Omar Ramsden, London 1934, 3in (7.5cm) high.
£350–400
$500–600 ⊞ BEX

▶ **A silver dish,** by Omar Ramsden, with central boss pierced as a seeded rose on wine-coloured enamel, 1923, 3in (7cm) diam.
£320–350
$450–500 ⋎ TEN

A pair of George II silver entrée dishes, by Paul Storr, 12in (30.5cm) long.
£7,500–8,500
$11,000–12,300 ⊞ MHB

▶ **A George III silver coffee biggin,** by Paul Storr, with wooden handle, engraved with an armorial, on a stand with three reeded lion paw supports and burner, London 1803, 12in (30.5cm) high, 45oz.
£4,000–4,600
$5,800–6,800 ⋎ DN

A George III silver beaker, by Paul Storr, London 1802–03, 4in (10cm) high.
£2,250–2,750
$3,300–4,000 ⊞ NS

A silver condiment set, by Paul Storr, London 1804, tray 17in (43cm) long.
£8,500–9,500
$12,500–13,500 ⊞ NOR

◀ **A George III silver tea urn,** engraved with two coats-of-arms, maker's mark of Paul Storr, London 1809 and 1810, 15in (38cm) high, 211oz.
£20,000–24,000
$29,000–35,000 ⋎ C

A George III silver coffee biggin, by Paul Storr, 11in (28cm) high, 53oz.
£5,000–6,000
$7,250–8,700 G(L)

A Regency silver four bottle decanter stand, by Paul Storr, with four cut-glass bottles, the stand with egg-and-dart border and lotus leaf supports, on lion mask and quilted supports, with central leaf-chased handle, London 1811, 8¼in (21cm) square, wood loaded base.
£8,000–9,000
$11,500–13,000 S

A silver salt, by Paul Storr, London 1813, 4¾in (12cm) wide.
£6,000–7,000
$8,800–10,000 S(NY)

A Regency silver coffee pot, by Paul Storr, London 1815, 10in (25.5cm) high.
£4,000–4,750
$5,800–6,800 WW

A pair of George III silver snuffer trays, by Paul Storr, London 1816–17, 9in (23cm) long.
£4,000–4,500
$5,800–6,500 NS

A George III silver bread basket, by Paul Storr, engraved with a coat-of-arms, London 1817, 10½in (26.5cm) wide, 65oz.
£35,000–40,000
$51,000–58,000 C

A silver toast rack, by Paul Storr, London 1834, 6in (15cm) long.
£2,000–2,300
$2,900–3,400 NOR

A pair of silver sauce tureens, covers and liners, by Paul Storr, after a design attributed to E. Hodges Baily, engraved with monogram and coronet, London 1817, 9¾in (25cm) wide, 135oz.
£32,000–36,000
$46,000–52,000 S(NY)

A George IV silver entrée dish, by Paul Storr, London 1822–23, 11in (28cm) long.
£5,500–6,500
$8,000–9,400 NS

▶ **A set of six silver-gilt teaspoons** by Paul Storr, hallmarked London, 1819–20, 6in (15cm) long.
£2,250–2,500
$3,500–3,500 NS

A William IV silver teapot, by Paul Storr, London 1832, 8½in (21.5cm) high.
£3,200–3,600
$4,500–5,300 MHB

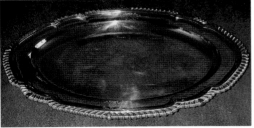

◀ **A sterling silver meat dish,** by Paul Storr, London 1835, 16¼in (41.5cm) long, 43oz.
£4,400–4,800
$6,500–7,000 SLI

A pair of silver meat dishes, by Paul Storr, with crest decoration, London 1834, 18in (45.5cm) long.
£7,500–8,500
$11,000–12,500 PAY

A Tiffany & Co silver-mounted cut-glass inkwell, with a miniature portrait of a lady in the top, 6in (15cm) high.
£800–900
$1,200–1,300 ⊞ JBU

A Tiffany & Co silver and mixed-silver Japanese-style creamer, spot-hammered and applied with vines spreading from the twig handle and bearing fruits of copper and Japanese gold, applied below the lip with a beetle, gilt interior, marked on base and numbered 7176-2336/3311, New York c1878, 4½in (11.5cm) long, 4oz.
£2,400–2,600
$3,500–3,800 ⚒ S(NY)

A Tiffany & Co silver jug, the neck and base chased with flowers on a matt ground above palmette leaves, with loop handle, underside with initials L. R. W., numbered 4706 9112, New York c1880, 8in (20.5cm) high, 30oz.
£5,500–6,500
$8,000–9,500 ⚒ S

A Tiffany & Co Japanese-style silver and mixed metal mantel clock, marked, c1880, 8¾in (22cm) wide.
£32,000–35,000
$46,500–51,000 ⚒ S(NY)

A Tiffany & Co silver water pitcher, the body applied with acanthus leaves alternating with tall sprays of bellflowers, the neck applied with grapevine spreading from the acanthus leaf handle, with engraved monogram below spout, marked on base and numbered 3077–7678, New York c1885, 7in (18cm) high, 29oz.
£35,000–40,000
$50,750–58,000 ⚒ S(NY)

A pair of Tiffany & Co silver five-light candelabra, New York c1885, 16½in (42cm) high, 115.5oz.
£10,000–12,000
$14,500–17,500 ⚒ S(NY)

A Tiffany & Co sterling silver basket, with pierced scrolled border and central monogram, c1890, 10½in (26.5cm) wide.
£650–800
$950–1,200 ⊞ SFL

A Tiffany & Co silver vegetable dish and cover, designed by Paulding Farnham, New York 1905, 15in (38cm) wide, 72oz.
£9,000–10,000
$13,000–14,500 ⚒ S(NY)

A Tiffany & Co sterling silver child's knife, fork and spoon, c1890, fork 7in (18cm) long.
£450–500
$650–700 ⊞ BEX

◄ **A Tiffany & Co sterling silver frame,** c1910, 14in (35.5cm) high.
£1,000–1,200
$1,500–1,800 ⊞ SHa

A Tiffany & Co silver and copper punchbowl, designed by Paulding Farnham, set with opals, marked on base, 1902, 21in (53.5cm) wide.
£13,000–15,000
$19,900–22,000 ⚒ S(NY)

A Sheffield-plated cruet stand,
by Bolton & Fothergill, c1769,
7in (18cm) high.
£400–450
$600–650 ⊞ CoHA

► **A pair of Sheffield-
plated wine coasters,**
with fluted sides, c1810,
5in (12.5cm) square.
£450–550
$650–800 ⊞ DIC

A pair of Sheffield-plated goblets,
c1790, 6in (15cm) high.
£300–350
$450–500 ⊞ JBU

◄ **A Sheffield-
plated funnel,**
c1825, 6in
(15cm) high.
£200–225
$290–325 ⊞ NOR

**A silver-plated
claret bottle
holder,** c1864,
12in (30.5cm) high.
£80–100
$120–150 ⊞ Har

A Sheffield-plated dish cross, 1780,
11in (28cm) wide.
£300–350
$450–500 ⊞ JBU

A Sheffield-plated sauce tureen,
c1820, 8in (20.5cm) wide.
£800–1,000
$1,200–1,500 ⊞ JBU

**A pair of close-plate candle
snuffers,** c1800, 8in (20.5cm) long.
£125–150
$180–220 ⊞ CoHA
Close-plate is a method of applying
a layer of silver foil to steel.

A silver-plated trolley coaster,
by Elkington & Co, c1860,
15in (38cm) long.
£1,650–1,850
$2,500–2,700 ⊞ JBU

A silver-plated cake basket, with
pierced border and reeded handle,
c1875, 9in (23cm) wide.
£85–95
$130–150 ⊞ SSW

**A pair of electro-plated parcel-gilt
five-light candelabra,** by Elkington
& Co, on four fluted pad feet, 1888,
26½in (67.5cm) high.
£3,500–4,500
$5,000–6,500 ⚒ Bon

**A Victorian silver-plated and
parcel-gilt-mounted etched glass
claret jug,** by Elkington & Co, 1887,
11in (28cm) high.
£1,250–1,500
$1,800–2,200 ⊞ PAY

**A set of four silver-plated
copper candlesticks,** 19thC,
10¼in (26cm) high.
£800–950
$1,200–1,400 ⊞ CoHA

A pair of Sheffield sauce tureens and covers, each with gadrooned borders and an armorial, the two handles with lions' masks, 19thC, 6in (15cm) diam.
£650–700
$950–1,000 ➶ DN

A Victorian silver-plated four-piece tea and coffee service, embossed with repoussé decoration, teapot with bird of prey finial.
£180–220
$260–320 ➶ PCh

A Victorian four-piece electro-plated Britannia metal tea service, by Mappin & Webb, c1880, large jug 9in (23cm) high.
£250–300
$350–450 ⊞ HofB

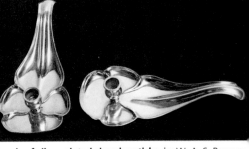

A Victorian silver-plated table centre épergne, 33in (84cm) high.
£2,400–2,800
$3,500–4,000 ➶ J&L

A late Victorian silver-plated stand, with cranberry glass liner, 6in (15cm) high.
£130–145
$190–200 ⊞ SPU

A pair of silver-plated chambersticks, by W. A. S. Benson, impressed marks, c1900, 10in (25.5cm) long.
£475–525
$700–750 ⊞ RUSK

An American Art Nouveau silver-plated tyg, by E. G. Webster & Son, Brooklyn c1900, 12in (30.5cm) high.
£500–550
$700–800 ➶ NOA

A silver-coloured metal beaker, by Josef Hoffmann for the Wiener Werkstätte, with beaded edges, 1905, 2½in (6.5cm) high.
£2,000–2,200
$2,900–3,200 ➶ S

A silver-coloured metal hand mirror, attributed to Joseph Hoffmann, slight damage to glass, c1905, 9¾in (25cm) wide.
£21,000–23,000
$30,500–33,500 ➶ S

A German silver-plated cigar box, decorated with enamelled portrait of a German officer, c1914–18, 5in (12.5cm) high.
£60–70
$90–100 ⊞ AnS

A silver-plated jam spoon, 1920s, 6in (15cm) long.
£12–15
$15–20 ⊞ FMN

A silver-plated egg stand, on claw feet, c1920, 9in (23cm) high.
£120–140
$175–200 ⊞ CoHA

A silver-plated cocktail set, with Bakelite dice-shaped handles, 1930s, largest 6in (15cm) long.
£35–40
$50–60 ⊞ BEV

A Jean Goulden silvered metal and enamel cigarette case, c1929, 3¼in (8.5cm) wide.
£4,000–4,500
$5,800–6,500 ➶ S

American Silver

merican silver has long reflected the diverse background of this country. In colonial times silversmiths emigrating from England, France and the Netherlands, influenced local styles and production methods. Today high retail and auction prices reflect the fact that early silver is very rare.

As America prospered, the quantity and quality of silver produced also grew. By 1861 a million and a half ounces of silver had been extracted from mines in California and Nevada. Prior to the mid-19th century discovery of vast silver deposits in the western states, much of the silver available came from Mexico and other countries, and the cost of the raw material remained relatively high. Labour saving innovations in silver fabrication that had begun in the Federal Period could not be fully utilized for mass production until the cost of the metal itself came down enough to attract the broader audience of middle class consumers.

From the 1860s, the level of skilled labour increased, designs became more elaborate and the consumer market expanded. In the latter part of the century much of the finishing work was still done by hand, such as chasing, engraving, applied ornamentation, and etching, which resulted in silver items of wonderful quality.

The silver business grew from a cottage industry to a major contributor to the US economy. At their peak, firms like Tiffany, Gorham, Reed & Barton and Whiting employed thousands of skilled and unskilled labourers in centres such as New York, NY, Providence, RI, and Taunton, MA. In the west, Shreve & Company flourished in San Francisco. The large volume of high quality silver that was produced during the last quarter of the 19th century is also noteworthy. During the Arts and Crafts movement of the late 19th and the early 20th century small companies such as the Kalo Shop in Chicago and Arthur Stone in Boston produced excellent quality, beautifully hand-crafted pieces.

People will argue which company produced the finest silver. Some will say Gorham's Martelé is the best because of its limited production and that it was all hand-made by the finest silversmiths of the day. Others will say Tiffany, because of its quality and design. There were many other companies represented during the great age of American silver production, such as Wallace, Towle, Samuel S. Kirk, and International Silver. The one thing they all have in common today is that their prices on the secondary market have increased and will continue to do so. **Connie MacNally**

An American silver can, by John Allen and John Edwards, modelled after a pottery example derived from China, engraved with a contemporary crest of an arm holding a bleeding heart, engraved c1800 with initials 'AS to MC', marked 'IE' and 'IA', Boston c1695, 4in (10cm) high, 6.2oz.
£44,000–50,000
$64,500–72,500 ⚒ **S(NY)**
John Allen (c1671–1760) and John Edwards (1671–1746) had a brief partnership just before 1700.

▶ **A set of four American silver table candlesticks,** by Samuel Kirk & Son, each on a pierced shaped base of flowers and foliage, the knopped stems rising to three ancient Egyptian busts, the bell-shaped sconces with everted pierced floral borders and detachable nozzles, stamped, Baltimore, Maryland c1845, 9¾in (25cm) high, 71oz.
£4,500–5,000
$6,500–7,000 ⚒ **S(NY)**

An American silver salver, by Edward Webb, with embossed rim of multiple mouldings, on a matching capstan foot, engraved underneath with contemporary initials 'S*P', the top marked 'EW', Boston c1700–10, 6in (15cm) diam, 5oz.
£7,000–8,000
$10,000–11,500 ⚒ **S(NY)**

A pair of American coin silver salts, by Jones, Ball & Co, Boston 1840, 2¼in (5.5cm) diam.
£320–360
$450–500 ⊞ **A&A**

Miller's is a price GUIDE not a price LIST

An American silver presentation fireman's trumpet, by Conrad Bard & Son, embossed and chased with floral sprays, engraved with presentation inscription and two suspension rims, Philadelphia c1845, 22in (56cm) long, 20oz.
£7,500–8,500
$11,000–12,500 ⚒ **S(NY)**

An American silver water pitcher, by Forbes & Son, the upper body with chased scrolling foliage framing the blank monogram reserve, the lower body chased with acanthus leaves in a stylized band, the multi-scroll handle chased with flowers and leaves, New York c1850, 14¾in (37.5cm) high, 43.5oz.
£1,800–2,000
$2,600–2,900 ♫ B&B

An 18thC-style American silver teapot, by Newell Harding & Co, the apple-shaped body chased at the shoulders with rococo decoration, bud finial, inscribed underneath, Boston, mid-19thC, 5½in (14cm) high, 16.5oz.
£1,500–1,800
$2,000–2,500 ♫ S(NY)

◄ **A pair of American silver vases,** chased with bands of foliage, the handles topped by bearded masks, initialled and dated '1863', 13in (33cm) high, 42oz.
£850–950
$1,200–1,400 ♫ S(NY)

An American silver vesta box and striker, modelled as a cigar, c1890, 4in (10cm) long.
£250–300
$350–450 ⊞ SFL

◄ **An American sterling silver punch ladle,** by Shreve, Crump and Low, 1868, 12¼in (31cm) long.
£250–300
$350–450 ⊞ A&A

An American silver soup tureen and cover, by Vanderslice & Co, retailed by George C. Shreve & Co, one side engraved with name and dated '1912', San Francisco c1870, 15in (38cm) wide, 88.5oz.
£3,200–3,600
$4,500–5,000 ♫ S(NY)

An American silver punch bowl, by James R. Armiger, with floral repoussé decoration and applied floral and shell cast border, Baltimore c1892, 12in (30.5cm) diam, 66oz.
£3,000–3,500
$4,400–5,000 ⊞ IHB

A late Victorian American silver heart-shaped box, embossed with floral decoration, maker's mark of Gorham, inscribed, 1895, with a silver dish commemorating Queen Victoria's Silver Jubilee.
£150–200
$220–290 ♫ Bon

A set of four American silver table candlesticks, by Marshall Field & Co, with baluster stems and detachable nozzles, decorated with putti and rococo ornament, Chicago, early 20thC, 9in (23cm) high.
£2,100–2,300
$3,000–3,300 ♫ S(NY)

A set of four American silver salts, by J. E. Caldwell, with shell-shaped bowls, raised on a pedestal foot modelled as a tortoise, three marked on base, one marked on underside of bowl, late 19thC, 2¾in (7cm) high, 29.5oz.
£3,500–4,000
$5,000–5,800 ♫ S(NY)

▶ **An American sterling silver dressing mirror,** chased and repoussé-decorated with birds and flowers, marked 'JR/925', c1900, 19½in (49.5cm) high.
£1,300–1,500
$1,900–2,100 ♫ NOA

Bowls

An American silver porringer, by Elias Pelletreau, marked 'EP', Southampton, New York c1760, 5¾in (14.5cm) diam, 7oz.
£3,300–3,650
$4,800–5,300 ⚒ S(NY)

Items in the American Silver section have been arranged in date order within each sub-section.

An American silver centrepiece bowl, by J. E. Caldwell & Co, the undulating wide rim applied with scrolling foliage, the foot rim applied with shells and scrolls, Philadelphia, late 19thC, 21in (53.5cm) diam, 120oz.
£3,100–3,500
$4,500–5,000 ⚒ S(NY)

▶ **An American silver bowl,** on a stepped circular spreading foot, the body inscribed 'The Manhattan Savings Bank, Institutional Exhibition of Champion Dogs Ch. Pugville's Imperial Imp II, February 1960', reproduction of an original by Paul Revere, 8in (20.5cm) diam.
£1,300–1,500
$1,900–2,100 ⚒ S(NY)
This bowl was awarded to the Duke and Duchess of Windsor's pug.

An American silver centrepiece bowl, by Shreve & Co, the wide rim cast and pierced with classical foliage and arches, San Francisco c1910, 24¼in (61.5cm) long.
£2,800–3,200
$4,000–4,500 ⚒ S(NY)

Cups

An American silver caudle cup, probably by John Coney, maker's mark 'IC' above fleur-de-lys on the base, Boston, dated '1676', 2in (5cm) high.
£4,200–4,800
$6,000–7,000 ⚒ RIT

An American silver mug, by Andrew Ellicott Warner, with double C-scroll handle, Baltimore, Maryland c1850, 3¼in (8.5cm) high, 6.5oz.
£200–250
$290–360 ⚒ RIT

An American silver repoussé floral pattern mug, by Samuel Kirk & Son, with double C-scroll handle, Baltimore, Maryland 1850, 4in (10cm) high, 8.5oz.
£260–300
$400–450 ⚒ RIT

Cutlery

An American silver dessert fork, by Ball, Black & Co, c1880.
£20–25
$30–35 PC

▶ **Five American sterling silver souvenir spoons,** c1915, 4in (10cm) long.
£30–40
$45–60 ⊞ YAN

Two American silver souvenir spoons, St Louis 1904 and Alaska 1909, 5in (12.5cm) long.
£60–70
$90–100 each ⊞ YAN

An American parcel-gilt Francis I pattern cutlery set, by Reed and Barton, comprising 251 pieces, engraved with initial 'S', Massachusetts, 20thC, 283oz.
£6,000–8,000
$8,700–11,600 ⚒ S(NY)

Dishes

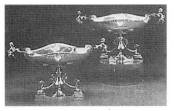

A pair of American silver comports, by Gorham, partly pierced with foliate designs, the handles modelled as demi-putti, openwork bases applied with leaf-tailed monsters, one with gilt interior, marked and No. 355, Providence, RI 1869, 14¼in (36cm) long, 60oz.
£1,600–1,800
$2,300–2,600 ✗ S(NY)

A pair of American silver vegetable dishes and covers, by Dominick and Haff, chased all over with flowers on a matted ground, bases with contemporary monograms, New York 1886, 11½in (29cm) wide, 85oz.
£2,800–3,200
$4,000–4,500 ✗ S(NY)

A pair of American silver-covered vegetable dishes, by Samuel Kirk & Son Co, repoussé and chased with Gothic scenes among flowers and foliage on a matted ground, similar ring handles, engraved on bases 'Gladys Heald Watts', marked and No. 243L, 1903–24, 10½in (26.5cm) wide, 64oz.
£2,800–3,200
$4,000–4,500 ✗ S(NY)

Jugs

An American silver-mounted cranberry glass claret jug, by Gorham, the body panelled and cut with branches of prunus, the silver neck chased with a collar of flowers, with hinged cover, Providence, RI 1888, 10½in (26.5cm) high.
£3,500–4,000
$5,000–5,800 ✗ S(NY)

A pair of American silver-mounted decanters, by T. B. Starr, with stamped foliate base and collar, initialled, c1900, 12in (30.5cm) high.
£800–900
$1,000–1,300 ✗ S(S)

An American silver jug, by Marshall Field & Co, with repoussé scenes of putti in scroll cartouches surrounded by flowers and rocaille, early 20thC, 10¼in (26cm) high, 41oz.
£1,000–1,100
$1,500–1,600 ✗ SK

Cross Reference
See Colour Review
(page 243)

An American silver-overlaid ewer, the rim and handle encased in silver, the body with foliate and scroll overlay decoration, with cartouche to front, on a spreading circular foot with frosted and cut base, with faceted silver overlay ball stopper, early 20thC, 11½in (29cm) high.
£1,400–1,600
$2,000–2,300 ✗ SK

Kettles

◀ **An American silver tea kettle-on-stand,** burner missing, marked on base of stand 'Ball Black and Co, W. F., New York', c1850, 17¼in (44cm) high, 91oz.
£1,400–1,600
$2,000–2,300 ✗ S(Cg)

▶ **An American silver kettle-on-stand,** with swing handle and burner, monogrammed, stamped 'Sterling, Howard & Co, New York, 1893', 12¼in (31cm) high, 34.5oz.
£230–250
$330–360 ✗ Bea(E)

An American silver kettle-on-stand, by Jones, Ball and Poor, chased and embossed with floral decoration, the handle with ivory insulating rings, Boston, mid-19thC, 9¼in (23.5cm) high, 24oz.
£550–650
$800–950 ✗ SK

Tea & Coffee Services

▶ **An American silver four-piece tea and coffee service,** by Thomas Fletcher, Philadelphia c1825, teapot 9in (23cm) high, 114oz.
£2,000–2,500
$2,900–3,600 ⚘ S(NY)

An American silver three-piece tea service, by John Burger, decorated with wheelwork bands, roundels and scrollwork, enriched with bright-cut details, engraved monogram 'A.C.S.', New York c1790, sugar urn 10in (25.5cm) high, 43oz.
£2,500–3,000
$3,600–4,400 ⚘ B&B

An American coin silver three-piece tea service, by Taylor and Hinsdale, monogrammed, New York, early 19thC, teapot 9½in (24cm) high, 90oz.
£1,600–2,000
$2,300–2,900 ⚘ SK

An American silver three-piece tea service, by J. and W. Moir, of ribbed pear shape, engraved monogram, New York 1845, 54.5oz.
£600–700
$900–1,000 ⚘ SK(B)

An American silver four-piece tea service, by Bogert for Tiffany & Co, with key pattern borders and urn finials, engraved with initial 'W', New York c1860, 78oz.
£2,200–2,500
$3,200–3,600 ⚘ S(NY)

An American silver five-piece tea and coffee set, by Eoff and Shepherd for Ball, Black & Co, including a silver-plated tray, with bright-cut borders, monogrammed 'JCS', New York c1860, 86.5oz.
£2,100–2,400
$3,000–3,500 ⚘ S(NY)

An American silver six-piece tea service, by William Gale & Son, heavily embossed with grapes and leaves, monogrammed, New York 1850–60, teapot 12¼in (31cm) high, 78oz.
£4,500–5,000
$6,500–7,000 ⚘ SK

▶ **An American sterling silver medallion coffee and tea service,** by William Gale & Son, New York c1862.
£7,500–8,500
$11,000–12,300 ⊞ YAN

An American silver five-piece tea and coffee service, by Dominick and Haff, with repoussé design of flowers and leaves, St Louis 1882, coffee pot 8¾in (22cm) high, 89.5oz.
£1,500–1,800
$2,000–2,600 ⚘ SLN

An American Baltimore-style sterling silver five-piece tea and coffee service, by Whiting Manufacturing Co, decorated with chased and repoussé roses and foliage, c1885–95, 74oz.
£2,500–3,000
$3,500–4,500 ⚘ NOA

An American silver part tea and coffee service, each piece on six paw feet, monogrammed and dated '1893', marked with maker's mark of a seahorse above initial 'S', 1893, 232oz.
£3,500–4,000
$5,000–5,800 ⚘ S(NY)

Chinese Export Silver

The designs of Chinese Export silver can be split into two categories: items which closely resemble the English styles of the 1800s and those which are undoubtedly of Chinese influence. The latter style, which can be elaborate and intricate, often features dragons, chrysanthemums or rural Chinese scenes, and is what makes collecting Chinese silver so interesting.

The early English-style pieces were made to satisfy the demand created by visiting merchants who found it cost effective to have copies of home-produced silver made locally despite the shipping costs. The Chinese silversmith would copy everything, including the hallmarks. In Britain it was illegal to copy town and assay office marks and gradually during the 1830s and 1840s the pseudo marks (English silver marks imitated and used on Chinese Export silver) were replaced by Chinese characters plus maker's mark.

The export silversmiths were based in Hong Kong, Canton and Shanghai. The most prolific producer was Wang Hing who operated from the 1870s to the 1920s in both Canton and Hong Kong. Generally speaking all the export silver produced was of high quality, roughly equivalent to sterling.

The China trade can be divided into four periods: Early China Trade, before 1785 which is generally unmarked; China Trade, 1785–1840 which has pseudo marks; Late China Trade, from 1840–1885 which has a mixture of Roman and Chinese letters, and Post China Trade, from 1885 which has Chinese marks only and was the most productive period but produced goods of inferior quality to the other periods. The export silver trade came to an end in the 1920s.

Affordable early Chinese Export silver is not easy to find as the number of collectors worldwide is growing and forcing prices up. However, Post China Trade pieces such as tea services, fruit bowls, punchbowls, goblets, condiments and snuff boxes can still be found at modest prices. These items are still much cheaper than their equivalent English or American counterparts, but the larger and rarer items from this period command higher prices.

As with all antique silver, before making a purchase novice collectors should start by handling pieces and reading as much as possible about them. Always take expert advice, and bear in mind that the condition of the item is of great importance.

Daniel Bexfield

A Chinese export silver mug, with presentation inscription, dated '1899', 3¼in (8.5cm) high.
£340–375
$500–560 ⊞ ELI

A Chinese export silver tea canister, by Wang Hing, the sides embossed with panels of Oriental landscapes and figural scenes, marked, late 19thC, 4½in (11.5cm) wide, 10oz.
£700–800
$1,000–1,200 ⚶ Bon

A Chinese export silver three-piece tea service and matching tongs, by Wang Hing, Shanghai c1900, teapot 5½in (14cm) high.
£950–1,100
$1,400–1,600 ⚶ B&B

A Chinese export silver two-piece clasp, 1930s, 2¾in (7cm) square.
£65–75
$95–110 ⊞ JBB

A Chinese export silver presentation bowl, by Wang Hing, decorated in relief with flowers, the handles in the form of dragons, Hong Kong c1900, 18½in (47cm) diam, 130oz.
£3,000–3,500
$4,500–5,000 ⚶ FBG

◀ **A Chinese export silver card case,** decorated with figural scenes, the reverse with foliate decoration and Chinese characters, marked '90', maker's mark of Wang Hing, 4in (10cm) high.
£280–320
$400–450 ⚶ Bon

Irish Silver

One of the features of the silver market in recent years has been the attention given to old Irish silver and its astonishing rise in value.

Plain pieces dating from 1780 are the most popular, particularly those bearing original armorials or crests, but more notable are the chased and decorative items made between 1739 and 1765. Fine examples of chinoiserie-decorated pieces from 1750–65 are beginning to command strong interest. While items from Galway and Kinsale are virtually impossible to find, value can still be found in fine Cork pieces such as those by George Hodder, Carden Terry and John Nicholson, who incidentally was one of the most gifted chasers in these islands. Pieces from Limerick are now extremely valuable, a single tablespoon can command £1,500–2,000 ($2,200–3,000).

The great rarity of fine Irish silver has only recently been noticed abroad. It is estimated that there are approximately 35–40 Queen Anne/George I Irish bullet teapots extant compared to thousands of London examples. This factor will continue to underline strong prices as supply cannot increase and demand will almost certainly do so. Generally it is estimated that the ratio of London to Dublin period silver is 150 to 1. Cork silver is perhaps five times scarcer than Dublin, and Limerick 20 to 30 times scarcer than Cork. A serious collector should focus on pieces of good authentic colour with original armorials or crests when possible (a good example of a superb armorial is the caster on page 264 of this book). One or two forgeries have surfaced in recent years and these have a dubious colour and never have correct arms. The design of the period Irish cartouche is quite different to the English example. Do not worry too much about missing date letters – that was common in Dublin c1738–85 – the design of the piece should be Irish not English.

Look out for forgeries. We recently noted a forgery of a freedom box, ostensibly Limerick but clearly made from a London toilet box with added engravings and forged mark of Joseph John. The piece should always look Irish with good colour and no added treatments, for example flagellation or plating.

A superb piece of Irish silver is a rare and highly collectable item which will prove increasingly valuable over time. It is still much cheaper than early American silver and probably just as scarce. A point worth remembering is that there are no examples in existence of the work of approximately 40 per cent of Irish silversmiths – so get hunting. **James Weldon**

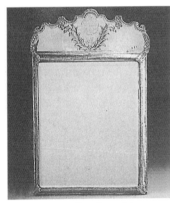

An Irish silver dressing table mirror, the ogee-moulded frame with a gadrooned border applied with stylized leaves at the corners, the centre engraved with a coat-of-arms, helm, crest and motto within engraved foliate scroll mantling and flanked by chased crossed fronds, with wood backing, maker's mark of John Humphreys, Dublin 1696–98, 28in (71cm) high.
£16,000–19,000
$23,000–27,500 ⚒ C
The arms are those of Thompson impaling Wilmot.

An Irish silver tankard, by David King, the tapering shape with twisted scroll thumbpiece, the handle with beaded rat-tail, the front engraved with a contemporary armorial, the cover engraved on top with a later crest, Dublin 1702, 6¾in (17cm) high, 23.75oz.
£4,500–5,300
$6,500–7,500 ⚒ P

An Irish silver-gilt cup and cover, by Thomas Sutton, engraved with contemporary arms on a foliate mantle, the cover engraved with a crest, Dublin 1724, 12¾in (32.5cm) high, 52.5oz.
£2,300–2,600
$3,300–3,800 ⚒ S(NY)

LOCATE THE SOURCE
The source of each illustration in Miller's can be found by checking the code letters below each caption with the Key to Illustrations, pages 311–314.

▶ **An Irish silver penal pyx,** by Thomas Sutton, Dublin 1730, 2in (5cm) diam.
£1,400–1,600
$2,000–2,300 ⊞ WELD
This was used by Roman Catholic priests to carry the host (bread) when the penal laws forbade the practise of Catholicism in Ireland.

A George II Irish silver kitchen pepper, by John Hamilton, Dublin 1730, 2in (5cm) high.
£1,200–1,400
$1,700–2,000 ⊞ WELD

A George III Irish silver sugar vase, possibly by Joseph Jackson, Dublin 1775, 9in (23cm) high.
£1,450–1,650
$2,000–2,400 ⊞ WELD

A George II Irish silver sugar caster, the body engraved with an armorial, maker's mark mis-struck, possibly William Betagh or Byrne, Dublin 1737, 7½in (19cm) high.
£5,000–5,500
$7,250–8,000 ⟋ DN

▶ **A George III Irish silver beaker,** by Michael Homer, c1778, 3¼in (8.5cm) high.
£1,600–1,750
$2,300–2,500 ⊞ WELD

▶ **A suite of Irish silver hunting buttons,** by Jane Stone, Dublin 1786.
£2,800–3,200
$4,000–4,700 ⊞ WELD

A pair of George III Irish silver buckles, by John Niddin, Dublin 1788, 3in (7.5cm) long.
£450–550
$650–800 ⊞ WELD

▶ **An Irish silver pair-cased Debaufre pocket watch,** signed Warner, Dublin c1790, 2¼in (5.5cm) diam.
£550–600
$700–850 ⊞ PT
This rare escapement, also known as a chaff-cutter, Ormskirk or club-footed verge, was the first frictional rest escapement invented by Debaufre in 1704.

A George III Irish silver box, by Samuel Neville, with inscription, presented by City of Dublin Corporation to James Twycross jeweller, Dublin 1808, 3¼in (8.5cm) diam.
£6,500–7,500
$9,500–11,000 ⊞ WELD

▶ **A pair of George II Irish silver candlesticks,** by John Letablere, Dublin 1748, 7in (18cm) high.
£4,500–5,500
$6,500–8,000 ⊞ WELD

◀ **A George III Irish silver soup tureen,** by John Lloyd, Dublin 1775, 15in (38cm) wide.
£13,000–15,000
$19,000–20,000 ⊞ WELD

An Irish silver pair-cased verge watch, by David Bigger, the movement with round pillars, pierced and engraved masked cock, Belfast c1780, 2in (5cm) diam.
£750–850
$1,100–1,300 ⊞ PT

Sets/pairs

Unless otherwise stated, any description which refers to 'a set' or 'a pair' includes a guide price for the entire set or the pair, even though the illustration may show only a single item.

▶ **A pair of Irish silver candlesticks,** by Gustavus Byrne, Dublin 1793, 10½in (26.5cm) high, 48oz.
£6,000–6,700
$8,700–9,700 ⊞ WELD

An Irish silver tea caddy, by Samuel Reily, with hinged cover and fitted lock, bright-cut decoration, engraved with a crest, later flower finial, Cork c1800, 4¼in (11cm) diam.
£3,200–3,600
$4,700–5,200 ⚒ JAd

An Irish silver caddy spoon, by Samuel Neville, Dublin 1810, 4in (10cm) long.
£260–320
$400–450 ⊞ STA

▶ **An Irish silver bright-cut presentation cup and cover,** by James Le Bass, Dublin 1816, 13in (33cm) high.
£1,800–2,000
$2,600–2,900 ⊞ SIL

◀ **An Irish silver hunting horn,** c1900, 8¾in (22cm) long.
£450–500
$650–750 ⊞ RTh

A Regency Irish silver box, the hinged cover with bright-cut engraved foliage, thistles, harps and crowns, the centre with the Cork coat-of-arms and Freedom motto, inscribed, maker's mark of Carden Terry and Jane Williams, Cork 1820, 3in (7.5cm) wide.
£2,200–2,500
$3,200–3,600 ⚒ CNY

A set of four Irish silver salts, by W. Nowlan, Dublin 1825, 4¼in (11cm) diam.
£1,800–2,000
$2,600–2,900 ⊞ SIL

Miller's is a price GUIDE not a price LIST

An Irish Republican silver letter opener, by William Egan, in the shape of a Celtic bird, with intertwined engraved and pierced decoration, inscribed and dated '1923, Cork 1922, 7in (18cm) long, 2oz.
£800–900
$1,100–1,300 ⚒ JAd

Baskets

A George III Irish silver basket, by Christopher Haines, Dublin 1785, 5in (12.5cm) high.
£1,200–1,500
$1,700–2,000 ⊞ WELD

Cross Reference
See Colour Review (page 244–245)

▶ **A George III Irish silver sugar basket,** by George West, with fluted swing handle, Dublin 1799, 7in (18cm) long, 7.75oz.
£600–700
$850–1,000 ⚒ L

A George III Irish silver sugar basket, by George West, with reeded border and swing handle, Dublin 1795, 7in (18cm) long.
£320–380
$450–570 ⚒ DN

▶ **A George III Irish silver bright-cut engraved sugar basket,** by William Bond, with reeded swing handle, Dublin 1803, 4in (10cm) long, 9oz.
£1,100–1,200
$1,600–1,800 ⚒ JAd

Bowls

A George I Irish silver bowl, by William Duggan, with inscription, Dublin 1726, 7¼in (18.5cm) diam.
£9,000–10,000
$13,000–14,500 ⊞ WELD
The desirability of this bowl is due to its excellent condition and the contemporary inscription, a feature which is rarely found.

A George II Irish silver bowl, maker's mark possibly John Christie, Dublin c1745, 6in (15cm) diam, 14oz.
£2,000–2,200
$2,900–3,200 ⚒ JAd

A George II Irish silver bowl, by Samuel Walker, the sides chased with trees, trailing vines and grape clusters, Dublin 1752–53, 7½in (19cm) diam, 18oz.
£5,000–6,000
$7,200–8,700 ⚒ P

A George III Irish silver bowl, by Matthew Walsh, Dublin 1780, 5in (12.5cm) diam.
£1,400–1,600
$2,000–2,300 ⊞ WELD

A George III Irish silver sugar bowl, by Matthew West, Dublin 1786, 5in (12.5cm) diam.
£1,200–1,300
$1,700–1,900 ⊞ WELD

▶ **An Irish silver bowl,** by West & Sons, with a band of Celtic-style ornament around the rim, presentation inscription, Dublin 1911, 9in (23cm) diam.
£520–575
$750–850 ⚒ S(S)

A George III Irish silver sugar bowl, by John Clark & Jacob West, the sides embossed with flowers, the front with a cartouche engraved with a crest, Dublin 1806, 5½in (14cm) diam, 8.5oz.
£450–500
$650–700 ⚒ P

◀ **An Irish silver two-handled porringer,** by Wakely & Wheeler, Dublin 1901, 9½in (24cm) long.
£700–800
$1,000–1,200 ⊞ SIL

Coffee Pots

An early George III Irish silver coffee pot, by J. West, Dublin 1765, 10½in (26cm) high.
£4,200–4,800
$6,000–7,000 ⊞ WELD

A George III Irish silver coffee pot, by John Lloyd, Dublin 1773, 13in (33cm) high.
£3,900–4,600
$5,500–6,500 ⊞ WELD

An Irish silver baluster-shaped coffee pot, by John Morton, embossed with shells, flowers and leaves, engraved with a crest, on pierced and chased shell and foliate feet, Dublin 1843, 9¾in (25cm) high, 31oz.
£700–800
$1,000–1,200 ⚒ DN(H)

An Irish silver coffee pot, with armorial engraving, rococo chased with flowers, scrolls and bearded masks, wood scroll handle, possibly by William Williamson, Dublin c1735, 9¼in (23.5cm) high, 34.75oz.
£1,800–2,000
$2,600–2,900 ⚒ S

Cutlery

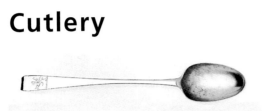

An Irish silver tablespoon, by Thomas Burke, Limerick
c1785, 9½in (24cm) long.
£650–750
$900–1,000 ⊞ WELD

A George III Irish silver hook-end basting spoon, with a
griffin crest, probably by Michael Keating, Dublin 1778,
11½in (29cm) long.
£320–350
$450–500 ⚒ P

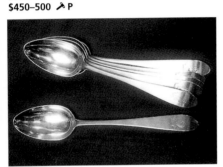

**Six George III Irish silver
Fiddle pattern dessert
spoons,** by Richard Sawyer,
each engraved with crest
above initials, Dublin
1813–15, 6.5oz.
£250–300
$350–450 ⚒ JAd

Six Irish silver tablespoons, by J. Shields,
Dublin c1786, 9in (23cm) long.
£800–900
$1,100–1,300 ⊞ WELD

**A set of George III Irish silver
cutlery,** comprising 101 pieces,
various makers, c1760–1812.
£5,500–6,500
$8,000–9,500 ⚒ S(NY)

Dish Rings

A George III Irish silver dish ring,
by John Lloyd, the sides pierced with
bands of foliate scrolls, semi-circles
and overlapping navettes, the centre
cartouche engraved with a boar's
head crest below and a shield charged
with the hand of Ulster, Dublin c1775,
7in (18cm) diam, 11.25oz.
£2,700–3,000
$4,000–4,500 ⚒ P
It would appear that the engraver
was not familiar with dish rings as
he had engraved the crest upside
down, erroneously assuming that
the wider part was the top rather
than the base.

An Irish silver dish ring, by Joseph
Jackson, Dublin c1775, 7½in (19cm) diam.
£7,500–8,500
$11,000–12,300 ⊞ WELD

An Edwardian Irish silver dish ring,
by West & Sons, the body pierced,
chased and engraved with various motifs,
Dublin 1906, 6¾in (17cm) diam, 9oz.
£1,750–2,000
$2,500–3,000 ⚒ JAd

Prices

The price ranges quoted in this
book reflect the average price a
purchaser might expect to pay
for a similar item from a similar
source. The price will vary
according to the condition,
rarity, size, popularity,
provenance, colour and
restoration of the item, and this
must be taken into account
when assessing values. Don't
forget that if you are selling it
is quite likely that you will be
offered less than the price range.

◄ **An Irish silver dish ring,** by
Wakely & Wheeler, decorated in Celtic
style, Dublin 1911, 7in (18cm) diam.
£2,200–2,500
$3,200–3,600 ⊞ SIL

**A George III-style Irish silver dish
ring,** by Thomas Weir, pierced and
chased with bands of scrolling foliage,
geometric design, scrolling foliate
swags within six plaques, with blue
glass liner, Dublin 1917, 9in (23cm)
diam, in a fitted case.
£1,400–1,600
$2,000–2,300 ⚒ JAd

Drinking Vessels

◀ **A Queen Anne Irish silver dram cup,** by Joseph Walker, Dublin 1702, 1½in (4cm) high.
£2,200–2,600
$3,200–3,800 ⊞ WELD

A pair of George III Irish silver loving cups, by Matthew West, Dublin 1786, 6in (15cm) high.
£2,500–3,500
$3,600–5,000 ⊞ WELD

◀ **A George III Irish silver mug,** by John Nicholson, Cork 1790, 2½in (6cm) high.
£1,200–1,600
$1,700–2,300 ⊞ WELD

▶ **An Irish flared cylindrical four-handled silver cup,** with square rim and angular handle supports, Dublin 1907, 7½in (19cm) high.
£675–750
$900–1,100 ⊞ WeH

A George III Irish silver loving cup, by Daniel McCarthy, Cork 1775, 7in (18cm) high.
£1,800–2,200
$2,600–3,200 ⊞ WELD

Jugs

A George II Irish silver cream jug, by James Douglas, Dublin 1752, 4in (10cm) high.
£1,200–1,400
$1,700–2,000 ⊞ WELD

An Irish silver cream or milk jug, by James Fray, in the shape of a pumpkin, Dublin c1830, 5in (12.5cm) wide, 19oz.
£440–500
$650–750 ⚒ MEA

An Irish silver covered jug, by J. Nowlan, Dublin 1833, 10¾in (27.5cm) high.
£3,200–3,500
$4,500–5,000 ⊞ SIL

An Irish silver cream jug and sugar bowl, by Weir & Sons, supported on three lion-mask and claw feet, both decorated with foliate scrollwork, fruit and a blank cartouche, Dublin 1902, 4½in (11.5cm) high, 13oz.
£420–460
$600–670 ⚒ P(E)

An Irish silver milk jug and sugar basin, decorated with Celtic motifs, Dublin 1922, 4½in (11.5cm) high, in original box.
£1,100–1,200
$1,500–1,700 ⊞ SIL

Sauce Boats

A pair of George III Irish bright-cut sauce boats, by R. Williams, Dublin c1785, 8in (20.5cm) long.
£3,800–4,200
$5,500–6,000 ⊞ WELD

An Irish silver sauce boat, by Matthew West, engraved with initials, on three shell and hoof feet, Dublin 1787, 8in (20.5cm) long, 9oz.
£1,400–1,700
$2,000–2,500 ✗ JAd

An Irish silver sauce boat, with scroll handle, on three cabriole legs and hoof feet, Dublin 1792, 8in (20.5cm) wide.
£430–480
$600–700 ✗ RTo

Serving Implements

◄ **A pair of Irish silver sugar nips,** Dublin 1750, 5½in (14cm) long.
£400–450
$580–650 ⊞ WELD

> **Miller's is a price GUIDE not a price LIST**

An Irish silver pudding slice, by James Graham, with ebonized turned wood handle and shell and scroll mount, the rounded triangular blade pierced with quatrefoils, foliage and a shell, the reverse engraved with a crest, no date letter, Dublin c1760, 13in (33cm) long.
£1,800–2,000
$2,500–3,000 ✗ CSK

A pair of George III Irish silver asparagus tongs, by William Law, Dublin 1785, 10in (25.5cm) long.
£650–750
$950–1,100 ⊞ WELD

A George III Irish silver punch strainer, by Michael Smith, Dublin 1793, 11½in (29cm) wide.
£1,400–1,600
$2,000–2,300 ⊞ WELD

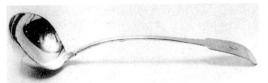

A George III Irish silver soup ladle, by Samuel Neville, Dublin 1808, 13½in (34.5cm) long.
£400–500
$600–750 ⊞ WELD

◄ **A George III Irish silver server,** Dublin 1819, 13½in (34.5cm) long.
£850–950
$1,300–1,500 ⊞ WELD

Snuff Boxes

A George II Irish silver snuff box, by Bart Stokes, c1750, 3in (7.5cm) wide.
£1,500–1,800
$2,200–2,600 ⊞ WELD

An Irish silver snuff box, by William Currie, Dublin 1760, 3in (7.5cm) wide.
£1,000–1,250
$1,500–1,800 ⊞ WELD

An Irish silver double snuff box, by John Townsend, each of cartouche form, with applied moulded body bands, the covers with leaf-carved thumbpieces and chased borders, the centres engraved with motto, City Arms of Cork and 'Royal Cork Artillery', Dublin 1855, on a walnut plinth, 7in (18cm) wide, 13oz.
£6,500–7,500
$9,500–11,000 ⚴ HAM
This was originally made for the officers of the Royal Cork Artillery and would have been mounted on a large table centrepiece, probably incorporating the horns of a ram's head and forming part of a typical officers' mess snuff mull.

Buyer' beware

When buying, always check hinges and mounts are not split or dented and that the lids close properly. Castle-top, battle and hunting scenes, or cast or enamelled decoration make the piece more desirable.

Teapots

▶ **An Irish bright-cut silver teapot,** by Jane Williams, the body with a monogram within a contemporary cartouche, engraved at the top with oak leaves, Cork c1790, 12¼in (31cm) long.
£1,100–1,300
$1,600–1,900 ⚴ HOK

A George III Irish bright-cut silver teapot, by James Le Bass, Dublin 1815, 11in (28cm) long.
£1,600–1,900
$2,300–2,700 ⊞ WELD

Cross Reference
See Colour Review
(page 244–245)

A George I bullet-shaped Irish silver teapot, by Thomas Bolton, Dublin 1717, 8½in (21.5cm) long.
£4,500–5,500
$6,500–8,000 ⊞ WELD

▶ **An Irish embossed silver teapot,** by James Fray, Dublin 1828, 12in (30.5cm) wide.
£1,200–1,400
$1,700–2,000 ⊞ SIL

Tea Services

▶ **An Irish silver four-piece tea service,** by Weir & Sons, the plain ground repoussé with bands of Celtic motifs, Dublin 1918, 80oz.
£1,200–1,500
$1,700–2,100 ⚴ P(HSS)

A William IV Irish silver three-piece tea service, by Edward Power, each on four foliate and scroll feet, Dublin 1831, teapot 7in (18cm) high, 54.5oz.
£1,800–2,000
$2,600–2,900 ⚴ L

▶ **An Irish silver four-piece tea service,** applied with chased Celtic open paterae, banding and prunts, maker's mark 'TW', Dublin 1930, 69.5oz.
£800–1,000
$1,100–1,500 ⚴ WW

Trays

A pair of Queen Anne Irish silver tazzas, by Edward Workman, Dublin c1710, 8½in (21.5cm) diam, 25oz.
£17,000–20,000
$24,500–29,000 ⊞ WELD

A George II Irish silver snuffer tray, by Alexander Brown, Dublin 1740, 7½in (19cm) long.
£1,400–1,600
$2,000–2,300 ⊞ WELD

A pair of George II Irish silver salvers, by Samuel Walker, Dublin 1752, 6in (15cm) diam.
£3,800–4,300
$5,500–6,300 ⊞ WELD

An Irish silver tray, with inscription on reverse, Dublin 1806, 6in (15cm) diam.
£800–900
$1,100–1,300 ⊞ SIL

An Irish silver salver, by James Le Bass, engraved with an armorial on four shell and scroll chased feet, Dublin 1812, 17in (43cm) diam, 76oz.
£2,000–2,200
$2,900–3,200 ↗ DN

▶ **An Irish silver salver,** with Celtic strapwork border incorporating mythical beasts and with applied bosses, possibly by West & Co, maker's mark obscured, Dublin 1913, 24in (61cm) diam, 148oz.
£2,500–3,000
$3,600–4,400 ↗ L&E

An Irish chased silver card tray, by J. Fray, Dublin 1840, 6in (15cm) diam.
£700–800
$1,000–1,200 ⊞ SIL

LOCATE THE SOURCE
The source of each illustration in Miller's can be found by checking the code letters below each caption with the Key to Illustrations, pages 311–314.

Wine Antiques

A George III Irish silver wine funnel, by William Bond, Dublin 1802, 4in (10cm) high.
£900–1,000
$1,300–1,500 ⊞ WELD

▶ **A pair of George III Irish silver coasters,** by John Sherwin, Dublin 1812, 6½in (16.5cm) diam.
£2,400–2,800
$3,500–4,000 ⊞ WELD

◀ **A George IV Irish silver two-handled wine cooler,** engraved with a coat-of-arms and presentation inscription, the upper section of the body embossed with two foliate scroll cartouches, each surmounted by an eagle, the lower section embossed with flowering acanthus leaves and flowers against a matted ground, with detachable liner, maker's mark of Edward Power & Edward Twycross, Dublin 1826, 11½in (29cm) high, 104oz.
£4,000–4,500
$5,800–6,500 ↗ Bon

Russian Silver

From the beginning of the Romanov Empire in 1613 until the revolution in 1917, Russia enjoyed a unique period of creativity and design under a single dynasty. In recent years Russian silver has become increasingly popular due to the variety of work that is available. Therefore, in collecting terms, there is something for everyone.

There are five main types of Russian silver: table silver, such as flatware, salts, spoons, beakers and candlesticks; tromp l'oeil work, literally 'trick of the eye', which was often translated in the design of the piece so that it resembled something else such as wood or material and is unique to Russia; guilloché and cloisonné enamel work, consisting of silver pieces with unique enamelling applied onto the surface of a finely-engraved background and also between hand-made silver wire borders; niello and lacquer work, involving a process of hand-applied alloys and cold enamel, mainly black and red in colour; silver filigree work, which involved pieces of hand-crafted silver wire originating from the East being adapted in a unique style.

The two main areas of production were Moscow and St Petersburg, with Odessa, Kiev and Kostroma being the main provincial towns which produced quality items. Makers from Moscow worth looking out for are Bolin, Khlebnikov (post-1871), Sazikov, Ovchinnikov, Saltykov, Semenova,

Vasilev and the Artels. Outstanding makers from St Petersburg include Grachev, Hahn Keibel, Khlebnikov (pre-1871), Morosov, Nicholls, Plincke and Sumin.

One maker not to be overlooked is Peter Carl Fabergé, who produced a wonderful variety of pieces. Working mainly in St Petersburg, but with workshops in Moscow, Odessa and Kiev, he employed some of the best craftsmen of the day, such as Michael Perchin and Henrik Wigström. As well as Fabergé having his own mark, each workmaster had an independent hallmark and was ultimately responsible for the quality of work produced from his workshop.

Hallmarks are not always easy to recognize as they are often in Russian Cyrillic and difficult to read. The most important is the 84 Zolotnik, the Imperial Russian silver mark which is the equivalent of the European .900 mark (see pp 8–9). The 88 and 92 Zolotnik marks, roughly equivalent to .925 and .950 silver, also appear. Next is the town mark, followed by the maker's mark.

There are many forgeries coming onto the market so beware! Buyers should purchase Russian silver pieces either from specialist dealers who can give expert advice, or auction houses that hold specialist Russian sales and can advise on prospective purchases.

Sheldon Shapiro

A pair of Russian silver beakers, by Timofej Filippow Silujanow, chased with strapwork, with gilt interiors, Assay Master A. K., Moscow 1761, 3¼in (8.5cm) high, 5oz.
£1,200–1,400
$1,800–2,000 ⚒ S(Am)

► **A Russian silver tea tray,** with pierced border, Assay Master Alexander Yashinkov, maker's mark 'T.P.', St Petersburg 1808, 25¼in (64cm) wide, 87oz.
£2,000–2,200
$2,900–3,200 ⚒ S(NY)

A Russian silver four-piece tea service, by Carl Siewers, fluted into panels, with ivory-fitted scroll handles and finials, gilt interiors, St Petersburg 1859, 64.5oz.
£1,600–1,800
$2,300–2,600 ⚒ S(Am)

A Russian silver caviar jar and vodka measure, with trompe l'oeil decoration, c1860, measure 5¼in (13.5cm) high.
£2,700–3,000
$3,900–4,400 ⊞ SFL

A Russian silver tray, by Adolf Sperr, Assay Master D. Tverskoi, engraved with the Imperial eagle, St Petersburg 1849, 27½in (70cm) wide.
£2,500–3,000
$3,600–4,400 ⚒ S(G)

► **A Russian silver presentation spoon,** the reverse of the bowl engraved with an inscription and scroll foliage, Moscow 1867, 7in (18cm) long.
£200–235
$300–350 ⊞ HofB

A pair of Russian silver-gilt salts, modelled as chairs, the covers engraved with calligraphy, the interiors with cockerels, Moscow 1873–74, 3in (7.5cm) high.
£650–800
$1,000–1,200 ✗ WW

A Russian silver samovar, engraved and with vacant cartouches, gilt-washed interior, ivory fittings, maker's mark 'MP', Moscow 1887, 15¾in (40cm) high, 114oz.
£4,500–5,000
$6,500–7,300 ✗ SLM

A pair of Russian silver candlesticks, the base with scrolling stylized dolphins, the stem with flat leaf motifs, restored, late 19thC, 13¾in (35cm) high, 26oz.
£500–550
$700–800 ✗ SK

An Imperial Russian silver cigarette case, with a scene of warriors, c1890, 4¾in (12cm) wide.
£500–550
$700–800 ⊞ SHa

A Russian silver-mounted cut-glass claret jug, by Ivan Khlebnikov, the spout in the shape of an oil lamp, the finial modelled as a swan, Moscow c1900, 14in (35.5cm) high.
£4,200–4,800
$6,000–7,000 ✗ S

A Japanese-style Russian silver-gilt seven-piece tea service, by Pavel Ovchinnikov, each piece applied with flowers, foliage and insects, with Imperial warrant, Moscow 1894, teapot 4½in (11.5cm) high, in original wooden case.
£14,500–16,500
$21,000–24,000 ✗ S

A Russian silver-mounted cut-glass claret jug, by Pavel Ovchinnikov, the mount decorated with stylized flowers, c1896, 10½in (26.5cm) high.
£1,000–1,200
$1,500–1,800 ✗ P

Boxes

A Russian silver-filigree box, set with turquoises, the cover with melon-shaped finial, 1863, 5in (12.5cm) high, 9.5oz.
£450–500
$650–700 ✗ S(Am)

A Russian parcel-gilt silver box, by Semenow/Saminkow, the sides engraved with cartouches enclosing a view of the Kremlin, with silver-gilt interior, Moscow 1874, 5¼in (13.5cm) high.
£950–1,150
$1,400–1,700 ✗ S(Z)

A Russian silver cigar box, the cover, sides and base engraved to simulate a wood grain finish with tax bands, the cover with internal inscription dated '1911', maker's mark 'N.K.', 6½in (16.5cm) long, 16oz.
£800–1,200
$1,200–1,800 ✗ BEA

Miller's is a price GUIDE not a price LIST

Enamel

▶ **An Imperial Russian gilded silver and *champlevé* enamel punchbowl,** with harp-shaped handles, rim with Cyrillic inscription, maker's mark 'AK', and '1896', Moscow, 10in (25.5cm) wide.
£4,500–5,000
$6,500–7,300 ⚒ JAA

A Russian silver and cloisonné enamel tazza, by Gustav Klingert, decorated with floral scrolls in blue and red on a turquoise ground, with white pellet bands, Moscow 1895, 5½in (14cm) high.
£500–600
$700–870 ⚒ S(S)

◀ **A Russian silver-gilt and shaded cloisonné enamel *kovsch*,** by Alexander Benediktovich Lyubavin, decorated with flowers and scrolls, the handle with a raised St Petersburg crest surmounted by a coronet, c1896, 7½in (19cm) long.
£900–1,000
$1,300–1,500 ⚒ S(S)

▶ **A Russian silver and *champlevé* enamel bracelet,** with a matching ring and pair of pendant earrings, Moscow 1899–1908, bracelet 2½in (6.5cm) diam.
£350–420
$500–600 ⚒ JAA

A Russian gilded silver and enamel lidded jar, with scrolling foliage in blue, brown, yellow and turquoise and an onion-shaped finial, marked, Moscow 1899–1908, 3½in (9cm) high.
£1,400–1,600
$2,000–2,300 ⚒ JAA

A Russian silver and enamel salver, the border polychrome-decorated with stylized foliage, the centre applied with the Imperial Order of St Andrew, c1900, 8¾in (22cm) diam.
£5,500–6,500
$8,000–9,500 ⚒ S(NY)

Technical Facts

Enamelling is a process by which a paste of coloured ground glass is applied to a gold, silver or copper base before being fired in a kiln to produce a hard, decorative surface.

▶ **A set of six Russian silver and enamel spoons,** the bowls decorated with circles and silver beads on a stippled silver ground, marked, Moscow c1908, 5¾in (14.5cm) long.
£1,200–1,400
$1,800–2,000 ⚒ JAA

A Russian gilded silver and shaded enamel cigarette case, by Ivan Saltykov, decorated with flowers on a pale blue ground, Moscow c1900, 3¾in (9.5cm) wide.
£1,800–2,000
$2,600–2,900 ⚒ S(NY)

Auction or dealer?

All the pictures in our price guides originate from auction houses and dealers. Look for the symbol at the end of each caption to identify the source.

When buying at auction, prices can be lower than those of a dealer, but a buyer's premium and VAT will be added to the hammer price. Equally, when selling at auction, commission, tax and photography charges must be taken into account. Dealers will often restore pieces before putting them back on the market.

Both dealers and auctioneers will provide professional advice, so it is worth researching both sources before buying or selling your antiques.

Fabergé

A Fabergé Louis XV-style silver jardinière, the lower part of the body cast and chased with lobes, the everted sides chased with shaped panels, with rocaille border and foliate side handles, on rocaille feet, maker's mark with Imperial warrant, Moscow 1880–93, with metal liner, 21½in (54.5cm) wide.
£17,000–19,000
$24,500–27,500 ✎ CNY

A Fabergé silver comport stand, with cut-glass bowl, on four ribbed supports terminating in hoofed feet, damaged, Moscow 1896, 10¾in (27.5cm) diam.
£4,000–4,500
$5,800–6,500 ✎ P

A Fabergé pearl, silver and enamel timepiece, with translucent oyster ground over moiré engine-turning, on a scrolled easel support, Workmaster H. Wigström, St Petersburg 1896–1908, 4in (10cm) high.
£14,000–16,000
$20,300–23,200 ✎ S(G)

▶ **A Fabergé gold, silver and enamel brooch,** converted from a buckle, the translucent lilac enamel on a sunburst field, signed 'KØ', Moscow c1900.
£2,300–2,600
$3,300–3,800 ✎ P

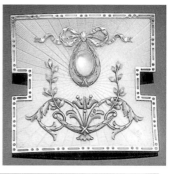

A Fabergé silver-mounted tazza, the red jasper column supporting a caryatid, with a wide agate dish on her head, Workmaster Julius Rappoport, St Petersburg, maker's mark, pre-1899, 6¾in (17cm) high.
£5,000–5,500
$7,000–8,000 ✎ CNY

A Fabergé silver-gilt overlaid and rose-diamond set nephrite vase, decorated with a floral pattern, c1900, 5in (12.5cm) high.
£17,000–20,000
$24,500–29,000 ✎ HAM

◀ **A Fabergé silver and blue enamel locket,** decorated with a diamond-set flower, Workmaster August Holmström, St Petersburg, c1900, 1½in (4cm) long.
£2,800–3,200
$4,000–4,500 ✎ S(NY)

▶ **A Fabergé silver-gilt and blue** *basse taille* **enamel cigar cutter,** painted with trailing foliage in white, with beaded rim and cast foliage thumbpiece to the cutter, Moscow c1905, 1½in (4cm) diam.
£7,200–8,000
$10,500–11,500 ✎ RBB

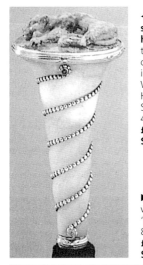

◀ **A Fabergé gem-set silver-gilt-mounted hardstone cane handle,** the top mounted with a carved recumbent tigress in reddish-brown agate, Workmaster August Hollming, maker's mark, St Petersburg 1908–17, 4in (10cm) high.
£11,500–13,000
$16,500–19,000 ↗ CNY

▶ **A Fabergé silver vase,** with glass liner, marked 'Moscow' 1908–17, 8½in (21.5cm) high.
£3,400–3,750
$5,000–5,500 ⊞ SHa

A Fabergé silver bonbonnière, embossed with a battlefield scene and enamelled with a red cross on a white field, the flange inscribed in Cyrillic with 'M.V.Steiger' and '10th November 1916', marked 'A.R.' for Anna Ringe, St Petersburg c1910, 1¾in (4.5cm) diam.
£1,400–1,600
$2,000–2,300 ↗ S(NY)

Icons

A Russian icon of the Kazan Mother of God, the veil and Christ's garments overlaid with seed pearls and paste stones, silver-gilt and repoussé halo, the borders with a silver repoussé and chased riza, 17thC, 12½ x 10½in (32 x 26.5cm).
£2,800–3,200
$4,000–4,500 ↗ JAA

A Russian icon of the Mother of God of Tenderness, with four saints on the borders, encased in a silver-gilt *oklad*, the garments composed of seed pearls, coral beads and semi-precious stones, maker's mark 'MT', 1844, 7 x 6in (18 x 15cm).
£2,300–2,700
$3,350–3,900 ↗ S

A Russian icon of a saint, painted on mother-of-pearl, in a silver and enamel frame, stamped 'AK 84', c1900, 2½ x 2¼in (6.5 x 5.5cm).
£150–180
$220–260 ↗ Bea(E)

Cross Reference
See Colour Review (page 245)

Niello

A Russian silver-gilt and niello beaker, the stippled sides with foliage and flowers within arched frames, maker's mark A. K. in script, Moscow 1838, 3¼in (8.5cm) high, 3.5oz.
£300–350
$450–500 ↗ P

A Russian silver and niello snuff box, decorated with a courtyard scene, stamped 'J. M. Etamat Xoyaa', late 19thC, 5in (12.5cm) wide.
£150–180
$200–250 ↗ FHF

A Russian silver and niello cup, with scrolling foliate and floral decoration on stippled ground, gilt interior, maker's mark 'AB', 19thC, 6½in (16.5cm) high, 9oz.
£500–550
$700–800 ↗ SLN

Scottish Silver

The statutes, which govern goldsmiths and silversmiths of Scotland, go back to the 15th century with the first statue formulated in 1457 to institute standards with penalties for their infringement. However, due to the remoteness of many of the smaller towns and villages, little control could be practically exercised over the silversmiths outside of Edinburgh and Glasgow. In the attempt to control the silver trade a further ordinance decreed that; a 'searcher' should be appointed in addition to the deacon to superintend the craft; a town mark should be used and silversmiths should be admitted to the craft before being allowed to work in silver. In 1681 the Edinburgh goldsmiths and silversmiths further regularized their craft by introducing date letters, using a 25 letter cycle (omitting J). The Glasgow craftsmen appear to have adopted a date letter in the same year, but during the 18th century its use was irregular and there is no sign of a deacon's mark.

Outside Edinburgh and Glasgow silver originated in a dozen or more towns from Banff to Wick. Silver from many of these provincial towns has become highly collectable and I strongly recommend collecting flatware with the following town marks and makers: BANF from Banff – William Simpson, John Keith, John McQueen; ELN from Elgin – Thomas Stewart, Charles Fowler, Joseph Pozzi; The Tower from Forres – John Raich, Patrick Raich; INS from Inverness – Alexander Stewart, Robert Naughten, Alexander MacLeod; Rose Mark from Montrose – Benjamin Lumsden, William Mull; PHD from Peterhead – William Ferguson, Alexander King; TAIN from Tain – Hugh Ross, Richard Wilkies; WICK from Wick – John Sellar.

Silver made by all of the above has substantially increased in value over the past ten years. For example, a Petershead teaspoon would have made £500 ($720) at auction ten years ago, but today a good example might make £2,500 ($3,500). Similarly a Wick toddy ladle would have made £550 ($800) ten years ago whereas today it could make £2,800 ($4,000).

When purchasing rare and unusual Scottish provincial flatware pieces always check the condition of the item very carefully. Make sure that the marks are clear, that there is no damage whatsoever and that the piece has not had any engraving removed. The price of a teaspoon, for instance, could be dramatically affected if damaged and be worth just a third of the value of a good example. The most popular items to collect are usually teaspoons, toddy ladles, sugar tongs and tablespoons.

Nicholas Shaw

A pair of Scottish silver table candlesticks, with turned stems, maker's mark 'I.C.', c1700, 5in (12.5cm) high, 14.5oz.
£6,000–7,000
$8,700–10,200 ⚖ L

A Scottish silver Warwick cruet set, by James Ker, with original bottles, Edinburgh c1735, 9¾in (25cm) high, 40oz.
£4,000–4,500
$5,800–6,500 ⊞ JSH

A George II Scottish silver Warwick cruet stand and fittings, the stand on four leaf-capped shell feet, with three casters each with pierced domed cover and baluster finial, with later monogram within motto and two silver-mounted cut-glass oil and vinegar bottles, the rococo cartouche engraved with a coat-of-arms, maker's mark of Douglas Ged, Edinburgh 1755, stand 10¼in (26cm) high, 52oz.
£4,500–5,500
$6,500–8,000 ⚖ C

◀ **A George III Scottish silver pap boat,** by Cunningham and Simpson, Edinburgh 1809, 4in (10cm) long.
£200–220
$290–320 ⚖ GAK

A George III Scottish silver goblet, by George McHattie, with gilt interior, Edinburgh 1813, 8¼in (21cm) high, 13.5oz.
£300–350
$450–500 ⚖ Bea(E)

Sets/pairs

Unless otherwise stated, any description which refers to 'a set' or 'a pair' includes a guide price for the entire set or the pair, even though the illustration may show only a single item.

A George III Scottish silver wine funnel, by W. and P. Cunningham, monogrammed, with gadrooned edging and shell clip, Edinburgh 1825, 5½in (14cm) high, 3.75oz.
£700–800
$1,000–1,200 ⚲ Bea

A Scottish silver christening mug, by John Sellar, with plain scroll handle, the body embossed and chased with a band of thistles and foliage centred by a scrolled cartouche engraved with a monogram, Wick c1830, 3¼in (8.5cm) high, 5oz.
£4,600–5,000
$6,500–7,250 ⚲ C(S)

A William IV Scottish silver three-piece tea service, with leaf-chased rims and feet, scroll handles, engraved with monograms, maker's mark 'AW', Edinburgh 1832, 49.5oz.
£800–900
$1,200–1,300 ⚲ DN

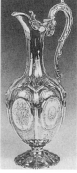

► **A Victorian Scottish silver claret jug,** by J. Mitchell, set with engraved panels of flowers and coats-of-arms, with scrolling handle, Glasgow 1852, 14in (35.5cm) high, 29oz.
£1,800–2,000
$2,600–2,900 ⚲ C(S)

A William IV Scottish silver salver, with shell and vine chased border, flat chased with flowers, foliate and shell scrolls and central monogram, on shell scroll bracket feet, possibly by William Cunningham, Edinburgh 1835, 10½in (26.5cm) diam, 24.5oz.
£450–550
$650–800 ⚲ DN

A George II-style Victorian Scottish silver tea kettle-on-stand, the scroll engraved body with presentation inscription, ivory swing handle, the stand with spirit burner and three shell supports, maker's mark 'RK', Edinburgh 1842, 16in (40.5cm) high, 70oz.
£1,800–2,200
$2,600–3,200 ⚲ Bri

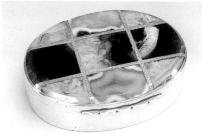

A Scottish silver table snuff box, by W. J. McDonald, the cover decorated with an agate chequered panel within silver framing, Edinburgh 1861, 3½in (9cm) wide.
£270–300
$400–450 ⚲ TMA

Four Scottish silver menu holders, by Hamilton and Inches, Edinburgh 1896, 2¾in (7cm) long.
£550–600
$800–870 ⊞ BEX

A Scottish silver-mounted horn snuff mull, the foliate repoussé-decorated cover with replaced paste gem, the tail with Cairngorm stone, 19thC, 9in (23cm) wide.
£480–530
$700–770 ⚲ CSK

► **A Regency-style Scottish silver four-piece tea service,** by Sorley, with partly fluted bodies, foliage and gadrooned rims, Glasgow 1902–03, 35oz.
£500–600
$700–870 ⚲ C(Sc)

◄ **A set of six Scottish silver plates,** by J. and W. Marshall, with gadrooned borders, engraved with a crest, maker's mark, Edinburgh 1867, 9in (23cm) diam.
£1,200–1,400
$1,750–2,000 ⚲ MCA

Cutlery

▶ **A set of four Scottish silver tablespoons,** by William Constable, Dundee c1800, 11½in (29cm) long.
£2,250–2,500
$3,300–3,600 ⊞ JBU

Six Scottish silver Fiddle pattern tablespoons, by John Pringle, engraved initial 'D' in script, Perth c1830, 12oz.
£500–550
$700–800 ⚶ P(NE)

Cross Reference
See Colour Review (page 246)

A Scottish silver 'Old Mother Hubbard' christening spoon and pusher, Glasgow 1930, spoon 4in (10cm) long, in original box.
£200–225
$290–325 ⊞ BEX

A Scottish silver Old English pattern canteen of cutlery, by James Crichton & Co, comprising 18 monogrammed place settings, Edinburgh 1886, in an oak and banded case.
£4,500–5,500
$6,500–8,000 ⚶ HYD

Jewellery

A Scottish silver pin, set with citrine and agate, 1¾in (4.5cm) diam.
£60–90
$90–130 ⊞ SPE

▶ **A Victorian Scottish silver and citrine brooch,** 1¾in (4.5cm) wide.
£100–140
$150–200 ⊞ SPE

▶ **A Scottish silver and agate brooch,** c1850, 3in (7.5cm) long.
£500–600
$700–870 ⊞ BWA

A Victorian Scottish silver brooch, in the shape of an owl and crescent moon, set with agate, 1½in (4cm) diam.
£120–160
$180–230 ⊞ PSA

A Scottish silver and hardstone bar brooch, 1860–80, 2½in (6.5cm) wide.
£425–475
$600–700 ⊞ WIM

Insurance values
Always insure your valuable antiques for the cost of replacing them with similar items, regardless of the original price paid. Both dealers and auctioneers will provide a valuation service for a fee.

A Scottish silver and hardstone brooch, 1860–80, 1¾in (4.5cm) wide.
£350–400
$500–600 ⊞ WIM

A Scottish silver brooch, set with citrine thistles, 1860–90, 2in (5cm) diam.
£120–135
$180–200 ⊞ WIM

A Scottish silver knot brooch, with green, blue and yellow agate, c1860, 2in (5cm) diam.
£250–300
$350–450 ⊞ BWA

◄ **A Scottish silver, agate and citrine penannular brooch,** c1860, 2½in (6.5cm) long.
£250–300
$350–450 ⊞ BWA

► **A Scottish silver and grey agate strap brooch,** c1860, 2½in (6.5cm) diam.
£300–350
$450–500 ⊞ BWA

A Scottish silver and grey agate strap brooch, c1860, 2½in (6.5cm) diam.
£350–400
$500–600 ⊞ BWA

A Scottish silver dagger pin, 1860–80, 3¼in (8.5cm) long.
£170–200
$250–300 ⊞ WIM

A Scottish silver and agate bracelet, c1870, 6in (15cm) long.
£350–450
$500–650 ⊞ BWA

A Scottish silver and hardstone brooch, 1860–80, 2in (5cm) diam.
£350–400
$500–600 ⊞ WIM

A Scottish silver and agate circular brooch, c1870, 2in (5cm) diam.
£250–300
$350–450 ⊞ BWA

A Scottish silver, agate and citrine brooch, c1870, 1½in (4cm) diam.
£160–200
$230–300 ⊞ BWA

◄ **A Scottish silver-gilt penannular brooch,** c1900, 2½in (6.5cm) diam.
£100–120
$150–180 ⊞ BWA
Celtic-inspired penannular brooches were very popular in Victorian times. The word penannular, meaning 'almost annular', relates to the shape, as it is a cleft ring. They were originally used to fasten cloaks.

Prices

The price ranges quoted in this book reflect the average price a purchaser might expect to pay for a similar item from a similar source. The price will vary according to the condition, rarity, size, popularity, provenance, colour and restoration of the item, and this must be taken into account when assessing values. Don't forget that if you are selling it is quite likely that you will be offered less than the price range.

Silversmiths
Bateman

Hester Bateman, the most famous of all women silversmiths, registered her first mark with the London Goldsmiths Co on 16 April 1761 when aged 52. She was widowed by John Bateman in 1760 and took over his metalwork business in Bunhill Row, London, transforming it into one of the most successful silversmithing workshops. Hester, and her sons John, Peter and Jonathan, who later married Ann, and their son William and grandson William II, became highly skilled silversmiths and produced some the best silver pieces of their generation. After Jonathan's death Ann also joined the partnership.

The main reason for their success was due to Hester's attention to detail and quality of design. All the pieces that left the workshop would be inspected to the highest standard and with this attitude the business grew. Many pieces of Hester's silver show identifying characteristics such as beading around the edges and the fine designs of bright-cut engraving. Keen collectors can recognize these pieces even before they look at the hallmarks. This awareness has helped many a collector and dealer searching through silver in shops, fairs and auctions.

The Batemans received many commissions from the City Guilds, private houses and religious establishments. One such item, requested by St Paul's Cathedral in London, was a Verger's wand, which can be seen in the Cathedral and is still in use today. I am sure Hester would be very proud of this.

Unlike most silversmiths who specialized in just one area of production, the Batemans were masters of many, producing fine wares right across the board from spoons, forks, serving utensils, dinner plates, goblets, salts, mustard pots, wine labels, funnels and coolers, teapots, cream jugs, butter shells, tea caddies, salvers, inkwells, important horse racing trophies and more. However, there is one item I cannot ever recall seeing made by any of the Batemans and that is a pair of candlesticks. The reason being, I feel, is that candlesticks would have been cast in silver and the Bateman' skills were in hammering, raising, planishing, burnishing and engraving.

In conclusion, Hester Bateman was a remarkable woman. Illiterate, widowed at 52 with a family to bring up, she turned a small metalwork business into a highly successful silversmithing company and is today one of the most sought after makers worldwide. All this happened over 200 years ago when there was no electricity or machines for mass production and the world was a very different place for women. **Daniel Bexfield**

A set of six silver teaspoons, by Hester Bateman, London 1786, 5in (12.5cm) long.
£350–400
$500–600 ⊞ BEX

A pair of silver sauce ladles, by Hester Bateman, London 1788, 7in (18cm) long.
£300–350
$450–500 ⊞ HCA

◀ **A George III silver teapot,** by Peter and Ann Bateman, with bright-cut neo-classical design, and an oval teapot stand, London 1794, 8in (20.5cm) wide.
£1,500–1,800
$2,200–2,600 ⚒ HYD

A pair of silver wine coolers, by William Bateman II, each with pedestal base and detachable rim and liner, engraved with the Royal cyphers of William IV and Adelaide on both sides, stamped 'Rundell Bridge et Co, Aurifices Regis Londini', London 1835, 10in (25.5cm) high, 228.5oz.
£30,000–34,000
$43,500–49,500 ⚒ S(NY)
The monograms 'WR' within garter motto and 'AR' within oak and reed wreath below the Royal Crowns are those of William IV and Adelaide, who were married in 1818.

A George III silver teapot, by Peter Ann and William Bateman, with thread edging, bright-cut decoration, green stained ivory pineapple finial and wood scroll handle, London 1800, 6½in (16cm) high, 15.25oz.
£1,100–1,300
$1,600–1,900 ⚒ Bea

A George IV silver three-piece Melon pattern tea service, by William Bateman, with shell, rose and foliate scroll borders and gilt interiors, 1827–28, 42oz.
£900–1,000
$1,300–1,500 ⚒ P(W)

Gorham Manufacturing Co

Established in 1831, Gorham is considered one of the leading silversmiths of 19th and early 20th century American silver. They produced an extensive range of silver from standard traditional wares to trend leaders inspired by such movements as Gothic and neo-classical revivals, Arts and Crafts and Art Deco. Their hand-made Arts and Crafts range, *Martelé*, included the highly desirable mixed metal items and like many American designs had its own style.

The Gorham family arrived in America during the early 17th century and by the time Jabez Gorham founded his silver company he was a fully fledged fifth generation American. Jabez served his apprenticeship under the silversmith Nehemiah Dodge and worked there from 1813–18. When the business fell on hard times Jabez continued alone and proved himself a successful businessman. From this period the Gorham company took shape and grew from strength to strength. Initially Gorham produced only traditional domestic wares such as flatware and hollow ware, popular with the expanding American population. During their first few decades Gorham silverware was very similar in design to pieces made in Victorian England, and they even patented some of these designs.

During the latter half of the 19th century demand began to change as trends and influences altered. Often beginning in Europe, certain design movements and methods were quickly adopted by American manufacturers like Gorham and Tiffany. Within many pieces and ranges one can see forms and decoration associated with Japanese design, neo-classical and gothic revivals. Gorham's finest period was the *Martelé* period, influenced by the Arts and Crafts movement in England and the work of such designers as Elviva, Irwine, Furber under William C. Codman, and other designers, came into its own at this time. The hand-made or hand-hammered period gave designers a blank page, enabling them to produce their work to resemble exclusive hand-crafted pieces. This was very appealing to aspiring members of society who were influenced by contemporary trends and culture. Manufactured silver items were also made to look more individual by applying copper, brass and lavish enamels. This was an important time for Gorham and can be seen as their heyday. They exhibited at international fairs and won several gold medals for their fine pieces. Items from this period are the grandest and are currently the most sought after, commanding high prices at auction.

Until their demise in the latter half of the 20th century Gorham were able to innovate, create and move with the times. Collectable in every way from spoons to presentation pieces, Gorham was very similar leading British silversmiths.

Loraine Turner

A milled coin silver six-piece coffee and tea service, by Gorham, the bodies with engraved foliate cartouches, monogrammed, Providence, RI, 1848–65, coffee pot 13in (33cm) high, 110oz.
£3,600–4,000
$5,200–5,800 ↗ SK

Cross Reference
See Colour Review (page 248)

A silver pitcher, by Gorham, with a broad die-rolled band of stylized foliate ornament, with contemporary cypher on the front 'RMT', Providence, RI, 1885, 10in (25.5cm) high.
£1,400–1,600
$2,000–2,300 ↗ S(NY)

A silver covered jar, by Gorham, the hammered surface applied with gold-washed Japanese-style prunus blossoms on engraved branches, late 19thC, 4¼in (11cm) high, 6oz.
£600–700
$900–1,000 ↗ SK

A .950 Standard silver bowl, by Gorham, *Martelé*, marked on base and with code 'CKC', Providence, RI, c1905, 11in (28cm) diam, 35oz.
£2,200–2,600
$3,200–3,800 ↗ S(NY)

▶ **A silver Egyptian-Revival centrepiece,** by Gorham, in the shape of a Nile barge, retailed by J. E. Caldwell, Philadelphia, marked on base and numbered '960', Providence, RI, 20in (51cm) long, 35oz.
£5,000–5,800
$7,000–8,500 ↗ S(NY)

Georg Jensen

Georg Jensen remains among the most sought after silverware in the world. Couple this worldwide demand against the company's inability to produce silverware today and one can begin to understand why the second-hand market for Georg Jensen silverware remains so buoyant – even in a depressed economic climate.

Auction prices remain robust for hollow ware, flatware and jewellery, with few pieces seeming to drop below estimate or failing to meet reserves. Georg Jensen is also the only silverware in the world where buyers can obtain a realistic price guide against identical new items being made today. After all, if you see a teapot retailing for £5,000 ($7,300) in a Georg Jensen shop window, it does not take much courage to work out that the identical teapot second-hand may be worth around £3,000 ($4,500).

Perhaps more importantly, buyers of Georg Jensen silverware are guided by the unique designs ranging from Arts and Crafts, Art Nouveau and Art Deco through to 1950s styles. Original 1950s pieces, particularly those designed by Henning Koppel, have been commanding very strong prices recently. It is extremely unusual to pick up a piece of Georg Jensen silverware that is not only beautifully designed, but also hand-crafted to an extremely high standard. Fakes and forgeries are mercifully rare – presumably because copies are too laborious and expensive to make.

So what is in demand? The answer is, not unexpectedly, the larger and the unusual, the one-off and therefore rare and more important pieces, which are commanding very high prices. Early jewellery and hollow ware, which is often set with semi-precious stones such as amber, chrysoprase or agate, is proving to be an increasingly strong market, while flatware is perhaps more stable with the Acorn pattern remaining the most popular. Hollow ware generally remains expensive in comparison, say, to many items of Georgian antique silver, but do not let the high prices put you off. Perhaps, because of its uniformity, reliable quality and design number system, Georg Jensen silverware is proving popular on the Internet with auction houses and dealers gaining increasing ground. The size of the market is substantial and international as a result of years of Georg Jensen silverware being exported from Copenhagen all over the world, particularly North America, Germany and Sweden.

Demand for this exceptional product looks set to stay for years to come and demand, after all, is what fuels the business of trading.

Alastair Crawford

◀ **A silver corkscrew,** by Georg Jensen, hallmarked, c1920, 4¼in (11cm) long.
£120–150
$180–250 ⊞ CS

A silver tray, by Georg Jensen, with slightly raised rim, notched decoration arranged in groups of three, having scrollwork handles with openwork foliate detail, monogram medallion, maker's marks 1925–32, London import marks for 1927, 17½in (44.5cm) wide.
£2,200–2,600
$3,200–3,800 ⚹ P

A pair of silver candelabra, by Georg Jensen, c1919, 11in (28cm) diam.
£25,000–30,000
$36,000–43,500 ⊞ SFL
These candelabra are of complicated construction and superb quality.

A sterling silver bowl, by Georg Jensen, No. 445, the hammered bowl with flaring rim, supported by foliate and bead openwork on stepped cup base, impressed marks, c1930, 8in (20.5cm) diam, 18oz.
£1,200–1,600
$1,800–2,300 ⚹ SK(B)

A pair of silver fish servers, by Georg Jensen, each decorated with a dolphin, c1930, 12in (30.5cm) long, in a fitted case.
£900–1,000
$1,300–1,500 ⚹ S

▶ **A pair of silver cufflinks,** by Georg Jensen, 1930s.
£120–150
$200–250 ⊞ DID

A silver bowl, by Georg Jensen, the rim with scrolling plant form decoration to two sides and underside, impressed mark and London import marks, dated '1931', 12½in (32cm) diam, 43oz.
£4,750–5,250
$7,000–7,500 ⚒ Mit

A canteen of table silver, by Georg Jensen, comprising 238 pieces, c1930.
£16,000–19,000
$23,000–27,500 ⚒ S

A pair of silver sugar tongs, by Georg Jensen, fully marked, London import marks, 1938, 4in (10cm) long.
£135–150
$200–220 ⊞ CoHA

A silver Blossom pattern five-piece coffee service, by Georg Jensen, with matching tray, numbered '2/2B/2D/2E', marked on bases, Copenhagen, post-1945, tray 22¾in (58cm) long, 222oz.
£11,500–13,500
$16,500–19,500 ⚒ S(NY)

A 68-piece canteen of silver-coloured metal cutlery, designed by Johan Rohde for Georg Jensen, Acanthus pattern, designed in 1915, the majority with Jensen marks for post-1945.
£3,500–4,000
$5,000–5,800 ⚒ S

A silver brooch, by Georg Jensen, modelled as a deer, No. 256, 1950, 2in (5cm) wide.
£200–225
$300–350 ⊞ DAC

▶ **A silver cocktail shaker,** by Georg Jensen, dated 'October 15th 1955', 13½in (34.5cm) high.
£2,500–3,000
$3,600–4,400 ⊞ SFL

A silver bracelet, by Georg Jensen, No. 188, designed 1960s.
£300–330
$450–500 ⊞ DAC

A silver pendant, designed by Nanna Ditzel for Georg Jensen, 1963, 2¼in (5.5cm) diam.
£300–350
$450–500 ⊞ ASA

▶ **A silver and quartz collar necklace,** designed by Torun for Georg Jensen, the quartz drop suspended from a tapering silver collar, signed, 1970.
£1,500–1,800
$2,000–2,500 ⚒ Bon

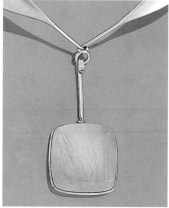

Cross Reference
See Colour Review (page 248–250)

A silver bowl, designed by Georg Jensen, post-1945, manufactured 1996, 15¾in (40cm) diam.
£8,500–10,000
$12,500–14,500 ⚒ BUK

Paul de Lamerie

Paul de Lamerie is without doubt the greatest silversmith of all time. He was born on 9 April 1688 in Bois-le-Duc in the Netherlands. His family came to London when he was three years old and they lived in Berwick Street, Soho. On arriving in London the family name of Souchay de la Merie was shortened first to De la Merie and later de Lamerie. In 1703, aged 15, he began a seven year apprenticeship with the highly respected master silversmith Peter Platel, acquiring the skills he needed for production as well as an understanding of design, and so went on to become the master silversmith of all time.

He received his freedom from the Goldsmiths Hall on 4 February 1713 and the following day registered his maker's mark and address as Windmill Street at the Hall. His workmanship was of such calibre that even as a young man he became known as the King of Silversmiths. With this reputation he received commissions from nobility, the Russian Court and Sir Robert Walpole, who patronized the workshop with numerous purchases. Many pieces are in private collections but his work can be seen in museums all over the world. One such item, a chandelier weighing well over a thousand ounces, hangs in the Kremlin. It is difficult finding pieces for sale, but reputable auction houses and dealers are still able to source pieces.

His early works were mainly pieces with clean simple lines influenced by the fashions of the Queen Anne period, but in 1730 he began to produce pieces in rococo design and it is these pieces which are most sought after by collectors and achieve the highest prices. His rococo pieces have been described as being buried in ornament, with such things as lions, sea monsters and urchins, shells and snakes, as well as cherubs and asymmetrical scrolls.

Much of his work was executed in Britannia standard silver, which was compulsory until 1720, but even after sterling was reinstated he chose to continue using the higher grade. Under pressure from his customers who wanted to save money, he eventually conceded to use the Sterling grade, but his standards did not waver. Whether plain or decorative, his wares were always pleasing to the eye and this is what projected him to stardom.

Paul de Lamerie was a shrewd business man who not only ran a workshop employing many silversmiths and apprentices, he was also in command of the retail side of the business. Many a silversmith went bankrupt due to lack of control over this aspect of their work.

He died on 1 August 1751, leaving behind a world full of the most wonderful pieces of silver ever produced.   **Daniel Bexfield**

A George II Britannia standard silver two-handled bell-shaped cup and cover, by Paul de Lamerie, applied with classical profiles and cartouches enclosing arms and a crest, gilt interior, London 1728, 12in (30.5cm) high, 95oz.
£122,000–135,000
$180,000–200,000 ⚹ S(NY)

> **Miller's is a price GUIDE not a price LIST**

▶ **A pair of George II silver sauce boats,** by Paul de Lamerie, the handles capped by monsters' heads, the sides centred by shells in chased cartouches below the gadrooned rims, the fronts engraved with arms, London 1744, 8½in (21.5cm) long, 42oz.
£105,000–115,000
$150,000–165,000 ⚹ S(NY)

A George II silver tot cup, by Paul de Lamerie, London 1736, 2in (5cm) high, 3oz.
£3,200–3,500
$4,500–5,000 ⚹ WW

A George II baluster mug by Paul de Lamerie, London 1736–37, 3¾in (9.5cm) high.
£10,000–12,000
$14,500–17,400 ⊞ NS

A George II mazarine, by Paul de Lamerie, pierced and engraved with scrolls and shells, later engraved with a coat-of-arms, 1745, 17½in (44.5cm) long, 26oz.
£3,000–3,500
$4,500–5,000 ⚹ C
The arms are those of Duncombe, Earls of Feversham.

Sampson Mordan

ampson Mordan (1790–1843) entered into the working world with an apprenticeship to John Bramah, who was a mechanic and inventor of the Bramah patent lock. It is here that Sampson would have learned about precision-made machinery which stood him in good stead for his future. He entered his first mark 'SM' at the Goldsmiths Hall on 26 June 1823 with his workshop at Castle Street, London.

Mordan patented a design for a silver propelling pencil on 20 December 1822. There has been much debate about who first patented a mechanical propelling pencil, but certainly Mordan was among the first to do so. With his patent Mordan went on to become the most accomplished pencil manufacturer, producing some very innovative designs. Whenever he made an item it would be constructed with the highest degree of precision and made from thick gauge silver. His ideal was that anything leaving his workshop would last a lifetime and this has clearly been realized as so many of his pencils are still in use today.

Upon his death two of his sons, Augustus and Sampson II continued the business with their father's ideology of quality, raising the company to new heights. They produced a vast range of personal and novelty trinkets that were new and innovative and which had a wide appeal. Items such as scent bottles, vinaigrettes and vesta cases have become greatly sought after by collectors especially if enamelled with interesting scenes and now sell for thousands of pounds. The enamelled pieces depict various subjects, for example soldiers in sentry boxes, golfers, erotic women, railway tickets, calling cards and hunting scenes.

The variety of pencils produced by the company almost exceed imagination. They were modelled as animals, boats, people, birds, tennis rackets, police truncheons, pistols, cutlery and even as Egyptian mummies. For example, they made a pencil two inches long that expanded to eight or nine inches, and a pig which produced a lead when its tail was pulled.

In 1870 Edmund George Johnson bought into the firm to become a partner and in 1881 he married Ada Florence Mordan, the second daughter of Augustus. That same year he became head of the company and continued its success. The Mordan & Co maker's mark is entered until 1941.

Even though there are many collectors of Mordan pieces it is still possible to pick up good examples today for relatively little money - it's just a matter of looking.

Daniel Bexfield

A Victorian die-stamped silver wine label, by Sampson Mordan, depicting four putti among fruiting vines, two above and two below the title scroll, pierced Claret, 1840.
£250–300
$350–450 P

A silver vesta case, by Sampson Mordan, London 1882.
£80–100
$100–150
PAY

A silver chatelaine, by Sampson Mordan, with penknife, corkscrew, pencil and *aide memoire*, London 1879–82, 15¼in (38.5cm) long.
£900–1,100
$1,300–1,600 AMH

A silver-mounted star-cut glass scent bottle and vinaigrette, by Sampson Mordan, London 1879, 4in (10cm) high.
£650–720
$1,000–1,100 THOM

A silver-mounted red glass double-ended scent bottle and vinaigrette, by Sampson Mordan, in the shape of opera glasses, c1880, 5½in (14cm) long, in a fitted case marked 'Face, Keen & Face, Plymouth'.
£820–920
$1,200–1,500 Som

Condition

The condition is absolutely vital when assessing the value of an antique. Damaged pieces on the whole appreciate much less than perfect examples. However a rare desirable piece may command a high price even when damaged.

◄ **A Victorian Stourbridge Burmese glass scent bottle,** the silver-gilt cap by Sampson Mordan, the glass bottle, with enamelled body graduating from brown to primrose and decorated with berries and a butterfly, attributed to Thomas Webb & Son, 4in (10cm) long, in original fitted case.
£380–420
$570–600 ⚒ P

A Victorian silver spiral fluted sovereign case, by Sampson Mordan, with hallmarks for London 1889–90, 1¼in (3cm) diam.
£300–350
$450–500 ⊞ NS

◄ **A silver vesta case,** modelled as an owl, the hinged head set with glass eyes, maker's mark of Sampson Mordan & Co, London 1895, 2¼in (5.5cm) high.
£1,200–1,400
$1,700–2,000 ⚒ Bon

A silver travelling ruler, by Sampson Mordan & Co, London 1901, case 3½in (9cm) long.
£600–675
$870–1,000 ⊞ HCA

A silver Queen Victoria memorial pin tray, by Sampson Mordan & Co, London 1902, 4½in (11.5cm) long.
£175–195
$250–280 ⊞ BEX

A silver-mounted cut-glass scent bottle, by Sampson Mordan & Co, with stopper modelled as a pharaoh's head, 1900, 6½in (16.5cm) high.
£450–550
$650–800 ⚒ G(B)

▶ **A pair of silver flower vases,** by Sampson Mordan & Co, with fluted rims, London 1902, 7in (18cm) high.
£400–450
$600–650 ⊞ THOM

An Edwardian silver pin cushion, by Sampson Mordan & Co, modelled as a chick, Chester 1907–08.
£235–275
$350–400 ⊞ NS

Cross Reference
See Colour Review (page 251)

A silver pig bookmark, by Sampson Mordan & Co, Chester 1907, 3in (7.5cm) high.
£340–380
$500–600 ⊞ THOM

A silver pin cushion, by Sampson Mordan & Co, modelled as a fish, 1908, 1½in (4cm) high.
£550–600
$800–870 ⊞ HCA

A set of four silver owl menu holders, by Sampson Mordan, Chester 1908–09, 1½in (4cm) high, in a fitted case.
£1,000–1,200
$1,500–1,800 ⊞ NS

Omar Ramsden

Omar Ramsden was born in 1873 and christened Omer, but later changed his name to Omar. He spent his early years in the USA but returned to Sheffield in Britain in 1887 aged 14 to start his apprenticeship. During this period he appreciated and learned the importance of mechanical production and techniques to the growing demand for mass market silver. At this time he met Alwyn Charles Ellison Carr, another pupil at the Sheffield School of Art, who was to become his great friend and partner. Together they studied at the Royal College of Art, at a time when the Arts and Crafts and Art Nouveau movements were developing, and these influences are evident in their work.

In 1897 Omar won a competition to design and produce a mace for the City of Sheffield. He and Alwyn decided to produce the piece as a joint venture and so set up a workshop at Stamford Bridge Studios, Chelsea, London. This was so successful that they became formal partners, registering their mark with the Goldsmiths Hall in February 1898.

They employed a number of workers whom they trained in silversmithing in order to carry out most of the work, leaving them free to design. As the business developed they found a ready market for their Arts and Crafts style, and so decided to expand. Another premises was obtained in Seymour Place, adjacent to Fulham Road, which became St Dunstan's Studio where they lived, designed and exhibited.

Both of them were staunch Roman Catholics, evidence of which can be seen in much of their work. They were commissioned for many ecclesiastical items such as chalices and mazer bowls. One such item, a magnificent monstrance, was requisitioned for Westminster Cathdedral.

During WWI Alwyn went off to the front line to fight, leaving Omar to manage the business. He returned as a wounded Captain in 1918 to find that Omar had excelled and the company was very buoyant, but in 1919 the partnership failed and they separated. Omar retained the expanded workshop and St Dunstan's, and with his organizational skills and business aptitude went from strength to strength.

Omar's trademark was that all his pieces were engraved 'Omar Ramsden me Facit' (Omar Ramsden made me), but this was not correct. All the work was carried out by his silversmiths and even the pieces that look like they have been hand raised from a single piece of silver were often cast and given a hammer finish to emulate a hand-made piece. Never the less this does not alter the quality, finish and design of the pieces that left the workshop.

Daniel Bexfield

A silver pendant necklace, by Omar Ramsden and Alwyn Carr, with interwoven tendrils surrounding a central green enamelled panel, maker's marks, London 1905, 3in (7.5cm) overall.
£1,700–2,000
$2,500–3,000 ⚒ S

▶ **A pair of silver spoons,** by Omar Ramsden, with decorated finials, 1931, 6¼in (16cm) long.
£500–600
$700–900 ⚒ P(B)

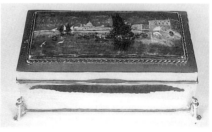

A silver box, by Omar Ramsden and Alwyn Carr, the top enamelled with a Venetian scene in naturalistic colours, London 1909, 6½in (16.5cm) long.
£5,000–5,500
$7,000–8,000 ⊞ SHa

A set of 12 silver and ivory knives and forks, by Omar Ramsden, London 1929.
£1,500–1,600
$2,000–2,500 ⊞ BEX

A silver salver, by Omar Ramsden and Alwyn Carr, with ropework edges, each corner set with chrysoprase, on four scroll and stump feet, base inscribed, 1913, 7in (18cm) square, 9.25oz.
£1,800–2,000
$2,600–3,000 ⚒ P

A silver tobacco box, by Omar Ramsden and Alwyn Carr, flat chased with arms and a motto 'Vincit Veritas' (Truth Prevails), London 1913, 3¼in (8.5cm) long, 3oz.
£1,100–1,300
$1,500–2,000 ⊞ PAY
The arms and motto are those of the Coote family.

Paul Storr

Paul Storr is in the premier league of British silversmiths and his pieces are highly sought after by collectors and museums. The items he produced are now two hundred years old and they will last for many centuries to come, for the qualiy of silversmithing was excellent and very thick gauge silver was used in the manufacturing process.

Paul's father, Thomas Storr, was a silver chaser by trade. Paul was born in 1771 and began his apprenticeship in 1785 with Andrew Fogelberg of Church St, Soho, London, when aged 14. Fogelberg, a Swedish-born silversmith acclaimed for the quality of his work, would have taught the young Storr the art and skill needed to manufacture to the highest degree. His first maker's mark was entered in May 1792 and is recorded as being in partnership with William Frisbee. This partnership obviously did not last for long as he entered another, solo, mark in January 1793. He concentrated on production of fine and elaborate presentation silver, some of it to royal commission, and as an interpreter of the French Empire style, but in a less formal manner, was instrumental in the development of the English Regency style.

In 1796 Storr opened his workshop at 20 Air Street, London, which had belonged to Thomas Pitts, another acclaimed silversmith. Between 1807 and 1819 he worked in association with Rundell, Bridge & Rundell, the Royal Goldsmiths to George III, making many of their more important silver pieces. During this time he produced a wide range of wares, mainly in the ancient Roman or rococo styles.

Paul Storr married Elizabeth Susanna Beyer, of the piano producing family, in 1801, and they had ten children. His work continued with the Royal Goldsmiths who supplied him with fresh designs from their numerous artists. It was decided that the Goldsmiths would open a workshop in Dean Street, Soho, to be run by Storr as the director, with the name Storr & Co, and maker's marks were registered accordingly.

Probably the most famous of all Storr's creations were his reproductions of the Warwick Vase. The original marble vase had been purchased by the Earl of Warwick in 1744 and engraved by Piranesi. His copies ranged in size from wine coolers to sugar bowls but were always of good weight.

Paul left Storr & Co in 1819 and set up in Gray's Inn Road. Three years later he entered into partnership with John Mortimer, and that lasted until his retirement in 1839, when he moved to Hill House, Tooting, London. He died on 18 March 1844 and is buried in Tooting churchyard.

Daniel Bexfield

A George III silver meat dish and cover, the gadrooned rim with anthemion, shell and acanthus, the border engraved with crests, engraved with a baron's armorials, maker's mark of Paul Storr, London 1808, 17in (43cm) long, 120oz.
£9,000–10,000
$13,000–14,500 ⚒ C(SP)

A George III silver teapot, by Paul Storr, the body with ribbed girdle above fluting, 1813, 13½in (34.5cm) wide, 37.25oz.
£2,000–2,200
$2,900–3,200 ⚒ P

A George III silver coffee pot, by Paul Storr, crested with two arms holding a dog below a gadrooned rim, the spout chased with acanthus leaves and anthemions, with ivory finial and scroll handle, London 1818, 8¾in (22cm) high, 29.5oz.
£2,000–2,500
$2,900–3,600 ⚒ S

A pair of Regency silver meat dishes, by Paul Storr, 1818, with mazarines and later domes, by John Bridge 1823, for Rundell, Bridge and Rundell, 23½in (59.5cm) wide, 620oz.
£35,000–40,000
$50,000–58,000 ⚒ S

◄ **A George IV silver candelabrum,** by Paul Storr for Storr and Mortimer, the triform base on four shell feet, each side with a cartouche enclosing armorials and a crest, six anthemion decorated scroll branches supporting drip pans and sconces with detachable nozzles, London 1825, 28½in (72.5cm) high, 246oz.
£29,000–34,000
$42,000–49,500 ⚒ S

Tiffany & Co

There is always a 'best' in everything, and the best in American silver from the mid-19th to the early 20th century was Tiffany & Co. American silver production at that time had reached its zenith, considered by people all over the world as the finest money could buy. Large companies like Gorham, Whiting, and Reed & Barton produced excellent silver, but Tiffany was exceptional. Winning award after award at international expositions, Tiffany established itself as the company for beautifully crafted, over-the-top pieces.

Tiffany has remained strong for more than a century. The more elaborate patterns in flatware, which include Japanese (or Audubon), Vine, Lap Over Edge, and Olympian, continue to escalate in value. According to Dr William Hood Jr, principal author of *Tiffany Silver Flatware 1845–1905, When Dining Was an Art,* serving pieces in these patterns, particularly Lap Over Edge, rarely come to auction, but when they do they far exceed their high estimates. This is proven by a set recently sold at auction, with 235 pieces of Lap Over Edge realizing £130,000/$189,500 (estimate £90,000–110,000/$130,000–160,000). The plainer, simpler patterns do not realize the prices commanded by the more ornate ones, but manage to remain popular and collectable all the same. Incredibly large services of flatware, with hundreds of pieces, always do well.

Tiffany's mixed-metal pieces, whether flatware or hollow ware, continue to bring ever higher prices at American sales. A set of 12 large Japanese-style teaspoons in silver with other metals realized £11,000/$16,000 (estimate £4,000–6,000/$6,000–9,000) at a recent auction. Another spectacular sale was of a silver and mixed-metal Japanese-style cup and saucer, c1880, which exceeded its estimate. Current sales at Christie's, Sotheby's, and Phillips continue to confirm this trend.

The Victorian hostess had a special serving and place piece for everything, from soup to nuts. Today, these pieces are recognized for their exceptional design and beauty, and the modern American hostess looks for new ways to display and use them. Odd pieces such as terrapin forks, bonbonnières and ice cream slices find innovative application as hors d'oeuvres forks, pea scoops and pie or cake servers.

Above all, Tiffany silver has stood the test of time. In antique shops and auction houses worldwide you can pick up a piece of silver and know that it is Tiffany, just from its weight, quality of design, and feel. Now, as when first produced, antique Tiffany silver commands more attention and higher prices.

Connie MacNally

A Tiffany & Co silver cutlery set, comprising 120 pieces, engraved 'F.S.F.', stamped on stems 'John Polhemus and Patent 1860'.
£3,500–4,000
$5,000–5,800 ↗ S(NY)

◄ **A Tiffany & Co silver ewer,** designed by Young and Ellis, decorated with grape vines, c1860, 16in (40.5cm) high.
£2,000–2,500
$2900–3,600
⊞ SFL

A Tiffany & Co sterling silver water jug, with erasure and later engraved monogram, slight damage, New York c1865, 11in (28cm) high, 52oz.
£3,500–4,000
$5,000–5,800 ↗ B&B

▶ **A Tiffany & Co five-piece tea service,** lightly chased with Indian-style foliage and a die-rolled girdle of Islamic and Oriental foliate designs, marked on bases, c1870, kettle-on-stand 14in (35.5cm) high, 117oz, and a silver-plated oval galleried tray.
£4,400–5,000
$6,500–7,500 ↗ S(NY)

A Tiffany & Co silver tureen and cover, the handles with beaded cube to centre and flat leaf terminals, with domed lid, monogrammed, 1875–91, 15in (38cm) long, 56oz.
£3,200–3,800
$4,500–5,500 ↗ SK

A Tiffany & Co sterling silver pierced comport, maker's mark of Edward Moore, c1880, 9in (23cm) diam.
£1,000–1,200
$1,500–1,800 ⊞ SHa

A Tiffany & Co silver six-piece tea and coffee service, the bombé bodies chased with spiral flutes and the necks with running bands of acanthus, matching handles, the bases marked and monogrammed, c1885, kettle-on-stand 15in (38cm) high, 185oz.
£7,000–9,000
$10,000–13,000 ⚒ S(NY)

A Tiffany & Co silver English King pattern cutlery set, comprising 12 each of dinner forks, salad forks, dinner knives, teaspoons, soup spoons and butter knives, New York c1890, 60oz excluding the knives.
£5,000–5,500
$7,250–8,000 ⚒ SK

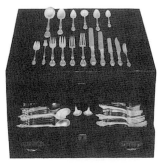

A Tiffany & Co silver Richelieu pattern cutlery set, comprising 410 pieces, monogrammed, New York c1895, 442oz excluding knives, in fitted mahogany case.
£20,000–25,000
$29,000–36,000 ⚒ S(NY)

A Tiffany & Co silver and other metals salad bowl, with hammered surface, the sides engraved with water plants, repeated in silver-gilt on the interior, the rim chased with overlapping lily pads applied with a brass crab and copper and brass insects, engraved with a contemporary monogram and crest, marked on base and numbered '5638-970-660, New York c1880, 15in (38cm) diam.
£25,000–30,000
$36,000–43,500 ⚒ S(NY)
This bowl is listed in Tiffany's ledgers as a salad bowl and is the only one listed. However, it is possible that it was originally one of a pair. The entry is dated December 1880 and the manufacturing cost of one bowl was $250 (£166).

A Tiffany & Co silver five-piece tea and coffee service, with monograms 'EHB' above applied girdles of flowers and scrolls, gadrooned rims, New York c1885, coffee pot 8½in (21.5cm) high, 95oz.
£3,000–3,500
$4,500–5,000 ⚒ S(NY)

A pair of Tiffany & Co silver covered serving dishes, the everted rims with moulded wave decoration, the domed lids with moulded bands and removable cast chrysanthemum finials, monogrammed, New York 1891–1902, 8½in (21.5cm) long, 75oz.
£2,200–2,600
$3,200–3,800 ⚒ SK

▶ **A Tiffany & Co silver punch ladle,** the gilt bowl with reeded band with embossed flower and a cast swallow attached to rim, monogrammed, New York, late19th/early 20thC, 15in (38cm) long, 8oz.
£2,400–2,700
$3,500–4,000 ⚒ S

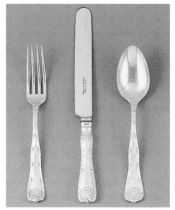

A Tiffany & Co silver assembled Wave Edge pattern cutlery set, comprising 111 pieces, monogrammed, New York 1884–91, 135oz.
£4,500–5,000
$6,500–7,250 ⚒ S(NY)

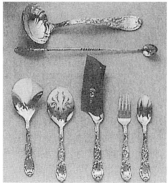

Nine Tiffany & Co silver Chrysan-themum pattern serving items, some engraved with monograms, New York c1885, 41oz.
£3,000–3,500
$4,500–5,000 ⚒ S(NY)

An American six-piece silver tea and coffee service, by Tiffany & Co, fluted oval with shell band borders, comprising tea pot, coffee pot, kettle-on-stand and burner, covered sugar bowl, milk jug and slop bowl, New York c1893, 154oz.
£6,200–6,800
$9,000–9,900 ⚒ S

A Tiffany & Co silver-mounted cut-glass claret jug, late 19th/early 20thC, 10¾in (27.5cm) high.
£320–350
$450–500 ✦ SK

A Tiffany & Co silver Wave Edge pattern table service, comprising 60 initialled pieces, New York c1900, 67oz.
£3,200–3,500
$4,500–5,000 ✦ S(NY)

A Tiffany & Co sterling silver pocket barometer, engraved 'H. W. B.', 1900, 4½in (11.5cm) high.
£250–280
$360–400 ⊞ REG

▶ **A Tiffany & Co sterling silver bowl,** the edge embellished in relief with an openwork design of clover and foliage, c1905, 12in (30.5cm) diam.
£1,200–1,400
$1,800–2,000 ⊞ SFL

A Tiffany & Co sterling silver vase, designed by John C. Moore, marked, c1910, 9in (23cm) high.
£1,100–1,250
$1,500–1,800 ⊞ SHa

A Tiffany & Co sterling silver bottle holder, marked 'John C. Moore', c1910, 6in (15cm) diam.
£900–1,000
$1,300–1,500 ⊞ SHa

A set of 12 Tiffany & Co silver finger bowls and stands, designed by Paulding Farnham, Renaissance pattern, with cut-glass liners, the plates initialled 'D,' the rims of the bowls engraved underneath with a name and date 'March 15th 1912', marked on bases and numbered '16181-3400', New York c1912, 6in (15cm) diam, 120oz.
£7,000–8,000
$10,000–11,500 ✦ S(NY)

◀ **A Tiffany & Co seven-piece silver tea and coffee service,** with matching two-handled tray, marked on bases, c1920, kettle-on-stand 12in (30.5cm) high, 276oz.
£9,500–12,000
$13,500–17,500 ✦ S(NY)

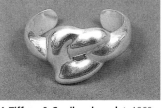

A Tiffany & Co silver bracelet, 1960s.
£230–250
$330–360 ⊞ GLT

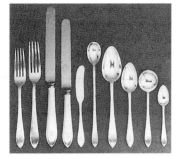

A Tiffany & Co silver Faneuil pattern cutlery service, comprising 131 pieces, the majority engraved with the same monogram, New York, 20thC, 167oz excluding knives.
£5,000–5,500
$5,800–8,300 ✦ S(NY)

A Tiffany & Co sterling silver cuff bangle, designed by Elsa Peretti, New York 1975, 3in (7.5cm) diam.
£450–500
$650–720 ⊞ DID

Cross Reference
See Colour Review (page 254)

A Tiffany & Co silver St Dunstan pattern cutlery service, comprising 137 pieces, all with monogram, in a fitted box, 154oz.
£4,000–5,000
$5,500–7,500 ✦ SLN

Silver Plate Techniques

To most of us the word plated suggests inferiority, a specious covering of something good to hide the cheap. Don't be put off! Many plated items are made as well, and sometimes better than those made of solid silver and cost much less. In times gone, by cheap labour could enable the sparing use of expensive materials to make some lovely things. Plated ware falls into two main categories, Old Sheffield Plate and Electroplate. Old Sheffield Plate was first made in the mid–18thC from sheets of silver fused to a thicker copper base by rolling. It is not particularly durable and in time the copper wears through in a noticeable manner. Electroplated items first appeared in the 1840s and copy the earlier designs and manufacturing techniques. Many pieces are available due to their robust construction and are often in good condition. Table and chamber candlesticks are good examples and can be purchased for less than their solid silver counterparts. The electroplating process involves the item, which is made of a base metal, usually nickel or copper, being placed in a tank of potassium cyanide solution. An electrode is then attached to the item, another electrode is connected to a piece of pure silver which is also in the tank. A low voltage electric current is then passed through and the base metal item becomes coated in silver by electrolysis. The longer the item is left in the solution the thicker the layer of silver becomes. Electroplated items usually bear the mark E.P.N.S. (Electroplated Nickel Silver). Today the thickness of the plating is measured in microns. Earlier plating was often marked 'A1' or 'Hotel Plate' which indicated a thicker layer of silver.

Bear in mind the following pointers when looking for Old Sheffield Plate: large hollow articles will have soldered seams, as the fused plate cannot be worked much by hammering; ornamental mounts should be made of thin stamped silver filled with lead and soldered in place, wear will cause this to become visible; interiors of cups can sometimes be gilded whereas the insides of larger items such as wine coolers and the bases of trays are tinned, giving a greyish look. Visible copper is acceptable if it is not too obvious.

Large pieces of Old Sheffield Plate can be good value at auction. Items such as trays and wine coolers are in increasing demand if in good condition. Look out for initials or armorials engraved upon an area of slightly greyish colour. This is a good sign of authenticity as it indicated plating of greater thickness to avoid the engraver cutting into the copper base. Pieces such as these can be relatively inexpensive as their large size can reduce their price. Smaller items are much in demand, pieces such as pretty pierced cream pails and sugar baskets, similar to their silver counterparts but at a third to half of the cost. Oddities in Old Sheffield Plate are well worth collecting, but can be expensive. Pieces such as cucumber slicers and folding toast racks are rare but more likely to be faked.

Early Sheffield Plate makers occasionally marked their work, often in a manner similar to marks found on contemporary silver. Watch out for makers such as Thomas Law (one of the earliest) and Matthew Boulton. The latter was probably the most famous, even though he worked in Birmingham. His mark is that of a sun struck twice, though this can be confused with the mark of Mappin & Webb, an equally good and collectable maker. The larger and duller the article the more genuine it is likely to be. Beware, however, of large items, particularly trays and wine coolers that are often decorated in the manner of Old Sheffield Plate but are entirely on copper without the filled silver mounts as described earlier.

There are specialist restorers and if the work is properly done is an enhancement to the piece. Sheffield plated items must never be re-plated unless one is not bothered about authenticity, or the originality of the item has been destroyed by excessive wear.

The best examples of electroplated silver were made by Elkington & Co, who developed and patented the process in 1841 and instituted a system of date letters and numbers. This adds spice to collecting their products, even humble spoons and forks. Their work is of the highest quality and the finish superb. Other quality makers were Martin Hall & Co, who specialized in cruets, condiments and spirit stands, Mappin Brothers, later Mappin & Webb, Walker & Hall and Henry Wilkinson & Co. All these makers, among many others, marked their wares as a guarantee of their quality and origin. As electroplate is hardly worth faking there is no need to worry on that score. However watch out for Victorian-looking items, particularly tea and coffee services, which although solidly spun or raised from nickel are coarsely engraved and finished, and have originated from the Middle East and India in recent years.

Electroplate does have a poor relative, known as E.P.B.M. (Electroplated Britannia Metal), which was developed at the end of the 18th century. It looks very much like pewter and was indeed used for pub measures, mugs and the like where low cost was required. It lends itself well to electroplating and because of simple manufacture became an inexpensive substitute for E.P.N.S., although its leaden feel will distinguish it and even when plated has a dull grey appearance. **Hugh Gregory**

Old Sheffield Plate

A Sheffield-plated coffee pot, with scrolled beech handle and acanthus leaf cast spout, stamped mark of four stylized 'B's on neck, c1760, 10½in (26.5cm) high.
£520–575
$750–850 ⚒ EH

A late George III Sheffield-plated argyle, with wood handle, 8½in (21.5cm) high.
£500–550
$700–800 ⚒ DN

A George IV Sheffield-plated coffee pot, with ribbed and leaf-capped repoussé swan neck spout and scroll wood handle, 11in (28cm) high.
£120–140
$175–200 ⚒ WW

▶ **A Sheffield-plated three-piece tea service,** with leaf-cast edges and scrolled fruitwood handle, with matching sugar pot and cream jug, c1835, teapot 7¾in (19.5cm) high.
£150–180
$200–250 ⚒ CGC

A Sheffield-plated fish slice, the blade pierced with foliate scroll decoration, with green stained ivory handle, unmarked, c1780, 12½in (32cm) long.
£450–500
$650–700 ⚒ Bon

▶ **A George III Sheffield-plated tea urn,** the body engraved with a contemporay armorial, the tap with an ivory handle, the crested cover with a ball finial, c1785, 22in (60cm) high.
£280–340
$400–500 ⚒ WW

A Sheffield-plated inkstand, with shell and gadroon chased borders and handle, on winged paw feet, with two square glass pots, early 19thC, 5in (13cm) wide.
£200–240
$300–350 ⚒ DN

A Sheffield-plated table, chased with rococo ornament, with oak backing, knopped column stem, on three paw feet, c1835, 24in (61cm) diam.
£6,000–6,500
$8,700–9,500 ⚒ S(NY)

A late George III Sheffield-plated tray, engraved with the arms of Pearce of Penzance, Cornwall, 24in (61cm) wide.
£400–440
$550–650 ⚒ DN

◀ **A Sheffield-plated ewer-form race trophy,** applied with an inscribed cartouche depicting two horses modelled in full relief, also applied with swags of flowers, acanthus and grapevine spreading from the branch handle, c1835–45, 34in (86cm) high.
£5,000–6,000
$7,500–8,500 ⚒ S(NY)
The inscription reads 'Croxton Park Races 1849'. A curious feature of this piece is the appearance on the back of the central cartouche of a mirror image of a map of the Italian coast, indicating the re-use of a copper plate used for map printing.

A Sheffield-plated standish, with foliate scroll borders, glass wells with hinged covers, chamber stick, detachable sconce, on lion paw feet, 19thC, 13½in (34.5cm) wide.
£440–480
$650–700 ⚒ N

A Sheffield-plated four-branch *épergne,* fitted with cut-glass centre bowl surrounded by smaller bowls, c1835–50, 14½in (37cm) high.
£1,500–1,650
$2,000–2,500 ⚹ NOA

A Sheffield-plated silver salver, 19thC, 10½in (26.5cm) diam.
£120–160
$175–225 ⊞ STA

A pair of Victorian Sheffield-plated communion flagons, by Martin Hall & Co, the hinged lids with urn knops, 16in (40.5cm) high.
£320–350
$450–500 ⚹ DA

Candelabra & Candlesticks

A pair of Sheffield-plated candlesticks, c1800, 11½in (29cm) high.
£250–300
$350–450 ⊞ PSA

LOCATE THE SOURCE
The source of each illustration in Miller's can be found by checking the code letters below each caption with the Key to Illustrations, pages 311–314.

A set of four Sheffield-plated candlesticks, the candleholders with detachable nozzles, early 19thC, 11¾in (30cm) high.
£400–450
$600–650 ⚹ WW

A pair of Sheffield-plated fluted candlesticks, applied with rococo shell, floral and C-scroll decoration, each with campana-shaped socket and detachable nozzle, probably re-plated, 11in (28cm) high.
£300–350
$450–500 ⚹ CSK

A pair of Sheffield-plated candelabra, with flame finials on reeded turned stems, double star mark, 19thC, 21in (53.5cm) high.
£525–575
$750–850 ⚹ AH

A pair of George III Sheffield-plated candelabra, by Matthew Boulton & Co, 19in (48cm) high.
£1,500–2,000
$2,000–3,000 ⚹ DN

A set of four Sheffield-plated candlesticks, two with detachable three-light candelabra branches, with acanthus leaf decorated reeded arms and central flambeaux finials, all with detachable sconces, tapering stems, decorated with double star marks, lacking two sconces, 13in (33cm) high and 21in (53cm) high overall.
£700–800
$1,000–1,200 ⚹ MCA

▶ **A pair of Sheffield-plated three-light candelabra,** 17in (43cm) high.
£500–600
$700–850 ⚹ Bea

Dishes & Bowls

A Sheffield-plated entrée dish and cover, the gadrooned rim with scroll acanthus at intervals, scroll leaf ring handle, c1810, 10in (25.5cm) diam.
£250–300
$350–450 ⊞ HofB

A pair of Sheffield-plated sauce tureens, c1820, 8in (20.5cm) wide.
£1,200–1,400
$1,750–2,000
⊞ DIC

A pair of Sheffield-plated entrée dishes and covers, probably by J. Watson & Sons, each supported on a two-handled warmer base with wooden detachable insulated feet, monogrammed, 1820–30, 13½in (34.5cm) wide.
£350–420
$500–600 ⚒ CGC

A pair of Regency Sheffield-plated entrée dishes, 12¾in (32.5cm) long.
£500–550
$700–800 ⚒ DN

A pair of Regency Sheffield-plated sauce tureens, with gadrooned borders and reeded shell scroll corners, the covers with lamp and pennant crest, leaf scroll ring handles, on leaf appliqué paw feet, 7½in (19cm) long.
£700–800
$1,000–1,200 ⚒ WW

A pair of Sheffield-plated entrée dishes and covers, with detachable handles, 19thC, 13in (33cm) long.
£320–350
$450–500 ⚒ PCh

A pair of William IV Sheffield-plated dishes and covers, the panelled sides with shell and foliage scrolling borders, the covers with detachable handles decorated with acanthus leaves, scrolls and flowerheads, 14¼in (36cm) long.
£200–250
$300–350 ⚒ WW

Wine Antiques

A George III Sheffield-plated wine cooler, with four reeded bands and loop handles, engraved with a crest, detachable liner and rim, c1800, 8¾in (22cm) high.
£650–720
$950–1,000 ⚒ WW

A Sheffield-plated wine coaster, with ogee sides and gadrooned rim, on a mahogany base, c1815, 6in (15cm) diam.
£150–180
$220–260 ⊞ JAS

◄ **A pair of Sheffield-plated wine coolers,** with foliage and shell rims, two reeded handles issuing from grapevines, detachable liner and collar, c1810, 11in (28cm) high.
£800–900
$1,000–1,300 ⚒ SLN

A pair of Regency-style Sheffield-plated wine coolers, fluted and with a band of shells and palmettes, reeded handles, c1820, 9¼in (23.5cm) high.
£3,000–3,500
$4,500–5,000 ⚶ B&B

A pair of Sheffield-plated wine coolers, the partly fluted campana form decoration with applied shells, engraved with arms, crest and motto, detachable rims and liners, c1820, 9½in (24cm) high.
£2,800–3,200
$4,000–4,700 ⚶ S(NY)

A pair of Sheffield-plated wine coolers, the campana form with shellwork rims and bases, bodies crested and applied with grapevine spreading from forked branch handles detachable liners, c1830, 12½in (32cm) high,
£2,600–3,000
$3,800–4,400 ⚶ S(NY)

A Sheffield-plated wine coaster, with mahogany base, c1840, 6in (15cm) diam.
£100–125
$150–180 ⊞ JAS

Miller's is a price GUIDE
not a price LIST

A George III Sheffield-plated wine cooler, with three reeded bands and loop handles, engraved with an armorial, 8¼in (21cm) high excluding handles.
£1,400–1,600
$2,000–2,300 ⚶ DN

A George III Sheffield-plated wine cooler, with gadrooned borders, part fluting and two reeded handles with satyr mask terminals, on a round base, engraved with crests and armorials, 9¼in (23.5cm) high.
£600–700
$870–1,000 ⚶ DN

A pair of Regency Sheffield-plated wine coolers, engraved with contemporary armorials, two wrythen grip handles with scallop shell appliqués, gadrooned borders with detachable liners, 8in (20.5cm) high.
£1,800–2,000
$2,600–2,900 ⚶ WW

A pair of Sheffield-plated wine coolers, early 19thC, 9in (23cm) high.
£1,400–1,700
$2,000–2,500 ⚶ AG

A Victorian Sheffield-plated plate magnum coaster, with pierced sides, 9½in (24cm) diam, on a wooden base.
£130–160
$190–230 ⚶ Mit

A pair of Sheffield-plated wine coasters, early 19thC, 5in (23.5cm) diam.
£350–400
$500–600 ⊞ ANT

A pair of Sheffield-plated wine ewers, decorated with floral and leaf scrolls, early 19thC, 12in (30.5cm) high.
£850–950
$1,300–1,400 ⚶ AAV

Silver Plate

A silver-plated salver, c1860,
11in (28cm) diam.
£60–75
$90–100 ⊞ STA

◄ A silver-plated wine pourer,
c1860, 3in (7.5cm) high.
£125–150
$180–220 ⊞ JAS

A silver-plated jewellery casket, by Elkington
& Co, decorated with relief panels of classical
figures and on four swan and shell feet, with
original velvet buttoned interior, stamped
'Philadelphia Exhibition 1876', 11in (28cm) long.
£340–380
$500–600 ⚒ GAK
Following the invention of the electric battery
in the early 19th century and the first
attempts to coat base metals with silver in
1840, the Birmingham firm of Elkington &
Co took out the first patent on the new
process of electroplating. Elkington
produced a huge range of items, both
functional and decorative, in the Victorian
period, contributing to all the major
international exhibitions and world fairs.

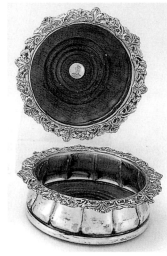

A silver-plated double wine coaster, on
spoked wheels, 19thC, each 6in (15cm) diam.
£220–260
$320–380 ⚒ GAK

An electroplated tobacco
jar, by Elkington & Co,
c1880, 9in (23cm) high.
£400–450
$600–650 ⊞ DIC

A pair of silver-plated coasters, with
crested wood bases, 19thC,
6¾in (17cm) diam.
£300–330
$440–480 ⚒ DN

A silver-plated candle snuffer, with silver handle, c1880,
10½in (26.5cm) long.
£50–60
$75–90 ⊞ TAC

A silver-plated tray, by Gorham,
with Bacchus mask figural decoration,
the interior with engraved and chased
geometric decoration, monogrammed,
19thC, 36in (91.5cm) long.
£460–550
$650–800 ⚒ FBG

► A silver-
plated bottle
label, 19thC,
1½in (4cm) wide.
£55–70
$80–100 ⊞ JAS

A silver-plated claret label,
19thC, 1½in (4cm) wide.
£35–45
$50–65 ⊞ JAS

◄ A silver-plated tray, with
gadrooned border and two foliate
handles, engraved in the centre with
an armorial, on chased feet, 19thC,
27in (68.5cm) wide.
£440–500
$650–700 ⚒ DN

A silver-plated embossed oval fruit dish, with grape scissors, c1885, 12in (30.5cm) wide, in original burgundy silk-lined case.
£250–275
$350–400 ⊞ DIC

A silver-plated travelling tea kettle and folding stand, designed by Dr Christopher Dresser for Hukin and Heath, with spirit burner, fully marked, c1890, 9in (23cm) high.
£200–250
$300–350 ⚒ CAG

An Arts and Crafts silver-plated chalice, by Philip Ashberry & Sons, c1890, 7½in (19cm) high.
£70–80
$100–115 ⊞ WeH

A silver-plated figural corkscrew, the handle and shaft modelled as a standing putti with a bunch of grapes in each hand, wire helix, possibly Scandinavian, 1890–1920, 6½in (16.5cm) high.
£240–280
$350–400 ⚒ P(B)

▶ **A Victorian silver-plated hip flask,** with snuff box, 5½in (14cm) long.
£120–150
$175–225 ⊞ ET

An American silver-plated wine cooler, by Gorham, with Greek key bands and two stag's head handles, interior bottle sleeve, late 19thC, 10in (25.5cm) high.
£2,500–2,750
$3,600–4,000 ⚒ SK

A silver-plated cut-glass cruet set, the stand in the shape of a golf ball and clubs, c1890, 3½in (9cm) high.
£120–140
$175–200 ⊞ MSh

A silver-plated spoon warmer, modelled as an egg with a chick perched on the shell, c1890, 5in (12.5cm) wide.
£280–320
$400–475 ⊞ SSW

A pair of electroplated urns, of compana form, relief-decorated with swags and gadrooning, on cylindrical rouge marble bases, late 19thC, 11¾in (30cm) high.
£180–200
$250–300 ⚒ P(B)

A pair of electrotype silvered chargers, the outer rim depicting astrological panels, the interior titled with months of the year and frolicking putti, late 19thC, 21in (53.5cm) diam.
£1,200–1,500
$1,750–2,250 ⚒ S(NY)

A Victorian gilt and silver-plated York and Lancaster Regiment officer's helmet plate, 4in (10cm) high.
£350–380
$500–575 ⚒ WAL

◀ **A barrister's silver-plated hammer,** c1900, 7¼in (18.5cm) long.
£60–70
$90–100 ⊞ WAB
The pointed end was used to break the seal on documents, and the hammer end to reseal them.

A **silver-plated pepper mill,** in the shape of a caster, c1920, 4¼in (11cm) high.
£60–70
$90–100 ⊞ CoHA

A set of Cristofle Gallia silvered-metal knife rests, each modelled as a stylized animal, in a presentation case, c1920, 11in (28cm) wide.
£850–950
$1,250–1,400 ⊞ ART

A silver-plated religious souvenir from Prague, 1920–30, 3in (7.5cm) high.
£12–15
$15–20 ⊞ DP

◄ A silver-plated corkscrew, modelled as a dog, 1930, 2½in (6.5cm) long.
£28–32
$45–50 ⊞ BEV

An Asprey's silver-plated cocktail shaker, 1930s, 8½in (21.5cm) high.
£450–550
$650–800 ⊞ ASA

A French silver-plated lift-arm lighter, c1930, 4in (10cm) high.
£50–55
$75–80 ⊞ HarC

A silver-plated hip flask, with raised panel and Art Deco decoration, 1930s, 3¾in (9.5cm) high.
£40–45
$60–65 ⊞ BEV

A silver-plated bottle opener in the shape of a donkey, 1930, 3½in (9cm) high.
£30–40
$45–60 ⊞ BEV

A silver-plated double measure, with a golf ball centrepiece, 1930s, 4¾in (12cm) high.
£30–35
$45–50 ⊞ BEV

A set of six silver-coloured metal Cannes oyster spoons, by Jean E. Puiforcat, each with maker's monogram, c1930, 5in (12.5cm) long.
£800–950
$1,200–1,400 ⚒ S

A Union Castle passenger ship's silver-plated sugar bowl, c1930, 4in (10cm) high.
£60–70
$90–100 ⊞ NC

A Stratton silver-plated Princess compact, with metal gravure Old Master design on lid and automatic opening inner lid, c1960, 3in (7.5cm) diam, with original figured grosgrain pouch.
£30–40
$45–60 PC

◄ A silver-plated miniature tea set, 20thC, largest 1in (2.5cm) high.
£40–45
$60–65 ⊞ TAC

Biscuit Boxes

◄ **A silver-plated biscuit barrel,** by Elkington & Co, decorated with figures in high relief, the hinged cover embossed with an ale-drinking figure sitting on a barrel, the spreading base with a band of flowers and leaves, 1874, 8¼in (21cm) high.
£330–360
$450–500 ✗ P(EA)

▶ **A glass biscuit box,** with silver-plated base and top, c1890, 7in (18cm) high.
£300–350
$450–500 ⊞ DIC

A Victorian folding double shell-shaped biscuit box, with pierced liner, cast rustic branch stand and handle, late 19thC, 8in (20.5cm) wide.
£380–440
$550–650 ✗ N

Candelabra & Candlesticks

A silver-plated-on-copper telescopic candlestick, 19thC, 11in (28cm) high extended.
£90–120
$130–180 ⊞ CoHA

A pair of silver-plated candelabra, each adapting with four or two branches, 19thC, 19in (48.5cm) high.
£1,300–1,500
$1,900–2,200 ⊞ DN

A Regency silver-plated telescopic candlestick, 19thC, 10in (25.5cm) high extended.
£80–90
$115–130 ⊞ AnSh

◄ **A pair of silver-plated candlesticks,** late 19thC, 12¼in (31cm) high.
£250–300
$350–450 ⊞ SPU

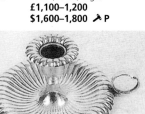

A pair of silver-plated chambersticks, c1900, 5in (12.5cm) diam.
£45–55
$60–80 ⊞ PSA

A pair of silver-plated candlesticks, the shaped triangular bases applied with three swans with shell supports, the sconces decorated with acanthus leaves, c1870, 6¼in (16cm) high.
£1,100–1,200
$1,600–1,800 ✗ P

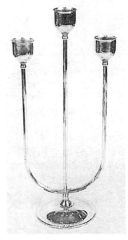

A pair of Art Deco silver-plated candelabra, 1930s, 12¼in (31cm) high.
£85–95
$120–140 ⊞ BET

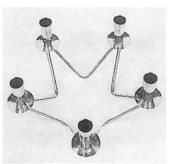

An Art Deco silver-plated candelabrum, 1930s, 10in (25.5cm) diam.
£50–60
$75–100 ⊞ BET

A pair of silver-plated four-light candelabra, the bases with two dolphin supports to the sphere and foliate column stems, with fine chain decoration, 21¼in (54.5cm) high.
£800–850
$1,200–1,300 ✗ L

Centrepieces

A pair of Victorian silver-plated comports, by Elkington & Co, the latticed tops with grape and leaf borders, supported by vine stems on stepped bases, date codes for 1845, 10½in (26.5cm) diam.
£1,200–1,700
$1,750–2,500 ⚖ HOLL

A silver-plated centrepiece épergne, the circular frame with ropework borders, the cut-glass bowl with wirework support, a framework supporting a dome with stiff-leaf decoration surmounted by a leafy knop finial, flanked by four branches each supporting a cut-glass bowl, raised on reeded claw feet, c1800, 14in (35.5cm) high.
£1,200–1,500
$1,750–2,250 ⚖ P

A 19thC silver-plated centrepiece, the central basket above a column formed by three semi-draped classical females, one branch incomplete, 21½in (54.5cm) high.
£700–800
$1,000–1,200 ⚖ MJB

A pair of silver-plated centrepieces, by Elkington & Co, modelled as palm trees with a deer and giraffe, marked for 1857, 18in (45.5cm) high.
£1,350–1,500
$2,000–2,200 ⚖ RBB

A Victorian silver-plated centrepiece, 17¼in (44cm) high.
£440–480
$650–700 ⚖ CGC

▶ **A Secessionist silver-plated metal and glass centrepiece,** with boat-shaped stand decorated with classical scenes, glass liner, stamped marks, inscribed in Swedish 'Julius Rohlen on his 50th Birthday, 27–10–1923', 1920–23, 18¼in (46.5cm) long.
£220–260
$320–380 ⚖ P(Ba)

A late Victorian silver-plated centrepiece, 24in (61cm) high.
£800–1,000
$1,200–1,500 ⊞ CoHA

Claret Jugs

◀ **A claret jug,** engraved with birds and flowers, with silver-plated mount, c1870, 12in (30.5cm) high.
£900–1,000
$1,300–1,500 ⊞ CB

▶ **A Victorian glass claret jug,** wheel-engraved with grapevine detail, with engraved silver-plated mounts and scrolled handle, c1875, 11in (28cm) high.
£230–260
$350–400 ⚖ GAK

A silver plate and glass claret jug, designed by Christopher Dresser, with vertical ivory rod handle and flat-hinged cover, maker's mark of Hukin and Heath, c1881, 8½in (21.5cm) high.
£1,650–1,800
$2,400–2,600 ⚖ S(NY)

Cutlery

A pair of silver-plated fish servers, with Japanese *Shibayama* handles, c1880, 12½in (32cm) long.
£550–650
$800–1,000 ⊞ SFL

A Victorian silver-plated flan slice, with ivory handle, 7¼in (18.5cm) long.
£15–20
$20–30 ⊞ TAC

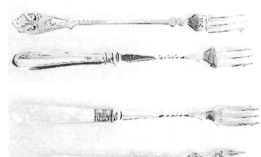

Two Victorian silver-plated pickle forks, with mother-of-pearl handles, longest 7½in (19cm).
£12–28
$15–40 each ⊞ TAC

A silver-plated jam spoon, c1910, 6½in (16.5cm) long.
£12–15
$15–20 ⊞ FMN

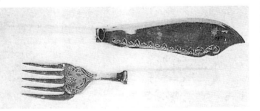

▶ **A canteen of silver-plated cutlery,** by Mappin & Webb, comprising 123 pieces, contained in two fitted drawers of a bow front walnut cabinet with claw-and-ball feet.
£1,200–1,700
$1,750–2,500 ↗ L

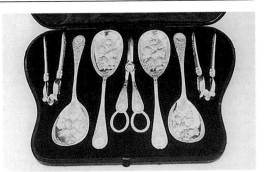

A set of four silver-plated fruit serving spoons, two grape shears and two pairs of nutcrackers, all with matching ornate handles, the serving spoons with gilt bowls, c1880, in a case.
£200–250
$300–350 ↗ GAK

▶ **A set of five silver-plated fruit spoons,** by Mappin & Webb, c1890.
£300–350
$450–500 ⊞ DIC

◀ **Two pickle forks,** one Victorian, silver-plated, with engraved handle, 7¼in (18.5cm) long, the other silver-handled, Sheffield 1917, 7½in (19cm) long.
£10–22
$15–30 each ⊞ TAC

Two Victorian silver-plated bread forks, one with ivory handle 8½in (21.5cm) long, the other with ebony handle 9¾in (25cm) long.
£35–45
$50–65 each ⊞ TAC

A silver-plated jam spoon, by Walker and Hall, c1920, 6¼in (16cm) long.
£15–18
$20–30 ⊞ FMN

◀ **A silver-plated fish knife and fork,** with bone handles, 1930s, 8in (20.5cm) high.
£35–40
$50–60 ⊞ BET

A silver-plated commemorative teaspoon, with enamelled terminal inscribed 'Canada' and embossed city scene on bowl, 4½in (11.5cm) long.
£9–10
$10–15 ⊞ TRE

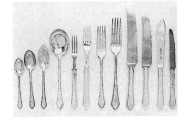

Decanters

▶ **A silver-plated stand,** with three spirit decanters, c1840, decanters 6¼in (16cm) high.
£450–500
$650–750 ⊞ **Som**

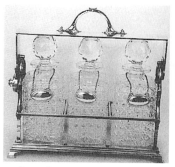

A silver-plated tantalus, with three cut-glass decanters, c1890, 13½in (34.5cm) high.
£700–800
$1,000–1,200 ⊞ **JIL**

Miller's is a price GUIDE not a price LIST

A silver-plated tantalus, with three cut-glass decanters, c1890, 12in (30.5cm) long.
£900–1,000
$1,300–1,500 ⊞ **GAS**

▶ **A silvered-bronze tantalus,** by Jacques Adnet, the glass bottles by Baccarat, c1935, 13in (33cm) wide.
£1,400–1,600
$2,000–2,300 ⊞ **ART**

Decorative Arts

A W. M. F. silver-plated pewter and glass bud dish, pierced and chased with rose-heads, the cut-glass liner etched with similar roses, stamped marks, c1905, 5¾in (14.5cm) wide.
£200–225
$300–350 ⊞ **DAD**

◀ **A silver-plated brass basket,** by the Wiener Werkstätte, with square perforations, impressed marks, c1905, 10½in (26.5cm) high.
£2,800–3,200
$4,000–4,700 ⚒ **DORO**

A W. M. F. silver-plated easel mirror, with classical female piper flanking bevelled plate, c1900, 16½in (42cm) high.
£1,000–1,200
$1,500–1,750 ⚒ **RBB**

A French silver-plated and green Bakelite bracelet, stamped 'Deposé', 1930s, 1¾in (4.5cm) high.
£220–250
$320–360 ⊞ **LBe**

◀ **An Art Deco silvered metal purse,** the mount and the belt hook cast in the shape of a bat with outstretched wings, set with green diamanté, 4in (10cm) wide.
£300–400
$450–550 ⚒ **CSK**

An Art Deco silver-plated fruit bowl, with Bakelite handles, 1930s, 11in (28cm) diam.
£120–150
$175–220 ⊞ **BET**

Dishes

A William IV silver-plated meat dome and warming stand, with loop handle and gadrooned border, on ball feet, 16in (40.5cm) wide.
£450–500
$650–750 ⊞ LHA

A Victorian silver-plated butter dish, in the shape of a boater, c1860, 3in (7.5cm) high.
£400–500
$600–750 ⊞ SFL

A pair of silver-plated fruit dishes, by Elkington & Co, in the shape of vine leaves with grapes, 1881, 13in (33cm) wide.
£350–400
$500–600 ⊞ DIC

A set of four silver-plated entrée dishes, with gadrooned borders and crests, foliate handles, 19thC, 11in (28cm) long.
£650–750
$950–1,100 ⚒ DN

A Victorian silver-plated covered turkey platter, with leaf and bead motif on the border, on scroll feet, 18in (45.5cm) high.
£600–650
$870–970 ⊞ LHA

A Victorian silver-plated breakfast dish, the revolving cover with floral decoration, on scroll feet, 15½in (39.5cm) long.
£260–300
$380–440 ⚒ Gam

A Victorian Renaissance-revival style silver-plated revolving tureen, by Mappin & Webb, with plain and pierced liners, on foliate scroll legs with lion's masks and paw feet, Sheffield/London, late 19thC, 13in (33cm) long.
£220–280
$320–420 ⚒ RIT

A Mappin & Webb silver-plated revolving tureen, with ivory handle, c1930s, 12½in (32cm) long.
£260–300
$380–450 ⊞ TAC

A Swedish silver-plated dish, 1930s, 9in (23cm) diam.
£50–60
$75–90 ⊞ MARK

◄ **A silver-plated soup tureen,** with gadrooned rim, two reeded acanthus scroll handles, the domed cover surmounted by a floral acanthus scroll handle, on four acanthus and paw feet, 16½in (42cm) long.
£650–700
$950–1,000 ⚒ SLN

A revolving silver-plated bacon dish, with drainer and liner, on four legs with rams' head masks, on bun feet, damaged, 19in (48.5cm) long.
£420–480
$600–700 ⚒ LF

A pair of silver-plated lidded sauce tureens, with gadrooned borders, on four scroll feet, 5½in (14cm) high.
£400–450
$580–650 ⚒ L

Two silver-plated and crested game dish covers, engraved with crests, largest 21in (53.5cm) long.
£270–320
$400–450 ⚒ MEA

Tea & Coffee Pots

A Regency-style silver-plated tea urn, the upturned foliate scroll handles and spigot with ivory knob, chased all over with foliate scroll motifs centering vacant cartouches, probably Sheffield c1830, 14¾in (37.5cm) high.
£400–450
$600–650 ⚲ RIT

A late Victorian electroplated tea and coffee service, possibly by Stacy, Henry and Horton of Sheffield, inscribed mark on underside, 19½in (49.5cm) wide.
£1,400–1,600
$2,000–2,300 ⚲ HCC

A silver-plated engraved coffee pot, c1870, 11in (28cm) high.
£300–350
$450–500 ⊞ DIC

A late Victorian teapot for China tea, by Hukin and Heath, the sides engraved with the Willow pattern, the flat hinged cover with a seated Chinaman finial, scroll wood handle.
£200–240
$300–350 ⚲ WW

▶ **An electroplated five-piece tea and coffee service,** tray 24in (61cm) long.
£900–1,200
$1,300–1,800 ⚲ Bea

A Victorian silver-plated coffee pot, engraved with arabesque and scroll patterns, scroll handle, greyhound finial to lid, c1850, 8½in (21.5cm) high.
£110–120
$160–180 ⚲ GAK

A late Victorian silver-plated teapot, 6½in (16.5cm) high.
£30–40
$40–60 ⊞ WN

Toast Racks

▶ **A Victorian White Star Line silver-plated toast rack,** 4in (10cm) wide.
£25–30
$35–45 ⚲ CaC

A silver-plated toast rack, with crossed cricket bats, stumps and a cricket belt, c1870, 7¼in (18.5cm) long.
£170–200
$250–300 ⊞ MSh

A silver-plated four-division toast rack, modelled as a car, c1900, 6in (15cm) long.
£250–275
$350–400 ⊞ SFL

LOCATE THE SOURCE
The source of each illustration in Miller's can be found by checking the code letters below each caption with the Key to Illustrations, pages 311–314.

◀ **A silver-plated toast rack,** c1900, 7in (18cm) high.
£55–65
$80–100 ⊞ ASAA

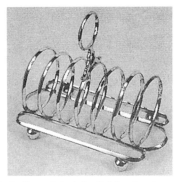

A silver-plated six-division toast rack, on ball supports, c1900, 6¾in (17cm) wide.
£35–40
$50–60 ⊞ PSA

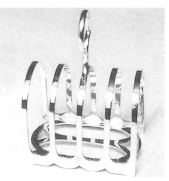

A silver-plated four-division toast rack, by Walker and Hall, c1910, 4in (10cm) long.
£45–55
$60–80 ⊞ ABr

A silver-plated four-division toast rack, 1920s, 3¼in (8.5cm) long.
£25–35
$30–50 ⊞ PSA

Trophies

A silvered bronzed model of Hippocampus, c1862, 9½in (24cm) high.
£250–280
$350–400 ⊞ SUC
Hippocampus was the steed of Neptune, Roman god of the sea. The mythical sea creature has the head and forelegs of a horse and the hindquarters and tail of a fish.

A silver-plated souvenir loving cup, from SS *Oxfordshire*, Bibby Line, 1920s, 1½in (4cm) high.
£18–20
$25–30 ⊞ BAf

◀ **A silvered spelter tennis trophy,** 1920s, 11in (28cm) high.
£150–200
$220–300 ⊞ WaR

A silver-plated two-handled trophy, inscribed 'The West Heath Dancing Cup, presented by Betty Vacani', on a turned stem with circular foot, on an ebonized plinth, 1958, 6½in (16.5cm) high.
£7,000–8,000
$10,250–11,500 ⊞ GOR
This cup was awarded to Lady Diana Spencer in 1976.

Writing

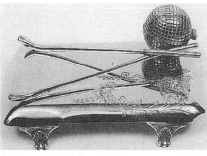

A silver-plated bird inkwell, c1870, 6in (15cm) high.
£250–300
$350–450 ⊞ BWA

A silver-plated inkwell, with two crossed clubs as a pen rest, and a mesh pattern ball as the well, c1890, 6¾in (17cm) long.
£180–220
$250–350 ⊞ MSh

▶ **An Art Nouveau silver-plated-on-copper double inkwell,** Germany c1900, 10in (25.5cm) long.
£450–550
$650–800 ⊞ ANO

A mid-European silver-plated desk seal, late 19thC, 4in (10cm) high.
£250–285
$350–425 ⊞ ChA

Glossary

acanthus: Classical ornament in the form of stylized leaf decoration based on the scalloped leaves of the acanthus plant.

amorini: Cupids or cherubs used in decoration.

annealing: Process for restoring the malleability of silver made brittle by hammering. The metal is heated until red hot and then immersed in cold water.

anthemion: Stylized ornament derived from classical architecture based on the honeysuckle flower.

applied work: Wire, moulding or cast pieces made separately and soldered on to the main body of a piece, to ornament or strengthen it.

armorial: Engraved crest or coat-of-arms.

assay: Testing metal to establish its purity.

baluster: Bulbous pillar shape, commonly used for vases, jugs and teapots, finials and the stems of some candlesticks and drinking vessels.

beading: Decorative border of tiny compact beads, either cast and applied or embossed.

beaker: A cup without stem, handle or cover, usually cylindrical in form.

biggin: A small coffee pot, with stand and heater for keeping coffee warm.

bleeding bowl: A shallow circular bowl with a single flat pierced handle.

brandy bowl: Wide, shallow silver bowl with handles used for warming and serving brandy.

bright-cut decoration: Type of engraving whereby the metal surface is cut creating facets that reflect the light.

Britannia standard: Higher standard of British silver used between 1697 and 1720; contains 95.8 per cent pure silver.

burnishing: Method of polishing metals by rubbing the surface with a hard smooth tool made of agate, to create a lustre.

caddy spoon: Spoon for taking a measure of tea from a caddy.

can or cann: A mug; the term is more common in the US.

candelabrum: Candlestick with arms and nozzles for two or more candles.

candlestick: Normally a single candleholder on a stem of columnar or **baluster** form.

canteen: A travelling set of knife, fork and spoon and perhaps beaker and small box.

caster: Vessel with a pierced cover, or sprinkling salt, sugar or ground pepper, usually in vase or similar form and often made in sets of three.

cartouche: Decorative shield, normally engraved, embossed or cast, and generally containing an inscription or coat-of-arms.

caster: Vessel with a pierced cover, for sprinkling salt, sugar or ground pepper, often made in sets of three.

casting: Process for making metal objects or their components, whereby molten metal is poured into a mould and then soldered to other parts.

chafing dish: Any dish which is provided with some means for keeping the food warm, such as a bowl for burning charcoal or a small lamp.

chalice: A large standing cup for wine in the Roman Catholic mass.

chamberstick: Utilitarian candlestick with a short stem and saucer-like base with a handle.

champlevé: Enamelling on metal, similar to **cloisonné**, in which a glass paste is applied to the hollowed-out design, fired and ground smooth.

chasing: Method of decorating silver using hammers and punches to push metal into a relief pattern; metal is displaced not removed.

chinoiserie: European fashion for decorating silver with Oriental figures and scenes, prevalent in the late 17thC and again in the mid-18thC.

chocolate pot: Similar to coffee pot but with a little lid in the cover through which a swizzle stick can be inserted for stirring the chocolate.

cloisonné: Enamelling on metal with divisions in the design separated by lines of fine metal wire. A speciality of the Limoges region of France in the Middle Ages, and of Chinese craftsmen to the present day.

coin silver: Silver of the standard used for coinage, ie .925 or sterling.

condiment: Small pot, often with glass or ceramic liner, for salt, pepper, mustard, etc.

cream jug: Small jug made in many forms in the 18th and 19thC, when cream was drunk with tea and coffee.

crest: Heraldic device surmounting a coat-of-arms, used to denote ownership.

cruet: Originally the vessels used for wine and water in the Christian ritual, later the collective term for a set of salt, pepper, oil and vinegar dispensers in a stand.

cut-card decoration: Flat shapes of applied silver used as decoration and for reinforcement.

diaper: Surface decoration composed of repeated diamonds or squares, often carved in low relief.

die-stamping: Method of pressing sheet silver between solid dies with complementary patterns to create or decorate an item.

dish cross: An 18thC device for keeping dishes warm, consisting of a central lamp with adjustable arms capable of holding dishes of various sizes.

engraving: Decorative patterns cut into the silver surface using a sharp tool; metal is actually removed.

entrée dish: A dish with a cover, sometimes made with a stand for a lamp.

épergne: Centrepiece consisting of a central bowl and several small detachable bowls to display and serve fruit and sweetmeats.

erasure: Removal of an existing coat-of-arms that is sometimes replaced by new arms.

étui: Small slim case for containing articles like scissors and needles, for ladies.

ewer: Large jug with a lip that is often part of a set including a basin.

faceted: Decorative surface cut into sharp-edged planes in a criss-cross pattern to reflect the light.

filigree: Openwork silver or gold wire panels.

finial: Decorative turned knob.

flagon: A tall type of tankard, uncommon after the mid-18thC, for beer or other liquor. They usually follow contemporary tankards in style.

flat chasing: Chasing on a flat silver surface, leaving an impression of the punched pattern on the back.

flatware: All flat and shallow tableware, such as plates and salvers, but more specifically applied to spoons and forks.

fluting: Pattern of concave grooves repeated in vertical, parallel lines.

gadrooning: Border composed of a succession of alternating lobes and flutes, usually curved. The opposite of **fluting**.

gauge: Thickness of a metal sheet or the diameter of a wire.

ghalian: Part of a hookah or hubble-bubble pipe.

gilding: Process of applying a gold finish to a silver or electroplated object.

goblet: A large wine cup.

hallmarks: Marks on silver that indicate it has been passed at assay. The term derives from the Goldsmiths' Hall, London, where the marks were struck.

hollow ware: Any hollow vessels, such as bowls and teapots.

knop: Decorative knob on lids, or the bulbous moulding, usually placed at the mid-point of the stem of a cup or candlestick.

kogo: A small incense box.

kovsch: Russian vessel used for measuring drink, often highly decorated for ornamental purposed from the late 18thC.

liner: Inner sleeve of a vessel, made of silver, plate or glass.

loading: System for strengthening and stabilizing hollow objects, such as **candlesticks** or candelabra, whereby an iron rod is secured inside the body using pitch or plaster of Paris.

martelé: Term for silverware with a fine, hammered surface first produced in France and later revived by the American silversmiths Gorham Manufacturing Co during the Art Nouveau period.

matting: Non-shiny texture produced by punching small dots or circles closely over the surface, commonly found contrasting with highly burnished surfaces.

mazarine: A flat pierced plate for straining food.

mazer: A silver-mounted wooden bowl on a foot. They were used for drink in the Middle Ages

monteith: Cooler for wine glasses, resembling a **punchbowl**, but with a notched, often detachable, rim to suspend the glasses over iced water.

mote spoon: Small spoon with a pierced bowl used to skim tea leaves, with a spike at the end of the stem to unblock the spout of the teapot.

moulding: Silver decoration cast in a mould.

muffineer: Another name for a **caster**, usually a small one

mug: A drinking vessel with a handle, normally smaller than a tankard and without a lid.

mustard pot: Until the mid-18thC mustard was served dry in a caster with an unpierced top. The more familiar pot for ready-mixed mustard appeared about 1760, usually with a blue glass **liner**.

nef: Highly ornate silver container, usually of German or French origin.

nickel: Any of various white alloys of copper, zinc and nickel used in electroplating as a base for coating with silver.

niello: Compound of silver, lead, copper and sulphur applied to metal and fired to create a shimmering black surface.

nozzle: On a **candlestick**, the detachable top in which the candle is placed.

nulling: Decorative carving in the form of irregular **fluting**.

openwork: **Pierced** decoration.

pap boat: A small oval bowl with a narrow lip for feeding infants or invalids.

parcel-gilt: Silver partially covered with gold.

patera: Small flat circular ornament, often in the form of an open flower or rosette.

patina: Fine, natural sheen of age on the surface of silver.

piercing: Intricate cut decoration, created by using a sharp chisel or fretsaw, and then punched.

plinth: Square base at the bottom of a candlestick column.

porringer: Two-handled dish, sometimes with a lid, originally used to hold porridge or gruel.

pouncebox: Often part of an inkstand, for sprinkling pounce on writing paper to prepare the surface before writing.

punchbowl: A large circular bowl, often with two drop-ring handles, for mixing and serving punch in the 17thC. They were later made as presentation pieces.

qajar: Iranian Dynasty established from 1794–1925.

quaich: A drinking cup with two handles, unique to Scotland.

raising: Process by which a piece of hollow ware is hammered into shape, using **annealed** silver.

rat-tail: Short ridge of silver applied to the back of spoon bowls to reinforce the joint at the handle.

rattles: Found in silver for babies in the 18th and 19thC. They had bells and corals (for teething) attached.

reeding: Decorative moulding composed of narrow parallel convex threadlike forms, usually confined to borders.

repoussé: Term for embossing. Relief decoration on metal is made by hammering from the reverse so that the decoration projects, then is finished from the front by **chasing**.

rococo: decorative style that originated in early 18thC France, characterized by elegant, elaborate decoration.

rolled edge: Edges of Sheffield plate or fused-plate articles were rolled to conceal the copper centre, which would otherwise be visible.

salt: A large ceremonial container for salt which took pride of place on the dining table before the centrepiece or *épergne*. It was gradually replaced in the 17thC by smaller, more convenient trencher salts or salt cellars.

salver: Flat dish, sometimes footed, for serving food or drink; similar to a tray but without handles and often with a moulded border and decorated with an engraved coat-of-arms.

sauce boat: A container for sauce. Early 18thC examples have a lip at each end, later ones are more like a low, elongated jug.

sconce: Candle socket of a **candlestick**. Also, a plate or bracket on the wall to which candle-holders could be attached.

scratchweight: Note made of the weight of a silver article at assay, usually hand engraved lightly on the base or reverse: any change from the original weight may indicate that the piece has been altered or overly polished; with silver in sets, such as plates, the number of the individual piece was often also inscribed on the base, which may help with building up a complete set.

scroll: Curved decoration, particularly used for handles.

shagreen: Untanned leather, originally the skin of the shagri, a Turkish wild ass; now used to refer to any granulated leather.

sheet: Sheet silver and sheet metal describe the panels of silver and plate used primarily in the manufacture of **candlesticks**.

silver-gilt: Solid silver covered with a thin layer of gold.

snuffer: Scissor-like implement for trimming and collecting wicks.

socle: Plinth

solder: Usually of lead, applied to repair cracks and holes.

spinel: Hard glassy minerals minerals occurring as octahedral crystals which are used as gemstones.

standard: Required amount of pure silver in an alloy.

standish: An old name for an inkstand.

sterling silver: British term for silver that is at least 92.5 per cent pure.

stirrup cup: Cup used for drinking prior to making a journey or going hunting, usually shaped as the head of an animal.

tankard: Mug with a hinged cover, usually for beer.

taperstick: Small **candlestick** for holding a taper (thin candle) for lighting pipes and melting wax.

tazza: Wide shallow bowl on a (central) stemmed foot.

teapot: Common from the 18thC, deviating early from the cylindrical form adopted by the coffee pot.

tea urn: Large vase-shaped alternative to the kettle. They had some popularity in the late 18th and 19thC.

tourmaline: Hard glassy minerals occurring in hexagonal crystaline form used in jewellery.

trencher salt: A small salt cellar, usually made in sets, one for each place setting, from the 17thC onwards.

tumbler cup/tumbler: Round-bottomed drinking vessel.

tureen: Large bowl on a foot for serving soup, usually with a cover.

tyg: Mug with three or more handles

vesta case: Ornate case for carrying matches.

vinaigrette: Small silver box with an inner **pierced** lid to hold a sponge soaked in a vinegar.

waiter: Small **salver**, less than 6in (15cm) diam.

wine taster: A small flattish bowl or cup, usually with a raised dome in the base.

Directory of Specialists

If you would like to contact any of the following dealers, we would advise readers to make contact by telephone before a visit, therefore avoiding a wasted journey.

Austria
Dorotheum, Palais Dorotheum, A-1010 Wien Dorotheergasse, 17 1010 Tel: 0043 1 515 600

Berkshire
Dreweatt Neate, Donnington Priory, Donnington, Newbury, RG14 2JE Tel: 01635 553553

Buckinghamshire
Hannah Tel: 01844 237899 Mobile: 07831 800774

Christopher Sykes, The Old Parsonage, Woburn, Milton Keynes, MK17 9QM Tel: 01525 290259

Cambridgeshire
Cheffins, 2 Clifton Road, Cambridge, CB2 4BW Tel: 01223 213343

Canada
Louis Wine Ltd, 140 Yorkville Ave, Toronto, Ontario, M5R 1C2 Tel: (416) 929 9333 www.louiswine.com

Devon
Bearnes, St Edmund's Court, Okehampton Str, Exeter, EX4 1DU Tel: 01392 422800

Timothy Coward Tel: 01271 890466

Gloucestershire
Corner House Antiques and Ffoxe Antiques, High Str, Lechlade, GL7 3AE Tel: 01367 252007

Greater Manchester
A. S. Antiques, 26 Broad Str, Pendleton, Salford, M6 5BY Tel: 0161 737 5938 Mobile: 07836 368230

Hampshire
Romsey Medal Centre, 5 Bell Str, Romsey, SO51 8GY Tel: 01794 324488

Hertfordshire
The Silver Collection Ltd Tel: 01442 890954

Kent
Glassdrumman Antiques, 7 Union Square, The Pantiles, Tunbridge Wells, TN4 8HE Tel: 01892 538615

Pantiles Spa Antiques, 4, 5 & 6 Union House, The Pantiles, Tunbridge Wells, TN4 8HE Tel: 01892 541377 Mobile: 07711 283655

Lincolnshire
Art Nouveau Originals, Stamford Antiques, Stamford, PE9 1PX Tel: 01780 762605

London
Amherst Antiques, Monomark House, 27 Old Gloucester Str, WC1N 3XX Mobile: 07850 350212

Antique Silver Vault, 31/32 London Silver Vaults, 53–65 Chancery Lane, WC2A 1QT Tel: 020 7430 1254

Argenteus Ltd, The London Silver Vaults, 53–65 Chancery Lane, WC2A 1QS Tel: 020 7831 3637 www.rfeldman.co.uk

A.H. Baldwin & Sons Ltd, 11 Adelphi Terrace, WC2N 6BJ Tel: 020 7930 6879

Paul Bennett, 48A George Str, W1H 5RF Tel: 020 7935 1555

Bentley & Skinner Ltd, 8 New Bond Str, W1Y 0SL Tel: 020 7629 0651

Daniel Bexfield, 26 Burlington Arcade, W1V 9AD Tel: 020 7491 1720 www.bexfield.co.uk

N. Bloom & Son Ltd, Bond Street Antiques Centre, 124 Bond Str, W1S 1DX Tel: 020 7629 5060 www.nbloom.co.uk

Bonhams & Brooks, Montpelier Str, Knightsbridge, SW7 1HH Tel: 020 7393 3900

John Bull (Antiques) Ltd, JB Silverware, 139a New Bond Str, W1Y 9FB Tel: 020 7629 1251 Mobile: 07850 221 468

Mary Cooke Antiques Ltd, 12 The Old Power Station, 121 Mortlake High Str, SW14 8SN Tel: 020 8876 5777

Didier Antiques, 58–60 Kensington Church Str, W8 4DB Tel: 020 7938 2537 Mobile: 07836 232634

Dix-Noonan-Webb, 1 Old Bond Str, W1X 3TD Tel: 020 7499 5022

I Franks, London Silver Vaults, 53–65 Chancery Lane, WC2A 1QS Tel: 020 7242 4035 www.ifranks.com

Hilltop Cottage Antiques, 101 Portobello Road, W11 Tel: 01451 844362 Mobile: 07773 658082

Koopman Ltd, The London Silver Vaults, 53–65 Chancery Lane, WC2A 1QS Tel: 020 7242 7624

Langfords, Vaults 8 & 10, London Silver Vaults, 53–65 Chancery Lane, WC2A 1QS Tel: 020 7242 5506 www.langfords.com

Sanda Lipton Tel: 020 7431 0866 www.antique-silver.com

Marks Antiques, 49 Curzon Str, W1Y 7RE Tel: 020 7499 1788 www.marksantiques.com

Nortonbury Antiques, BMC Box 5345, WC1N 3XX Tel: 01984 631668 Mobile: 07774 174092

Percy's (Silver) Ltd, London Silver Vaults, 53–65 Chancery Lane, WC2A 1QS Tel: 020 7242 3618 www.percys-silver.com

Phillips, 101 New Bond Str, W1Y 0AS Tel: 020 7629 6602

Piers Rankin, 14 Camden Passage, N1 8ED Tel: 020 7354 3349

Schredds of Portobello, 107 Portobello Road, W11 2QB Tel: 020 8348 3314 www.schredds.com

Shapiro & Co, Stand 380, Gray's Antique Market, 58 Davies Str, W1Y 5LP Tel: 020 7491 2710

The Silver Fund Ltd, 40 Bury Str, St James's, SW1Y 6AU Tel: 020 7839 7664

Sotheby's, 34–35 New Bond Str, W1A 2AA Tel: 020 7293 5000

William Walter Antiques Ltd, London Silver Vaults, 53–65 Chancery Lane, WC2A 1QS Tel: 020 7242 3248 www.williamwalter.co.uk

Nottinghamshire
Neales, 192 Mansfield Road, Nottingham, NG1 3HU Tel: 0115 962 4141

Oxfordshire
Payne & Son, 131 High Str, Oxford, OX1 4DH Tel: 01865 243787

Republic of Ireland
James Adam & Sons, 26 St Stephen's Green, Dublin 2 Tel: 00 3531 676 0261

Hamilton Osborne King, 4 Main Str, Blackrock, Co Dublin Tel: 353 1 288 5011

Mealy's, Chatsworth Str, Castle Comer, Co Kilkenny Tel: 00 353 56 41229

The Silver Shop, Powerscourt Townhouse Centre, St Williams Str, Dublin 2 Tel: 00 3531 6794147

J. W. Weldon, 55 Clarendon Str, Dublin 2 Tel: 00 353 1 677 1638

Scotland
Bow Well Antiques, 103 West Bow, Edinburgh, EH1 2JP Tel: 0131 225 3335

Decorative Arts @ Doune, Stand 26, Scottish Antique and Arts Centre, By Doune, Stirling, FK16 6HD Tel: 01786 461 439 Mobile: 07778 475 974

Lyon & Turnbull, 33 Broughton Place, Edinburgh, EH1 3RR Tel: 0131 557 8844

Phillips Scotland, The Beacon, 176 St Vincent Str, Glasgow, G2 5SG Tel: 0141 223 8866

Phillips Scotland, 65 George Str, Edinburgh, EH2 2JL Tel: 0131 225 2266

Shropshire
Teme Valley Antiques, 1 The Bull Ring, Ludlow, SY8 1AD Tel: 01584 874686

Somerset
ASA Antiques, 5–10 Bartlett Str, Bath, BA1 2QZ Tel: 01225 312781

D & B Dickinson, The Antique Shop, 22 & 22a New Bond Str, Bath, BA1 1BA Tel: 01225 466502

Surrey
S & A Thompson Tel: 01306 711970

East Sussex
Gorringes Auction Galleries, Terminus Road, Bexhill-on-Sea, TN39 3LR Tel: 01424 212994

Gorringes inc Julian Dawson, 15 North Str, Lewes, BN7 2PD Tel: 01273 472503

West Sussex
Nicholas Shaw Antiques, Great Grooms Antiques Centre, Parbrook, Billingshurst, RH14 9EU Tel: 01403 786656/01403 785731 Mobile: 07785 643000

Sotheby's Sussex, Summers Place, Billingshurst, RH14 9AD Tel: 01403 833500

Rupert Toovey & Co Ltd, Star Road, Partridge Green, RH13 8RA Tel: 01403 711744

U.S.A.
Argentum, 414 Jackson Str, San Francisco, CA 94111 Tel: 001 415 296 7757

Butterfields, 220 San Bruno Avenue, San Francisco, CA 94103 Tel: 00 1 415 861 7500

Hartman Rare Art Inc, 306 East 61st Str, New York 10021 Tel: 001 212 207 3800

Imperial Half Bushel, 831 North Howard Str, Baltimore, Maryland 21201 Tel: 001 410 462 1192

R & P Kassai, LLC, 14W 45th Str, New York 10036 Tel: 001 212 302 7010 www.kassai.com

The McNally Company Antiques, 6033-L&M Paeso Delicias, PO Box 1048, Rancho Santa Fe, California 92067 Tel: 001 858 756 1922 www.mcnallycompanyantiques.com

New Orleans Auction Galleries, Inc, 801 Magazine Str, AT 510 Julia, New Orleans, Louisiana 70130 Tel: 00 1 504 566 1849

M.S.Rau, 630 Royal Str, New Orleans, LA 70130 Tel: 001 504 523 5660 www.rauantiques.com

Jolie Shelton, 1326 West Pinhook Road, Lafayette, Louisiana 70503 Tel: 001 337 237 3000

Skinner Inc, 357 Main Str, Bolton, MA 01740 Tel: 00 1 978 779 6241

Sloan's Auctioneers & Appraisers, Miami Gallery, 8861 NW 18th Terrace, Suite 100, Miami, Florida 33172 Tel: 00 1 305 592 2575/800 660 4524

Sotheby's, 1334 York Avenue, New York, NY 10021 Tel: 00 1 212 606 7000

Wakefield-Scearce Galleries, 525 Washington Str, Shelbyville, Kentucky 40065 Tel: 001 502 633 4382 www.Wakefield-Scearce.com

Warwickshire
The Antique Shop, 30 Henley Str, Stratford-Upon-Avon, CV37 6QW Tel: 01789 292485

West Midlands
Frank H. Fellows & Sons, Augusta House, 19 Augusta Str, Hockley, Birmingham, B18 6JA Tel: 0121 212 2131

Wiltshire
Woolley & Wallis, Salisbury Salerooms, 51–61 Castle Str, Salisbury, SP1 3SU Tel: 01722 424500

Worcestershire
Howards of Broadway, 27A High Str, Broadway, WR12 7DP Tel: 01386 858924

Key to Illustrations

Each illustration and descriptive caption is accompanied by a letter code. By referring to the following list of auctioneers (denoted by *) and dealers (•) the source of any item may be immediately determined. Please note that inclusion of an item in this book does not guarantee that the item, or any similar item, is available for sale from the contributor. Advertisers are denoted by †.

If you require a valuation for an item, it is advisable to check whether the dealer or specialist will carry out this service and if there is a charge. Please mention Miller's when making an enquiry. Having found a specialist who will carry out your valuation it is best to send a photograph and description of the item to the specialist together with a stamped addressed envelope for the reply. A valuation by telephone is not possible. Most dealers are only too happy to help you with your enquiry. However, they are very busy people and consideration of the above points would be welcomed.

A&A • Antiques & Art, 116 State Street, Portsmouth, NH 03802 U.S.A. Tel: 603 431 3931

AAV * Academy Auctioneers & Valuers, Northcote House, Northcote Avenue, Ealing, London W5 3UR Tel: 020 8579 7466 www.thesaurus.co.uk/academy/

ABB * Abbotts Auction Rooms, Campsea Ashe, Woodbridge, Suffolk IP13 0PS. Tel: 01728 746323

ABr No longer trading

AEF • A & E Foster Tel: 01494 562024

AG * Anderson & Garland (Auctioneers), Marlborough House, Marlborough Crescent, Newcastle-upon-Tyne, Tyne & Wear NE1 4EE Tel: 0191 232 6278

AH * Andrew Hartley, Victoria Hall Salerooms, Little Lane, Ilkley, Yorkshire LS29 8EA Tel: 01943 816363 ahartley.finearts@talk21.com

ALiN • Andrew Lineham Fine Glass, The Mall, Camden Passage, London N1 8ED Tel: 020 7704 0195/ 01243 576241 Mobile: 07767 702722 www.andrewlineham.co.uk

AMH • Amherst Antiques, Monomark House, 27 Old Gloucester Street, London WC1N 3XX Mobile: 07850 350212 amherstantiques@monomark.co.uk

ANG • Ancient & Gothic, Bournemouth, Dorset BH7 6JT Tel: 01202 431721

ANO • Art Nouveau Originals, Stamford Antiques, Stamford, Lincolnshire PE9 1PX Tel: 01780 762605 anoc@compuserve.com

AnS • The Antique Shop, 30 Henley Street, Stratford-Upon-Avon, Warwickshire CV37 6QW Tel: 01789 292485

AnSh No longer trading

ANT • Anthemion, Cartmel, Grange Over Sands, Cumbria LA11 6QD Tel: 015395 36295 Mobile: 07768 443757

ARE • Arenski, The Coach House, Ledbury Mews North, Notting Hill, London W11 2AF Tel: 020 7727 8599/020 7229 9575 arenski@netcomuk.co.uk www.arenski.com

ART • Artemis Decorative Arts Ltd, 36 Kensington Church Street, London W8 4BX Tel: 020 7376 0377/020 7939 9900 Artemis.w8@btinternet.com

ASA • A. S. Antiques, 26 Broad Street, Pendleton, Salford, Greater Manchester M6 5BY Tel: 0161 737 5938 Mobile: 07836 368230 as@sternshine.demon.co.uk

ASAA • ASA Antiques, 5–10 Bartlett Street, Bath, Somerset BA1 2QZ Tel: 01225 312781

ATQ • Antiquarius Antiques, 131/141 King's Road, Chelsea, London SW3 5ST Tel: 020 7351 5353 antique@dial.pipex.com

B * Boardman Fine Art Auctioneers, Station Road Corner, Haverhill, Suffolk CB9 0EY Tel: 01440 730414

B&B * See **BB(S)**

B&L * Bonhams and Langlois, Westaway Chambers, 39 Don Street, St Helier, Jersey JE2 4TR Channel Islands Tel: 01534 22441

BaN • Barbara Ann Newman, London House Antiques, 4 Market Square, Westerham, Kent TN16 1AW Tel: 01959 564479

BAf • Books Afloat, 66 Park Street, Weymouth, Dorset DT4 7DE Tel: 01305 779774

Bal • A.H. Baldwin & Sons Ltd, 11 Adelphi Terrace, London WC2N 6BJ Tel: 020 7930 6879

BB(S) * Butterfields, 220 San Bruno Avenue, San Francisco, CA 94103 U.S.A. Tel: 00 1 415 861 7500

Bea * Bearnes, 1 Southernhay West, Exeter, Devon EX1 1JG Tel: 01392 219040

Bea(E) * Bearnes, St Edmund's Court, Okehampton Street, Exeter, Devon EX4 1DU Tel: 01392 422800

BET • Beth, GO 43–44, Alfies Antique Market, 13–25 Church Street, Marylebone, London NW8 8DT Tel: 020 7723 5613

BEV • Beverley, 30 Church Street, Marylebone, London NW8 8EP Tel: 020 7262 1576

BEX •† Daniel Bexfield, 26 Burlington Arcade, London W1V 9AD Tel: 020 7491 1720 antiques@bexfield.co.uk www.bexfield.co.uk

BGA • By George Antique Centre, 23 George Street, St Albans, Hertfordshire AL3 4ES Tel: 01727 853032

BHA • Bourbon-Hanby Antiques Centre, 151 Sydney Street, Chelsea, London SW3 6NT Tel: 020 7352 2106

BHa • Judy & Brian Harden Antiques, PO Box 14, Bourton-on-the-Water, Cheltenham, Gloucestershire GL54 2YR Tel: 01451 810684

BKK • Bona Art Deco Store, The Hart Shopping Centre, Fleet, Hampshire GU13 8AZ Tel: 01252 616666

Bon * Bonhams & Brooks, Montpelier Street, Knightsbridge, London SW7 1HH Tel: 020 7393 3900 www.bonhams.com

Bon(G) * Bonhams & Martel Maides Ltd, Allez St Auction Rooms, 29 High Street, St Peter Port, Guernsey GY1 4NY Channel Islands Tel: 01481 713463/722700

Bon(M) * Bonhams & Brooks, St Thomas's Place, Hillgate, Stockport, Greater Manchester SK1 3TZ Tel: 0161 429 8283

BQ • The Button Queen, 19 Marylebone Lane, London W1M 5FE Tel: 020 7935 1505

BR * Bracketts, Auction Hall, The Pantiles, Tunbridge Wells, Kent TN1 1UU Tel: 01892 544500 www.bfaa.co.uk

Bri * Bristol Auction Rooms, St John's Place, Apsley Road, Clifton, Bristol BS8 2ST Tel: 0117 973 7201 www.bristolauctionrooms.co.uk

BSA • Bartlett Street Antiques, 5–10 Bartlett Street, Bath, Somerset BA1 2QZ Tel: 01225 466689

BUK * Bukowskis, Arsenalsgatan 4, Stockholm, Sweden-SE111 47 Tel: 08 614 08 00 / info@bukowskis.se www.bukowskis.se

BWA • Bow Well Antiques, 103 West Bow, Edinburgh, Scotland EH1 2JP Tel: 0131 225 3335

C * Christie, Manson & Wood Ltd, 8 King Street, St James's, London SW1Y 6QT Tel: 020 7839 9060

C(G) * Christie's (International) S.A., 8 Place de la Taconnerie, 1204 Geneva, Switzerland. Tel: 00 4122 319 1766

C(S) * Christie's Scotland Ltd, 164–166 Bath Street, Glasgow G2 4TG Scotland Tel: 0141 332 8134

C(Sc) * See **C(S)**

C(SP) * Christie's, Unit 3 Park Lane, Goodwood Park Hotel, 22 Scotts Road, Singapore Tel: (65) 235 3828

CaC * Cato Crane & Co, Liverpool Auction Rooms, 6 Stanhope Street, Liverpool, Merseyside L8 5RF Tel: 0151 709 5559 www.cato-crane.co.uk

CAG * The Canterbury Auction Galleries, 40 Station Road West, Canterbury, Kent CT2 8AN Tel: 01227 763337

CB • Christine Bridge, 78 Castelnau, London SW13 9EX Tel: 07000 445277

CCG • Cynthia O'Connor Gallery, 17 Duke Street, Dublin 2, Republic of Ireland Tel: 00 353 679 2177.

CDC * Capes Dunn & Co, The Auction Galleries, 38 Charles Street, Off Princess Street, Greater Manchester M1 7DB Tel: 0161 273 6060/1911

CGC * Cheffins, 2 Clifton Road, Cambridge CB2 4BW Tel: 01223 213343 www.cheffins.co.uk

ChA No longer trading

CHe • Chelsea Clocks & Antiques, Stand H3–4, Antiquarius Market, 135 Kings Road, London SW3 4PW Tel: 020 7352 8646

CNY * Christie, Manson & Woods International Inc., 502 Park Avenue, (including Christie's East), New York 10022 U.S.A. Tel: 001 212 636 2000

CoHA •† Corner House Antiques and Ffoxe Antiques, High Street, Lechlade, Gloucestershire GL7 3AE Tel: 01367 252007 jdhis007@btopenworld

CRA • Cranks Antiques, Powerscourt Townhouse Centre, Dublin 2, Republic of Ireland

CS • Christopher Sykes, The Old Parsonage, Woburn, Milton Keynes, Buckinghamshire MK17 9QM Tel: 01525 290259

CSK * Christie's South Kensington Ltd, 85 Old Brompton Road, London SW7 3LD Tel: 020 7581 7611 www.christies.com

DA * Dee, Atkinson & Harrison, The Exchange Saleroom, Driffield, Yorkshire YO25 7LJ Tel: 01377 253151 exchange@dee-atkinson-harrison.co.uk www.dee-atkinson-harrison.co.uk

DAC • Didcot Antiques Centre now Trading as Vetta Decorative Arts, Oxfordshire

DaD No longer trading

DAD • Decorative Arts @ Doune, Stand 26, Scottish Antique and Arts Centre, By Doune, Stirling FK16 6HD Scotland Tel: 01786 461 439 Mobile: 0378 475974 gordonfoster@excite.co.uk

DBA • Douglas Bryan Antiques, The Old Bakery, St Davids Bridge, Cranbrook, Kent TN17 3HN Tel: 01580 713103

DD * David Duggleby, The Vine St Salerooms, Scarborough, Yorkshire YO11 1XN Tel: 01723 507111 auctions@davidduggleby.freeserve.co.uk www.davidduggleby.com

DDM * Dickinson Davy & Markham, Wrawby Street, Brigg, Humberside DN20 8JJ Tel: 01652 653666

DIC • D & B Dickinson, The Antique Shop, 22 & 22a New Bond Street, Bath, Somerset BA1 1BA Tel: 01225 466502

DID • Didier Antiques, 58–60 Kensington Church Street, London W8 4DB Tel: 020 7938 2537 Mobile: 07836 232634

DN * Dreweatt Neate, Donnington Priory, Donnington, Newbury, Berkshire RG14 2JE Tel: 01635 553553 fineart@dreweatt-neate.co.uk

DN(H) * Holloways (RICS), 49 Parsons Street, Banbury, Oxfordshire OX16 5PF Tel: 01295 817777 enquiries@hollowaysauctioneers.co.uk www.hollowaysauctioneers.co.uk

DNW * Dix-Noonan-Webb, 1 Old Bond Street, London W1X 3TD Tel: 020 7499 5022

DOC * Dockree's, Landmark House, 1st Floor, Station Road, Cheadle Hulme, Cheshire SK8 5AT Tel: 0161 485 1258

DORO * Dorotheum, Palais Dorotheum, A-1010 Wien, Dorotheergasse 17, 1010 Austria Tel: 0043 1 515 600

DP • No 7 Antiques, 7 High Street, Dulverton, Somerset TA22 9HB Tel: 01398 324457

DQ • Dolphin Quay Antique Centre, Queen Street, Emsworth, Hampshire PO10 7BU Tel: 01243 379994/37994 www.dolphin-quay-antiques.co.uk

E * Ewbank, Burnt Common Auction Room, London Road, Send, Woking, Surrey GU23 7LN Tel: 01483 223101 www.ewbankauctions.co.uk

EH * Edgar Horn Fine Art Auctioneers, 46–50 South Street, Eastbourne, East Sussex BN21 4XB Tel: 01323 410419 www.edgarhorns.com

EIM • Christopher Eimer, PO Box 352, London NW11 7RF Tel: 020 8458 9933

EKK • Ekkehart, U.S.A. Tel: 001 415 571 9070

EL * Eldred's, Robert C Eldred Co Inc, 1475 Route 6A, East Dennis, Massachusetts 0796 U.S.A. Tel: 00 1 508 385 3116

ELI • Eli Antiques, Stand Q5 Antiquarius, 135 King's Road, London SW3 4PW Tel: 020 7351 7038

EMC • Sue Emerson & Bill Chapman, Bourbon Hanby Antiques Centre, Shop No 18, 151 Sydney Street, Chelsea, London SW3 6NT Tel: 020 7351 1807

ET • Early Technology, Monkton House, Old Craighall, Musselburgh, Midlothian EH21 8SF Scotland Tel: 0131 665 5753 michael.bennett-levy@virgin.net www.earlytech.com

EXC • Excalibur Antiques, Taunton Antique Centre, 27–29 Silver Street, Taunton, Somerset TA13DH Tel: 01823 289327/0374 627409

F&C/ * Finan & Co, The Square, Mere, Wiltshire BA12 6DJ
FW&C Tel: 01747 861411

FBG * Frank H. Boos Gallery, 420 Enterprise Court, Bloomfield Hills, Michigan 48302 U.S.A. Tel: 001 248 332 1500

FFAP * Freeman Fine Art Of Philadelphia Inc, 1808 Chestnut Street, Philadelphia U.S.A. PA 19103 Tel: 001 215 563 9275

FHF * Frank H. Fellows & Sons, Augusta House, 19 Augusta Street, Hockley, Birmingham, West Midlands B18 6JA Tel: 0121 212 2131

FHM No longer trading

FMN • Forget-Me-Not Antiques, Over the Moon, 27 High Street, St Albans, Hertfordshire AL3 4EH Tel: 01727 53032/01923 261172

G * Gorringes Auction Galleries, Terminus Road, Bexhill-on-Sea, East Sussex TN39 3LR Tel: 01424 212994 bexhill@gorringes.co.uk www.gorringes.co.uk

G(B) * Gorringes Auction Galleries, Terminus Road, Bexhill-on-Sea, East Sussex TN39 3LR Tel: 01424 212994 bexhill@gorringes.co.uk www.gorringes.co.uk

G(L) * Gorringes inc Julian Dawson, 15 North Street, Lewes, East Sussex BN7 2PD Tel: 01273 472503 auctions@gorringes.co.uk www.gorringes.co.uk

GAK * Keys, Aylsham Salerooms, Off Palmers Lane, Aylsham, Norfolk NR11 6JA Tel: 01263 733195 www.aylshamsalerooms.co.uk

Gam * Clarke Gammon, The Guildford Auction Rooms, Bedford Road, Guildford, Surrey GU1 4SJ Tel: 01483 880915

GAS • Gasson Antiques, P O Box 7225, Tadley, Hampshire RG26 5YB Tel: 01189 813636 Mobile: 07860 827651

GAZE * Thomas Wm Gaze & Son, Diss Auction Rooms, Roydon Road, Diss, Norfolk IP22 3LN Tel: 01379 650306 www.twgaze.com

GEM • Gem Antiques, 28 London Road, Sevenoaks, Kent TN13 1AP Tel: 01732 743540 www.gemantiques.com

GH * Gardiner Houlgate, The Bath Auction Rooms, 9 Leafield Way, Corsham, Nr Bath, Somerset SN13 9SW Tel: 01225 812912 gardiner-houlgate.co.uk

GIO • Giovanna Antiques, Bourbon & Hanby Antiques Centre, Shop 16, 151 Sydney Street, London SW3 6NT Tel: 020 7565 0004

GLa • Glassdrumman Antiques, 7 Union Square, The Pantiles, Tunbridge Wells, Kent TN4 8HE Tel: 01892 538615

GLT • Glitterati, Assembly Antique Centre, 6–8 Saville Row, Bath, Somerset BA1 2QP Tel: 01225 426288

GOO • Gooday Gallery, 14 Richmond Hill, Richmond, Surrey TW10 6QX Tel: 020 8940 8652 Mobile: 077101 24540

GOR * See G(L)

GTH * Greenslade Taylor Hunt Fine Art, Magdelene House, Church Square, Taunton, Somerset TA1 1SB Tel: 01823 332525

Hal * Halls Fine Art Auctions, Welsh Bridge, Shrewsbury, Shropshire SY3 8LA Tel: 01743 231212

HAM * Hamptons International, Baverstock House, 93 High Street, Godalming, Surrey GU7 1AL Tel: 01483 423567 fineart@hamptons-int.com www.hamptons.co.uk

HAN • Hannah Tel: 01844 237899 Mobile: 078 31 800774

Har/ • Hardy's Collectables/Hardy's Clobber, 862 & 874
HarC Christchurch Road, Boscombe, Bournemouth, Dorset BH7 6DQ Tel: 01202 422407/473744 Mobile: 07970 613077

HARP • Harpers Jewellers Ltd, 2/6 Minster Gates, York YO1 7HL Tel: 01904 632634 harpers@talk21.com www.vintage-watches.co.uk

HCA • Hilltop Cottage Antiques, 101 Portobello Road, London W11 Tel: 01451 844362 Mobile: 0777 365 8082 noswadp@AOL.com

HCC * H C Chapman & Son, The Auction Mart, North Street, Scarborough, Yorkshire YO11 1DL Tel: 01723 372424

HCH * The Cotswold Auction Company Ltd, The Coach House, Swan Yard, 9–13 Market Place, Cirencester, Gloucestershire GL7 2NH Tel: 01285 642420 info@cotswoldauction.co.uk www.cotswoldauction.co.uk

HEB • Hebeco, 47 West Street, Dorking, Surrey RH4 1BU Tel: 01306 875396 Mobile: 07710 019790

HEI • Heirloom Antiques, 68 High Street, Tenterden, Kent TN30 6AU Tel: 01580 765535

HEL • Helios Gallery, 292 Westbourne Grove, London W11 2PS Tel: 077 11 955 997 heliosgallery@btinternet.com www.heliosgallery.com

HofB • Howards of Broadway, 27A High Street, Broadway, Worcestershire WR12 7DP Tel: 01386 858924

HOK * Hamilton Osborne King, 4 Main Street, Blackrock, Co Dublin, Republic of Ireland Tel: 353 1 288 5011 blackrock@hok.ie www.hok.ie

HOLL * Holloways (RICS), 49 Parsons Street, Banbury, Oxfordshire OX16 5PF Tel: 01295 817777 enquiries@hollowaysauctioneers.co.uk www.hollowaysauctioneers.co.uk

HSS * Phillips, 20 The Square, Retford, Nottinghamshire DN22 6XE Tel: 01777 708633

HUM • Humbleyard Fine Art, Unit 32 Admiral Vernon Arcade, Portobello Road, London W11 2DY Tel: 01362 637793 Mobile: 0836 349416

HYD * Hy Duke & Son, Dorchester Fine Art Salerooms, Dorchester, Dorset DT1 1QS Tel: 01305 265080

ICO • Iconastas, 5 Piccadilly Arcade, London SW1 Tel: 020 7629 1433 iconastas@compuserve.com

IHB • Imperial Half Bushel, 831 North Howard Street, Baltimore MD 21201 U.S.A. Tel: 001 410 462 1192 patrick.duggan@worldnet.att.net www.imperialhalfbushel.com

J&L No longer trading

JAA * Jackson's Auctioneers & Appraisers, 2229 Lincoln Street, Cedar Falls IA 50613 U.S.A. Tel: 00 1 319 277 2256

JACK • Michael Jackson Antiques, The Quiet Woman Antiques Centre, Southcombe, Chipping Norton, Oxfordshire OX7 5QH Tel: 01608 646262 mjcig@cards.fsnet.co.uk www.our-web-site.com/cigarette-cards

JAd * James Adam & Sons, 26 St Stephen's Green, Dublin 2, Republic of Ireland Tel: 00 3531 676 0261

JAS • Jasmin Cameron, Antiquarius, 131–141 King's Road, London SW3 4PW Tel: 020 7351 4154

JBB • Jessie's Button Box, Great Western Antique Centre, Bartlett Street, Bath, Somerset BA1 5DY Tel: 0117 929 9065

JBU • John Bull (Antiques) Ltd, JB Silverware, 139a New Bond Street, London W1Y 9FB Tel: 020 7629 1251 Mobile: 07850 221 468 ken@jbsilverware.co.uk www.jbsilverware.co.uk

JES • John Jesse, 160 Kensington Church Street, London W8 4BN Tel: 020 7229 0312

JH * Jacobs & Hunt, 26 Lavant Street, Petersfield, Hampshire GU32 3EF Tel: 01730 233933 www.jacobsandhunt.co.uk

JHW • John Howkins, 1 Dereham Road, Norwich, Norfolk NR2 4HX Tel: 01603 627832

JIL • Jillings Antique Clocks, Croft House, 17 Church Street, Newent, Gloucestershire GL18 1PU Tel: 01531 822100 Mobile: 07973 830110 clock@jillings.com www.jillings.com

JNic * John Nicholson, The Auction Rooms, Longfield, Midhurst Road, Fernhurst, Surrey GU27 3HA Tel: 01428 653727

JSH * Jack Shaw & Co, The Old Grammar School, Skipton Road, Ilkley, Yorkshire LS29 9EJ Tel: 01943 609467

JSM * J & S Millard Antiques, Assembly Antiques, 5–8 Saville Row, Bath, Somerset BA1 2QP Tel: 01225 469785

JWA * J.W.A. (UK) Limited, P.O. Box 6, Peterborough, Cambridgeshire PE1 5AH Tel: 01733 348344

KID * George Kidner, The Old School, The Square, Pennington, Lymington, Hampshire SO41 8GN Tel: 01590 670070 www.georgekidner.co.uk

L * Lawrence Fine Art Auctioneers, South Street, Crewkerne, Somerset TA18 8AB Tel: 01460 73041

L&E * Locke & England, 18 Guy Street, Leamington Spa, Warwickshire CV32 4RT Tel: 01926 889100 www.auctions-online.com/locke

L&T * Lyon & Turnbull, 33 Broughton Place, Edinburgh EH1 3RR Scotland Tel: 0131 557 8844

LBe * Linda Bee, Art Deco Stand L18–21, Grays Antique Market, 1–7 Davies Mews, London W1Y 1AR Tel: 020 7629 5921

LBr * Lynda Brine, Assembly Antiques Centre, 5–8 Saville Row, Bath, Somerset BA1 2QP Tel: 01225 448488 lyndabrine@yahoo.co.uk www.scentbottlesandsmalls.co.uk

LF * Lambert & Foster, 102 High Street, Tenterden, Kent TN30 6HT Tel: 01580 763233 www.lambertandfoster.co.uk

LHA No longer trading

LJ * Leonard Joel Auctioneers, 333 Malvern Road, South Yarra, Victoria 3141 Australia Tel: 03 9826 4333 decarts@ljoel.com.au www.ljoel.com.au

LT * Louis Taylor Auctioneers & Valuers, Britannia House, 10 Town Road, Hanley, Stoke-on-Trent, Staffordshire ST1 2QG Tel: 01782 214111

MARK • 20th Century Marks, 12 Market Square, Westerham, Kent TN16 1AW Tel: 01959 562221 lambarda@msn.com

MAT * Christopher Matthews, 23 Mount Street, Harrogate, Yorkshire HG2 8DQ Tel: 01423 871756

MB • Mostly Boxes, 93 High Street, Eton, Windsor, Berkshire SL4 6AF Tel: 01753 858470

MCA * Mervyn Carey, Twysden Cottage, Benenden, Cranbrook, Kent TN17 4LD Tel: 01580 240283

MCO • Mary Cooke Antiques Ltd, 12 The Old Power Station, 121 Mortlake High Street, London SW14 8SN Tel: 020 8876 5777

MEA * Mealy's, Chatsworth Street, Castle Comer, Co Kilkenny, Republic of Ireland Tel: 00 353 56 41229 info@mealys.com www.mealys.com

MED * Medway Auctions, Fagins, 23 High Street, Rochester, Kent ME1 1LN Tel: 01634 847444

MGe • Michael C. German, 38B Kensington Church Street, London W8 8EP Tel: 020 7937 2771

MHB • M. H. Beeforth. silver@meegan.co.uk www.antique-silverware.com

Mit * Mitchells, Fairfield House, Station Road, Cockermouth, Cumbria CA13 9PY Tel: 01900 827800

MJB * Michael J. Bowman, 6 Haccombe House, Netherton, Newton Abbot, Devon TQ12 4SJ Tel: 01626 872890

ML • Memory Lane, Bartlett Street Antiques Centre, 5/10 Bartlett Street, Bath, Somerset BA1 2QZ Tel: 01225 466689

MM • Michael Marriott, 588 Fulham Road, London SW6 5NT Tel: 020 7736 3110

MoS • Morgan Stobbs Mobile: 07702 206817

MRW • Malcolm Russ-Welch, PO Box 1122, Rugby, Warwickshire CV23 9YD Tel: 01788 810 616

MSh • Manfred Schotten, The Crypt Antiques, 109 High Street, Burford, Oxfordshire OX18 4RG Tel: 01993 822302

MSW * Marilyn Swain Auctions, The Old Barracks, Sandon Road, Grantham, Lincolnshire NG31 9AS Tel: 01476 568861

N * Neales, 192 Mansfield Road, Nottingham NG1 3HU Tel: 0115 962 4141

NAW • Newark Antiques Warehouse, Old Kelham Road, Newark, Nottinghamshire NG24 1BX Tel: 01636 674869 enquiries@newarkantiques.co.uk

NC • The Nautical Centre, Harbour Passage, Hope Square, Weymouth, Dorset DT4 8TR Tel: 01305 777838

NOA * New Orleans Auction Galleries Inc, 801 Magazine Street, AT 510 Julia, New Orleans, Louisiana 70130 U.S.A. Tel: 00 1 504 566 1849

NOR • Nortonbury Antiques, BMC Box 5345, London WC1N 3XX Tel: 01984 631668 Mobile: 07774 174092 nortonbury.antiques@virgin.net www.antiquesweb.co.uk/nortonbury

NS •† Nicholas Shaw Antiques, Great Grooms Antiques Centre, Parbrook, Billingshurst, West Sussex RH14 9EU Tel: 01403 786656/785731 Mobile: 07785 643000 silver@nicholas-shaw.com www.nicholas-shaw.com

OBS • The Old Button Shop, Lytchett Minster, Poole, Dorset BH16 6JF Tel: 01202 622169

OD • Offa's Dyke Antique Centre, 4 High Street, Knighton, Powys LD7 1AT Wales Tel: 01547 528635/528940

Oli * Olivers, Olivers Rooms, Burkitts Lane, Sudbury, Suffolk CO10 1HB Tel: 01787 880305

P * Phillips, 101 New Bond Street, London W1Y 0AS Tel: 020 7629 6602 www.phillips-auctions.com

P(B) * Phillips, 1 Old King Street, Bath, Somerset BA1 2JT Tel: 01225 310609

P(Ba) * Phillips Bayswater, 10 Salem Road, London W2 4DL Tel: 020 7229 9090 www.phillips-auctions.com

P(C) * Phillips, Cardiff.

P(Ch) * Phillips, Chichester.

P(E) * Phillips, 38–39 Southernhay East, Exeter, Devon EX1 1PE Tel: 01392 439025

P(EA) * Phillips, 32 Boss Hall Road, Ipswich, Suffolk IP1 5DJ Tel: 01473 740494

P(Ed) * Phillips Scotland, 65 George Street, Edinburgh EH2 2JL Scotland. Tel: 0131 225 2266

P(F) * Phillips, Folkestone.

P(G) * Phillips Fine Art Auctioneers, Millmead, Guildford, Surrey GU2 5BE Tel: 01483 504030

P(Gen) * Phillips Geneva, 9 rue Ami-Levrier, CH-1201 Geneva Switzerland Tel: 00 41 22 738 0707

P(HSS) * Phillips, 20 The Square, Retford, Nottinghamshire DN22 6XE Tel: 01777 708633

P(L) * Phillips Leeds, 17a East Parade, Leeds, Yorkshire LS1 2BH Tel: 0113 2448011

P(NE) * Phillips North East, 30/32 Grey Street, Newcastle-Upon-Tyne, Tyne & Wear NE1 6AE Tel: 0191 233 9930

P(O) * Phillips, 39 Park End Street, Oxford OX1 1JD Tel: 01865 723524

P(S) * Phillips Fine Art Auctioneers, 49 London Road, Sevenoaks, Kent TN13 1AR Tel: 01732 740310

P(Sc) * Phillips Scotland, The Beacon, 176 St Vincent Street, Glasgow Scotland G2 5SG Tel: 0141 223 8866

P(Sy) * Phillips Sydney, 162 Queen Street, Woollahra, Sydney, NSW 2025 Australia Tel: 00 612 9326 1588

P(WM) * Phillips, The Old House, Station Road, Knowle, Solihull, West Midlands B93 0HT Tel: 01564 776151

PAY • Payne & Son, 131 High Street, Oxford OX1 4DH Tel: 01865 243787 silver@payneandson.co.uk www.payneandson.co.uk

PC Private Collection

PCh * Peter Cheney, Western Road Auction Rooms, Western Road, Littlehampton, West Sussex BN17 5NP Tel: 01903 722264/713418

PFK * Penrith Farmers' & Kidd's plc, Skirsgill Salerooms, Penrith, Cumbria CA11 0DN Tel: 01768 890781 penrith.farmers@virgin.net

PSA • Pantiles Spa Antiques, 4, 5, 6 Union House, The Pantiles, Tunbridge Wells, Kent TN4 8HE Tel: 01892 541377 Mobile: 07711 283655 psa.wells@btinternet.com www.antiques-tun-wells-kent.co.uk

PT • Pieces of Time, (1–7 Davies Mews), 26 South Molton Lane, London W1Y 2LP Tel: 020 7629 2422 info@antique-watch.com www.antique-watch.com

Q2 • Q2, Antiquarius Antique Market, 131/141 King's Road, Chelsea, London SW3 5ST Tel: 020 7351 5353

Rac/ RAC • Field, Staff & Woods, 93 High Street, Rochester, Kent ME1 1LX Tel: 01634 846144

RBB * Brightwells Ltd, Ryelands Road, Leominster, Herefordshire HR6 8NZ Tel: 01568 611122 fineart@brightwells.com

REG • Regatta Antiques, Antiques Centre, 151 Sydney Street, Chelsea, London SW3 6NT Tel: 020 7460 0054

RID • Riddetts of Bournemouth, 177 Holden Hurst Road, Bournemouth, Dorset BH8 8DQ Tel: 01202 555686

RIT * Ritchie Inc., D & J Auctioneers & Appraisers of Antiques & Fine Arts, 288 King Street East, Toronto, Ontario M5A 1K4 Canada Tel: (416) 364 1864

RMC • Romsey Medal Centre, 5 Bell Street, Romsey, Hampshire, SO51 8GY Tel: 01794 324488 post@romseymedals.co.uk www.romseymedals.com

RRA • Rambling Rose Antiques, Marcy & Bob Schmidt, Frederick, MD, U.S.A. Tel: 301 473 7010

RTh • The Reel Thing, 17 Royal Opera Arcade, Pall Mall, London SW1Y 4UY Tel: 020 7976 1840

RTo   *   Rupert Toovey & Co Ltd, Star Road, Partridge Green, West Sussex RH13 8RA Tel: 01403 711744 auctions@rupert-toovey.com www.rupert-toovey.com

RUL   •   Rules Antiques, 62 St Leonards Road, Windsor, Berkshire SL4 3BY Tel: 01753 833210/01491 642062

RUSK   •   Ruskin Decorative Arts, 5 Talbot Court, Stow-on-the-Wold, Cheltenham, Gloucestershire GL54 1DP Tel: 01451 832254

S   *†   Sotheby's, 34–35 New Bond Street, London W1A 2AA Tel: 020 7293 5000 www.sothebys.com

S(Am)   *   Sotheby's Amsterdam, De Boelelaan 30, 1083 HJ, Amsterdam, Netherlands Tel: 00 31 20 550 22 00

S(Cg)   *   Sotheby's, 215 West Ohio Street, Chicago, Illinois 60610 U.S.A. Tel: 00 1 312 670 0010

S(G)   *   Sotheby's, 13 Quai du Mont Blanc, Geneva, CH-1201 Switzerland Tel: 00 41 22 908 4800

S(NY)   *   Sotheby's, 1334 York Avenue, New York, NY 10021 U.S.A. Tel: 00 1 212 606 7000

S(S)   *   Sotheby's Sussex, Summers Place, Billingshurst, West Sussex RH14 9AD Tel: 01403 833500

S&S   *   Stride & Son, Southdown House, St John's Street, Chichester, West Sussex PO19 1XQ Tel: 01243 780207

SAS   *   Special Auction Services, The Coach House, Midgham Park, Reading, Berkshire RG7 5UG Tel: 0118 971 2949 www.invaluable.com/sas/

SFL   •†   The Silver Fund Ltd, 40 Bury Street, St James's, London SW1Y 6AU Tel: 020 7839 7664 dealers@thesilverfund.com www.thesilverfund.com

SHa   •†   Shapiro & Co, Stand 380, Gray's Antique Market, 58 Davies Street, London W1Y 5LP Tel: 020 7491 2710

SIL   •   The Silver Shop, Powerscourt Townhouse Centre, St Williams Street, Dublin 2, Republic of Ireland Tel: 00 3531 6794147

SK   *   Skinner Inc, The Heritage On The Garden, 63 Park Plaza, Boston, MA 02116 U.S.A. Tel: 001 617 350 5400

SK(B)   *   Skinner Inc, 357 Main Street, Bolton, MA 01740 U.S.A. Tel: 00 1 978 779 6241

SLI   •†   Sanda Lipton. Tel: 020 7431 0866 webmaster@antiques-silver.com

SLL   •   Sylvanna LLewelyn Antiques Tel: 020 7598 1278 www.silvanna.com

SLM   *   Sloan's Auctioneers & Appraisers, Miami Gallery, 8861 NW 18th Terrace, Suite 100, Miami, Florida 33172 U.S.A. Tel: 00 1 305 592 2575/ 800 660 4524

SLN   *   Sloan's, C. G. Sloan & Company Inc, 4920 Wyaconda Road, North Bethesda, MD 20852 U.S.A. Tel: 00 1 301 468 4911/669 5066 www.sloansauction.com

SnA   •   Snape Maltings Antique & Collectors Centre, Saxmundham, Suffolk IP17 1SR Tel: 01278 688038

Som   •   Somervale Antiques, 6 Radstock Road, Midsomer Norton, Bath, Somerset BA3 2AJ Tel: 01761 412686 Mobile: 07885 088022 ronthomas@somervaleantiquesglass.co.uk www.somervaleantiquesglass.co.uk

SPE   •   Sylvie Spectrum, Stand 372, Grays Market, 58 Davies Street, London W1Y 1LB Tel: 020 7629 3501

SPU   •   Spurrier-Smith Antiques, 28, 30 & 39 Church Street, Ashbourne, Derbyshire DE6 1AJ Tel: 01335 343669/342198/344377

SSW   •   Spencer Swaffer, 30 High Street, Arundel, West Sussex BN18 9AB Tel: 01903 882132

STA   •   Michelina & George Stacpoole, Main St, Adare, Co Limerick, Republic of Ireland Tel: 00 353 61 396 409

STG   •   Stone Gallery, 93 High Street, Burford, Oxfordshire OX18 4QA Tel: 01993 823302

STH   •   Steppes Hill Farm Antiques, Steppes Hill Farm, Stockbury, Nr Sittingbourne, Kent ME9 7RB Tel: 01795 842205

SUC   •   Succession, 18 Richmond Hill, Richmond, Surrey TW10 6QX Tel: 020 8940 6774

SUL   •   Sullivan Antiques (Chantal O'Sullivan), 43–44 Francis Street, Dublin 8, Republic of Ireland Tel: 00 3531 4541143/4539659

SWO   *   G. E. Sworder & Sons, 14 Cambridge Road, Stansted Mountfitchet, Essex CM24 8BZ Tel: 01279 817778 www.sworder.co.uk

TAC   •   Tenterden Antiques Centre, 66–66A High Street, Tenterden, Kent TN30 6AU Tel: 01580 765655/7658

TAR   •   Lorraine Tarrant Antiques, 23 Market Place, Ringwood, Hampshire BH24 1AN Tel: 01425 461123

TB   •   Millicent Safro, Tender Buttons, 143 E.62nd Street, New York, NY10021, U.S.A. Tel: (212) 758 7004

TC   •   Timothy Coward Tel: 01271 890466

TEN   *   Tennants, The Auction Centre, Harmby Road, Leyburn, Yorkshire DL8 5SG Tel: 01969 623780

TGa   •   No longer trading

THOM   •   S. & A. Thompson. Tel: 01306 711970 Mobile: 07770 882746

TIH   No longer trading

TMA   *   Brown & Merry, Tring Market Auctions, The Market Premises, Brook Street, Tring, Hertfordshire HP23 5EF Tel: 01442 826446 sales@tringmarketauctions.co.uk www.tringmarketauctions.co.uk

TRE   •   No longer trading.

TRL   •   Thomson, Roddick & Medcalf, Coleridge House, Shaddongate, Carlisle, Cumbria CA2 5TU Tel: 01228 528939

TRM   *   Thomson, Roddick & Medcalf, 60 Whitesands, Dumfries, DG1 2RS Scotland Tel: 01387 255366

TVA   •   Teme Valley Antiques, 1 The Bull Ring, Ludlow, Shropshire SY8 1AD Tel: 01584 874686

TWD   •   The Watch Department, 49 Beauchamp Place, London SW3 1NY Tel: 020 7589 4005 thewatch.dept@virgin.net www.watchdept.co.uk

VB   •   Variety Box, 16 Chapel Place, Tunbridge Wells, Kent TN1 1YQ Tel: 01892 531868

WaR   •   Wot a Racket, 250 Shepherds Lane, Dartford, Kent DA1 2PN Tel: 01322 220619 wot-a-racket@talk21.com

WAB   •   Warboys Antiques, St Ives, Cambridgeshire Tel: 01480 463891 john.lambden@virgin.net

WAC   •   Worcester Antiques Centre, Reindeer Court, Mealcheapen Street, Worcester WR1 4DF Tel: 01905 610680

WAL   *   Wallis & Wallis, West Street Auction Galleries, Lewes, East Sussex BN7 2NJ Tel: 01273 480208 auctions@wallisandwallis.co.uk www.wallisandwallis.co.uk

WDG   *   William Doyle Galleries, 175 East 87th Street, New York 10128 U.S.A. Tel: 212 427 2730

WeH   •   Westerham House Antiques, The Green, Westerham, Kent TN16 1AY Tel: 01959 561622/562200

WELD   •†   J. W. Weldon, 55 Clarendon Street, Dublin 2, Republic of Ireland Tel: 00 353 1 677 1638

WIM   •   Wimpole Antiques, Stand 349, Grays Antique Market, 58 Davies Street, London W1Y 2LP Tel: 020 7499 2889

WL   *   Wintertons Ltd, Lichfield Auction Centre, Wood End Lane, Fradley, Lichfield, Staffordshire WS13 8NF Tel: 01543 263256

WN   •   What Now, Cavendish Arcade, The Crescent, Buxton, Derbyshire SK17 6BQ Tel: 01298 27178/23417

WW   *   Woolley & Wallis, Salisbury Salerooms, 51–61 Castle Street, Salisbury, Wiltshire SP1 3SU Tel: 01722 424500

YAN   •   Yanni's Antiques, 538 San Anselmo Avenue, San Anselmo, CA 94960 U.S.A. Tel: 001 415 459 2996

ZEI   •   Zeitgeist, 58 Kensington Church Street, London W8 4DB Tel: 020 7938 4817

Index to Advertisers

Index

Italic page numbers denote colour pages; **bold** numbers refer to information and pointer boxes

Sale Highlights
of Silver

ON SOTHEBYS.COM

Scottish sterling silver coffee/hot water pot, Edinburgh, 1938
Offered by Daniel Bexfield Antiques, a Sothebys.com Associate
Estimate: $700 – 1,000
Sold: $977.50

Silver Centrepiece Bowl
Estimate: $1,200 – 1,500
Sold: $2,530

German Monumental Silver Flagon, in Medieval style, late 19th century
From the Pabst Brewing Company Stein Collection
Estimate: $10,000 – 15,000
Sold: $10,063

An important Wiener Werstaette
'Fern Fronds' silver bowl by
Otto Prutscher, circa 1920s
Offered by Burton Brook Farm,
a Sothebys.com Associate
Estimate: $25,000 – 35,000
Sold: $24,950

Sothebys.com

for a complete listing of special auctions, please log on to www.sothebys.com/specialauctions

The Silver Collection Limited
Telephone/Fax 00 44 (0)1442 890954 Mobile 07802 447813